Implementing
Government Policy Initiatives:
The Thatcher Administration 1979-83

The RIPA, founded in 1922, is the leading independent British institution concerned with policy-making and administration in the public sector. Its aims are to help improve the effectiveness of public administration and to increase public understanding of institutions, processes and policies in the public service. It is concerned both with the needs of public authorities and also with the needs of the public they serve.

OTHER RIPA PUBLICATIONS

Politics, Ethics and Public Service
Bernard Williams, John Stevenson, Professor F.F. Ridley, Sir Kenneth Couzens, Alexander Grey, Peter Jay

Developing the FMI Principles: Changes in Process and Culture
Proceedings of an RIPA/Peat, Marwick, Mitchell & Co. Seminar

Privatizing Public Enterprises
David Steel and David Heald (eds.)

Contracting Out in the Public Sector
Proceedings of an RIPA conference

Policy Analysis and Evaluation in British Government
Andrew Gray and Bill Jenkins (eds.)

Job Satisfaction in Public Administration
P.B. Beaumont and M. Partridge

Royal Commissions and Departmental Committees of Inquiry
Dr Martin Bulmer

The Home Office: Perspectives on Policy and Administration
James Callaghan, Lord Allen of Abbeydale, Sir Cyril Philips, Michael Zander, Lord Windlesham, Hugo Young

Parliament and the Executive
Professor J.A.G. Griffith, Sir Kenneth Clucas, Frank Field MP, Sir Cecil Clothier

Management Information and Control in Whitehall
Proceedings of an RIPA/Peat, Marwick, Mitchell & Co. seminar

Allies or Adversaries? Perspectives on Government and Industry in Britain
Sir Keith Joseph, Sir Leslie Murphy, Sir William Barlow, Alan Lord, Ray O'Brien, John Smith

Implementing Government Policy Initiatives: The Thatcher Administration 1979-83

Edited by
Peter Jackson

ROYAL INSTITUTE OF PUBLIC ADMINISTRATION

First published in 1985

Published by the Royal Institute of Public Administration, 3 Birdcage Walk, London SW1H 9JH

Printed in England by Victoria House Printing Co., 124/130 Tabernacle Street, London EC2

ISBN 0 900628 38 3

CONTENTS

Contributors

Peter Jackson is Director of the Public Sector Economics Research Centre and Professor of Economics at Leicester University where he specializes in public expenditure analysis. He is also Director of Studies at the Public Finance Foundation. The author of many academic articles he has co-authored, with C.V. Brown, *Public Sector Economics* (Martin Robertson, 1978) and, with S. T. Cook, *Current Issues in Fiscal Policy* (Martin Robertson, 1980) and is the author of *The Political Economy of Bureaucracy* (Phillip Allan, 1982). He is editor of the journal *The Social Studies Review* and was editor of the RIPA publication *Government Policy Initiatives 1979-80: Some Case Studies in Public Administration* (RIPA, 1981).

David Steel is Assistant Director of the National Association of Health Authorities. Until July 1984 he was Lecturer in Politics at the University of Exeter where he specialized in public administration. Since completing a doctoral thesis at Nuffield College on the British Transport Commission, he has written extensively on the nationalized industries and central government. He is co-author (with the late Ronald Brown) of *The Administrative Process in Britain* (Methuen, 1979). With David Heald, he has been researching and publishing on various dimensions of the Government's programme for privatizing public enterprises, including editing *Privatizing Public Enterprises* (RIPA, 1984).

David Heald is a part-time Lecturer in Management Studies at the University of Glasgow where he specializes in finance and public sector management. He is the author of *Public Expenditure: Its Defence and Reform* (Martin Robertson, 1983) and joint editor, with David Steel, of *Privatizing Public Enterprises* (RIPA, 1984). Also a qualified accountant, with experience of both the public and private sectors, he has acted as specialist adviser to the Treasury and Civil Service Committee and the Committee on Scottish Affairs.

Phil Beaumont is Senior Lecturer in Industrial Relations at the University of Glasgow. He has a long standing research interest in public sector industrial relations, being the author, with Andrew Thomson, of *Public Sector Bargaining* (Saxon House, 1978), *Government as Employer - Setting an Example?* (RIPA, 1981) and, with Mark Partridge, *Job Satisfaction in Public Administration* (RIPA, 1983). He has recently been involved in large research projects concerning industrial relations in local government and the personnel management function in the NHS (in Scotland).

Stephen Wilks is Lecturer in Politics at the University of Liverpool. He qualified as a chartered accountant before taking up an academic career which included a doctorate at the University of Manchester. He has written widely on issues of industrial politics and is the author of *Industrial Policy and the Motor Industry* (Manchester University Press, 1983) and co-editor (with Kenneth Dyson) of *Industrial Crisis: A Comparative Study of the State and Industry* (Basil Blackwell, 1985). He is the Research Co-ordinator for the Economic and Social Research Council's programme of research on Comparative Government Industry Relations.

Justin Meadows is a Research Fellow in the Public Sector Economics Research Centre at the University of Leicester. Since joining the Centre from local government in 1979 he has worked on a number of research projects in the area of local government finance and central-local relations. He is co-author (with Peter Jackson) of 'UK Local Government: Alternative Macroeconomics Strategies' in *New Research in Central Local Relations* edited by Mike Goldsmith (Gower 1985). He is currently a specialist adviser to the Committee of Experts on Local and Regional Finance of the Council of Europe.

Alan Murie is Senior Lecturer in Urban Studies at the School for Advanced Urban Studies at the University of Bristol. He has for a number of years specialized in teaching and research on housing and housing policy issues. He has written extensively on these topics and his most recent publications include *Housing Inequality and Deprivation* (Heinemann, 1983) and a number of papers on recent policy developments published through SAUS. Between 1980 and 1981 he acted as specialist adviser to the House of Commons Environment Committee for their enquiries into council house sales and the housing implications of public expenditure plans 1980-81 to 1983-84.

Rudolf Klein is Professor of Social Policy and Director of the Centre for the Analysis of Social Policy at the University of Bath. Before turning academic, he was a journalist with the London *Evening Standard* and the *Observer*. He is joint editor of *Political Quarterly* and was, for five years, a specialist adviser of the Social Services Committee. He has written extensively about public expenditure, social policy and health politics. His most recent books are *The Politics of the National Health Service* (Longman, 1983) and, as editor with Michael O'Higgins, *The Future of Welfare* (Blackwell, 1985).

Adrian Webb is Professor of Social Administration, Director of the Centre for Research in Social Policy in the Department of Social Sciences at Loughborough University. His primary interests are in the study of policy processes and the health and personal social services. He has published extensively in these fields. He is a member of the Council of Tribunals.

Gerald Wistow is Deputy Director of the Centre for Research in Social Policy in the Department of Social Sciences at Loughborough University. He is primarily interested in policy processes as they relate to client groups at the interface of health, local authority and non-statutory agencies. He has published widely on joint planning, joint finance and the personal social services. He is co-author with Adrian Webb of *Whither State Welfare* (Royal Institute of Public Administration, 1982) and *Planning, Need and Scarcity: Essays on the Personal Social Services* (Allen and Unwin, 1985, in press).

Susanne MacGregor is Senior Lecturer in Political Sociology at Birkbeck College, University of London. She is the author of *The Politics of Poverty* (Longman, 1981) and co-author of *Dealing with Drug Misuse: Crisis Intervention in the City* (Tavistock, 1984). She has written extensively on social policy, homelessness and drug misuse in particular and is a scientific adviser to DHSS's Homelessness and Addiction Research Division Group.

Roger Williams is Professor in the Departments of Government and Science and Technology Policy at the University of Manchester. His particular interests are in the field of government and technology. He is the author of *The Nuclear Power Decisions* (Croom Helm, 1980) and of numerous other books and articles in the technology and government field. He has a first degree in physics and has worked as an operational research scientist and a science adviser.

PREFACE

The 1979/83 Conservative Government was elected to office on the basis of a manifesto which was seen at the time to be radical. Many long held and cherished views about the role of government in a modern mixed economy were challenged and the post-war social democratic consensus grounded upon the economic philosophy of Keynesianism was swept aside.

When considering the social and economic history of this recent period, a number of fundamental questions can be asked. Were the policies contained in the manifesto really so radical? What problems did the in-coming government face when it tried to implement these policies? This volume is not a political evaluation of the successes and short-comings of the 1979-83 Conservative Government. Rather it is an exercise in the study of the implementation of policies, especially policies which are not incremental, in the sense that they are departures from that which has gone before.

Each author in this volume is an authority in his/her subject area and was given the task of setting down the details of the more significant policies in their subject area. The next stage was to consider the implementation problems. This volume is a follow up to an earlier study which was reported as P.M. Jackson (ed), *Government Policy Initiatives 1979-80: Some Case Studies in Public Administration* in 1981. Given that the previous study looked at the first 18 months of the Government's term in office it was obviously incomplete. This report completes the picture. Unfortunately between the first report and the second, three subject areas have been omitted: Law and Order; Education and Transport. The reason for this is simply that their authors were unable to contribute to the second volume due to other commitments and to find replacements would have delayed publication.

It is to be hoped that these authoritative accounts will be of value to students of public administration and policy analysis who will find in each chapter a summary of some of the policy changes along with an examination of the problems of implementation. Each chapter has a detailed set of references which students can follow up.

Ideas come and go. There is competition between academics and other social thinkers who present their thoughts and views in the popular and the financial press in the hope of catching the eye and capturing the mind of politicians who might act upon their teachings. The press and the media seek out the spectacular and highlight conflicts. This is what sells today's news. The media prefer simple messages – balance the budget; control the money supply; cut taxation. These simple ideas have an appeal. They resemble home truths and are easy to package. The complex technical arguments of the middle ground do not grab the headlines. They are, instead, burdened by a set of conditional and qualifying clauses. Simple line messages refer to a simple, non-complex world in which there is certainty, conviction and strong belief. The world is, unfortunately, not like this. It is, instead, complex, messy and uncertain with the result that doubt and qualification are the order of the day. To believe otherwise is to be extremely naive.

None of the chapters in this volume can be called naive. They display in all its richness the complexities and ambiguities of the real world in which policies have to be implemented. It is such a policy environment which causes the problems and limits the success of policies. It is upon the reef of complexity that the hopes of many policy makers are dashed.

A number of books appraising the Thatcher Government have preceded this one. They include Peter Riddell's *The Thatcher Government* (Martin Robertson, 1983); William Keegan's *Mrs Thatcher's Economic Experiment* (Allan Lane, 1984) and a collection of essays collected and edited by Stuart Hall, *Thatcherism* (Pluto Press 1982). Our volume is distinguished from these on a number of counts. First, there is no ideological or political party stance taken: each author has his/her own political views but these do not form the core of their essays. Second, both the depth and breadth of the coverage of this volume is greater.

As with the previous volume we are indebted to the Leverhulme Trust who provided a grant to RIPA to cover the costs of bringing together the researchers and the Editor and drawing their conclusions into a common form.

Peter Jackson
Leicester 1985

1

Policy Implementation and Monetarism: Two Primers

Peter Jackson

It is only if we have complete confidence in our ability to control economic pressures, whatever their strength (and to control them at the precise time when they need to be controlled), that the sort of understanding given by Keynes is enough. Otherwise we must know something about the longer-run consequences of policies; we must have an assurance that policies adopted to deal with a monetary emergency, will not set up, in the longer run, pressures which are greater than we can hope to withstand. (J R Hicks, *The Trade Cycle*, 1950, p.1)

Hick's warning about using economic models to guide policies has not received sufficient attention. Indeed, it would be possible to extend the argument generally to all policies based upon social science models. The policy prescriptions gleaned from these analytical systems can be extremely misleading especially with regard to their long run consequences. One reason for this state of affairs is that the structural parameters whose values influence mainly the long run behaviour of the system are much more difficult to estimate than the parameters whose values have important effects on short run behaviours. A set of important structural parameters that is frequently omitted from analysis, certainly by the economist, is the implementation system.

Those who prescribe policy actions and generate blue-prints for governments to follow take the implementation system as given. It is regarded as some external, neutral and unproblematic set of relationships. Policy decisions are somehow translated into actions which generate the desired outputs of the socio-political system. This 'black box' approach to policy analysis has permeated the literature for some time now and serves little useful purpose in trying to understand why policy outcomes *ex post* are not equivalent to those intended *ex ante*. The full title of Pressman and Wildavsky's (1973) classic work on policy implementation was *Implementation: How Great Expectations in Washington are Dashed in Oakland or Why It's Amazing That Federal Programs Work At All. This*

Being a Saga of the Economic Development Administration as Told by Two Sympathetic Observers Who Seek to Build Morals on a Foundation of Ruined Hopes.[1] Whilst the book's title might gain the prize for being the longest it does clearly give the reader a flavour of what to expect. The first part of this chapter examines and develops some of the issues of policy implementation which were identified by Pressman and Wildavsky.

The policies introduced by the 1979/83 Conservative Government were regarded by many to be radical and innovative. They broke the Keynesian mould which had turned out earlier post-war policies and sought to replace it with an alternative based upon free market and monetarist principles. The second part of this Chapter takes a look at fundamental teachings of monetarism and free market economics. A non-technical approach is adopted in an attempt to get across the spirit of monetarism to a wider audience which is probably not familiar with the finer points of economic analysis. Whilst an attempt has been made to ensure that no particular proposition is compromised, the reader should appreciate that what might appear to be a set of simple statements are, in fact derived from a complex set of technical arguments.

Problems in the Implementation of Policy

There has been a general lack of interest in the problems of policy implementation, with more emphasis and attention being given to policy formation and design and policy evaluation. Policy implementation is however, quickly becoming recognized as a problem area and one which should be taken into account when judging *a priori* the feasibility of projects or policies or when evaluating, *ex post*, the success or failure of a policy programme. Over the past ten years a literature has developed which seeks to provide a more careful examination of the issues of policy implementation.[2]

The importance of the implementation process has recently been stressed by a number of policy analysts especially in their explanations of why policies failed to achieve the results expected of them. Thus, Williams (1982)[3] concluded that implementation was the Achilles heel of the Johnson administration's social policy... So, figuring out how to do implementation better is a crucial policy need across all levels of government. When considering the implementation of the 1979/83 Conservative Government's Manifesto, which is the subject of the chapters which follow, it is necessary to bear in mind the basic conditions which increase the probability of the successful accomplishment of a policy. The converse is what factors can result in policy failure (or government failure)?[4]

For a policy to be feasible, and therefore to possess some chance of success a number of constraints must be satisfied:

(1)   Is the programme *budget feasible*? That is, have sufficient resources

been allocated to achieve the objectives specified in the policy statement. It is easy to pass laws, but if insufficient resources are allocated to them then implementation becomes difficult if not impossible. To the extent that the policy is not budget feasible it will soon run out of funds and will fall short of its stated objectives. A school without a roof; a motorway which stops one mile from its final destination; or a hospital without nursing staff are extreme and contrived examples of the kind of policy disasters which can arise. But how can this come about? Poor cost information or the complete lack of costings when decisions are made is a frequent reason. A failure to consider the recurrent costs (staffing, debt charges etc) of capital programmes is frequently a source of subsequent budgetary problems, as is the wishful thinking of some governments that the resources will appear from somewhere.

(2) Is the programme *technically feasible*? A policy blue-print just like the blue-print of an aircraft or a bridge must be based upon some minimal understanding of the principles of the system to which it applies. To answer the questions 'will the aircraft fly' or 'will the bridge fall down?' requires references to be made to aerodynamics, physics etc. But as any engineer knows, in getting something from the drawing board stage into an operational prototype there are many problems to be faced on the way. Whilst physical principles do undoubtedly govern the design stage, much more is learned when flying the prototype and seeking out the limits of the physical system. The same kind of argument applies to the implementation of economic and social policies. If socio-economic policies are designed with reference to principles that do not bear a close relationship to the way in which actual economies or social systems behave then they are likely to fail. Alternatively, if the policy objectives are to be achieved in the knowledge that the policy instruments will not be effective given the existing structure of the economy then, prior to implementing the policy, a series of structural/institutional changes need to be made. Unfortunately too frequently policies which are implemented are predicated upon mistaken beliefs about how the socio-economic system operates and no amount of political rhetoric will change the structure of the system. Structural change requires deliberate action and takes a while to effect, which means that in their haste to achieve some outcome prior to the next election cycle politicians will be tempted to push through policies without taking sufficient time to create the necessary conditions for success. Some might of course argue that the belief system upon which policies are based or the policy instruments should be changed. That might not, however, be politically feasible given that beliefs and the specification of policy

instruments are tied up with the ideological stance of the government. A monetarist is more likely to institute changes that will bring the structure of the economy into line with his schema rather than adopt Keynesian policy instruments which might stand a better chance of success given the prevailing structure of the economy. Since the structure of the economy includes the set of property rights along with other rights, then such changes will affect the distribution of incomes.

(3)   Is the programme *legally feasible?* An *a priori* condition for the implementation of new policies might be a change in the law as in the case of structural adjustments. This obviously takes time and can delay the achievement of policy objectives.

These constraints place obvious barriers on the implementation process both in terms of its direction and pace. But there are other considerations which can result in policy failure. The objective(s) of the policy might be poorly defined and ambiguous, or many conflict with one another. Moreover, policies tend to become more complex when they are translated into action. It is a mistake to distinguish too sharply the difference between policy making and policy implementation since in effect they both tend to merge. As the policy is implemented it becomes more clearly defined and is firmed up (concretized). Often, however, this learning process results in the conclusion that the original policy specification was technically infeasible. This will either require complete abandonment of the policy, a sea change, or structural alterations of the kind discussed above which will make the policy feasible.

Implementation takes place through organizations peopled by agents with their own particular self interests. It is too idealized a view to regard these individuals as neutral agents within the implementation process. The reality of political life impinges at many different points on the implementation process. Policy implementation requires negotiation especially with those that the policy is likely to affect. During the negotiation stage the original policy can change its form as new bargains are struck. Conflicts between policy objectives and between different programmes, as they affect different groups of individuals, become apparent during the negotiation process. Trade offs and choices have to be made which can move the final policy outcome further away from its original intention.

The recognition that there exist negotiation constraints on the implementation of new policies only arises within pluralistic political systems, i.e. a pluralism of interest and values. Governments cannot impose solutions. If they are to be feasible then they have to be negotiated and bargained. This will take time and will involve costs, as the rules of the game defining the interactions between individuals and groups have to be agreed. Not only are there the direct bargaining costs of gathering and processing information but there is the opportunity cost of delaying the consumption of the benefits arising from the policy whilst negotiations are taking place. The implementation of policies in pluralistic systems implies that persuasion rather than confrontation will characterize the bargaining process. Partnership arising from a negotiated outcome increases the chances of feasibility and effectiveness of the policy. Within such a political system the government cannot assume compliance. That is, it cannot, for example, unilaterally establish a framework for economic activity and assume all other parts of the system will fall in line. Failure to recognize the pluralism of the political system can result in policy failures.

Policy is implemented via individuals. The less clearly defined the policy objectives the greater is the scope for individual discretion in the interpretation of what the policy is all about. Within organizations scope exists for communication failures and the distortion of information. This is also true for a system of local governments. The achievements of many national goals (employment, equality etc.) are subject to local determination irrespective of the allocation of formal powers. A system of local governments within a pluralistic society implies that local decision makers will attempt to adapt policies and re-interpret them according to the local circumstances that they face. The centre's attempts to gain control over the implementation of policy will, unless it is handled properly, result in conflicts.[5] Barrett and Hill[6] summarize it thus;

> The essence of our argument is that many so called implementation problems arise precisely because there is tension between the normative assumptions of government – what ought to be done and how it should happen – and the struggle and conflict between interests – the need to bargain and compromise – that represent the reality of the process by which power/influence is gained and held in order to pursue ideological goals.

The implementation of socio-economic policies is undertaken in environments which are both complex and uncertain. Not only does this imply that in many cases there is a great deal of ignorance about the cause and effect relationships of policies but it also suggests that policy makers should be prepared to be disappointed in the results of many of their policies. They should, therefore, stand ready to learn about the behaviour of the socio-economic system through the information generated from the implementation of their policies. Our understanding of the complex relationships that make up the socio-economic environment is sufficiently incomplete that we do not know with certainty that the application of a particular policy will have the desired effects. In order to alleviate the effects of unemployment, inflation, poor housing, poverty etc it is necessary to have some clear idea of the causes of these conditions.

In the face of complexity and uncertainty governments should be more prepared than they have been to couch their policy statements in probabilistic terms. This serves at least two purposes. First, it does not create unrealistic expectations in the minds of citizens and it would enhance the credibility of government if in the event these policies should fail. Second, it would permit and allow governments to pursue policies with a greater degree of flexibility. Rather than become tied into a particular stance from the outset, a government could admit its prior uncertainty and declare its willingness to make adjustments en route as it learns about the system from experience.

The origins of complexity and uncertainty are many. The number of possible inter-relationships in society makes it difficult to know how individuals and groups of individuals will react to a particular policy when implemented. Socio-economic systems are not determined in the same sense that physical systems are. The behaviour of the weather is not influenced by the information provided by weather forecasts nor is the track of an election affected by the scientist's knowledge of its physical properties. Individual agents operating and behaving in socio-economic systems are, however, influenced in their behaviour by the knowledge used to formulate and design policies. They are reactive and will, especially when policies are intended to control their behaviour, adjust in order to minimize the effects of the policy. In other cases, the information system, upon which the policies are based, is also available to individuals whose expectations and beliefs are influenced by that information. Thus, a forecast of inflation will affect the expectations of businessmen and trades unions and will modify their behaviour. The businessmen fearing the impact of inflation will cut back on their investment plans whilst trade unions will press for higher wages. As a consequence a 'stagflation' arises and any policies based on the original forecast are unlikely to be sufficiently appropriate to deal with the emergent situation.

Socio-economic policy making, therefore, takes place in an environment which is not static. It is dynamic and continually adapting as individuals within it learn from and react to change, arising not only from the policies themselves but from influences outside the local environment. Successful policies need to be flexible and policy makers themselves need to be reactive. This view of policy making does, however, generate a number of analytical problems. If individuals know that government will change and react in response to their reactions then that information, no matter how uncertain, will influence the behaviour of individuals in subsequent periods. A complex set of games and strategies, actions and reactions can, therefore, emerge with one side trying to be one jump ahead of the other. This is very similar in essence but not identical to the notion of the 'U' turn in policy making. If it is known that eventually, say close to an election, a government will relax some set of controls then that will influence the expectations and the behaviour of individuals such that the success of the controls will be confounded. In these cases, rather than being flexible, the government must employ rigid policies and let it be known clearly that it will not budge. Uncertainty of policy outcomes arises because no government has the power nor the resources to control all relevant dimensions of the socio-economic environment. Not only is there the uncertainty originating from the reactive behaviour of individuals but a number of exogenous factors play an important role also. In a small open economy like that of the UK many decisions and influences external to it and beyond the control of government can have a devastating impact on what happens. An increase in US interest rates relative to those in the UK will affect UK exchange rates, inflation, order books and employment. The same also applies to an increase in the world price of oil or the world price of wheat following a drought. Very often, therefore, the success or failure of policy has nothing to do with the ability of government. Rather it is the reflection of both the endogenous complexity of the socio-economic system and the exogenous uncertainties which are the inescapable features of the decision maker's reality.[7]

Bureaucratic Inertia

It should be clear from this discussion that the problems of implementation are not viewed entirely as a set of technocratic issues, in the sense that economic institutions become the independent variable and all that is necessary is to get the institutions right and everything else will fall into place. However, since 1979 a number of the Government's policy advisers seem to have taken just such a technocratic view. They have argued that one of the main impediments to the successful implementation of the Government's new and radical policies has been 'bureaucratic inertia'.

The UK civil service had become accustomed to consensus and had helped to create it. It did not particularly wish radical change. This has led many commentators to remark that whilst the incoming 1979 Conservative Government had a radical set of policies it did not have a sufficiently radical machinery of government capable of putting these changes into effect. Malcolm Rutherford[8] expressed it this way: 'there is an implicit acknowledgement that the civil service was not able readily to adapt to a radical prime minister. When Mrs Thatcher came into power in 1979 she wanted to break with the post-war consensus...' Bureaucratic or organizational inertia is not a novel idea but has become the focus of considerable attention recently; see Olson (1983). The essential idea is that organizational sclerosis arises from organized interests which act collectively to undermine the implementation of new arrangements or new policies. It is similar to the problems already discussed in connection with the implementation of policy in a pluralistic society.

One of the main proponents of the bureaucratic inertia thesis was Sir John Hoskyns, former head of Mrs Thatcher's No. 10 Policy Unit.[9] Sir John's thesis was that the task facing the 1979 Government was the fundamental transformation of Britain's political economy but that this was beyond the technical competence of Whitehall and Westminster. A radical reform of the political and governmental system was a precondition of Britain's recovery. His solution was not to rely upon career politicians at Westminster but to bring in high quality outsiders into top civil service posts (a politicization of the civil service) whilst at the same time reducing Minister's workloads to free them from day to day survival and to enable them to concentrate on strategy and innovation. Similar views were expressed by Strauss,[10] another personal adviser to Mrs Thatcher: 'Few would dispute the belief that radical organizational changes are essential for progress. But, however radical a government's legislative intentions, nothing much tends to happen when the reform which has been agreed on requires a major change in behaviour and attitude, a shift in the culture to be brought about by the governmental insiders who are given the business of making the changes happen. . . The insiders either deliberately stifle new ideas or they are genuinely incapable of executing them'. Both Hoskyns and Strauss did not reserve their criticisms for the civil servant. They also considered that many politicians, including ministers, were not sufficiently rigorous or imaginative in their thinking.

It is not too surprising to learn that there has been no official response by means of a reply to these criticisms from the civil service. However, a number of coded messages have been transmitted by retired senior civil servants. In 1983 Lord Bancroft,[11] who was head of the civil service from 1978/81, in a lecture given at the London School of Economics, was critical of Mrs Thatcher's approach to civil servants which seemed to be to ask 'is he one of us?' Bancroft argues, suppose the answer was 'yes', then that civil servant should quit the service and become a party politician. He was very bitter about the erosion of the civil service ethos which had taken one and a quarter centuries to build but could be destroyed in a decade. Sir Douglas Wass[12] in the 1983 Reith Lectures rejected the concepts of an inner cabinet and the Prime Minister's own department and spoke out against the politicization of the civil service. He admitted that the machinery for reaching many decisions was defective and that many wrong decisions had been made in the past. But he was also critical of Cabinet decision making which did not seem to engage in periodic assessments of policies to see if they were on target. There was, he argued, a need for Cabinet reviews based upon systematic study and a need for Cabinet members to be more imaginative and to get away from the 'don't rock the boat' mentality. The reality which seemed to prevail, however, was that too many Cabinet members and ministers generally were too ready to protect their image and promote their political careers. This had an adverse effect on the quality of decisions.

There can be no doubt that poor decision making, a lack of strategy and vision, and bad management of the delivery of services will all conspire to promote policy failure. It does, however, remain an interesting but open question how much these factors have contributed to policy failures in the UK. Given the uncertainties and complexities which are inherent in pluralistic systems a much broader perspective is essential when discussing policy implementation.

Finally, governments can survive (politically) in uncertain environments by almost disengaging themselves from the socio-economic system. Rather than giving the impression that governments can, in fact, do anything about solving social and economic problems, which was the predominant view for most of the post-war period, a government might suggest that there is very little that it can do and that the pursuit of such policies is neither the appropriate nor the legitimate role of the State. This is, in effect, what the Thatcher Government has done. It has redefined the role of the State as being one which creates the 'conditions' for certain things to happen, e.g. investment, growth, employment creation. The actual realization of these outcomes does not depend upon government *per se*. Instead It depends upon individuals' efforts in the pursuit of these goals through market forces. Governments will create the necessary (but sufficient?) conditions by improving incentives (tax reductions etc), reducing interest rates, holding down inflation and removing legal impediments. This could mean that in future governments will not be judged in terms of policy failures because their response to such charges will be, 'we created the right conditions; you failed to respond'. Political debate will then be shifted to arguing about what are and what are not the appropriate conditions.

The Political Economy of the UK

The 1979 Conservative Government's economic programme captures the teachings of monetarism and supply side economics. Control the money supply and inflation will automatically fall; reduce taxes and this will create incentives that will generate a bounty of economic growth. But what exactly are these concepts?

What is Monetarism?

Fifteen years ago 'monetarism' was a highly specialized school of thought which was only discussed in the academic journals. Now it is, like its predecessor 'Keynesianism', a household word and is one of the principal elements of the Government's economic philosophy. Like Keynesianism, monetarism, whilst frequently referred to, is seldom understood. This might be because the term monetarism is not unambiguous and is often used as an umbrella term under which a number of distinct economic concepts are gathered. If one is to talk about a government being monetarist as opposed to Keynesian in its approach to economic policy making it is necessary to know what these terms mean.

The term 'monetarism' was coined by Karl Brunner in 1968.[13] Brunner used the term to summarize three conclusions drawn from monetary economics:

(1)   monetary impulses are an important factor accounting for variations in output, employment and prices;

(2)   movements in the money stock are the most reliable measure of the thrust of monetary impulses;

(3)   the behaviour of the monetary authorities dominates movements of the stock of money over business cycles.

These propositions are compared to the Keynesian policies during the post-war period which had emphasized the control of interest rates without much regard to the implications for the money supply. Monetarists blamed the resulting inflation on this growth of the money supply. Reductions in interest rates which had been aimed at stimulating the components of aggregate demand (namely consumption and investment) increased the money supply which in turn promoted an inflation which wiped out the gains made for aggregate demand. Keynesian policies which were aimed at expanding demand and, thereby, reducing unemployment had, it was advocated, generated inflation as a side effect. This inflation would, it was argued, destroy jobs in the long run.

These monetarist propositions were based on the work of Milton Friedman and his associates. Since the mid 1950s Friedman had actively pursued a research programme which sought to determine the impact of monetary impulses on the real economy (output and employment levels) - see Friedman (1956, 1958, 1959, 1966, 1970);[14] Friedman and Meiselman (1963)[15] and Friedman and Schwartz (1963).[16] This work concluded that the demand for money balances was stable and predictable and not sensitive to the rate of interest, so that changes in the supply of money would have important consequences for the economy. In particular from their pioneering monetary study of the history of the US economy Friedman and Schwartz formulated a monetarist theory of business cycles. Cycles, they argued, are explained in terms of changes in the rate of monetary growth. The nominal quantity of money is the major determinant of aggregate demand, i.e. nominal GNP is caused by real factors (capital accumulation, productivity changes, increases in labour supply).

Probably the best known monetarist proposition is that which links the money supply with inflation - inflation is everywhere a monetary phenomenon.[17] This assertion follows from the now famous identity:

$$M V = P Y$$

where M is the stock of money; V is the velocity of circulation of the money stock; P is the general level of prices and Y is the volume of transactions or the real level of output of the economy. Since Y is equivalent to real GNP it follows that the product PY is money or nominal GNP. The relationship is a national income accounting identity which must be true by definition.

Monetarists argue that following a monetary impulse M, the effect will either flow into a change in prices P or a change in real output Y. This is required to maintain the identity, because Friedman's earlier studies had shown the demand for money, and hence V, to be constant (or at least stable enough to be predictable). Further empirical work by Friedman and his associates had shown that over the short run (up to 12 months) following an increase in the money stock, real output increased but that this was eventually dissipated and gave way to price increases after about two years. The lag between an increase in the money stock and prices was long and variable.

> Because prices are sticky, faster or slower monetary growth initially affects output and employment. But these effects wear off. After about two years the main effect is on inflation. (M Friedman, 'Defining Monetarism', *Newsweek* 12 July, 1982)

The monetarist's theory of inflation generated much heated controversy. First, monetarists were called upon to explain how an increase in the money stock was transmitted into price rises. The transmission mechanism that they gave assumed that individuals had some desired demand for money: this depended upon their planned transactions. If the actual stock of money held exceeded the desired demand for money balances then they would get rid of these surplus balances by spending them. The real level of expenditure (output) would increase over the short run as indicated above. After this initial impact on real spending demand would exceed supply and prices would start to rise. Thus the monetary impulse would eventually work into higher prices. Another possible route was via high wages. The increased money stock gave firms additional liquidity which would be used to finance higher money wages in excess of productivity increases. This would then feed through in higher prices.

Keynesians, who did not dispute the identity, did, however, subscribe to an alternative transmission mechanism and viewed the underlying behaviour of the economy differently. They argued that the excess money stock caused interest rates to rise as individuals moved out of money into other financial assets in their portfolios. This increase in interest rates would cause some items of real expenditure which were interest elastic (e.g. inventories and housebuilding) to be cut back. Thus Keynesians recognized the importance of money for the real economy but saw it operating via a different route and having a weaker impact on prices.

Because monetarists assumed the demand for money to be stable (i.e. V stable) they concluded that if a government wanted to stabilize the economy then what they should do is to set the money stock M to grow in line with the projected increase in output. That simple rule Friedman argued would ensure price stability (no inflation). Monetarists favoured the setting of macro-economic policy rules rather than letting the authorities pursue discretionary interventions. Using Keynesian policies in the past, attempts had been made with fiscal policy (tax and expenditure changes) to 'fine tune' the economy. The success of this fine tuning had been called into question. Indeed, many contended that frequent interventions by the government had destabilized the economy and political business cycles had been set up. Thus, another distinction between monetarists and Keynesians emerged: Keynesians preferred discretionary interventions to control the macro-economy whilst monetarists preferred establishing simple policy rules and sticking to them.

Keynesians and monetarists also differed over their interpretation of the stability of the demand for money. If V is not stable then it becomes very difficult to set a simple monetary rule of the kind described above. For example, if Y is thought to grow at 5% and M is set to grow along with it then, if V is constant, prices will not change. If, however, V suddenly and unpredictably fell by 10%, then MV would fall by 5% to maintain the identity P and/or Y would also need to fall by 5%. It, therefore, becomes necessary to know much more about V.

Monetarists have tended to concentrate upon the transactions demand for money which is probably reasonably stable (see below). Money is, however, held for purposes other than for transactions: it is held for precautionary motives and for speculation. Taken together this means that V tends to be unstable and dependent in part upon interest rates. As M is controlled then V tends to adjust as a compensation for the monetary control - new forms of money as a medium of exchange emerge and institutional changes occur. There will always be some change in the money stock which will dominate velocity changes but it must be appreciated that these changes might be quite large with significant impacts on the real economy through interest rate effects.

Another problem which arises is the possible endogeneity of the money supply. Does the money supply respond to changes in the demand for money or is it purely exogenous, i.e. under the control of the authorities? If the demand for money increases faster than the supply then interest rates will rise. This increase in interest rates not only cuts back the demand for money but it can result in the creation of new forms of money. Thus, the money supply is, in part, endogenous. In terms of the identity of $MV = PY$, if the authorities cut back M the rise in interest rates can induce an increase in new forms of M and a rise in velocity, with the final result that MV does not change. By assuming V to be stable monetarists are assuming a zero price elasticity of demand for money. In other words they believe the money market to be inflexible. This is, however, at variance with their beliefs about markets generally and doesn't even seem to be empirically true.

There is no such thing as a distinct monetarist model of the economy despite attempts to construct one. Many monetarist propositions, instead of being derived from formal models, are drawn from supplementary empirical hypotheses which are asserted and vaguely defined. Stein,[18] who is himself a monetarist, has argued that monetarism rests upon empirical work. Generally speaking monetarists believe that markets adjust quickly and that the adjustments take place through prices rather than quantities. This contrasts sharply with Keynesians who see markets being inflexible, adjusting slowly and adjusting through quantities.

It would be a mistake to assume that all monetarists agree with one another. One area in which this is noticeable is over the degree of monetary control which is required. Economists such as David Laidler (and Friedman) favour a gradual reduction in the money supply. Gradualists would set modest money supply targets over the medium term, judging the success of the policy over two or three years and not month to month or quarter to quarter. On the other hand, there are others who advocate a big bang reduction or 'cold turkey' approach to monetary control. According to Hayek gradualism simply stretches out the misery of the recession.

> You can cure inflation suddenly or gradually. Politically it is impossible to do it gradually. To put it crudely, I would say that it is possible to create 20% unemployment for six months if you can hold out the hope that things will get better after that. You cannot have 10% unemployment for 3 years. (Hayek, *The Times*).

Another set of empirical propositions which were gathered under the monetarist's umbrella relate to the public sector deficit. Keynesians had long argued that a deficit would stimulate output and employment. The increase in taxation following the rise in output would then finance the deficit. Empirical work by Andersen and Jordan[19] found that monetary policy was quick and powerful whilst fiscal policy was impotent. The original Andersen and Jordan study, however, has now been discredited by Goldfeld and Blinder[20] but it did generate considerable interest in the possibilities that fiscal policy might 'crowd out' private sector economic activity (for a survey see Jackson 1984).[21] It has always been recognized by Keynesians that an increase in public spending must result in a corresponding displacement of private spending £1 for £1 at full employment. At less than full employment crowding out will be partial.

Public sector deficits do, however, have important financial consequences which Keynesians until recently ignored. To sell government bonds it may be necessary for the authorities to offer them at an attractive price. This will force up interest rates. A similar effect exists if the fiscal policy is pursued with a fixed money supply. Certain categories of private spending (consumption and investment) are sensitive to interest rates, which means that these will fall following the increase in interest rates precipitated by the fiscal policy. The net effect of the fiscal policy depends upon the sensitivity of private spending to the interest rates. At one extreme the rise in public spending is matched by a decline in private spending. In that case crowding out is 100% complete. In practice, however, crowding out is incomplete because private spending is not as interest elastic as monetarists assume.

Crowding out can also take place through exchange rates and imports. The rise in interest rates, following the public sector deficit, if they are higher relative to interest rates elsewhere in the world will promote an increase in the exchange rate. This will cause imports to rise and exports to fall. Public sector deficits might also cause an increase in the money supply. This can happen if they are financed through the banking system or if the rapid rise in interest rates cause the authorities to intervene and expand the money supply in an attempt to stop interest rates rising further.

For these reasons monetarists argue that fiscal policy should not be used as an element of the government's macro-economic policy. First, crowding out renders it impotent and second it has destabilizing effects through its impact on interest rates and the money supply. Public sector deficits should be minimized and it is a frequent call from monetarists that the budget be balanced. Fiscal policy would then be used purely to allocate resources to social policies.

Whether or not deficits affect interest rates is an empirical question. Even leading monetarists are not in agreement over this. Asked if public sector deficits affected interest rates Robert Lucas[22] replied 'It's possible but I think the effect is hard to detect. I can't rule out the possibility of a crowding out effect but there are just so many forces acting on interest rates that it is a tough job to sort them out. I think that the major effect probably has to do with inflationary expectations'. Anna Schwartz[23] conceded that we do not have any information to sort out inflationary expectations from crowding out effects of budget deficits on interest rates.

In the final analysis those who advocate balanced budgets do so on the basis of some ill-defined market psychology. Financial markets are more stable and less nervous with balanced budgets because they believe that a balanced budget implies zero inflation. On the other hand governments could do much to educate financial markets that they should not necessarily associate inflation with budget deficits, especially when there is a high level of unemployment. This is, of course, an empty plea when governments themselves don't believe it.

During the 1970s a new strand was added to classical monetarism. This came from a number of American economists but is particularly associated with the work of Robert Lucas[24] and Thomas Sargent; it is referred to as the 'new classical' or the new conservative macro-economics. Their work arose from a dissatisfaction with Keynesianism. In particular they preferred to view business cycles as caused by random shocks to the economic system and so they based their analysis upon the study of stochastic processes. Given the length of the lags in any economic system, which are due to the time it takes to make decisions and the time it takes to accumulate capital, these shocks become converted into serially correlated movements in output and employment. In the short-run firms are assumed to cut prices and profits whereas in the long run they make redundancies.

The new conservative macro-economics is based upon an over-riding faith that markets will respond rapidly. In particular they believe that prices adjust quickly. This is a faith that they share in common with the supply side wing of monetarism. Supply siders argue that Keynesians have spent too long concentrating upon the demand side of the economy. Indeed, Keynesian fine tuning was often referred to as demand management. Sir Geoffrey Howe in his budget statement, 10 March 1981 (Col 760) argued that 'Our problem in recent years has not been a lack of final demand'. It was, he went on to argue, a problem of the supply side of the economy's lack of competitiveness, low productivity, high wage costs (see also Treasury and Civil Service Committee 232, II, April 1981, para. 20). The policies advocated by the supply siders included the abolition of any unwarranted institutional constraints which inhibited the free working of the market system. These include: minimum wage legislation, trades unions, exchange controls, market regulation.

Lucas and his associates had some powerful things to say about the conduct of monetary and fiscal policy. An important element in any inflationary process is the formation of expectations. Individuals do not only take into account information about where the economy has come from and where it is today, they have a mental map which they use to work out where the economy might be moving to. This map is based upon a set of beliefs about how the economy behaves. Such beliefs need not be true because they can be self-fulfilling. Suppose, for example, the government announces money supply figures which are well above their trend value. Decision makers will then believe that this will cause higher inflation in subsequent periods. Their response will be to renegotiate their contracts to take account of the higher expected inflation. Thus, wages will increase and interest rates will rise. The consequence of this is that inflation will, in fact, increase!

If expectations are indeed formed in this way, then governments must announce their targets and stick by them. If the public believes that a change in policy will be introduced or that the government will make a U turn then this will be incorporated into individuals' expectations and will frustrate the original policy. Moreover, the theory stresses unexpected changes in monetary growth or any kind of economic surprise. It is surprise events which, by definition, have not been built into expectations that shock the economic system. Another feature of economic reality which this group stress is that economic agents find it difficult to distinguish between transitory and permanent changes (shocks) and between absolute and relative price changes. Economic agents make decisions on the basis of highly imperfect limited information which will have important consequences for resource allocations and distributions.

Fiscal supply siders gained a great deal of attention in the 1970s, especially through the fiscal containment movement of California's proposition 13. The best known of these economists was Arthur Laffer who gave his name to the 'Laffer curve'. The ideas contained in the Laffer curve are simplistic and not worthy of serious consideration except that they were taken seriously by the policy makers. What the curve shows is that as the tax *rate* rises, tax revenue increases but that there exists some tax rate beyond which tax revenues then fall. In other words at that point disincentives have set in. No-one, Keynesian or otherwise, would dispute this proposition. Discussions of the disincentive effects of taxation are known (see Brown and Jackson 1982).[25] What is in dispute is the notion that our tax system has reached the point that these disincentive effects are causing tax revenues to fall. There is no such evidence. Laffer and his associates provided none, but instead, proceeded with their campaign by making assertions. Nevertheless, it did give right-wing politicians a pseudo-academic argument to call for budget and tax reductions.

Monetarists frequently tend not to recognize market imperfections and market failures. When they do they advocate policies which will make structural changes, thereby opening up and liberating trade. Monetarists are ideologically committed to favouring market resource allocations and the market place as the origin of income distributions and the final arbiter between competing economic claims. They emphasize government failure, bureaucratic inertia and the destabilizing impact of governments who pursue discretionary macro-economic policies. Monetarists also tend to be libertarians in their social philosophy (see Hayek (1967)[26] and Friedman (1953)[27]). Their aim is to get government off the backs of the people; to reduce the scope of bureaucratic meddling and decision making; to return freedom of choice (via the market) back to individuals and to give only the minimalist night-watchman role to the state.

In the final analysis a great deal of the paraphernalia and intellectual baggage that is referred to as monetarism is nothing more than the classical economists pre-Keynesian belief that the economy is, or soon will be, in demand/supply equilibrium. But as Hahn [28] and a number of other commentators have argued, 'there is no convincing theoretical support for the view that the economy will eventually reach a satisfactory equilibrium (e.g. one where unemployment is at the natural rate). Only quite rudimentary and implausible models show that much' (p.82, Memorandum to Treasury and Civil Service Committee, 1980). On fiscal supply side economics, Anna Schwartz[29] has argued 'I think that the supply side promise was oversold. It was political sweet talk'; whilst Robert Lucas[30] points out 'the idea that cutting taxes generally would stimulate the system enough to increase revenue – which is what I think is the key claim of supply side economics – doesn't have any foundation whatsoever, either in fact or in theory'.

Whilst monetarism started out as a distinct set of empirical propositions about the importance of monetary impulses in explaining business cycle behaviour, it soon became overloaded by popular commentators who lumped any right-wing economic policies under the general heading of monetarism. This has led to confusion and has devalued the term. Many monetarists, especially Friedman, object to this broadening of the term. Whilst they are willing to subscribe to Brunner's original definition, they are not willing to associate themselves to the ideas of the new conservative macro-economics with their belief in Austrian economics and libertarian ideals. 'The controversies over monetarist theory and policy have been so extensive and its current influence so ubiquitous that numerous variants have been specified, just as the Eskimos have so many words for snow. But they have no single word for snow in general, nor is there any single monetarist model ... therefore take monetarism as a general body of thought stressing the pervasive importance of the general stock of money in macro-economic relationships, especially those determining quantities denominated in money such as money income'.[29]

As a body of thought, not only is monetarism ambiguous but it is also incomplete. Monetarist theories and the empirical work used to support them have been subjected to the most severe criticism. One well known monetarist is quite candid about the amount of work that remains to be done: 'Economists like myself or Milton Friedman who attach great importance to changes in the quantity of money as causing a depression have got a hard theoretical problem on our hands. Why should the changes in the quantity of money – basically a unit's change – alter decisions people make about production, employment, and so forth? That's the great puzzle with business cycle theory. Why doesn't a purely nominal variation in the number of dollars in circulation simply change the general price level and nothing else'.[32]

Despite the theoretical and empirical weaknesses of the corpus of monetarist statements they have gained popular appeal. To understand this it is necessary to stand outside of standard economic analysis and to approach the issue as a problem in the sociology of knowledge.

Monetarism Comes to Britain

How did monetarism come to Britain, the nation of the Keynesian revolution? The sociology of knowledge of that period has still to be written but a number of strands in the argument can be presented. How economic ideas come to be accepted and integrated into policies is a fascinating topic which has been relatively ignored by economists and political scientists. Keegan[33] has provided some insight but the story remains incomplete.

There was a general disenchantment with the standard Keynesian policy paradigm in the 1970s as the world moved into the turbulent years of stagflation. Accelerating inflation in world commodity and food prices; the floating of the dollar; the quadrupling of the world price of oil in 1973/74 and the slump in output found Keynesian principles wanting. In the face of these difficulties a vacuum emerged which was to be filled by alternative policies. Keynes himself always produced economic analysis in response to the problems of the age but his Keynesian successors seemed, at the time, to be incapable of generating solutions to the problems of stagflation. Harry Johnson[34] commenting on the monetarist counter-revolution wrote;

> New ideas win a public and a professional hearing not on their scientific merits but on whether or not they promise a solution to important problems that the established orthodoxy had proved itself incapable of solving.

Two influential journalists who had visited the USA in the 1960s and had been converted to monetarist ideas were Sam Brittan of the *Financial Times* and Peter Jay of the London *Times*. Whilst it would be a mistake to suggest that the financial press was so powerful to bring about a revolution in economic thought it is nevertheless important in forming the ideas of others, especially politicians and their personal advisers. Jay and Brittan, along with private sector think tanks such as the Institute for Economic Affairs, did much to introduce into Britain the monetarist creed and to popularize it. Also, the work of Bacon and Eltis[35] should not go unmentioned in this connection. Their book did much to divide the nation into two parts: the wealth creating manufacturing sector and the wealth consuming parasitical public sector. From the mid-1970s, this physiocratic notion of the need to create wealth was an integral part of the supply side message. It also did much to provide an intellectual foundation for those crude policies that were aimed at rolling back the frontiers of the state. This could now be done in the name of expanding the wealth creating base of the economy.

Work carried out in the Bank of England, the Treasury, university departments and various research institutes seemed to suggest that the structure and behaviour of the UK economy was suitable for the introduction of monetarist policies. Before giving serious consideration to controlling the money supply for anti-inflation policy purposes it was essential to know if there was a stable demand for money. Many UK studies suggested that the demand for money in the UK was indeed stable, although subsequent analysis has called these results into question (these and other empirical studies are reviewed in detail in the next chapter). The empirical link between money supply changes and prices in the UK is weak and few studies have managed to find this relationship. Indeed, in 1980 the money stock increased by almost 20%. This, according to monetarist principles, should have resulted in a rise in the general price level two years later. Instead inflation fell to about 5% p.a. in 1983/84!

Whilst a limited amount of evidence suggests that the monetarists' simple propositions about the behaviour of the economy could be formulated into policy rules, that evidence was never strong enough for it to be used as the spearhead of a monetarist policy counter-revolution. In retrospect it is really quite amazing how such a motley collection of economic studies could have served as the foundation for a radical change in economic policy making. It was the force of circumstances which brought these monetarist ideas from the background to centre stage. Politicians actively pursuing economic policies of an interventionist type suddenly found that in the conditions of the 1970s previous policies did not work well. They were, therefore, receptive to new ideas which included monetarist propositions. The Callaghan-Healey administration had run up a series of large public sector deficits in an attempt to deal with stagflation. This resulted in a run on the pound sterling as international speculators anticipated runaway inflation and a devaluation of sterling. In order to balance the books the IMF was approached for a loan. This loan was granted on the condition that the UK government would undertake to cut back its public spending, control the money supply, and reduce the public sector deficit. The first UK monetarist government was, in fact, a Labour Government.

Conclusion

The remainder of this book examines the implementation of economic and social policies against the background of the revolution which has taken place in the design of policies. How easy was it to implement these new policies? What were the difficulties of getting them from the drawing board blue-print stage to actually producing policies which would work well? This chapter has sought to provide a framework within which these questions might be answered. The implementation of policies in a complex, uncertain, pluralistic system faces many difficulties. Which impediments were more more important than others? That is the subject matter of the chapters which follow.

Notes and References

1. J. Pressman and A. Wildavsky, *Implementation*, University of California Press, 1973.
2. E.C. Hargrove, *The missing link*, Urban Institute, Washington DC, 1975; C. Hood, *The limits of administration*, John Wiley, 1976; L. Gunn, Policy and the policy analyst, Paper presented to Public Administration Conference, York, 1980, mimeo; A. Dunsire, *Implementation in a bureaucracy: the execution process*, Martin Robertson, 1978; P.M. Jackson, *The political economy of bureaucracy*, Philip Allan, 1982.
3. W. Williams, 'The study of implementation: an overview', in W. Williams (ed), *Studying implementation*, Chatham House Publishers Inc., 1982.
4. A literature on the failure of government, ungovernability and planning disasters has recently grown up. See J. Cornford, *The failure of the state*, Croom Helm, 1975; A. King, Overload: problems of governing in the 1970s, *Political Studies*, 23, 1975; R. Rose,

Overload governments: the problem outlined, *European Studies Newsletter*, 1975; S. Brittan, The economic contradictions of democracy, *British Journal of Political Science*, April 1975; M. Crozier, 'The crisis of democracy' in M. Crozier, S. Huntington and J. Watanuki (eds), *The crisis of democracy*, New York University Press, 1975.

5. The literature on economic planning in socialist/centralized economics has recognized these problems for some time. See J. Kornai, *Overcentralization in economic administration*, Oxford University Press, 1959; A. Berliner, *Factory and manager in the USSR*, Cambridge Mass., 1957; M. Ellman, Changing views on central economic planning, *ACES Bulletin*, Spring 1983.

6. S. Barnett and M.J. Hill, *Report to the SSRC Central Local Government Relations Committee on the Core or Theoretical Component of the Research on Implementation*, mimeo.

7. Some of these issues are taken up by Shonfield (*The use of public power*, OUP, 1982) in which he argues that successful intervention by government has become increasingly difficult because (a) the instruments of economic policy are big, clumsy and slow moving and (b) fine adjustments and fine tuning are required but this is not feasible.

8. Malcolm Rutherford, *Financial Times*, 25 November 1983.

9. Sir John's statements are found in two articles which he wrote in *The Times*; Strip down the state machine and start again, 16 February 1983 and Take off the blinkers: think for a change, 22 November 1983.

10. N. Strauss, The case for more live wires in Whitehall, *The Times*, 19 January 1984.

11. A report of Lord Bancroft's lecture is found in Hugo Young, The mandarins strike back, *Sunday Times*, 11 December 1983.

12. Sir Douglas Wass, *Government and the governed*, BBC Reith Lectures 1983, Routledge and Kegan Paul, 1984.

13. K. Brunner, The role of money and monetary policy, *Federal Reserve Bank of St. Louis Review*, July 1968.

14. M. Friedman, Studies in the quantity of money, Chicago University Press, 1956; M. Friedman, 'The supply of money and changes in prices and output' in *The relationship of prices to economic stability and growth*, Papers submitted by panelists appearing before the Joint Economic Committee, 85th Congress, 2nd session, 1958, 241-256; M. Friedman, The demand for money: some theoretical and empirical results, *Journal of Political Economy*, 67, 1959, 327-358; M. Friedman, Interest rates and the demand for money, *Journal of Law and Economics*, 9, 1966, 71-86; M. Friedman, A theoretical framework for monetary analysis, *Journal of Political Economy*, 78, 1970, 193-238.

15. M. Friedman and D. Meiselman, 'The relative stability of monetary velocity and the investment multiplier in the United States, 1897-1958', in *Stabilization Policies*, a series of Research Studies prepared for the Commission on Money and Credit, Englewood Cliffs, New Jersey, 1963, 165-268.

16. M. Friedman and A. Schwartz, Money and business cycles, *Review of Economics and Statistics*, 1963, 32-64.

17. M. Friedman, The role of monetary policy, *American Economic Review*, March, 1968 (reprinted in *The Optimum Quantity of Money*, Ch. 5).

18. J.L. Stein, 'Introduction: The monetarist critique of the new economics' in Stein (ed), *Monetarism*, North Holland Amsterdam, 1976.

19. L.C. Andersen and J.L. Jordan, Monetary and fiscal actions: a test of their relative importance in economic stabilization, *Federal Reserve Bank of St. Louis Review*, 50, 1968, 11-24.

20. S.M. Goldfeld and A.S. Blinder, Some implications of endogenous stabilization policy, *Brookings Papers on Economic Activity*, 1972, 585-640.

21. P.M. Jackson, *Macroeconomic activity and local government behaviour*, Report presented to Central/Local Government Relations Panel of ESRC, 1984.

22. R. Lucas, Commentary in the *Manhattan Report on Economic Policy, III, (4)*, July 1982.

23. A. Schwartz, Commentary in the *Manhattan Report on Economic Policy*, II, (4) July 1982.

24. R.E. Lucas, Econometric policy evaluation: a critique, *Carnegie Rochester Conference*

Series on Public Policy, Vol 1, 1976.
25. C.V. Brown and P.M. Jackson, *Public sector economics*, Martin Robertson, 1982.
26. F.A. Hayek, *Studies in philosophy, politics and economics*, Routledge, 1967.
27. M. Friedman, *Essays in positive economics*, Chicago University Press, 1953.
28. F. Hahn, Memorandum presented to Treasury and Civil Service Committee, 1980.
29. A. Schwartz, *op. cit.*
30. R. Lucas, Commentary, *op. cit.*
31. R. Portes, 'Central planning and monetarism: fellow travellers', Birkbeck College Discussion Paper in *Economics*, 80, July 1980.
32. R. Lucas, *op. cit.*, p.6.
33. W. Keegan, *The Thatcher experiment*, 1984.
34. H.G. Johnson, The monetarist counter revolution, *American Economic Review*, 1971.
35. R. Bacon and W. Eltis, *Britain's economic problem: too few producers*, 2nd ed., Macmillan, 1978.

2

Perspectives on Practical Monetarism

Peter Jackson

The cure for inflation is simple to state but hard to implement.(M. Friedman and R. Friedman, p.316, 1980)[1]

Mrs Thatcher and her Government came to power in 1979 with what was regarded at the time as a radically new approach to the management of the British economy. In the run up to the general election of that year the Conservative Party had promised to put the nation on a fundamentally different course which would revitalize the economy and improve incentives for individual efforts. To do this it was to rely more than previous governments had upon the dynamics of market forces and the benefits of entrepreneurship. What the Thatcher Government did was to embrace the emergent popular perceptions of the nation's problems: a perception created in part by its own party thinkers such as Sir Keith Joseph and his team of advisers at the Centre for Policy Studies.

After four years in office, few of the Government's economic objectives were achieved. The June 1983 general election was not won on the basis of economic success. Many changes had been made but the economy stubbornly refused to turn. Whilst inflation had been reduced the price paid for this success was a dramatic increase in unemployment. The incoming 1979 Conservative Government had always argued that it would take more than one term of office to change the structure of the economy and the effects of decades of post-war policy, and to shift public attitudes. What they did not seem to appreciate was just how difficult this would prove to be. Moreover, the Government's particular economic strategy, which can usefully be referred to as practical monetarism, had never been implemented before. There was no guarantee that what appeared to be technically feasible in blue print form could be translated from the drawing board into something that would produce the desired results.

Much of the Government's first term in office was devoted to defining in more detail the elements of its practical monetarism. As the Government learned how to implement its new policies, the ride for the economy was bumpy. It was like learning to drive a revolutionary new car which was still in the early prototype stages of its development. As the driver crunches his way through the gears, periodically stalling the engine, he slowly learns about the internal workings of the engine along with what the car is capable of doing and what it cannot do without over straining the system. On a test run there should be no casualties - even the driver should survive. Carrying out experiments on an economy, however, is likely to produce casualties unless safety-nets are built in to protect them. In this case the unemployed and the poor have been the casualties of the 'Thatcher experiment'.

This chapter reviews the problems which the Thatcher Government encountered in implementing its new economic strategy. One important lesson learned from this whole episode is that the British economy is more resilient than is often supposed. Having faced a decade of financial instability from 1969-1979, followed by an injection of deflationary policies unprecedented during the post-war period, the economy remains, if battered, nevertheless intact. This lesson tells the observer as much about the nature of British society as it does about the robustness of the economy.

The Becalming of Keynesian Economics

After 30 years of increasing governmental attempts, by all parties, to stabilize the economy through fiscal means,[2] to redistribute income and to promote full employment a counter-revolution had taken place which called into question the Keynesian legacy. The post-war social democratic consensus assumed that policies, based upon broadly Keynesian thinking, would provide economic stability, growth and prosperity. It was also the age of 'corporatism', an implicit cooperative alliance between industry labour and government embodied in, for example, the tri-partite meetings held by the National Economic Development Office.

The counter-revolution of Thatcherism and practical monetarism was to sweep away much of that post-war economic infrastructure. The UK's economic ills were blamed upon Keynesianism and excessive doses of corporatism.[3] Cooperation and corporation were to be replaced by 'conviction politics'.[4] The focal point of the counter-revolution was a philosophy based upon a more limited role for government; the replacement of the maintenance of full employment, as the primary economic policy objective, by that of the elimination of inflation.

The success of the counter-revolution in obtaining the support of the popular vote was, in part, due to the advertising campaign which the Conservative Party had employed in order to project the message and the image of its new philosophy. But the timing was also right. The sentiments of the British electorate were suitably receptive to this new message which offered hope. The 1970s had been a series of one economic problem after another: a period of what has come to be known as 'stagflation', the simultaneous occurrence of inflation and recession. Stagflation had been ruled out as a possibility by Keynesian policy makers and yet it did happen. This disillusionment with Keynesianism and its apparent inability to counteract stagflation provided a vacuum which alternative policies rushed in to fill.

The causes of the UK economy's poor economic performance during the 1970s became the centre of debate. Keynesians blamed the accelerating inflation upon the world oil price shock, food price rises and commodity price increases which set in train a price-wage spiral. They also noted the impact which the discovery of North Sea oil had upon an economy which had recently moved to a system of floating exchange rates. The unemployment which accompanied this inflation was, the Keynesians argued, the result of the system's adjustment to the oil price hike. To contain both the inflation and the unemployment they advocated the imposition of price and wage controls; a policy which the Labour Government did in fact pursue post-1976. This policy was neither popular with industry nor the trade unions. It eroded profits, interfered with the free workings of the market, and upset free wage negotiation and collective bargaining.

The Labour Party's opposition came from an increasingly articulate anti-Keynesian group who proposed the use of monetarist solutions to the economy's problems. They persistently argued that the UK economy's problems were deep rooted and went back much further than the oil price rise. The current economic difficulties were the result of years of overstimulative fiscal and monetary policies. Successive governments had run deficits in order to gain votes. The expansionary fiscal policies and the associated deficits had fuelled inflation.[5] Moreover, expansionary public spending had to be paid for from taxation which, it was asserted, eroded incentives and destroyed entrepreneurship.

The anti-Keynesians also argued that post-war economic growth and stability had nothing to do with Keynesian policies. During most of the post-war period the engine of economic growth, propelled by the automobile and the white goods industries, had generated sufficient income to make unpleasant choices between, for example, profits and wages, unnecessary. The fruits of growth had allowed conflicts to be resolved. But all the time the mixed economy was being eroded. The entrepreneurial spirit was being dulled, whilst the horn of plenty was full and, in some cases, overflowing. Moreover, in periods of growth and prosperity, managerial mistakes could be absorbed and go unnoticed; wage increases in excess of productivity growth could be granted and generally a quiet life could be pursued by avoiding excessive risk taking in investments and other ventures. But this was not sustainable. What the 1973 oil price hike did was to rip away the paper which had been covering the cracks of weakness in the structure of the UK economy: it exposed the inherent contradictions of the post-war mixed capitalist economy.

Keynesians did not come to the rescue. Their arguments against the alternative economic policies could only be conducted at the level of technical economic analysis, which had very little appeal to the popular vote. Discredited publicly by their apparent lack of success, they could only assert that the new untried policies would not work as simply as their advocates suggested. What the 1979 General Election did prove was that at least some of the British electorate were willing to give the new policies a chance.

Part of the collapse of Keynesianism was due to a shift in the underlying political basis upon which such policies depended for their successful implementation. When Keynes wrote in the 1920s and 1930s, each nation state was responsible for its own economic policy. Whilst this remains true, the environment through which these policies are implemented has changed. There is now a greater international interdependence in economic affairs. National economic sovereignty is as much an illusion today as it was for Ramsay MacDonald and Philip Snowdon in 1931. But not only was this a problem which post-war Keynesianism had faced, it was to be confronted by Mrs Thatcher's economic policies also. In a global, highly interdependent financial community, the success of one nation's economic policy is contingent upon the changes which the other major economies make to their policies.

TINA 364

What made the Thatcher Government's economic policies different? Some have mistakenly argued that it was the use of monetary targets which distinguished the 1979/83 Government from its predecessors. But monetary targets had been introduced by the previous Callaghan-Healey administration. Indeed, the introduction of British practical monetarism can be traced back to 1976 when Mr Healey, who was then the Chancellor of the Exchequer, signed the IMF Letter of Intent. The Thatcher Government's strand of monetarism was more than just setting monetary targets, it included a package of structural readjustments, trades union reforms and a fiscal strategy which would be compatible with financial stability. Based upon the neo-liberal counter revolution, referred to above, it embraced an idealization of the market place and the writings of neo-liberal economists such as Milton Friedman and Fredrick von Hayek, along with the new classical economists such as Robert Lucas in the USA and Patrick Minford in the UK. The economic philosophy pursued was, therefore, a pot-pourri of different strains of right wing economic thinking. Herein lay one of its difficulties – were these different strands compatible with one another at an intellectual, let alone a practical level?[6]

The distinguishing feature of the 1979 Government's policies was that it made the elimination of inflation the primary target of economic policy whilst to all intents and purposes suspending short-term stabilization policies. Ever since the publication of the 1944 all party White Paper on full employment, which had been drawn up by Beveridge and Keynes, the primary objective of economic policy had been the maintenance of full employment. This was to be achieved by means of the instruments of fiscal policy, accompanied by a monetary policy that would ensure stable interest rates. The money supply was not an instrument of control. The Thatcher Government reversed the roles of fiscal and monetary policies in addition to making the elimination of inflation its primary objective. Fiscal policy was relegated to an accommodating position with monetary policy, in particular control of the money supply, calling the tune. Specifically it was the public sector borrowing requirement (PSBR), which was part of the money supply that had to be controlled. If taxation was also to be reduced, then public spending had to be brought under strict control. In other words, there was no role for an independent fiscal policy: all fiscal instruments had to be made compatible with the Government's money supply targets.

This policy was supported by the Government's new classical advisers, who argued at a technical level, that the short-run benefits of fiscal policy as measured, for example, in terms of reductions in unemployment, were short lived. All that the fiscal stimulus did was to generate inflation which eventually resulted in higher unemployed.[7] The elimination of inflation was intended to provide a stable environment that would result in plans being made by industry that would create jobs. This produced a series of statements made by ministers that it was not in the power of governments to create jobs and employment. Rather, governments should generate the conditions that are conducive to job creation. Moreover, the Government's advisers claimed that the deflationary impact of imposing tight money supply targets would not produce unemployment. Any impact on employment would be short lived. As the inflation fell, employment would be generated.

The details of the 1979 Government's economic policies are found in their pre-election manifesto.

> To master inflation, proper monetary discipline is essential with publicly stated targets for the rate of growth of the money supply. At the same time a gradual reduction in the size of the government's borrowing requirement is also vital... It will do yet further harm to go on printing money to pay ourselves without first earning more... The state takes too much of the nation's income; its share must be steadily reduced... The reduction of waste, bureaucracy and over government will yield substantial savings. We shall cut income tax at all levels to reward hard work, responsibility and success.

In a letter sent to the Treasury and Civil Service Committee's 'Memorandum on Monetary Policy' (HC 450) Sir Geoffrey Howe elaborated these objectives:

> The Government have also eschewed all the apparatus of formal incomes

policies which have failed in the past and led to distortion in the labour market... the Government do not intend to intervene in individual wage negotiations except where they are inevitably involved as direct employers.

The Government intends to restore a broad balance of power in the framework of collective bargaining.

. . . the poor trend in our trade performance in recent years, which reflects the UK's industrial performance is a matter for concern.

So far as taxes are concerned, our primary concern is that both the structure and the level should not discourage enterprise but should permit hard work and initiative to be rewarded.

It was part of the Government's economic strategy to stick rigidly to its announced plans. There would be no U turns as there had been in the past. The reason for previous U turns in policy had been that as soon as the going became rough, governments had relaxed their policy stance in the fear that their popularity would be damaged. This meant that economic agents, businessmen, wage negotiators etc behaved in the expectation that the policy stance would be relaxed. The consequence was that policies were less effective than they otherwise might have been. The Thatcher style of government was that no U turn or relaxation of policy would be made. Decision makers could base their plans on the expectation that the Government would stand by its announced policies over the medium term. By announcing money supply targets for the medium term (four years ahead) the Government was in effect signalling that inflation would come down. It was assumed by policy makers that businessmen and trades unionists would base their price and wage decisions on these announced targets and thereby produce the desired outcome, namely a reduction in the rate of inflation. If there had been a hint that the money supply targets would be subsequently relaxed then the price and nominal wage decisions would have been based on the expectation that inflation was going to be higher than the Government was announcing. The result would then have been an actual rate of inflation in excess of that desired.

The success of the Government's economic strategy depended crucially not only upon the reasoning which lay behind this kind of inflation psychology and decision making but also upon its ability to control the money supply, the PSBR and government spending. Moreover, the whole strategy rested upon economic relationships which were in dispute. Were these strong unambiguous relationships between the money supply and inflation; between the PSBR and the money supply; between the PSBR, interest rates and investment; and between taxation and incentives?

In 1980 364 of the UK's university economists, including the most senior professors and previous advisers to governments signed an open letter arguing that the Government's policies were unlikely to bring inflation permanently under control without causing a massive increase in unemployment. They invited the Government to think again and to consider alternatives. The reply was simple and direct: 'there is no alternative' (TINA).

The 1979 Government's economic strategy was, therefore, more than just money supply targets. It shifted emphasis away from demand side management of injecting demand into the system (by increasing government spending or reducing taxes) when unemployment was rising, and concentrated instead upon supply side policies: improving incentives through tax reductions; pursuing the market ethic through privatization programmes and the sale of council housing; improving collective bargaining; reducing the number of government regulations; and increasing labour productivity in the belief that jobs would only be created and sustained in the long run if British industry was competitive in cost terms both at home and abroad.

The Medium-Term Financial Strategy (MTFS)

The centre piece of the Government's macroeconomic strategy was the medium-term financial strategy. This was without doubt an important innovation in the design of economic policy. It was one of the first attempts to integrate monetary and fiscal policies by making sure that they were compatible with one another. This was a significant departure from previous Keynesian policies which had ignored the financial consequences of fiscal policies. The MTFS was the 1979 Conservative Government's equivalent to the National Plan introduced by the 1964 Labour Government of Harold Wilson. Like the National Plan, the MTFS was to prove to be difficult to implement.

The MTFS was a set of plans introduced in the budget of March 1980, detailing targets for the growth of the money supply and other financial variables such as the public sector borrowing requirements (PSBR). It set these targets a number of years ahead (four years). As such, it was the first attempt to produce a system of financial planning as an integral part of the economic management of the UK. The aim of the MTFS was to provide a framework for financing an acceptable rate of growth at a tolerable rate of inflation. In the past many plans for growth had been unsustainable over the long run because they ran into financing constraints, balance of payments' difficulties, and inflation. By presenting the MTFS the Government was in effect announcing that its plans for reducing inflation were credible because it had established a set of money supply targets which were consistent with the achievement of its objectives.[8]

The MTFS operated by gradually reducing the rate of growth in the money supply, sterling M3(£M5) – see Appendix to this chapter for the definition of £M3. Along with the targets for the growth in £M3 the Government also produced targets for the PSBR to ensure that there would not be undue pressure placed on interest rates. There was no exchange rate policy and no wages policy. These were left to market forces.

The structure of the MTFS was simple enough and was presented in the

Financial Statement and Budget Report (the 'Red Book') at the time of the budget. Whilst Denis Healey had used money supply targets these had only been set one year ahead: the money supply targets of the MTFS were set for a number of years ahead. For the fiscal year 1979 the target for £M3 was 10% with a permissible range of 8% - 12%. The target and its associated range were to be reduced by 1% p.a. so that by 1983 the target would be 6% within a range of 4% to 8%. This was a slow and gradual reduction in the money supply. During 1978, the year before the Government took office, £M3 had grown by 12%. The Government was, therefore, not introducing a sharp reduction in the money supply. Their objective was to bring down the money supply without causing a credit crunch.

In 1979 the monetarist's greatest virtue was the simplicity of their message: a message which had been easy to get across to the electorate. Inflation was always and everywhere a monetary phenomenon. All that governments had to do was to control the money supply and inflation would automatically fall. What was not fully appreciated at the time was that there would be problems involved in implementing such a simple message. The successful implementation of a policy depends, *certis paribus*, upon it being firmly grounded upon an understanding of how the world actually operates. Was the MTFS firmly grounded? To answer this general question a number of supplementary questions are considered:

(1)   which measure of money should the Government control? Did the Government choose the correct measure of money when formulating the MTFS?
(2)   does the money supply act as a reliable indicator of the state of the economy?
(3)   is there an unambiguous and strong relationship between the money supply and (a) inflation (b) the PSBR?
(4)   can the money supply be controlled?

Unless the Government is able to measure, interpret, and control the key variables of its plan then it is like a ship's captain navigating with a faulty compass and without a rudder to his ship. Just how robust was the MTFS?

Which Measure of the Money Supply?

It frequently comes as a surprise to discover that there is more than one possible measure of money. These are given a variety of labels, M_0, M_1, M_2, M_3, £M3, PSL1 PSL2, to name but the more popular measures. What distinguishes one definition of money from another is its *liquidity*: i.e. how quickly the assets which make up money can be used to buy something. Notes and coins are the most liquid forms of money. The alternative definitions of money are set out in Appendix 1.

When formulating its MTFS the Government, therefore, had a number of alternative measures of the money supply to choose from when setting its money supply targets. The measure which was actually chosen was Sterling M3 (£M3). Was this, however, the most appropriate measure and what factors should influence such a choice?

A useful measure of the money supply should have the following characteristics:

(1)   it should have a long run of data measuring it so that its behaviour can be studied in terms of its suitability and in relation to the behaviour of other economic variables such as prices and nominal GNP;

(2)   it should be controllable.

The Bank of England[9] rejected M1 on the grounds that estimates of it were of a low quality and that data referring to it existed for a few years only. Studies by Artis and Nobay[10] and Goodhart and Crocket[11] found that M3 gave a good statistical explanation of changes in nominal GNP but no consideration was given to *causation*. In fact, in a later study Williams, Goodhart and Gowland[12] rejected the idea that the changes in the money supply caused changes in GNP.

Studies of the relative stability of the different measures of money indicated that £M3 was the more stable.[13] From these, and other studies, it was eventually decided that of all the possible measures of the money supply, the £M3 was probably the best for the purposes of formulating the MTFS. This choice was not free of criticism.

£M3 as an Indicator

What information does £M3 give to policy makers? It was assumed that changes in £M3 would give signals about changes in the pressure of demand within the economy. If money (£M3) is held for the purpose of effecting transactions (demand), then an increase in £M3 reflects an increase in demand. A rapid increase in demand, it was assumed, will result in price rises, i.e. inflation. To cut back on inflation it is necessary to reduce demand, and to reduce demand it is necessary to reduce the means of making demand effective (i.e. reduce the money stock).

The chain of reasoning set out in the previous paragraph essentially amounts to the monetarist theory of inflation. All depends upon the supply of money. As with any chain its strength depends upon its weakest link. It will be shown subsequently that this chain has a number of weak links but, in the meantime, the link that will be considered is this: how reliable is £M3 as a measure of transactions and hence the pressure of demand?

There are a number of problems associated with using £M3 as an index of the pressure of demand. First, £M3 is not held only for transactions purposes. Part of it is held for transactions, some of it is used as liquidity against uncertainty, and part of it is held for speculation. It is, therefore, difficult to disentangle the message when £M3 changes. Is it changing because the volume of transactions has increased, or is its change a reflection of an increased demand for liquidity brought about by greater uncertainty? Second, £M3 contains an interest rate component and will, therefore, be sensitive to changes in interest rates.[14] That is, interest is paid on some of the assets which go to make up £M3. Thus, £M3 will rise as interest rates rise if people decide to invest more in these assets. Such increases have nothing to do with an increase in the volume of transactions and will not be inflationary.

The third difficulty associated with £M3 is the statistical series used to measure it was badly distorted as a result of the imposition of the monetary controls used during the 1970s. In their attempt to bring the money supply under control the authorities imposed direct controls in the form of 'the corset' on bank lending, periodically between 1973 and 1978 and then continuously for two years from June 1978. The corset restricted the amount of interest bearing liabilities that the banks could bid for and hence the amount of lending that they could do. As a consequence these 'lost deposits' were simply diverted outside of the banking system to other parts of the financial sector. This process was called dis-intermediation. The result was, however, that £M3 became less and less useful as an indicator. When, in June 1980, the corset was removed, as part of the Government's policy of deregulation, re-intermediation took place. The funds which had by-passed the banks came flooding in again. Between June 1980 and June 1981 £M3 rose by 19% – well outside of the Government's targets.

A more appropriate tactic would have been to remove the corset prior to the implementation of the MTFS. It was well known that the £M3 series was badly distorted because of the imposition of the corset and disintermediation. This would have allowed the financial system to adjust and for the Government to set realistic money supply targets which had some chance of being met. As it was, the Government chose a sequence for the implementation of its policies which guaranteed that the money supply targets of the first year of the MTFS would be breeched. Why did it do this? Was it badly advised – did its advisers not realize the scale of the disintermediation which had taken place or was the Government too impatient to delay the implementation of its new system?

It is clear that £M3 was not a useful indicator of the pressure of demand in the economy. Too many other factors in addition to the volume of transactions influenced £M3. This caused problems for the interpretation of changes in £M3 and made it too clumsy an indicator for policy. It was for these reasons that the Government towards the end of its first term of office looked to new alternative measures of the money supply. That which seemed to shadow transactions and the pressure of demand most closely and which did not suffer from the problems of £M3 was M_0. Rather than rely upon a single indicator the Government seemed to minimize its risks by referring to a set of indicators comprised mainly of £M3, PSL2, and M_0. Whilst it continued to set £M3 targets, the Government began to take account of the growth in these other measures, directing its policy to a progressive and sustained reduction in the rate of growth of all of them.

Not only was £M3 a poor indicator it suffered the fate of all economic indicators that after a while they lose their usefulness and meaning. This is because of 'Goodhart's law', named after Dr Charles Goodhart, Chief Economic Adviser to the Bank of England:

> Any statistical regularity will tend to collapse once pressure is placed upon it for control purposes... In 1970 it was believed that there were a number of important economic regularities which could be manipulated for short-run control purposes – the Phillips Curve, the demand for money function, the consumption function. During the early 1970s these regularities became unstuck one after another. They are regularly glued together again, down in the econometric workshops, but they no longer carry the same bright conviction. *The Times*, 8 February 1980)

Money Supply and Inflation

The sole purpose of the MTFS and control over the money supply was to bring down the rate of inflation. In the previous section the argument linking the money supply to inflation was set down. Increases in the money supply were seen to result in an increase in demand which in turn caused prices to rise. If the supply of money rises faster than the demand for it, individuals will wish to get rid of it. Money is not held for its own sake but is used as a medium of exchange. To get rid of unwanted money balances individuals spend them and this pushes up demand. Prices will eventually rise.

The gulf which separates monetarists and Keynesians is not as wide as is often supposed. Most neo-Keynesians would agree that at some point a rapid increase in the money supply will cause prices to rise. Where they do disagree with monetarists is where this point lies and how big the price increases are. For a strict monetarist, inflation is always a monetary phenomenon and its cure is a reduction in the money supply. The Keynesian theory of inflation is much more complex and pays more attention to how prices are actually formed in an economy; supply responses to the increase in demand; and cost factors, including external costs to the UK economy. Thus, whilst an increase in the money supply will cause demand to rise, a Keynesian would argue that this need not result in a price rise if the supply of goods and services is increased. The money supply increase will, therefore, result in an increase in output and employment and not inflation up until the economy reaches its full employment level of output.

To resolve the difference between monetarist and Keynesian theories of inflation it is necessary to consider the available empirical evidence. In the previous section it was shown that £M3 was not a useful indicator of the pressure of demand. Is there, however, any measure of money which is closely associated with inflation? Holly and Longbottom; Benstock and Longbottom; Budd, Holly, Longbottom and Smyth,[15] using a variety of statistical causality tests, conclude that £M3 causes wholesale prices with a lag of between 1¼ and 4¾ years. These studies are, however, problematic and the length of the lags are quite incredible. A Treasury study, reported in Wren-Lewis (1981), found that increases in £M3 caused increases in retail prices but again the lags were incredibly long. Hendry, in his evidence to the House of Commons Treasury and Civil Service Committee criticized the Wren-Lewis Study as being nothing more than a data mining exercise whilst Hendry and Ericcson[16] were critical in their review of the Friedman and Schwartz[17] study which claimed that changes in the money supply accounted for the UK cycle in nominal GNP. Hendry and Ericcson concluded that 'the failure by Friedman and Schwartz to present test evidence pertinent to their main assertions leaves those void of credibility'.

A study of UK inflation carried out by Bade and Parkin[18] found that £M3 caused inflation under *flexible* exchange rates. Under fixed exchange rates, however, domestic monetary policy caused neither inflation nor output fluctuations:

> The empirical findings are of course tentative. They certainly are not regarded as an unshakable body of dogma... The research agenda suggested by the results give a high place to investigating more thoroughly the effects of exogenous foreign variables on domestic prices and incomes.

This conclusion of Bade and Parkin, which is in accordance with that of Williams, Goodhart and Gowland[19] indicates clearly that even at the time of writing the relationship between money supply and inflation is nowhere near settled. Controversy abounds, so that strong statements about the need to control the money supply in order to control inflation, as embodied in the MTFS, are statements of faith and much to do with political rhetoric.

During the 1980s, £M3 failed to foreshadow price changes. Any statistical relationship that might have existed seemed to have broken down. This was confirmed in a Treasury study reported in Johnson.[20] Between February 1980 and December 1980 £M3 rose by 23% but prices have continued to fall. Was this an example of Goodhart's Law or was the relationship between £M3 and inflation much more complex and much weaker than the Government and its advisers had supposed?

If Bade and Parkin and a growing number of others are correct and the origins of the UK's inflation do lie outside the economy then this presents the Government with an entirely different set of economic management problems. First, economic policies will be reactive to exogenous influences rather than actively promoting change. Any domestic initiatives could be swamped by external forces if these are relatively stronger. Thus, domestic stability sought by systems such as the MTFS, can easily be upset by external factors which lie beyond the control of governments. Second, it would appear that in a highly integrative and interrelated international economic system, joined together through the mediating influences of flexible exchange rates, economic stability will require international cooperation. Global stability will demand coordination of the economic policies of each country - especially those of the big six: USA, Germany, Japan, France, Italy and the UK. The lack of success in reaching agreement in recent economic summits does not give much indication of hope that such cooperation would be feasible. The distribution of the benefits of cooperation will be an obvious source of disagreement and each participant will need to be convinced that the net benefits of cooperation exceed those available to a country going it alone. Indeed, it is possible that in order to maximize the benefits to the group as a whole a country would need to implement policies which would otherwise have been politically unpopular. Economic sovereignty is thus called into question. The problem nevertheless remains. In a highly integrated economy with a system of floating exchange rates uncoordinated economic policies can generate unwelcome side effects.

Finally, it will be recalled from chapter 1 that the monetarist's equation of exchange linking changes in the money supply to inflation ($MV = PQ$) depended upon V being constant. Studies carried out by the Bank of England and others during the 1970s had found that the demand for money (£M3), i.e. V in the above equation, was relatively stable. This, therefore, provided a justification for using monetary policy to control inflation or at least to influence GNP (i.e. PQ). If V, however, was found to be unstable changes in the velocity of circulation could offset changes in M.

Further studies of the stability of the demand for money (£M3) especially those by Haache[21] and Artis and Lewis[22] found that the velocity of circulation was increasingly unstable over time. The velocity of circulation had been changing at about 3% p.a. as a result of both financial innovation and interest rate changes. Thus, as V was rising this would offset the influence of reductions in M. This made £M3 inadequate as an instrument of monetary policy.

Can the Money Supply be Controlled?

The efficacy of the Government's macro-economic strategy depended crucially upon its ability to control the money supply. Is £M3, therefore, under the control of the monetary authorities?

During most of the post-war period, successive governments had used direct controls over bank lending in their attempts to control the money supply. This was implemented in conjunction with interest rate policy. By increasing the price of money and credit (i.e. interest rates) it was assumed that individuals would cut back on their demand for money. In 1971 the Heath Conservative administration abandoned direct controls and introduced their 'Competition and Credit Control' policy. Bank lending, and hence the money supply, was to be controlled through interest rate differentials which were established by the forces of competition between banks and other financial intermediaries in the money markets.

Competition and Credit Control was not a success and during the 1970s governments were forced to rely upon direct controls over bank lending such as the 'corset' (op. cit). When the Conservative Government came into power in 1979 Mrs Thatcher set up an enquiry into monetary control which resulted in the publication of the Green Paper, in 1980, *Monetary Control* (Cmnd. 7858).

The Treasury and the Bank of England disagreed over the best means of controlling the money supply. It was the Treasury's view that the monetary authorities should control the money supply directly through the monetary base of the system[23] irrespective of the impact that this would have on interest rates. On the other hand the Bank of England was worried about the high rates that would result from monetary base control. Their concern was that the high interest rates would cause financial instabilities which would spill over into the real sector of the economy, producing bankruptcies and unemployment. The Bank preferred, therefore, to control the money supply by manipulating interest rates. As the money supply increased at a rate faster than the target range then interest rates would be raised, thereby making bank borrowing more expensive.

It was the Bank of England, in particular the Governor of the Bank, Sir Gordon Richardson, which won this dispute. Some have argued that having lost the battle the Government became less committed to the MTFS, but the war continued. Richardson's successor was a political appointment and was more monetarist in his thinking. By 1983 Nigel Lawson in his Mansion House speech announced that narrow money M_0 would be the main focus of monetary policy and would determine interest rates. Even then the Bank of England continued to argue that interest rates should be set not in relation to M_0 but after considering a whole set of liquidity measures.

This whole episode raises the interesting question about the relationship between the Bank of England and the Treasury (Government) in the sphere of economic policy making. If the Bank of England is not sympathetic and is not prepared to implement the Government's monetary policy then what? After all the Government is dependent upon the Bank's contextual and specialist knowledge of the financial system to design and implement its monetary policy.

Whilst the MTFS was a new system of financial management the

Government did not introduce a new system of monetary control. Instead it used a complex and clumsy system in which the PSBR was to play a central role. Since it was argued that the PSBR contributed directly to the growth of the money supply and that the PSBR also caused interest rates to rise, then any attempt at controlling the money supply must also involve control over the PSBR.

The link between the PSBR, interest rates and the money supply requires more explanation. It was the Government's belief that increases in the PSBR caused interest rates to control the money supply. The rises in interest rates caused by the PSBR, therefore, reduced its scope to control the money supply. Thus in order to return more degrees of freedom to the Government attempts were made to control the PSBR.

Friedman,[24] in his evidence to the House of Commons Treasury and Civil Service Committee, was very critical of the UK system of monetary control. He agreed with UK Keynesians that there was no obvious link between the PSBR and interest rates. In his opinion the PSBR did not necessarily cause interest rates to rise. It was, therefore, not necessary to control the PSBR for the purpose of monetary control. Friedman was, however, an advocate of monetary base control and disagreed strongly with the strategy of using interest rates to control the money supply.

The Government's deregulation of the banking system and its abolition of the corset made its conduct of monetary policy more difficult. The whole control system rested upon the sensitivity of the private sector's demand for money to interest rate changes. As it turned out, the private sector's demand for money was not sufficiently interest elastic. The recession which set in after 1979 resulted in distress borrowing by the corporate sector from the banks. This caused bank lending and hence the money supply to rise. The Government's response to the increase in the money supply was to raise interest rates. The increase in interest rates placed cash flow problems on the corporate sector, which resulted in a further round of distress borrowing and further increases in the money supply. A spiral was, therefore, established in which corporate sector borrowing, caused in part by the Government's restrictive monetary policy, resulted in money supply increases and further monetary restrictions. The changes recorded in £M3 were interpreted incorrectly. It will be recalled from the previous discussion that the Government assumed that increases in £M3 reflected increases in transactions. In this case this was not so.

To control the money supply by relying solely on interest rates, unaided by direct controls, requires that the Government be in a position to forecast the credit demands of all sectors of the economy. This exercise was not only beyond the technical competence of the Government, given the current state of economic intelligence, but it required a degree of sophistication in economic forecasting which the Government denied was possible. Following the anti-scientism of writers such as Hayek, the

Government had argued that little store should be placed in forecasts of economic magnitudes.

The money supply process was and remains, improperly understood. None of the major forecasting models had a satisfactory explanation of the dynamics of money supply. How was it, therefore, possible to control with precision a system that was improperly understood? The answer is that it was not. The choice of £M3 was based upon flimsy evidence; the relationships between £M3, inflation and output were ambiguous and weak, and by the time the MTFS came to be implemented these relationships were breaking down. Moreover, the stability of £M3 was not as certain as had been supposed. Finally, the Government made a tactical error by abolishing the corset after the MTFS had been set in train, and it was only later that it discovered just how difficult it was to control monetary aggregates.

Gradually the Government played down the centrality of the MTFS and looked at alternative money aggregates such as M_0. Today the MTFS remains and will continue to be an integral part of any Government's economic strategy. The first four years of the MTFS were undoubtedly a period of learning. This was the first time that such a strategy had been implemented. The principal lesson that was learned from the exercise was that monetary policy was much more difficult to implement than was originally supposed.

Successful Targeting?

How successful was the Government in meeting the money supply targets of the MTFS? The previous discussion has indicated that controlling the money supply is complex because the money supply behaves in a way that is improperly understood.

The money supply growth targets and outcomes are shown in Table 1.

TABLE 1   Target Growth for £M3 and Outcomes

Budget	1979/80	1980/81	1981/83	1982/83	(%) 1983/84
1980	7–11	7–11	6–10	5–9	4–8
1981			6–10	5–9	4–8
1982				8–12	7–11
1983					7–11
Outcome	16¼	19¼	13	11	8–6*

Source: Bank of England
* estimate

It is clear from the evidence in Table 1 that the Government's success in meeting its £M3 growth targets was a complete failure, especially in the first three years of MTFS. These targets were revised upwards between successive budgets. Thus, the target range set for 1982/83 in the 1980 budget was 5%-9% which was then revised upwards to 8%-12% in 1982. The outcome for 1982/83 was 11%, but when the budget for 1982 was set it would by then have been clear that the money supply trend was such that the original target range would not have been met.

How Tight was Monetary Policy?

Failure to meet the money supply targets might indicate that the Government's monetary policy was relaxed, but this is an inappropriate means of judging the tightness of the Government's monetary stance. To find out about the severity of the Government's monetary policy it is necessary to consider the growth of the money supply in relation to other economic aggregates such as GNP and to examine what was happening to other measures of the money supply and liquidity. Sterling M3 is not the most appropriate measure of the transactions demand for money. Thus whilst £M3 might be lax, other money aggregates such as M_0 might be tight. To judge the tightness of monetary policy it is therefore necessary to look outside of the MTFS and the targets for £M3.

Does it matter if monetary policy is too tight; after all, a tightening of the money supply was supposed to bring down inflation. Will this not simply mean that inflation will be brought under control more quickly? It is possible to bring down a patient's raging fever by immersing him in ice cold water; however, the doctor runs the risk of causing heart failure and killing the patient. The same applies to the control of inflation. If the money supply is set too tight, interest rates will be forced up and the economy will be pushed into recession with severe consequences for unemployment. Setting targets for the money supply is, therefore, a complex task. They need to be finely balanced – set tight enough to bring down the rate of inflation but not so tight that unemployment rises. Such precision, however, requires knowledge about the money supply process and the ability to control it – qualities which it was suggested above that governments did not possess.

The failure of £M3 to fall within the target range has already been noted; however, £M3 is not a reliable indicator of the volume of money required to finance transactions. A more suitable indicator is M_0, which can be seen from Figure 1 has been falling since 1978. Using the measure M_0, monetary policy was much tighter than £M3 figures would suggest. Also, the liquidity measure PSL2 did not change significantly between 1979 and 1981 and fell from 1981/82, thereby giving an indication of a tightening of liquidity in the economy. Again, as before, this suggests that £M3 was not the most appropriate indicator to use when setting monetary policy. By pinning too much on the £M3 indicator the Government ran the

CHART 1.12   Monetary growth, percentage changes on a year earlier for banking months March, June, September and December

(a) **narrow aggregates**   *(b)* **broad aggregates**

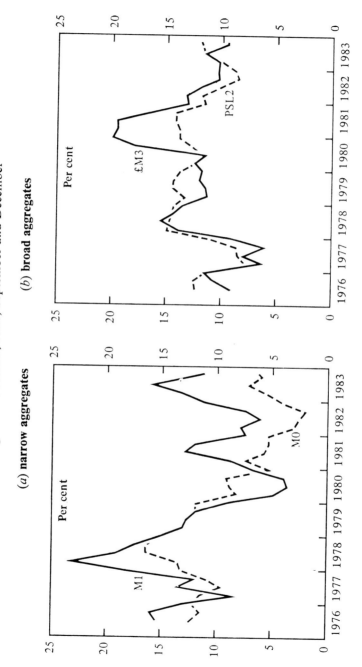

risk of deflating the economy.

Another useful indicator is the real money supply. This is set out in Table 2. Whilst real £M3 rose, real M1 fell. Since M1 is a measure which is closer to M_0 and the volume of transactions, this reduction in real M1 is an indication that the Government's monetary policy was much tighter than it supposed at the time.

TABLE 2   The United Kingdom Real Money Supply (annual percentage changes)

	M1	£M3	PSL2
1971 11 to 1972 11	+7.1	+14.7	+12.3
1972 11 to 1973 11	+2.8	+12.5	+8.4
1973 11 to 1971 11	−13.5	+1.9	−2.1
1974 11 to 1975 11	−7.3	−12.2	−11.5
1975 11 to 1976 11	−0.6	−6.7	−3.4
1976 11 to 1977 11	−5.5	8.4	−7.8
1977 11 to 1978 11	+13.4	+7.3	+6.8
1978 11 to 1979 11	+1.5	+1.9	+3.8
1979 11 to 1980 11	−12.3	−4.7	−7.4
1980 11 to 1981 11	−1.5	+4.4	+1.7
1981 11 to 1982 11	−1.6	+2.0	+0.2
1982 11 to 1983 11	+10.2	+7.0	+7.7
1983 May to December	+5.9	+5.4	+4.9

The increase in the series for M1, £M3 and PSL2 (Private Sector Liquidity) deflated by the rise in retail prices.

Towards the end of its first term in office the Government started publishing on a more regular basis data on M_0 and liquidity aggregates: PSL1 and PSL2. This was an indication that the Government was relying less and less upon targeting £M3 but was, instead, examining the information provided by a wide range of money aggregates. Targets for £M3 were still published, with the result that it ceased to be at all clear what the Government's monetary stance really was. What significance did the Government place upon deviations of £M3 from its targets and how did they react to information about the trend in M_0?

The Fiscal Strategy

The Government's macro-economic strategy started off as a set of money supply growth targets and ended up as a fixed strategy and PSBR targets. Reductions in the PSBR were justified for two reasons. First, it was believed that increases in the PSBR would increase interest rates. This would limit the Government's ability to control the money supply through interest rate changes. Moreover, it was argued that the increase in interest rates would constrain private sector investment which was thought to be interest elastic. Second, there was a fear that the government deficit (PSBR) would be monetized, i.e. that it would cause an increase in the money supply.[25] For these reasons the Government's advisers pressed hard for a controlled reduction in the PSBR as a percentage of GNP. Some went so far as to argue in favour of annual balanced budgets, whilst others advocated balancing the budgets over a number of years.

If a much smaller proportion of public spending was to be financed from borrowing, then this automatically suggested that taxation had to accept a greater share of the financing requirement. One of the Government's economic objectives, however, was to reduce the burden of taxation in an attempt to restore incentives. Thus, if the Government was reducing both borrowing and taxation, this implied that public spending must also be tightly controlled.

Reductions in public spending as a percentage of GNP were not only the consequence of economic policy; the Government also argued on ideological grounds for constraints to be placed on the scope and power of the State, thereby increasing personal freedoms and liberties.

In their Manifesto, the Conservatives had advocated an increase in public spending for law and order and defence. If these items were to be increased, whilst the total was to be constrained, then this implied that other areas such as education, personal social services and housing had to fall.

The Government's fiscal strategy was as full of hidden complexities and ambiguities as was its Medium-Term Financial Strategy. First, the strategy was based upon a weak theoretical structure. It was more an article of faith than a well established set of facts that tax reductions would improve incentives[26] or that reductions in the PSBR would ease the pressure off interest rates and thus help any expansion in private investment. Thus, the reduction in the top marginal rate of personal income tax from 83% to 60% in Howe's first budget provided a few top tax-payers with a windfall income gain without any change in incentives. Also, private sector investment tends to be more sensitive to demand and profitability than to interest rates.[27]

The second problem with the fiscal strategy is that the PSBR is a very difficult magnitude to control. Since government borrowing is the arithmetic difference between two very large magnitudes (i.e. tax revenues and public spending)— any small deviation in taxation or public spending from target can result in a big divergence in the PSBR from its target. If public spending is only 1% above its target, whilst tax revenue is 1% below, then the PSBR will be 2% above its target. To bring public spending under control the Government introduced an elaborate set of institutions which strained its relations with both local government and the nationalized industries. Because these sectors contributed to the PSBR the Government attempted to centralize its control over public spending decisions of local authorities and the pricing decisions of nationalized industries.

Targeting the PSBR during a recession is almost an impossible task. As the economy moves into recession unemployment rises and, along with it, public spending on unemployment benefits. At the same time, the tax revenues flowing to the exchequer fall because the unemployed do not pay income taxes, the revenues from national insurance payments fall, and expenditure tax revenue declines. Unless the Government is able to forecast unemployment and the loss of tax revenue accurately, then the PSBR targets will not be achieved. In practice the Government did not forecast unemployment well (see Table 3). The March 1980 unemployment forecasts were a disaster. As time went on the unemployment forecasts improved.

TABLE 3   Unemployment Forecasts

	1979/80	1980/81	1981/82	1982/83	1983/84
March 1980	1.25	1.6	1.8	1.8	
March 1981		1.8	2.5	2.7	2.7
March 1982			2.6	2.9	
Feb 1983				2.7	3.0
Actual Outturn	1.26	1.82	2.6	2.8*	2.9*

Notes:
1. Figures are expressed in millions; they are average unemployment figures for the year for GB, excluding school leavers.
2. * there was a change in the official definition of unemployment which excluded about 170,000 - 190,000 previously recorded.

The PSBR targets and outcomes are shown in Table 4.

TABLE 4   PSBR Targets as a % of GDP

Budget	1979/80	1980/81	1981/82	1982/83	1983/84
1980	4.75	3.75	3.00	2.75	1.50
1981			4.25	3.25	2.00
1982				3.50	2.75
1983					2.75
Outcome	5.00	5.50	3.50	3.25	3.25

Source : Treasury

Not only were the PSBR targets not met but they were revised upwards between successive budgets. This, in part, reflects the severity of the recession which was much worse than was expected. Despite the depth of the recession, fiscal policy became increasingly tighter, as can be seen from the PSBR outcome data. Public sector borrowing as a percentage of GDP continued to fall year after year. Keynesian policy would have made use of the automatic stabilizers[28] built into the economy, but the Government's monetarist stance over-rode all of the automatic stabilizers, placing a fiscal as well as a monetary squeeze on the economy. The combined effect of the Government's monetary and fiscal policies was to push the economy deeper into recession. A vicious cycle was set up. As the economy moved further into recession, the PSBR had a tendency to rise. To prevent this happening, public spending was further restrained, removing demand from the private sector and contributing to the rise in unemployment.

How severe was the Government's fiscal policy? To answer this question some commentators use the PSBR data. If there is a deficit on the public sector's account, then this is used to signal that fiscal policy was relatively relaxed and injecting a stimulus to the economy. Inflation and unemployment, however, badly distort the information provided by the crude PSBR. This means that in order to be a useful indicator of fiscal policy the PSBR needs to be adjusted for the impact of inflation and unemployment.

As unemployment rises this forces up the PSBR. It has been estimated that during 1981/82 the annual costs to the Exchequer (in terms of lost tax revenues and increased public spending) of each additional unemployed person was about £6,000 p.a. This has led to the production of a number of alternative measures of the PSBR, each making some adjustment for unemployment effects. These include, the Full Employment Budget (FEB) surplus/deficit, the demand weighted PSBR and the cyclically adjusted PSBR. Each differs in the way in which the unemployment cost adjustments are made.

What would the PSBR figures have looked like if they had been adjusted for unemployment? The projected £11 billion PSBR for 1981/82 was on a full employment basis equivalent to a budget *surplus* of £2 billion (see Dilnot and Morris[29]). Adjusted PSBR figures compared to actual are shown in Table 5.

TABLE 5   PSBR Adjusted for Unemployment (% of GDP)

	Actual	Adjusted
1978/79	−5.4	−4.9
1979/80	−5.0	−3.7
1980/81	−5.5	−1.7
1981/82	−3.5	+2.5
1982/83	−3.3	+3.5

Notes: a negative means a deficit and a positive a surplus.

Sources:
1. *National Income and Expenditure*, 1984 edition.
2. W.H. Buiter and M.H. Miller, Centre for Labour Economics Discussion Paper 179, November 1983, London School of Economics

When the PSBR data have been adjusted for the effects of

unemployment, then the deficit is much smaller than supposed for 1981/82 and 1982/83 was in surplus. Thus, the Government's fiscal stance was much tighter than the crude PSBR data suggested. The Government, however, did not seem to be interested in the adjusted PSBR. First, it would have required it to make public its unemployment forecasts, which it was not prepared to do. Second, from the perspective of the MTFS it was the actual PSBR which impacted on financial markets and had a potential influence on interest rates. 'In setting fiscal policy in the Budget, the size of the PSBR is judged, above all, in relation to the Government's intention to leave room for a fall in interest rates within the overall financial discipline needed to reduce inflation. This requires a reduction in the nominal PSBR as a proportion of GDP over the medium term... the acid test of the PSBR is the level of interest rates at which it can be financed'. (*Treasury Economic Progress Report*, No 144, April 1982).

The unadjusted PSBR is a meaningless target for economic policy. It is not a useful statistic of the Government's fiscal stance. Borrowing by the nationalized industries, and central and local government for *capital* purposes will not have the same economic consequences as borrowing to pay for current spending, e.g. on public employee wages, pensions etc. Moreover, the total PSBR figure contains public sector borrowing to finance private sector capital spending. The PSBR is distorted by inflation and unemployment. Finally, the PSBR has a limited impact upon interest rates. The PSBR statistics, like the money supply aggregates, are very complex data and changes in their magnitudes are the resultant of many different forces. Using such statistics as targets for policy puts the Government on a high risk course of action unless it has the technical competence to unscramble the signals which these statistics contain. As the MTFS and its associated fiscal strategy was implemented, it became increasingly clear that the Government was unsure of how to interpret its policy targets.

Over the lifetime of the MTFS money supply targets became less important, whilst the PSBR targets assumed a greater significance. But did the Government have PSBR targets? Middleton,[30] giving the official Treasury view, has argued that the PSBR had not become a target but was instead simply to be made compatible with the MTFS: 'the lower the PSBR, the lower interest rates can be for a given monetary target. That is not a case for making a target out of the PSBR', (p.11). Whilst this might have been the official 'view', the financial community came to place greater importance on the PSBR figures because a failure to meet the PSBR 'targets' within the MTFS indicated likely interest rate changes with possible gains/losses to be made on the gilt edged market.

Public Expenditure and Taxation

Did the Government manage to control the growth of public spending and was its tax policy such that incentives were improved?

The first Public Expenditure White Paper published by the Thatcher Government in March 1980 reduced the projected increases in public spending envisaged by the outgoing Labour Government. At the same time they planned to increase expenditure on law and order and defence. Thus, the composition of total public expenditure was planned to change. What was actually achieved?

Public expenditure outturns, compared to March 1980 targets, are shown in Table 6.

TABLE 6   Public Expenditure Targets and Outturns 1978/79 - 1983/84

	1978/79	1979/80	1980/81	1981/82	1982/83	1983/84
March 1980 Plan	100.0	99.6	99.6	98.7	96.5	95.8
Outturn	100.0	100.0	103.3	105.7	107.0	108.0

Source: T. Ward reported by P. Riddell, *Financial Times*, 28 January 1984

Notes:
1.   Index 1978/79 = 100
2.   Public spending is shown at constant prices.

It had been the intention that public expenditure would fall in real terms by 4.2% over the 5 years of the plan. Instead, public expenditure increased by 8.0% in real terms. Why was this and was it the experience of all elements of public spending? Differences in the real rate of increase in various public expenditures, are shown in Table 7.

TABLE 7   Percentage Change in Programmes between 1978/79 and 1983/84 (in real terms)

Energy	+62%
Employment Measures	+61%
Agriculture, fisheries, food	+40%
Law and Order	+33%
Social Security	+26%
Defence	+23%
Health and Personal Social Services	+16%
Transport	+8%
Arts and Libraries	+7%
Education and Science	+1%
Overseas Aid	−17%
Trade and Industry	−29%
Housing	−34%

Source: *The next ten years: public expenditure and taxation into the 1990s*, Cmnd. 9189, HMSO

The increase in energy expenditure is largely assistance to the coal industry, whereas the growth in defence expenditure is a reflection of a shift in Government priorities towards defence, the increase in NATO costs and the Falklands conflict. Expenditure on social security, the largest component of total public spending, increased rapidly because the number of pensions had increased by 650,000 and the number receiving disability allowances also rose. The increase in unemployment from 1.26 million in 1979/80 to 2.77 million added considerably to social security costs. Public expenditure did, however, fall in some areas, particularly local authority capital spending on housing. Cutbacks in public sector capital spending have adverse effects upon the level of employment over the short run and, in particular, result in increased local unemployment in the construction industry.

The increase in public expenditure meant that the Government was unable to make the tax reductions which it had planned to. Taxation as a percentage of GNP increased from 345 in 1978/79 to 405 in 1982/83. This was, of course, due in part to the fall in real GNP as a consequence of the recession. In 1979 the basic rate of income tax was cut from 33% to 30%. The top marginal rate of income tax was reduced from 83% to 605. At the same time, however, Value Added Tax was raised from 8% to 15%. Not only did this add 45 to the retail price index but it was highly regressive in its incidence. Those on low incomes paid very little income tax but spent more of their income of VAT'able goods compared to those on higher incomes. Moreover, the new financing limits for the nationalized industries forced those industries such as gas, water, electricity and transport to raise their prices. The output of these industries feature large in the budgets of the poor. At the same time local authorities faced reductions in the levels of grant-in-aid which they received from central government. The result was that whilst domestic rates increased, subsidies given to local authority rents fell. Again, on a proportional basis it was the poor who suffered most.

Tax thresholds fell between 1979/80 and 1981/82 but since then they have increased. In 1981 personal tax allowances were not increased, despite the 15% rate of inflation in that year. Finally, national insurance contributions rose both for employees and for employers, who also had to pay a surcharge. By how much did the tax burden rise? Assuming that taxes refer to income taxes, VAT, excise duties and national insurance contributions, then to return taxes from their 1983/84 level to their 1978/79 level would require cutting the basic rate of income tax by 9 pence in the £.

Economic Outcomes: Inflation, Unemployment, and the Exchange Rate

Controlling the rate of growth of the money supply was supposed to bring down the rate of price inflation without producing adverse effects on the real sector of the economy, measured in terms of output and unemployment. How successful was the Government's anti-inflation policy?

The main economic indicators are shown in Table 8. Changes in inflation, unemployment and national income (real GNP) are shown between 1979 and 1984 both for the UK and the OECD countries.

TABLE 8   UK and OECD Economic Indicators

INFLATION	*May 1979*	*May 1984*	*Change in % points*			
UK	10.3%	5.1%	−5.2%			
OECD	9.7%	5.4%	−4.3%			
UNEMPLOYMENT	*1979*	*May 1984*				
UK	5.5%	13.4%	+7.9%			
OECD	5.1%	8.3%	+3.2%			
NATIONAL INCOME (real GNP, 1979 = 100)						
	1979	*1980*	*1981*	*1982*	*1983*	*1984*
UK	100	97.4	96.1	98.3	101.4	103.9
OECD	100	101.2	103.2	102.7	105.2	109.7

Sources: OECD Main Economic Indicators and OECD Economic Outlook

Prior to the 1983 election, at the end of its first term, the Government made great play of the fact that it had brought down inflation, whilst the rise in unemployment had been caused by the world recession which was outside of the Government's powers of control. A glance at the summary statistics in Table 8, however, suggests a number of doubts about this interpretation of events.

The UK's inflation rate was brought down in line with the rate of inflation in all other OECD countries. There was nothing spectacular about the Government's achievement. Indeed, many other OECD countries such as Italy, managed to bring their inflation rates down without using monetary policies.

One of the striking differences between the UK and other OECD countries is that the OECD countries managed to bring their inflation rates down without paying such a large price in terms of lost output and increased unemployment. Whilst UK unemployment increased by 7.9% points, unemployment in OECD countries only rose by 3.2% points. The rise in UK unemployment was blamed on the world recession but evidence of this cannot be found. The real output of OECD countries, as measured by real GNP, rose steadily by almost 10% between 1979 and 1984 whereas UK real output only rose by 4% over the same period, having first fallen between 1979 and 1981. It was rather a distortion of statistics for Conservative politicians to claim, prior to the election, that real GNP had increased by 5.3% points between 1981 and 1983, or about 2.5% p.a. Choice of 1981 as a base year gives this result. The reality is that the economy was depressed for three years and then slowly pulled up prior to the election.

Total real GNP figures, as shown in Table 8, however, hide the details of what was happening to the components of total output. What, for example, was happening to manufacturing output? Table 9 shows the changes which occurred in some of the major sectors of UK industry.

TABLE 9   Changes in Production by Industry 1979/83

Energy	15.3%
Manufacturing	−13.2%
Engineering	−12.6%
Textiles, Clothing	−27.4%
Construction	−10.3%
Consumer goods	−11.0%

Source: *Monthly Digest of Statistics*, HMSO

Note: The industries are those of the SIC 1980.

Total output increased because of the importance of the growth in the energy sector, in particular the growth in production of North Sea oil.

The increase in unemployment was caused by the massive loss in output in major sectors of UK industry; losses which are masked by looking at aggregate statistics. In 1982 the UK became a net importer of manufactured goods for the first time in 200 years since the advent of the industrial revolution. Employment in the manufacturing sector fell from 7.1 million in 1979 to 5.5 million in 1983. Between 1979 and 1983 UK manufactured export volume was down by 2% despite a real growth in world markets of 20% over the same period. A manufacturing trade balance surplus of £5,566 million was transformed into a deficit of £2,148 million by 1983.

What caused this decline in output and the increase in import penetration? A number of factors can be suggested:

(1)   The tightness in monetary and fiscal policy was much more severe than was thought. This was demonstrated earlier. A direct consequence of a severe monetary and fiscal policy was to deflate the economy. Order books were cut back.

(2)   Whilst inflation eventually fell, it increased dramatically in the first year of the Government's term. When they came into office in 1979 inflation was running at just above 10% p.a. By the third quarter of 1980 it reached a high of 22%. This rapid increase was caused by a variety of factors, including, increases in VAT; oil prices; nationalized industries' prices, and public sector wages, following the implementation of the Clegg recommendations. These price rises promoted a wage explosion and further price increases. The wage and price increases reduced the international competitiveness

of UK exports, orders were lost and bankruptcies followed. It also made imports relatively cheaper and so import penetration advanced.

(3) The increase in UK inflation caused nominal interest rates to rise relative to overseas rates (see Table 10). Moreover, attempts to control the money supply had also forced up interest rates. These favourable interest rate relativities, coupled with the confidence that North Sea oil revenues imparted to foreign exchange dealers, forced up the exchange rate. The higher interest rates increased the demand for Sterling as foreigners invested their short term funds in the UK. Not only did this boost the Sterling exchange rate; the short term highly liquid foreign funds expanded the money supply. The rise in the exchange rate made imports cheaper whilst it made exports more expensive. UK export markets were lost whilst domestic markets were given over to imported goods.

TABLE 10 Exchange and Interest Rates

	London Banks Base Rate (%)	Effective Exchange Rate (1975=100)	£/US$ Exchange Rate
1978	9.09	81.5	1.9197
1979	13.68	87.3	2.1223
1980	16.32	96.1	2.3281
1981	13.27	95.3	2.0254
1982	11.93	90.7	1.7489
1983	9.83	83.3	1.5158

Source: *Financial Statistics*, HMSO

If the Government had adopted a more relaxed attitude to monetary and fiscal policy, by using more suitable indicators such as M_0 and the full employment budget balance, then interest rates would not have increased by such a large margin and the exchange rate would not have appreciated with its damaging consequences. The Government, however, refused to pursue an active exchange rate policy because to do so would have been to interfere with free market forces.

Tight monetary policy, tight fiscal policy, high interest rates and a high exchange all combined to deflate the economy. Output fell, imports increased, exports fell, stocks increased, unemployment rose and inflation came down. Why did inflation fall?

The Government has found it difficult to argue that its monetary policy brought down inflation because the £M3 targets were not met. However, the stock of money used for transaction purposes, M_0, did fall. There are a number of factors which contributed to the decline in the rate of inflation. The increase in unemployment moderated money wage increases in the private sector, whilst cash limited public expenditure acted as an implicit incomes policy for the public sector. However, the rise in the exchange rate reduced the price of imported manufactured goods and also the prices of imported raw materials. Between 1979 and 1983 the all items commodity price index fell by 14% points.

Conclusions

The outcome of Mrs Thatcher's economic experiment was only successful in one dimension; the rate of inflation fell. But did inflation fall because of the Government's monetary policy or did other external factors act to bring prices down? Whilst the economic history of the 1979/83 period has been recorded it will be interpreted and debated for many years to come. Debate will centre upon issues such as what actually happened in much the same way as current generations of economists discuss the recession of the 1920s and 1930s.

Did the Government's tight monetary and fiscal policies, its single minded determination to bring down inflation and its abandonment of the full employment objective precipitate the longest and most severe recession which the UK has had since the 1930s?

Despite the failure of the Government's economic strategy to reduce taxes and to restore incentives, to give a dynamic boost to British industry, and to assist in the creation of growth and prosperity, the Medium Term Financial Strategy should not be regarded as a failure *per se*. The MTFS was an important innovation but the issue is, was it implemented in the best way? One of the essential features of the MTFS is that it allows the coordination of monetary and fiscal policies by taking into account the financial flows which follow from any fiscal policy. This must in years to come be regarded as a significant policy innovation.

There is, however, an infinity of monetary and fiscal policy mixes that might exist. The Government's choice of one of these mixes was based upon faulty information, because imperfect indicators such as £M3 and the unadjusted PSBR were used. Failure of the Government's policy should not, therefore, be construed as a failure of the PSBR *per se*. It was a failure to implement the MTFS properly that resulted in difficulties in problems for the economy. Future developments in the design of economic policy within the context of the MTFS must pay more regard to which indicators are to be used and how the information that they provide should be interpreted. At the same time government policy making needs to recognize that the world is a highly complex and uncertain place. Policies based upon simple axioms and maxims, therefore, run a high risk of resulting in catastrophe. Moreover, because the world is uncertain and because the conditions upon which policies were predicated change rapidly, then Governments need to do more than they have done in designing contingency plans. This approach would resolve the question of whether or not the Government is making a U turn or not.

The message of monetarism is simple to state and lends itself to pre-election rhetoric. Whilst the depression of the late 1920s and 1930s was an external event that the Government had to respond to, the recession of the 1980s was of the Government's making. Over tight monetary and fiscal policies and the loss of overseas markets, due to an over-valued Pound (£), resulted in an erosion of demand, falling investment, rising inventories, bankruptcies and an explosion in the numbers unemployed. The Government's advisers could counter that the policies had not been successful because they had not been pursued with sufficient vigour. If only the Government had reduced the money supply more quickly and had been more strict with the trades unions to bring down real wages then the economy would not have responded by increasing unemployment. In other words, to break inflationary expectations quickly, it is thought by some economists that a cold sharp shock to the economy (the cold turkey approach to monetarism) is preferable to the gradual monetarism which the Government pursued.

No matter where the Government turns, it faces criticism from those who claim it was too monetarist and from those who claim it wasn't monetarist enough. Despite the Government's protestations and claims to the contrary, alternative policies did exist. It would have been possible to negotiate some kind of incomes policy; when unemployment exceeded the 10% mark it would have been possible to apply a mild reflation without running the risks of increasing inflation; it would have been possible to have an exchange rate policy; finally, a more sensitive approach to the social costs of its policies would not have gone amiss. When it claimed that 'there is no alternative' (TINA), the Government was signalling that no other policy mix was feasible within the context of its ideology, the pursuit of free market forces. Each of these alternative policies implied greater government involvement. Any benefits from the efficiency gains of liberated and free markets are small compared to the inefficiencies and social costs of mass unemployment.

If the Thatcher Government really did want to revive British industry, then why did it allow interest and exchange rates to rise to crippling levels? Why was the employer's national insurance surcharge not cut? Why was demand cut? Did the Government value its own ideology more than the costs inflicted upon the economy? These questions will be debated for years to come. The Thatcher Government broke the mould of post-war Keynesianism and consensus politics and replaced them with the conviction of monetarism. This was innovatory and revolutionary and distances the Thatcher Government from the lukewarm monetarism of Callaghan and Healey. The Medium Term Financial Strategy was an innovation in policy design. What the Thatcher Government did, however, was to demonstrate clearer than any other post-war Government has managed to that policy innovations can be enormously costly and that the price of policy mistakes has to be paid for years to come.

Appendix

UK Definitions of the Money Supply

Alternative definitions of the money supply focus upon a different range of assets which are regarded as performing the functions of money. Those definitions which are currently in use in the UK are:

Narrow Money (money held predominantly for spending)

	Amount (Oct 1983) (£ billion)
Cash : Notes and coins held by public	11.5
M_0 : Monetary base : cash plus bank's till money and operational balances at Bank of England	12.8
NIBMI: Non-interest bearing M1 (or 'retail M1') : notes and coin plus non interest bearing private sector sight deposits at UK banks	30.8
M1 : as above but including all private sector sight	42.0
M2 : Transactions balances : Notes and coins plus all private sector deposits in banks and building societies held for transaction purposes (i.e. less than £100,000)	112.4

Broad Money (money held for spending and/or as a store of value)

£M3 : Sterling M3 : Notes and coin plus all Sterling bank deposits held by UK private and public sectors	100.3
PSL2 : Private Sector Liquidity (broad definition) : Notes and coin plus private sector Sterling bank deposits plus holdings of money market instruments (e.g. Treasury Bills) plus short term building society deposits and National Savings	162.3

Velocity is defined as nominal GDP divided by money supply
i.e. MV = PT where PT is nominal GDP
$$V = \frac{PT}{M} \text{ (true by definition)}$$

Balance Sheet identities:
Increase in £M3 equals:
Public Sector Borrowing Requirement (PSBR)
(minus) sales of public sector debt to UK non-bank sector
(plus) increase in Sterling lending to overseas residents
(minus) external finance of public sector
(minus) increase in overseas sterling deposits
(minus) increase in foreign currency deposits net of foreign currency assets
(minus) increase in non-deposit liabilities of banks.

i.e. in general terms:
>   Increase in £M3 equals:
>   PSBR
>   − Gilt sales
>   + increase in bank lending
>   equals DCE (Domestic Credit Expansion)
>   + net external flows
>   − increase in non-deposit liabilities
>   equals increase in £M3

Notes and References

1. M. Friedman and R. Friedman, *Freedom to choose*, 1980.
2. By fiscal means, I refer to the Government's public expenditure and taxation policies, broadly defined.
3. Some influential observers, such as the late Andrew Shonfield had hypothesized that the UK had suffered from an inadequate amount of corporatism when compared to more successful economies such as Sweden and Japan.
4. The term 'conviction politics' has never been clearly defined or analysed. Some would regard it as a euphemism for dogmatism. What it seems to mean is the singleminded pursuit of a set of policies which are not subject to negotiation and hence modification when implemented. Such an approach to politics seems to negate the pluralistic nature of British political life.
5. A lack of monetary and financial discipline had also fuelled inflationary pressures. In order to keep interest rates down the Government's expansionary fiscal policies had been accommodated by increases in the money supply.
6. Lucas was a Keynesian who had changed his mind. But the new classical school was as much a reaction against old fashioned monetarism as it was against Keynesianism. Basically, the new classical school was predicated on the belief that the market would adjust rapidly so that deflationary monetary policies would act quickly on prices without causing increases in unemployment.
7. Mr Callaghan had made a similar argument in his now famous speech to the Labour Party's 1976 annual conference.
8. This was predicated on the beliefs of the new classical (also called rational expectations) school referred to earlier. Tighter money supply targets would cause decision makers to revise downwards their expectations of the likely rate of inflation.
9. See the *Bank of England Quarterly Bulletin* for 1973, and the 1980 Green Paper on *Monetary Control*, Cmnd. 7858.
10. M. Artis and A.R. Nobay, Two aspects of the money debate, *National Institute Economic and Social Review*, August 1969.
11. C.A.E. Goodhart, and A.D. Crockett, The importance of money, *Bank of England Quarterly Bulletin*, 10(2), June 1970.
12. D. Williams, C.A.E. Goodhart, and D.H. Gowland, Money income and causality, *American Economic Review*, 66 (3), June 1976.
13. There is much controversy surrounding the statistical analysis of money supply data to ascertain stability. This debate is reviewed in P.M. Jackson, *Macro-Economic activity and local government behaviour*, Public Sector Economics Research Centre, University of Leicester, 1975. See C.A.E. Goodhart and A.D. Crockett, *op.cit.*, L.L. Price, The demand for money in the UK; a further investigation, *Bank of England Quarterly Bulletin*, 12 (1), March 1972, 43-55; M. Artis and M. Lewis; The demand for money in the UK, *Manchester School*, June 1976, 147-77.

14. Friedman and other monetarists assume that the demand for money is not sensitive to interest rates and that any change in demand for money is due entirely to changes in income (transactions). In other words the money supply is partly endogenous and not completely exogenous as monetarists claim.
15. S. Holly and A. Longbottom, The empirical relationship between the money stock and the price level in the UK: a test of causality, London Business School Economic Forecasting Unit Discussion Paper: Discussion Paper, No. 78, July, 1980; M. Benstock and A. Longbottom, Portfolio balance and inflation in the UK, London Business School Economic Forecasting Unit Discussion Paper No. 79, 1980; A. Budd, S. Holly, A. Longbottom and D. Sunny, Does monetarism fit the facts? London Business School Economic Forecasting Unit Discussion Paper, September 1981.
16. D.F. Hendry, and N.R. Ericcson, Assertion without empirical basis: an econometric appraisal of Friedman and Schwartz monetary trends in the UK in *Monetary trends in the United Kingdom*. Bank of England Panel of Academic Consultants, Panel, Paper No. 22, October 1983.
17. M. Friedman and A. Schwartz, *Monetary trends in the United Kingdom*, Chicago University Press, 1982.
18. R. Bade and M. Parkin, Is Sterling M3 the right aggregate? Mimeo, 1982.
19. Williams, Goodhart and Gowland, *op. cit.*
20. R.B. Johnson, The demand for non-interest bearing money in the UK, *Treasury Working Paper*, 1983.
21. G. Haache, The demand for money in the UK since 1971, *Bank of England Quarterly Bulletin*, 14 (3), September 1974.
22. Artis and Lewis, *op. cit.*
23. The 'monetary base' is defined as notes and coins in circulation plus private banks' deposits at the Bank of England.
24. M. Friedman, Memorandum to Treasury and Civil Service Committee, Session 1979/80, published in *Memorandum on monetary policy*, HC 720, July, HMSO, 1980.
25. The PSBR only adds to the money supply if it is financed through the banking system: see Appendix.
26. For a review of the evidence relating to tax incentives in the UK see C.V. Brown and P.M. Jackson, *Public sector economics* 2nd ed, Blackwell, 1983.
27. See the evidence presented to the Wilson Committee.
28. Automatic stabilizers refer to the changes in tax revenues and government spending which occur automatically over the trade cycle. These are distinguished from discretionary changes in these magnitudes. Thus, as the economy moves into recession public spending increases, as too does the PSBR. This prevents demand in the economy falling too much. By setting PSBR targets the Government wiped out the benefits of automatic stabilizers.
29. A. Dilnott and G.N. Morris, The Exchequer cost of unemployment, *Fiscal Studies*, November 1984.
30. P. Middleton, Evidence to House of Commons Treasury and Civil Service Committee, HC 163 - II, HMSO, 1980.

Bibliography

M. Artis and D. Currie, 'Monetary and exchange rate targets: a case for conditional targets' in P. Sinclair and W. Eltis (eds), 1981.
M. Artis and M. Lewis, *Monetary control in the UK*, Philip Allan, 1980.
A.B. Atkinson, 'Unemployment benefits and incentives' in J. Creedy (Ed), *The Economics of Unemployment in Britain*, Butterworth, 1981.
A.B. Atkinson and J. Flemming, Unemployment social security and incentives, *Midland Bank Review*, 1978.

A.D. Bain, 'Finance in the mixed economy' in Lord Roll (Ed) *The Mixed Economy*, Proceedings of Section F (Economics) of the British Association for the Advancement of Science, Macmillan, 1982.

C.R. Barrett and A.A. Walters, The stability of Keynesian and monetary multipliers in the United Kingdom, *Review of Economic and Statistics*, XLVII (4), November, 1966.

R.A. Batchelor, 'British economic policy under Margaret Thatcher: a mid-term examination: a comment on Darby and Lothian' in *Carnegie Rochester Conference Series on Public Policy*, 18, 1983, 208-220.

BEQB, Does the money supply matter?, *Bank of England Quarterly Bulletin*, 13 (2), June 1973.

BEQB, Reflections on the conduct of monetary policy, *Bank of England Quarterly Bulletin*, 18, (1), March 1978.

W.H. Buiter and M. Miller, The Thatcher experiment: the first two years, *Brookings Papers on Economic Activity*, 1981, 315-367.

W.H. Buiter and M. Miller, Monetary policy and international competitiveness, *Oxford Economic Papers*, 1981.

R.T. Coughlan, A transaction demand for money, *Bank of England Quarterly Bulletin*, March 1979.

J.T. Cuddington, Money income and causality in the United Kingdom and empirical investigation, *Journal of Money Banking and Credit*, August 1981, 342-51.

R. Davies, Friedman on Thatcher: four out of 10 so far, *Observer*, 26 October 1982.

R. Dornbush, Expectations and exchange rate dynamics, *Journal of Political Economy*, 84, 1976, 1161-1176.

D. Fisher, The demand for money in Britain: quarterly results 1951/67, *Manchester School*, December 1968, 328-44.

P.J. Forsyth and J.A. Kay, The economic implications of North Sea oil revenues, *Fiscal Studies*, 1980.

M. Friedman, *A programme for monetary stability*, Fordham University Press, 1969.

C.A.E. Goodhart, *Monetary theory and practice*, Macmillan, 1983.

C.W.J. Granger, Investigating causal relations by econometric models and cross spectral methods, *Econometricaly*, July 1969, 37.

J. Grice and A. Bennett, The demand for £M3 and other aggregates in the UK, *HM Treasury Working Paper*, 1981.

D.F. Hendry, 'Predictive failure and modelling in macroeconomics: the transactions demand for money', in P. Ormerod (Ed), *Economic Modelling*, Heinemann, 1979.

J.R. Hicks, *Critical essays in monetary theory*, Oxford University Press, 1967.

H.M. Treasury and Bank of England, *Monetary control*, Cmnd. 7857, HMSO, 1980.

House of Lords, *Select Committee of the House of Lords on Unemployment*, HMSO, 1982.

P.M. Jackson, Macroeconomic activity and local government behaviour. Report presented to Central/Local Government Relations Panel of ESRC, 1984.

N. Kaldor, Memorandum to Treasury and Civil Service Committee, Session 1979/80 published in *Memorandum on monetary policy*, HC 720, HMSO, 1980.

N.J. Kanavagh and A.A. Walters, Demand for money in the UK 1877-1961: some preliminary findings, *Bulletin of the Oxford University Institute of Economics and Statistics*, May 1966, 93-116.

V. Keegan, So much for relying on invisibles: can we have our manufactures back please?, *Guardian*, 23 January 1984.

D. Laidler and M. Parkin, The demand for money in the UK 1956-67, *The Manchester School of Economic and Social Research*, XXXVIII (3), September 1970, 187-208.

H. Mayer and H. Taguchi, Official intervention in foreign exchange markets, Bank for International Settlements, Discussion Paper 6, March 1983.

D. Metcalfe, Special employment measures: an analysis of wage subsidies, youth schemes and worksharing, *Midland Bank Review*, Autumn/Winter, 1982.

M. Miller, Monetary control in the UK, *Cambridge Journal of Economics*, 1979.

M. Miller, The medium term financial strategy: an experiment in coordinating monetary and fiscal policy, *Fiscal Studies*, 1982.

M. Miller, The 1982 Budget, *Fiscal Studies*, 3, 1982.

M. Miller, 'Inflation adjusting the public sector financial deficit' in J.A. Kay (ed), *The 1982 Budget*, Institute for Fiscal Studies, 1982.

R. Miller and J. Wood, *What price unemployment?* Hobart Paper, Institute of Economic Affairs, 1982.

P.A. Minford, Memorandum to Treasury and Civil Service Committee, Session 1979/80 published in *Memorandum on monetary policy*, HC 720, July, HMSO, 1980.

P. Minford, The nature and purpose of UK macroeconomic models, *Three Banks Review*, 125, March 1980 3-27.

P. Minford, The 1982 Budget, *Fiscal Studies*, 3, 1982.

P. Minford, Statement published in Laurie Millbank Gilt Edge Seminar Report, 1982.

P. Minford, *Unemployment cause and cure*, Martin Robertson, 1983.

C.N. Morris and A.W. Dilnott, Modelling replacement ratios, Institute for Fiscal Studies, Working Paper No. 40, 1982.

S.J. Nickell, The effects of unemployment and related benefits on the duration of unemployment, *Economic Journal*, 1979.

S.J. Nickell, The determinants of equilibrium unemployment in Britain, *Economic Journal*, 1982.

OECD, *Budget financing and monetary control*, Paris, 1981.

A. Okun, *Prices and quantities*, Oxford: Basil Blackwell, 1981.

J. Ruberry and R.J. Tarling, Women in the recession, *Socialist Economic Review*, 1982.

Runnymede Trust, *Race and immigration*. Issue Paper 159, September 1982.

C.A. Sims, Money income and causality, *American Economic Review*, 62, September 1972.

C. Trinder, Pay of employees in the public and private sectors, *National Institute Economic and Social Review*, August 1981.

W. Wells, The relative pay and employment of young people. Department of Employment Research Paper 42, 1983.

M. Wickens, Inaugural Lecture, University of Southampton Discussion Paper 8114, 1981.

F. Williams, Monetarism handled badly - Friedman, *The Times*, 21 October 1982.

J. Williamson, The exchange rate system, Institute for International Economics, Washington, 1983.

Wilson Committee. *Review of the functioning of financial institutions*, Cmnd. 7937, HMSO, 1980.

S. Wren-Lewis, The role of money in determining prices: a reduced form approval, Treasury Working Paper 18, March 1981.

3

The Privatization of Public Enterprises 1979-83

David Steel and David Heald

The privatization of public enterprises was one of the most important and distinctive features of the record of the 1979-83 Conservative Government. No fewer than twelve statutes were enacted empowering ministers to sell assets or shares and to relax statutory monopoly powers. Progress in implementing these provisions was more limited but nonetheless, by the dissolution in May 1983, the Government had already effected the most radical shift in the boundary between the public and private sectors of industry since 1951.

The Conservative Manifesto for the 1979 General Election[1] provided little guide as to the scale or scope of this programme. It contained only four pledges:

(1)   to offer to sell back to private ownership British Shipbuilders and British Aerospace, giving their employees the opportunity to purchase shares;
(2)   to sell shares in the National Freight Corporation to the general public in order to achieve substantial private investment in it;
(3)   to relax bus licensing to enable new services to develop, particularly in rural areas, and to encourage new private operators;
(4)   to review all the activities of the British National Oil Corporation.

In practice, however, the Government went a great deal further than this. By May 1983, firm proposals had been announced for over twenty enterprises (the only major omission being the National Coal Board) and many of them had been implemented successfully. Indeed, most

---

This chapter is an analysis of the privatization programme up to the end of the Government's first term in June 1983, and was written shortly afterwards. The second term programme is examined in D. Steel and D. Heald (Eds), *Privatizing Public Enterprises: Options and Dilemmas* (RIPA, 1984). A substantially similar paper was presented to a conference at the University of Texas in spring 1984 and will be published in W. Glade (ed), *State Shrinking: A Comparative Inquiry into Privatization*.

unusually, the Government's enthusiasm for this radical cause gathered momentum, rather than waned, as its term of office progressed.

The Government's record, in this as in other areas, marks a significant break with past Conservative practice. The 1951-55 Government denationalized only steel, which had barely been nationalized, and road haulage (and parts of both industries remained in public ownership). The 1970-74 Government talked ambitiously about denationalization before it took office but actually achieved no more than minimal change. This break with precedent reflects the important change of direction that occurred in Conservative economic policy generally and in its attitude towards the public sector in particular during its period in opposition between 1974 and 1979. The focus of this chapter is on the scope of the programme and on the methods adopted and difficulties encountered in implementing it. First, however, it will be helpful to outline briefly the context in which it has been pursued and the arguments ministers have adduced in its support (but no attempt will be made here to assess their validity).[2]

Why Privatize?

The Government's policies towards public enterprises were part of its general programme of reducing state activities and freeing market forces. In this context, privatization has two main elements: *denationalization* - the sale of assets and/or shares, regardless of whether the state retains a partial holding in an enterprise; and *liberalization* - the relaxation or abolition of statutory monopoly powers. This distinction and the definition of these terms are important because the word privatization, scarcely heard in the UK before 1979, has come to be used so frequently and in such diverse contexts that its meaning has become imprecise. Almost any policy designed to reduce the scale or limit the scope of the public sector or to encourage private provision of services that were previously supplied publicly is now labelled privatization. In relation to central and local government, it sometimes means selling assets (for example, the sale of motorway service areas and new town land and buildings) but more often it refers to the contracting out to the private sector of the provision of services which continue to be financed by the taxpayer (for example, local authority refuse collection and disposal services and the ancillary services of the national health service). It has also been applied to the policy of transferring the financing of public services from taxes to charges (for example, in relation to council housing).[3]

As these examples illustrate, the Government has been sympathetic to privatization in all parts of the public sector. However, it has approached the privatization of public enterprises with particular enthusiasm and determination. In part this reflects the greater ease with which such a policy can be applied to already free-standing units. More important has been the undisguised hostility of most Conservative politicians towards the nationalized industries, which stands in contrast to their much greater ambivalence about the public non-market sector, seen for instance in their declarations on the NHS during the first half of 1983.

The unpopularity of the nationalized industries among Conservative politicians is not new. In the past, however, they have been content to criticize the industries' record and to resist strongly any proposals to extend public ownership but they have not engaged in significant denationalization. The tougher line that developed during the 1970s can be attributed to two developments. First, external criticism of the industries intensified and some of their problems increasingly came to be regarded as insoluble. Thus, during the period, the industrial relations problem of the UK economy transferred from its traditional home in private manufacturing to the public sector, especially the nationalized industries.[4] In such a climate, the serious problems of certain undertakings, notably the British Steel Corporation, have had reverberations for other public enterprises, irrespective of their own performance. Second, there was a significant shift in the Conservative Party as its leaders renounced the pragmatism of their predecessors and espoused the revived doctrines of monetarism and free market economics. This change, both in the substance and style of Conservative politics, is crucially important to an understanding of the emphasis laid upon privatization and of the determination with which it has been pursued. It is therefore important to look briefly at the arguments that ministers have used in support of their proposals.

Four recurring arguments can be identified, although not all of them apply to each case of privatization. Three, concerning efficiency, economic freedom and pay bargaining, relate to both elements of privatization – denationalization and liberalization; the fourth, concerning public sector borrowing, to denationalization only.

The first, and probably the most widely used, argument in favour of privatization concerns efficiency. Ministers believe that public enterprises are intrinsically less efficient than private enterprises because they are insulated from the disciplines of the capital and product markets. They do not have to compete for capital in the open market, nor do most of them have to meet consumers' wishes in order to remain in business. With the sanctions of bankruptcy and takeover removed, and with no private shareholders to satisfy, managers of public enterprises are alleged to have little incentive to promote the efficient use of the resources at their disposal. In any case, their efforts to do so have frequently been frustrated by government intervention in pursuit of macro-economic and income redistribution objectives. Privatization is advanced as a solution to all these problems. The abolition or relaxation of statutory monopolies will, it is claimed, promote efficiency through competition in the market-place; denationalization   will   restore   market   disciplines;   and   partial denationalization will, by introducing pressures to attract and maintain private capital, increase incentives to operate efficiently and make government intervention more difficult because of the private interests involved.

Second, the Government argues that public ownership threatens economic freedom. In so far as public enterprises enjoy statutory monopoly powers or are able to use their market strength to compete 'unfairly', they limit consumers' freedom of choice. In addition, the very fact of public ownership impinges upon economic freedom because the government is depriving individuals of income or capital and forcing them to hold 'implied shareholdings' which they might not privately choose. On this argument,[5] freedom is therefore fostered by extending competition and by reducing the public sector so as to allow individuals to keep a higher proportion of their wealth in the form they themselves choose. Similarly, part of privatization's appeal to the Government relates to its desire to boost wider share ownership among the population and among an enterprise's employees in particular. This is seen as a means of increasing the stability of the private enterprise system as a whole and of individual companies. Indeed, Mr Nicholas Ridley, MP, then the Financial Secretary to the Treasury, claimed that privatization, rather than nationalization, would lead to 'real public ownership – that is ownership by the people'.[6]

Third, there is a more pragmatic argument concerning pay bargaining in the public sector. This problem has been prominent in Conservative Party debate since the conflict with the miners in 1974, which precipitated the fall of the Heath Government. It is argued that, whereas trade unions in the private sector know that an excessive pay award may lead to bankruptcy no equivalent constraint exists in the public sector. This led many Conservatives to believe that it would be impossible to withstand pay claims in those sectors in which workers have the power to hold the nation 'by the jugular vein' and that the problem could be solved only by removing access to Exchequer funds.[7] Denationalization potentially has this effect: liberalization also contributes to the solution of this problem by making it more difficult for managers to pass on excessive pay increases to consumers by raising prices.

Fourth, the Government's determination to arrest monetary growth has led it to pay attention to reducing public sector borrowing. Denationalization can contribute to this process in two ways: the sale of public assets generates an immediate cash flow to the Exchequer; and the creation of hybrid enterprises (those in which the state retains a partial shareholding) enables their borrowing to be defined out of the Public Sector Borrowing Requirement (PSBR). Under present conventions, the borrowing of the nationalized industries is included in the PSBR regardless of its source.[8] In contrast, although practice is rather confused, the borrowing of companies (irrespective of the proportion of their shares held by the state) has in the past usually been excluded. Thus the external finance from non-government sources of Rolls-Royce, although wholly-owned by the state, has never been included in the PSBR. However, when public corporations have been converted into Companies Act companies, they have been excluded only after the share sale, not on incorporation. The new test is said to be the question of whether effective control has passed out of the Government's hands (though the proportion of shares retained makes this in itself problematical).[9]

An evaluation of the Government's case for privatizing public enterprises is outside the remit of this chapter which concentrates upon the implementation of the programme. The principal arguments have been outlined only to explain the enthusiasm which ministers have shown for privatization and the determination with which they have sought to overcome the practical problems which have arisen in putting it into practice. They are, however, also relevant to the assessment, in the final section, of the Government's success at the end of its first term of office in achieving its objectives.

The Government's Record

The annex to this chapter outlines the privatization programme of the 1979-83 Government in a form which utilizes the distinction made earlier between denationalization and liberalization (with the result that several enterprises appear in both parts). Its length provides a rough indication of the scale of the programme.[10] By May 1983, the Government had either privatized or taken steps in this direction in relation to all or part of no fewer than 25 public enterprises.

In assessing the significance of this record, three qualifications need to be made. First, some of the undertakings involved, such as Amersham International (formerly the Radiochemical Centre) and the British Sugar Corporation, are of minor importance in relation to the public sector of industry as a whole. Second, several of the larger enterprises were affected only marginally. Thus, the Post Office's letter monopoly was relaxed only in areas such as express mail and the transfer of mail between document exchanges and it was solely the subsidiary activities of British Rail, such as hotels, shipping and property, and of British Leyland that were included. Third, less progress was made in implementing many of the most far-reaching proposals affecting major public enterprises, such as the sale of British Gas' oil interests and the abolition of its monopoly rights over the purchase of North Sea gas and its sale to industry, and the sale of 51% of British Telecommunications (British Telecom). Nonetheless, during its first four years in office, the Government succeeded in raising £1440 million through sales of public enterprise assets,[11] in converting four major undertakings into companies with just under 50% private shareholding, and in making significant reductions in the restrictions on entry into two important sectors of the economy.

A distinguishing feature of the denationalization measures has been that in the most important cases it has only been partial. Earlier denationalizations, such as steel and road haulage in the 1950s, were outright in the sense that public assets were simply sold to private bidders. On this occasion, however, the entire assets of an enterprise or all of its shares have been sold in only a few instances, such as Amersham International, most of British Rail's hotels and some of the National Enterprise Board's subsidiaries (e.g. Ferranti, International Computers and Fairey Holdings). The more usual approach has been to introduce private capital through the creation of hybrid companies in which the Government has retained a holding of just under 50%. This happened in the case of British Aerospace, Cable & Wireless,[12] the oil-producing side of the British National Oil Corporation (Britoil), and the British Transport Docks Board (Associated British Ports), and was planned for British Airways (for which legislation was enacted in 1980) and British Telecom (for which legislation was introduced in the final session of the 1979-83 Parliament but which lapsed at the dissolution). It was also intended for the National Freight Corporation (although the Government planned to retain at most only a very small shareholding). However, the recession which hit the road transport industry very severely, caused postponement of its flotation and eventually the Government sold the undertaking instead to a consortium of its employees, backed by a group of major banks.

As far as liberalization is concerned, the main developments have occurred in two sectors: transport and telecommunications. Route licensing in the bus industry has been eased, making the entry of private operators on to profitable routes much easier and allowing both public and private bus operators to compete more vigorously with British Rail, notably in the provision of inter-city express services. The Government has also taken steps towards deregulating domestic air routes, with private operators, such as British Midland, being granted licences for routes hitherto reserved for British Airways. The most far-reaching changes, however, have been in the telecommunications industry where, at the same time as technological changes are challenging the exclusive position of British Telecom, the Government has made progressively further inroads into its statutory monopoly, starting with the supply, installation and maintenance of most equipment and later extending to the resale of British Telecom's network for value-added services and to the provision of competing transmission services (with the first rival system, run by the Mercury Consortium for business users, receiving a licence in February 1982).

Implementation of the Programme

Only a very limited privatization programme had been declared as

Conservative policy before the Government took office. However, more far-reaching proposals had been made in 1978 by a Conservative Party research group under the chairmanship of Mr Nicholas Ridley MP, whose unpublished report was leaked to *The Economist*.[13] Its recommendations, which caused some embarrassment to the Shadow Cabinet at the time, resemble much more closely than the Manifesto the programme that actually evolved between 1979 and 1983.

In fact, the programme appears to have developed in a rather piecemeal and *ad hoc* manner. Important questions, such as the proportion of shares to be retained in hybrid companies, received little prior attention. Indeed, the Government has never really provided a proper justification for its decision to retain about 50%, especially as the logic of its general arguments in favour of privatization suggests that the process should be complete. Ministers have, however, on a number of occasions pointed to British Petroleum (in which the Government had had a stake of about 50% since 1914)[14] as a successful model. The capacity of the market to take up large share issues was also an argument for limiting the size of any one sale and for moving in stages in those cases in which ministers stated that the government holding might be reduced further in the future.

Two examples provide clear illustration of the way in which the programme evolved. In the case of the British National Oil Corporation (BNOC), the Government displayed considerable indecision. Its first proposal — to sell some of its offshore assets — had to be abandoned amidst almost universal condemnation. Two different methods of injecting private capital then emerged: one, to issue revenue bonds to the public, the return on which would be related to revenues from specified BNOC fields in the North Sea; the other, to divide BNOC into two parts: trading (which would remain wholly state-owned) and production (part of which would be sold to the public). The latter proposal was first announced in late 1979 but the introduction was twice delayed, ostensibly because of congestion in the parliamentary timetable, but more likely in the face of formidable practical difficulties in splitting the Corporation and opposition from within the Cabinet (notably from the Treasury and the Foreign Office). As a result, the revenue bond proposal was adopted and preparations were made for the launching of the scheme in the autumn of 1981. However, the appointment of Mr Nigel Lawson to replace Mr David Howell as Secretary of State for Energy in September 1981 resulted in a last-minute reversion to the more radical option, reflecting his determination to overcome the practical and political obstacles that had daunted his predecessor.

The second example is British Telecom. Initially, the Government's approach to liberalization was cautious, proposing only to end British Telecom's monopoly of the supply, installation and maintenance of equipment other than the subscriber's first telephone. However, prompted by two reports it commissioned from enthusiastic supporters of liberalization (Professors Michael Beesley and Stephen Littlechild),[15] it became increasingly radical, first authorizing the use of British Telecom's network by private operators to supply services to third parties and the provision of competitive transmission services (Beesley), and later deciding to end the first telephone monopoly and to permit competition in international communications (Littlechild). In this case too, the Government showed indecision over methods of injecting private capital. After prolonged discussions, the Chancellor announced in his 1982 Budget that agreement had been reached for British Telecom to raise funds through the issue of so-called Buzby Bonds. Within a matter of weeks, however, this plan had been abandoned in favour of the more drastic option of privatizing British Telecom through the sale of equity shares.

On the methods of privatization, there are also clear signs of haste and improvization. Little, if any, preparatory work appears to have been undertaken and officials did not have any blueprints to take down from the shelves. Although each of the denationalization schemes followed a broadly similar pattern, there are a number of interesting variations, on such questions as whether the Government should appoint directors to serve on the boards of hybrid companies (for example in British Aerospace and Britoil but not Associated British Ports and British Airways) and the setting of a statutory ceiling on the public stake in such companies (in British Aerospace only), which cannot be explained in terms of the special circumstances of particular enterprises. Similarly, with regard to liberalization surprisingly little prior thought seems to have been given to important issues such as who should regulate the new competitive regime in the gas and telecommunications industries: the minister, the public enterprise itself or a special regulatory body. Moreover, it was widely regarded as unsatisfactory that the Littlechild Report and the Government's conclusions on its recommendations were published only during the Committee Stage of the Telecommunications Bill.

In a few cases the Government was able to sell shares under existing powers (for example, the sale of its shareholding in the British Sugar Corporation and part of its holding in British Petroleum). Generally, however, legislation was required to effect both denationalization and liberalization: for the former, to establish companies registered under the Companies Act to which the assets of existing public corporations could be transferred and to provide for the sale of shares; for the latter, to repeal statutory restrictions upon entry and to lay down a framework for competition in the future.

Both processes have proved to be extremely complex, involving a large number of legal and practical issues. To a certain extent, the task was simplified by the use of enabling legislation, leaving ministers to fill in the details later, a device which also suited the Government's tight timetable.[16] Nonetheless, either in the legislation itself or during the passage of the legislation through Parliament, ministers were required to provide a considerable amount of detail about their intentions, for example in relation to the constitutions of the new companies and about methods of regulation. In this, as well as at the later stage of offering shares for sale, the Government depended heavily upon a wide array of well-paid advisers, notably lawyers and merchant bankers. The split of BNOC posed special difficulties, because of the complex participation agreements the Corporation had concluded with private oil companies and because everything had to be resolved in three-way negotiations between the Department of Energy and the two successors of the original corporation (BNOC and Britoil), each backed by their teams of legal and financial advisers.

In this process, the Government was helped to a considerable extent by the cooperation of the affected enterprise. In only a few cases did their boards oppose the substance of the Government's proposals (in rather more, concern was expressed about timing and, in relation to liberalization proposals, to safeguarding the position of public suppliers). In 1979, a spirited campaign by the board of BNOC, led by its founder chairman Lord Kearton, persuaded the Government not to sell profitable oilfields and to accept instead forward sales of oil as its contribution towards the reduction of the PSBR in 1979-80. However, this rebuff led ministers to search hard to find a new chairman who was enthusiastic about privatization, eventually recruiting a City financier, Mr (now Sir) Philip Shelbourne, who in conjunction with Nigel Lawson played a key role in the launching of Britoil.

The most successful case of opposition to date has been the British Gas Corporation. Under the leadership of its formidable chairman, Sir Denis Rooke (whom the Government re-appointed in 1981), it has resisted the Government's attempts to privatize *parts* of its undertaking, requiring ministers to issue formal directions, and succeeded in stalling over the disposal of its showrooms and over the sale of its 50% interest in the Wytch Farm oilfield in Dorset (for which a direction was issued in October 1981 but which had still not been sold at the dissolution) and of its offshore oil interests.[17] British Telecom and British Shipbuilders also voiced opposition to privatization, particularly in so far as it endangered the integrity of their undertakings. Otherwise, resistance has been exceptionally weak. In many cases, privatization has been welcomed as a means of escaping the harsh financial controls being exerted by the Government over profitable nationalized industries. Moreover, the recruitment of Shelbourne is not the only example of the Government using its powers of appointment to further its policy objectives (for example, appointing Sir John King and Ian MacGregor as chairmen of British Airways and British Steel respectively and not re-appointing union leader Mr Clive Jenkins, the General Secretary of ASTMS, to the board of BNOC).

In legislative terms, the Government's record in obtaining endorsement of its proposals is impressive. In four parliamentary sessions, it introduced thirteen privatization bills (Table 1) and all but one of them reached the statute book (the exception being the Telecommunications Bill which was lost only because of the early dissolution) virtually unscathed. In two cases, a guillotine motion had to be introduced but this was indicative only of the opportunities parliamentary procedures provide for the Opposition to delay progress (including an eleven hour speech by Mr John Golding MP on the Telecommunications Bill) and not of any difficulties the

TABLE 1 Privatization Legislation

Title	Date of Commons Second Reading	Date of Royal Assent	Enterprises affected
British Aerospace Act 1980	November 1979	May 1980	British Aerospace
Civil Aviation Act 1980	November 1979	November 1980	British Airways
Industry Act 1980	November 1979	June 1980	National Enterprise Board, Scottish and Welsh Development Agencies
Transport Act 1980	November 1979	June 1980	National Freight Corporation, National Bus Company, Scottish Transport Group and municipal operators
Atomic Energy (Miscellaneous Provisions) Act 1981	February 1981	July 1981	Radiochemical Centre
British Telecommunications Act 1981	December 1980	July 1981	Post Office (posts and telecommunications), Cable and Wireless
Iron and Steel Act 1981	March 1981	July 1981	British Steel Corporation
Transport Act 1981	January 1981	July 1981	British Railways Board, British Transport Docks Board
Oil and Gas Enterprise Act 1982	January 1982	June 1982	British Gas Corporation, British National Oil Corporation
Transport Act 1982	February 1982	October 1982	National Bus Company
British Shipbuilders Act 1983	November 1982	May 1983	British Shipbuilders
Energy Act 1983	November 1982	May 1983	Electricity Boards
Telecommunications Bill 1982	November 1982	—	British Telecommunications

Government experienced in winning comfortable majorities for its proposals.

Its record in this respect reflects its large majorities in both Houses of Parliament and the enthusiasm of its own supporters, not least in mid-term when the macro-economic outlook was bleak and privatization provided a valuable tonic for dispirited backbenchers. It was further helped by the unprecedented weakness of the Labour Opposition which seemed more interested in its own internal divisions than in effective opposition to controversial legislation on the details of which ministers were often vulnerable. The attitude of the House of Lords, which caused the 1974-79 Labour Government serious problems with aircraft and shipbuilding nationalization, was significant. The fact that the Government extended its programme far beyond its 1979 Manifesto was not greeted by the chorus of protest which would occur were a Labour Government to push through nationalization measures outside its manifesto commitments.

In contrast, the Government's progress at the second stage of denationalization – that of actually selling shares – was much less impressive. With only a few exceptions, the sales were delayed, in most cases by a substantial period. For this and other reasons too, the proceeds from this source were significantly lower than ministers intended and fell short of the targets which were set for special sales of assets as part of the drive to reduce the PSBR (see Table 2 which is discussed in the next section).

A major reason for this shortfall was the poor financial health of some of the leading candidates for denationalization, caused by the severity of the recession and various special problems affecting particular enterprises. This led to abandonment of the plan to sell shares to the public in the National Freight Company (which instead was sold to its staff); to indefinite postponement of the flotation of British Airways for which legislation was enacted in October 1980; to substantial delay in the sale of shares in Associated British Ports (which occurred seventeen months after the necessary legislation received the Royal Assent); and to delay and modification[18] of the proposal to denationalize British Shipbuilders (ironically one of the few commitments included in the 1979 Manifesto). Problems such as these encouraged the Government to bring forward some of the commercially strongest enterprises, such as Cable & Wireless and Britoil, to which its general arguments appeared much less applicable. Moreover, the sale of Britoil – the largest to date – in a highly depressed oil market resulted in proceeds only about half of the initial forecast.

For other reasons too, the Government experienced difficulties in raising as much as it might have hoped. The management of new issues is never easy and various special factors, largely but not entirely beyond its control, compounded these problems. The size of most of the offers and the publicity surrounding them, not least as a result of the Labour Party's threats of renationalization either with no compensation or 'with compensation of no more than that received when the assets were sold',[19] meant that the Government and its City advisers were working in virgin territory. The Government itself also imposed various restrictions on most of the sales, for instance to limit foreign purchases and to secure wide dispersal of ownership.

Problems such as these exacerbated the difficulties of deciding upon the best methods of sale. The Government's desire to help the small investor led it to choose a fixed price offer for the first three flotations: British Aerospace, Cable & Wireless and Amersham International. In one sense, these sales were highly successful in that they were heavily oversubscribed (2.4 times for British Aerospace, 4.6 times for Cable & Wireless and 24.6 times for Amersham). However, such oversubscription, together with the premium at which the initial dealing took place, suggests that the selling prices could have been fixed at a higher level and that assets were disposed of at less than market value. Indeed, this aspect of the Amersham sale in particular caused the Government considerable embarrassment and its methods of selling shares were criticized by the Public Accounts Committee in April 1982.[20] These criticisms led the Government to decide that the largest sale to date, that of Britoil, should be by tender but with special arrangements for small investors. Again, however, it was embarrassed by the outcome. Only just over 25% of the shares were taken up, the remainder being left in the hands of the underwriters, as a result of last-minute nerves on the part of the financial institutions about the prospects for the oil market. Two months later, the Government's problems were compounded by a 35 times oversubscription for the shares of Associated British Ports for which it had reverted to a fixed price offer.

Despite these problems, ministers could claim with some justification that the conclusion of these sales was in itself a considerable achievement. If the transfer of ownership is more important than the price secured, this is a fair claim. Moreover, as far as Amersham and Britoil were concerned, last-minute changes in the market's assessment of the offers were the Government's undoing, and in the latter case ministers argued that the 'loss' was borne by the underwriters rather than the taxpayer as it was they who were left with the bulk of the offer in their hands and the Exchequer received in full the money it had expected at the time of the offer on sale.

One potential problem that did not materialize during this first phase of the privatization programme was effective trade union opposition. With higher unemployment, falling membership (but not union densities), anti-trade union legislation and hostile public opinion, the unions have not been looking for additional battlefields. Thus, although opposed to privatization in principle, most unions appeared to accept the inevitable and did little to resist the implementation of the Government's plans. Only in two cases did the threat of significant industrial action materialize in the form of one-day strikes against the disposal of gas showrooms and the

Government's plan to sell a 51% stake in British Telecom. Both were well-supported and the showrooms action was claimed to have met with some success. However, it was management opposition which was decisive in persuading ministers to delay (officially, on the ground that new safety legislation would be needed first).

The Government embarrassed the unions by skilful exploitation of concessionary issues of employee shares which have proved highly popular. Although a negligible proportion of the total, they are rich in public relations value. There were also two special cases of employee involvement: a management-led consortium, but with more extensive shareholding and the support of four of the five unions involved (but not the largest, the Transport and General Workers' Union) bought the National Freight Company in 1982; and the National Union of Railwaymen became a shareholder in Gleneagles Hotels, a company established to run three of British Rail's Scottish hotels – a tactic designed to protect its negotiating rights and which, although not welcomed by the Government, had the effect of compromising the union's opposition to privatization.[21]

Assessment of the Government's Record

As befits a controversial programme, the Government's record in privatizing public enterprises during its first term of office has been the subject of widely differing verdicts. Some, both supporters and opponents, have regarded the scale of the programme as impressive, going far beyond anything previously achieved, whereas others have expressed disappointment that after four years the core of the 'problem', the public enterprise heartland such as coal, electricity, gas and railways, remained largely unscathed. The share flotations have been heralded as successful, or at least satisfactory, by some financial commentators and condemned as disastrous, and even scandalous, by others. As for implementation generally, ministers have both been congratulated on their good fortune (for example in the lack of effective parliamentary and trade union opposition) and commiserated on their bad luck (for example in the volatility of the stock market and the economic recession).

It is as yet premature to attempt a comprehensive assessment of the Government's record for the programme is by no means completed, as the 1983 Conservative Manifesto and subsequent ministerial speeches indicate.[22] Moreover, many of the effects will be apparent only in the long term. Nonetheless, it is useful to look at experience up to May 1983 in order to gauge the progress that the Government had made in achieving the objectives which it had set for the programme.

Of the four aims outlined earlier, the reduction of the PSBR was prominent during this first phase of the programme. Given the Government's preoccupation with the PSBR, it is not surprising that denationalization appeared as an attractive option, especially as an alternative to making cuts in public spending. This goal strengthened

TABLE 2   Proceeds from Special Sales of Assets
(£million cash)

	1979-80	1980-81	1981-82	1982-83
TARGET (a)	**1,000**	**500**	**500**	**600**
1. PRIVATIZED NATIONALIZED INDUSTRIES AND PUBLIC SHAREHOLDINGS (b)	**336**	**126**	**305**	**380**
Sale of shares in British Petroleum		276	8(c)	
Sale of shares held by National Enterprise Board	37	83	2	
Sale of shares in British Aerospace		43		
Sale of shares in Cable and Wireless			182	
Sale of shares in British Sugar Corporation			44	
Sale of shares in Amersham International			64	
Sale of shares in National Freight Company			5	
Sale of shares in Britoil (first instalment)				334(d)
Sale of shares in Associated British Ports				46
Sale of shares in other companies	23			
2. OTHER ASSET SALES	**34**	**279**	**189**	**108**
Sale of land and buildings owned by various public bodies (e)	34	56	88	31
Sale of motorway service area leases		28	19	4
Receipts from 7th and 8th rounds of offshore oil licensing		195		33
Sale of oil stockpile			63	33
Sale of other stocks			19	7
TOTAL 1 + 2	**370**	**405**	**494**	**488**
3. REVENUE OFFSETS				
Advance payments to BNOC for oil	622	(49)	(573)	—
Stamp Duty and VAT	7			
GRAND TOTAL (1 + 2 + 3)	**999**	**356**	**(79)**	**488**

Sources: HM Treasury, *Economic Progress Report*, No. 145, May 1982 (targets); Cmnd. 8789, *The Government's expenditure plans 1983-84 to 1985-86* and H.C. Deb. 27 July 1983, col. 453 (outturns).

Notes:

(a) Comparison of actual proceeds against target is complicated by the switch from volume to cash planning in the 1982 Public Expenditure White Paper (Cmnd. 8494). The target figures listed in the table ignore this complication, as have Government pronouncements. They are taken from the Treasury's *Economic Progress Report* and do not in all cases agree with the figures in successive Public Expenditure White Papers.

(b) To these totals, there need to be added the proceeds of various sales which have remained within the businesses concerned, for instance British Rail and British Steel, even if effectively offset by equivalent reductions in Exchequer finance.

(c) The Government's nil-paid rights in the 1981 rights issue.

(d) Includes repayment of a debenture of £88 million with interest. The second instalment of £293 million (investors paid for their shares in two instalments) was received in April 1983.

(e) New towns, water authorities, Property Services Agency, Crown Agents, Forestry Commission.

ministers' resolve to overcome the many practical problems that confronted them and influenced the order in which proposals were implemented. However, the amounts actually raised were trivial in the context of public expenditure totals.

For each financial year, the Government fixed a target for 'special sales of assets'. Table 2 sets out these targets and the outturns achieved. The Government's definition of asset sales extends beyond the privatization of public enterprises. The table, therefore, has been broken down to distinguish between those sales which form part of the privatization programme as it has been defined here (Section 1) and other asset sales (Section 2). Section 1 shows that over four financial years just £1147 million (cash) was raised, of which just over 50% accrued from the BP and Britoil sales. To this total, there needs to be added the proceeds of various sales which have remained within the businesses concerned, such as British Rail and British Steel, even if effectively offset by equivalent reductions in Exchequer finance.[23]

Assessment of the Government's record in terms of its own targets is complicated.[24] In 1979-80 the outturn appears to have been remarkably close to the target. However, the figures were manipulated by the inclusion of the proceeds of forward sales of BNOC's oil (Section 3) which accounted for over 60% of the sums raised. Moreover, this device simply shifted cash flow forward, causing negative figures when the practice ceased such that, although in 1981-82 the asset sales achieved (Sections 1 and 2) were in line with the Government's target, they were more than offset by this factor. The outturn in other years was also influenced by the inclusion of rather dubious items such as the premiums on North Sea oil licences (which in 1980-81 accounted for almost 50% of asset sales) and the sale of oil stockpiles.

Quite apart from the delays which have occurred and the depressed state of the oil market, the benefit to the Exchequer has been limited because of the need to provide certain companies with new capital (e.g. British Aerospace) and to fund deficiencies in pension funds (e.g. the National Freight Company). In the longer term, privatization may also have some adverse budgetary implications for the Exchequer. If denationalization leads to a rationalization of activities, the PSBR could be increased as a result of redundancy payments and unemployment pay.[25] Liberalization is also likely to have the effect of limiting the ability of public enterprises to continue the practice of cross-subsidization. Many of the advocates of privatization see its elimination as a major gain. However, the Government's position is ambiguous, reflecting the political pressures, not least from Conservative MPs, to maintain services, such as those in rural areas, which are generally believed to be cross-subsidized. If competition diminishes the profitability of those parts of a business which have financed cross-subsidization in the past, the Government will have either to incur higher public expenditure on explicit subsidies or to build continued cross-subsidization into the new arrangements (as it is doing in the case of British Telecom's licence) if it is to avert a drastic reduction in the provision of unprofitable 'social' services.

Another way in which the programme contributed to reducing the PSBR was through the creation of companies – both hybrid and wholly private – whose borrowing, as soon as flotation occurred, was excluded from the PSBR. By May 1983, four enterprises – British Aerospace, the National Freight Company, Britoil, and Associated British Ports – had been taken out. As Cable & Wireless and the Radiochemical Centre (now Amersham International) were Companies Act companies before privatization, only that part of their external finance which came from the Exchequer was ever included. Again, therefore, the effect upon the PSBR was modest. It should also be noted that the same result could have been achieved with rather less difficulty simply by altering the definition of the PSBR, a change which has been widely advocated and which would bring the UK into line with a number of other countries. Indeed, the Government has itself demonstrated that the rules are not immutable. Traditionally, as has been mentioned above, those public enterprises taking the Companies Act company form, even with 100% state shareholding, had their external finance from non-government sources excluded from the PSBR. On that basis, once a public corporation becomes a Companies Act company, it should have been excluded. However, the Treasury has decided that the new companies should be excluded only after control has passed to the private sector with that being taken to occur after a 50% share sale. Such a ruling has enabled ministers to claim that the 'benefit' of reducing the PSBR can be achieved only in this way.[26]

An attempt to secure wider share ownership influenced the Government's choice of method of sale and led it to give preferential treatment to small investors in the allocation of shares. However, in no case was the proportion of shares held by small shareholders significant (although it would of course have been lower but for the Government's action). Moreover, in the case of British Aerospace, there was a dramatic 83% fall in the number of shareholders in the ten months following flotation.[27] The slide in the price of Britoil shares to 157p in February 1983 (compared with the striking price of 215p) must also have caused ministers some embarrassment, as the shares which were taken up went almost exclusively to private individuals who, unlike the financial institutions, were less able to respond to the last-minute fears about the future of oil prices.[28] The Government met with greater success in its attempt to promote employee shareholding. Around 100,000 employees took advantage of the opportunities which were offered, representing about 90% of the total eligible workforce. However, the proportion of the total equity acquired by employees was negligible, ranging from 4.3% in Associated British Ports to just 0.1% in Britoil.[29]

In the longer term, the success or failure of the programme will be judged by its effects upon the quality and efficiency of service provision. As far as consumer choice is concerned, there is no question that the programme has in various sectors, notably buses and telecommunications, opened up new opportunities. However, the Government's success in promoting competition can be assessed only once the market has settled down. In the bus industry, for example, relaxation of the licensing system brought in a large number of new operators but many of them have already gone out of business.

In other sectors, a serious conflict has emerged between the Government's denationalization and liberalization objectives. Whether denationalization of itself will lead to more competition or less depends heavily upon the circumstances of each case, such as the technology of the industry and the prevailing market structure. Moreover, in order to raise as much money as possible from denationalization, there are obvious attractions in selling an enterprise to a company already operating in the relevant sector and in providing the new operator with a degree of protection. Ministers have recently demonstrated a growing awareness of these tensions within the privatization programme and have asserted the primacy of the liberalization objective.[30] However, the Government's record casts doubts upon such assertions. Various decisions, such as British Steel's joint ventures with the private sector and the merger between Seaspeed and Hoverlloyd, former competitors in the provision of cross-Channel hovercraft services, had the effect of limiting competition. Similarly, liberalization of the provision of telecommunications network has been extremely hesitant with just one rival to British Telecom being granted a licence and with a guarantee that no further networks will be licensed at least until 1990. Most embarrassing of all to those ministers who espouse competition must have been European Ferries' bid for British Rail's subsidiary, Sealink.

Instead of rejecting it immediately on the ground that it would have given European Ferries 80% of the cross-Channel market, the Government reached this decision only after it had received an adverse report from the Monopolies and Mergers Commission. Such tensions between denationalization and liberalization arise even more seriously in relation to a number of the current front-runners for flotation, such as British Airways and British Telecom, and will test to the full the relative priority attached by the Government to these two objectives.

The question of whether privatization will lead to greater efficiency can also be answered only in the long term. The present evidence on the respective merits of private and public enterprise is far from conclusive.[31] Certainly the belief in the superiority of the private sector is widely held. However, it is difficult to isolate the effects of ownership from other factors such as size. Moreover, the turnround in the finances of a number of public enterprises since 1979 suggests that quality of management may be crucial. In any case, a policy of selling off the most profitable or efficient enterprises, thus leaving the public sector with the troublesome lossmakers, has clear implications for the future image and performance of the nationalized sector.

A particular aim of the Government in this area has been to free these undertakings from ministerial intervention. Only experience will tell whether privatization will have this effect. Problems are particularly likely to arise in relation to the new hybrid companies.[32] Despite the continuing substantial public shareholding, ministers insist that they will not intervene in such companies' commercial affairs other than in exceptional circumstances, such as an attempt to alter the articles of association so as to permit a higher proportion of foreign ownership. It remains to be seen, however, whether this stance holds in the face of political and economic pressures. There have already been a few signs of parliamentary pressure upon ministers to take a closer interest and the fact is that almost all of the new hybrids operate in sectors such as defence, energy and communications, in which ministers retain major responsibilities.

Another source of pressure to intervene is likely to come from industrial relations. Weakening public sector trade unions has been an important strand in the privatization programme. Since 1979, however, its salience has been moderated by the effects of high levels of unemployment upon union activity. In addition, those enterprises privatized during the Government's first term of office were not those with a record of difficulty in this respect. As privatization moves into areas of potential confrontation, such as telecommunications, gas, and electricity, where there is the prospect of disrupting the entire economy, it will be seen whether governments will be able to resist the pressures upon them to become involved in the resolution of disputes.

Conclusions

This brief analysis provides some indication of the complexity of reaching an overall assessment of the Government's record, especially when the programme is incomplete and before many of the longer-term consequences have emerged. Nonetheless, a few concluding observations can be made. First, the Government has demonstrated that, with sufficient determination, it is possible to overcome the practical difficulties of implementing privatization, and its achievements by the end of its first term of office exceeded the expectations of virtually all informed commentators. On the other hand, except in telecommunications and oil, the changes which it had effected by May 1983 in the public sector of industry may reasonably be regarded as limited. The Conservative 1983 Manifesto and developments since the General Election make it clear that the Government intends to take the programme considerably further but, as it digs deeper into the core of this sector, so the problems of implementation will increase.

ANNEX
The Privatization of Public Enterprise
The Government's Record 1979-83

I.   Denationalization

Proposal	*Progress*
BRITISH AEROSPACE Conversion into Companies Act company and sale of about 50% of its shares.	Legislation enacted in May 1980; transfer to company in January 1981; sale of 51.6% shares in February 1981.
BRITISH AIRWAYS Conversion into Companies Act company and sale of 'a substantial minority shareholding' (probably 49%).	Legislation enacted in November 1980; implementation delayed by BA's financial problems at least until 1984; among measures to raise cash, sale of subsidiary, International Aeradio, in 1982.
BRITISH GAS CORPORATION Sale of (i) British Gas' 50% interest in Wytch Farm oilfield in Dorset; (ii) its 900 showrooms; and (iii) its offshore oil business.	(i) Direction issued in October 1981, sale repeatedly delayed, now due in 1984; (ii) & (iii) legislation enacted in June 1982, sale of (iii) planned for 1983-84 but sale of (ii) postponed due to need for additional legislation on safety of appliances and their installation.
BRITISH LEYLAND Sale of various subsidiaries.	Sales to date include Prestcold (refrigerators), agricultural tractor and forklift truck businesses.
BRITISH NATIONAL OIL CORPORATION Originally sale of offshore assets; later, division of BNOC into two (trading and production) and sale of majority stake (initially 51%) in production business; restricted role for BNOC.	Original proposals abandoned in 1979; legislation enacted in June 1982; split of BNOC and creation of Britoil in August 1982 and sale of 51% shares in November 1982; various restrictions effected.
BRITISH PETROLEUM LTD. Sale of 10% of state shareholding.	Sold in November 1979, reducing combined Treasury and Bank of England holding from 51% to 46%; further reduced to 39% by 1981 rights issue.

BRITISH RAIL Transfer of subsidiaries (hotels, ferries, hovercraft and non-operational property) to holding company and sale of at least a majority interest (timing and manner of sale to be decided by British Rail).

British Rail Investments Ltd. created in November 1980; legislation permitting sale of shares enacted in July 1981; merger of Seaspeed (BR) and Hoverlloyd in October 1981; sale (in most cases outright) of property, laundries and 26 (out of 29) hotels with 2 others leased pending estate development; sale of Sealink to European Ferries blocked by Monopolies Commission.

BRITISH SHIPBUILDERS Partial privatization whether by sales of subsidiaries or joint ventures with private sector.

Legislation enacted in May 1983.

BRITISH STEEL CORPORATION Sale of between 15 and 25% of BSC either through specific sales of subsidiaries or by way of joint ventures with private sector (Operation Phoenix).

Legislation enacted in July 1981; three joint ventures launched in 1981 and 1982; sale of Redpath Dorman Long in 1982.

BRITISH SUGAR CORPORATION Sale of Government's 24% shareholding.

Sold in July 1981.

BRITISH TELECOMMUNICATIONS Conversion into Companies Act company and sale of 51% of its shares.

Telecommunications Bill lost at dissolution in May 1983.

BRITISH TRANSPORT DOCKS BOARD Conversion into Companies Act company (called Associated British Ports) and sale of about 50% of its shares.

Legislation enacted in July 1981; transfer to company in December 1982; sale of 51.5% shares in February 1983.

CABLE AND WIRELESS LTD. Sale of just under 50% of its shares.

Legislation enacted in July 1981; sale in October 1981.

NATIONAL BUS COMPANY Joint ventures with private sector in express coach and holiday businesses and in certain property developments and improvements.

Legislation enacted in October 1982.

NATIONAL ENTERPRISE BOARD To sell £100m assets in 1979-80 and generally to dispose of its shareholdings 'as soon as commercially practicable'; powers to be severely restricted; Board to be merged with National Research Development Corporation and renamed as British Technology Group (thus confirming its revised emphasis on assisting new high technology ventures).

Released from obligation to sell £100m in 1979-80; legislation enacted in June 1980; by May 1983 sales amounting to over £150m, of which the most important were Ferranti, International Computers and Fairey Holdings; transfer of British Leyland and Rolls-Royce to Department of Industry in 1980-81; new guidelines issued in August 1980; operational merger in July 1981.

NATIONAL FREIGHT CORPORATION Conversion into Companies Act company and sale of 'all or virtually all' of its shares.

Legislation enacted in June 1980; transfer to company in October 1980; following delay in flotation due to recession, company sold to consortium of managers and employees backed by group of major banks in February 1982.

RADIOCHEMICAL CENTRE LTD. (renamed Amersham International Ltd.) Sale of up to 100% of its shares (held by UK Atomic Energy Authority).

Legislation enacted in July 1981; sale of all its shares in February 1982.

II. Extending Competition

| *Proposal* | *Progress* |

BRITISH GAS CORPORATION Abolition of British Gas' monopoly rights over the purchase of North Sea gas and its sale to industry.

Legislation enacted in June 1982.

BRITISH TELECOMMUNICATIONS Initially liberalization of supply, installation and maintenance of all equipment other than first telephone and maintenance of private branch exchanges; following Beesley Report (1981), use of BT network by private companies to supply services to third parties (ii) and provision of additional transmission services (iii); following Littlechild Report (1983), abolition of 'first telephone' monopoly and greater freedom in use of BT network (iv); creation of office of Director General of Telecommunications to supervise telecommunications industry (v).

Legislation enacted in July 1981; (i) to be phased in between 1981 and 1984; (ii) private companies permitted as from October 1981 to use BT circuits to supply special services which BT is not ready to supply and to supply all such services (but not merely to-sell capacity) as from April 1982; (iii) Mercury Consortium licensed in February 1982 to provide an independent telecommunications system (designed for business users); (iv) and (v) included in Telecommunications Bill which fell at dissolution in May 1983.

BUS AND COACH SERVICES Relaxation of licensing controls permitting greater competition with municipal and nationalized operators (National Bus Company, Scottish Transport Group).

Legislation enacted in June 1980; new system into force in October 1980.

ELECTRICITY Encouragement of private generation of electricity by empowering private firms to sell electricity to local electricity boards on fair terms and to use National Grid, and repealing statutory prohibition on generation as a main business activity.

Legislation enacted in May 1983.

POST OFFICE Limited relaxations of postal monopoly (e.g. express mail, bulk mail between document exchanges).

Legislation enacted in July 1981; express mail monopoly ended in November 1981; licences permitting document exchanges to transfer mail and charities to carry Christmas cards issued in late 1981.

Notes and References

1. Conservative Party, *The Conservative Manifesto 1979*, 1979.
2. Such an assessment is provided in D.A. Heald and D.R. Steel, Privatizing Public Enterprise: An Analysis of the Government's Case, *Political Quarterly*, July 1982, 333-49.
3. These four uses of the term 'privatization' are discussed in D.A. Heald, *Public Expenditure: Its Defence and Reform*, Martin Robertson, 1983, Chapter 13.

4. See, for example, the figures published by the Department of Employment in H.C.Deb, 25 November 1982, cols. 571-2.
5. It is an argument which raises fundamental issues about the relationship between markets and freedom which are beyond the scope of this chapter but which are thoroughly discussed in D.A. Heald, *op.cit.*
6. Quoted in *Economic Progress Report*, HM Treasury, May 1982, p.1.
7. See, for example, the report of a Conservative research group whose unpublished conclusions were leaked to *The Economist*, 27 May 1978.
8. Present practice is set out in the report of the Treasury and Civil Service Committee on the financing of the nationalized industries (HC 348, 1980-81, Appendix 18).
9. There has been almost no public discussion of the implications of different levels of public shareholding for public control. At first sight, it might appear that ministers regard 50% as the crucial threshold. However, the Government has not adhered to this view in every case, sometimes stating that control would pass out of its hands despite the retention of a 51% stake and at other times insisting upon the sale of significantly more than 50% for this to occur. Moreover, no one would suggest that in the private sector control cannot be exercised unless a single shareholder holds more than 50% of the voting shares.
10. Despite the efforts made here to define privatization, the boundaries of the programme remain rather imprecise. For example, public bodies sold surplus assets, such as land, long before privatization was conceived and for reasons unconnected with the present arguments. Similarly, various developments, such as the creation of joint ventures, can - and have - been regarded in some quarters as extensions rather than reductions in the public sector ('creeping nationalization').
11. £1147 million was raised during the financial years 1979-80 to 1982-83 (Table 2) and a further £293 million in April 1983.
12. In March 1983, the Government shareholding fell to just over 45% when Cable & Wireless issued additional shares in connection with the purchase of shares in the Hong Kong Telephone Company. Following the General Election, it was further reduced to 22% when the Government decided to sell half of its remaining stake.
13. *The Economist*, 27 May 1978. Ridley was then a backbencher but he has been a minister in the Government since 1979 and, since 1981, he has had responsibilities in relation to privatization, first as Financial Secretary to the Treasury and, from October 1983, as Secretary of State for Transport.
14. Ironically, they have done this at the same time as they were taking steps to reduce the Government's stake in BP (from 51% to 46% in 1979; to 39% in 1981; and to 32% in September 1983).
15. M.E. Beesley, *Liberalization of the Use of British Telecommunications' Network*, Department of Industry, 1981; S.C. Littlechild, *Regulation of British Telecommunications' Profitability*, Department of Industry, 1983.
16. This device was adopted most dramatically in the most complicated case, that of Britoil. The relevant parts of the Oil and Gas Enterprise Act are very short (just four pages) and use was made of 'scheme-making' powers modelled on those of the Transport Act 1968.
17. At an early stage in the row, Rooke challenged the Government to privatize the entire corporation rather than to dismember it. After the 1983 General Election, there were reports that his bluff was going to be called.
18. Instead of denationalizing British Shipbuilders as a whole, the Government has been considering the sale only of its profitable parts, notably the naval shipyards.
19. Confusion as to the Labour Party's intentions reflected the strains between the PLP and the Annual Conference and within the PLP itself. The phrase quoted here is from the Party's 1983 Manifesto, *The New Hope for Britain*.
20. Tenth Report from the Committee of Public Accounts (HC 189, 1981-82).
21. This course of action was too expensive to repeat in other cases in which the NUR's efforts were focused upon preserving as far as possible its negotiating rights and protecting its members' interests rather than upon outright opposition to the sales.

22. See, for example, the speech made by the Financial Secretary to the Treasury, Mr. John Moore MP, at the annual conference of stockbrokers, Fielding, Newson Smith, on 1 November 1983.

23. For example, in 1982-83, £35 million was raised from the sale of British Rail hotels and £60 million from British Airway's subsidiary, International Aeradio (H.C.Deb, 27 July 1983, col. 453).

24. Comparison of actual proceeds against target is complicated by the switch from volume to cash planning in the 1982 Public Expenditure White Paper (Cmnd. 8494). The target figures used in this paragraph and in Table 2 ignore this complication, as have Government pronouncements. They have been taken from the Treasury's *Economic Progress Report* and do not in all cases agree with the figures in successive Public Expenditure White Papers.

25. This point is made by A.T. Peacock and G.K. Shaw in *The Public Sector Borrowing Requirement*, University College at Buckingham, Occasional Papers in Economics No. 1, 1981. Interestingly, this study was commissioned by the Centre for Policy Studies and a first draft was presented to a seminar organized by the Prime Minister's Policy Unit and chaired by Professor Alan Walters, then the Prime Minister's economic adviser.

26. Perhaps the most overt abuse of the PSBR argument for denationalization can be found in Mr Patrick Jenkin's statement on the future of British Telecom, reproduced in *The Future of Telecommunications in Britain*, Cmnd. 8610, 1982.

27. Tenth report from the Committee of Public Accounts (HC 189, 1981-82), Appendix II.

28. The price subsequently improved (although the shares were still at a 41p discount at the time that the second instalment was due) and by the time of the General Election the discount had been reduced to 9p.

29. Speech of the Financial Secretary to the Treasury, November 1983, press release, p.11., H.C. Deb., 29 July 1983, cols. 731-2.

30. *Ibid*, 16.

31. A recent review of the evidence is provided by R. Millward, 'The comparative performance of public and private enterprise' in Lord Roll (ed.) *The Mixed Economy*, Macmillan, 1982, 58-93.

32. These problems are developed in D.R. Steel, Government and the new hybrids: a trail of unanswered questions, *Fiscal Studies*, February 1984.

4

Public Sector Manpower, Wages and Industrial Relations 1979-83

Phil Beaumont

In this overview chapter I outline the evidence available at the time of writing (August - September 1983) on three related matters; manpower, wages and industrial relations in the public sector for the period 1979-83. This chapter is quite different to the one in the earlier RIPA volume in that here I avoid discussion of (i) past trends in public sector employment, and (ii) the background to, and evolution of, the present Government's policies towards the public sector; my concentration is almost solely on results and outcomes during the period under consideration. In presenting my material I will tend to follow, wherever possible, the traditional division of the public sector into central government (very largely the civil service), local government and the public corporations (very largely the nationalized industries). As background to the more detailed discussion to come, however, I set out below in Table 1 the changes in public sector employment, by major categories, over the period 1976-1982.

The contents of Table 1 indicate that total public sector employment increased from 7,310,000 in 1976 to 7,444,000 in 1979, but by 1982 had fallen by some 408,000 (5.5%) to a figure of 7,036,000. By mid-1982 there were some 7 million employees in the public sector, which comprised some 1.8 million employees in public corporations, 2.3 million in central government and 2.9 million in local authorities. The decline in public sector employment over the three years to mid-1982 was considerably less than that in the private sector where some 1,621,000 jobs were lost; a 10.1% fall.

This much larger fall in private sector employment has important implications for Government policy towards the public sector, a point that is strongly emphasized by no less a person than Walter Eltis in the following extract:[1]

> Halting, or indeed reducing the growth of government employment has only very slight beneficial effects on government finances in conditions of high unemployment. These policies will, of course, entirely fail to raise the

country's growth potential - their true *raison d'etre* - if industry and commerce cannot re-employ the workers the government makes redundant. In these circumstances, manpower cuts in the public services will be extremely damaging to economic welfare, and largely irrelevant to government efforts to reassert financial control. The manpower cuts in general government envisaged by the present Conservative Government are of the order of 3-5% and not 33% of central government employment as a whole. Their net effect on the Government's borrowing requirement and on the necessary taxation and the monetary aggregates is likely to be very slight indeed.

In short, the Eltis and Bacon argument, which seems to have been so much accepted by the present Government, was developed with reference to a relatively full employment economy, a reference point of limited, to say the least, relevance to Britain in recent years. Accordingly, with this economic context firmly in mind, we now turn to consider the employment position in central government where we concentrate on the civil service and, to a lesser extent, the national health service.

Central Government Manpower

The Government's target with regard to the civil service is that it was to be reduced from 732,000 (at May 1979 when it assumed office) to 630,000 by April 1984, a 14% reduction in staffing levels over a five year period. The figures set out in Table 2 below suggests that the Government is reasonably well on course to achieve this targeted reduction.

If we concentrate solely on the 'all departments total' then there has been a reduction from 732,300 in 1979 to 648,900 in April 1983; an 11.4% reduction over the period. Moreover, the 1983-84 supply estimates indicate that the Government expect to achieve their originally stated target; indeed their estimated total for April 1984 is a civil service total of 628,316. The relevant figures in this regard are set out in Table 3.

The figures in Tables 2 and 3 raise the obvious question of how such reductions were, and are to be, achieved. At present we lack an analysis of the source of these reductions over the full period in question, but results are available for 1980-81 and 1981-82 separately. These are set out below in Table 4.

The above results indicate that the bulk of the savings resulted from 'general streamlining', which involved the accumulation of a large number of individually small changes; changes that could involve improvements in efficiency or the lowering of standards. A rather smaller number came from privatization, particularly in 1980-81, while implementation of the numerous proposals suggested by Sir Derek Rayner produced just under 4,000 reductions in 1980-81 (of which 1,000 came from new PAYE procedures), with rather more in the following year. Some useful illustrative examples of the type of key, small changes noted above are set out in a talk by Michael Heseltine to a branch of the British Institute of Management.[2]

TABLE 1 UK Public Sector Employment 1976-1982 by Major Categories[1]

Thousands

	General government				Local authorities							Public corporations			
	Central government														
Mid-year	HM Forces and women's services	National health service	Other central government	Total central government	Education services	Health and social services	Construction	Police (incl civilians)	Other local authorities	Total local authorities	Total	Nationalized industries (incl Post Office)	Other public corporations	Total public corporations	Total public sector
1976	336	1,146	832[3]	2,314[3]	1,568	319	165	187	777	3,016	5,330	1,690	290[3]	1,980[3]	7,310
1977	327	1,155	823	2,305	1,556	322	155	184	767	2,984	5,289	1,803[4]	286	2,089[4]	7,378[4]
1978	318	1,175	814	2,307	1,563	334	155	183	762	2,997	5,304	1,774	287	2,061	7,365
1979	314	1,197	808	2,319	1,587	344	156	189	784	3,060	5,379	1,777	288	2,065	7,444
1980	323	1,228	776[5]	2,327[5]	1,556	346	152	195	778	3,027	5,354	1,744	294[5]	2,038[5]	7,392
1981	334	1,264	761	2,359	1,505	350	143	200	768	2,966	5,325	1,586[6]	281	1,867[6]	7,192
1982[2]	324	1,287	735	2,346	1,483	352	132	201	763	2,931	5,277	1,487	272[7]	1,759[7]	7,036

1 Appendix 2 gives details of the definitions and coverage of the sectors and sources of the statistics and major changes in them between 1976 and 1982.

2 Preliminary estimates based upon data covering nearly 95 per cent of the general government sector; these should not be regarded as accurate to the last digit shown.

3 The Property Services Agency (Supplies Division) was reclassified to public corporations from 1976.

4 Most of the aerospace and shipbuilding industries were nationalized in 1977, resulting in the transfer of about 150,000 from the private sector.

5 The establishment of HMSO from 1 April 1980 as a trading body implies the transfer of about 6,000 to public corporations.

6 British Aerospace was reclassified to the private sector in February 1981 reducing public corporations' employment by about 73,000.

7 Cable and Wireless was reclassified to the private sector in October 1981 and National Freight Corporation in February 1982, together reducing public corporations by about 28,000.

Note: Components may not add to totals because of rounding.

Source: Howard Morrison, Employment in the public and private sectors 1976 to 1982, Economic Trends, February 1983, 84.

TABLE 2   Civil Service Staff Analysis by Ministerial Responsibilities

Full-time equivalent² (thousands)

	1977 1 April	1978 1 April	1979 1 April	1980 1 April	1981 1 April	1982 1 April	1 October	1983 1 January	1 April
Agriculture Fisheries and food	15.5	14.6	14.5	14.3	13.6	13.1	12.9	12.8	12.7
Chancellor of the Exchequer's Departments:									
Total³ ⁴	129.3	128.9	128.2	119.0	114.9	121.0	118.7	118.5	117.4
Customs and Excise	29.3	28.8	28.8	27.2	26.8	26.2	25.7	25.6	25.4
Inland Revenue	83.9	85.2	84.6	78.3	75.6	74.0	73.4	73.6	73.1
Department for National Savings	12.2	10.9	10.8	10.4	10.0	9.1	8.6	8.5	8.3
Treasury and others	3.9	4.0	4.0	3.1	2.5	11.7	11.0	10.8	10.6
Education and Science	4.0	3.7	3.7	3.7	3.6	3.5	3.5	3.5	3.5
Employment⁵	52.5	53.7	53.6	50.7	53.8	58.7	57.9	57.6	57.9
Energy	1.3	1.3	1.3	1.3	1.2	1.1	1.1	1.1	1.1
Environment⁶ ⁷	61.5	57.3	56.0	51.7	47.0	42.1	40.9	40.5	39.4
Foreign and Commonwealth	12.4	12.1	12.1	11.6	11.4	11.1	11.0	11.0	11.1
Home	32.6	33.2	33.5	34.1	35.4	34.6	34.7	35.0	35.1
Industry	9.7	9.5	9.5	9.1	8.8	8.3	7.9	7.8	7.7
Scotland⁹	13.0	13.5	13.7	13.6	13.6	13.4	13.3	13.2	13.1
Social services	98.3	99.5	100.9	98.9	100.1	98.0	96.7	96.9	96.4
Trade	10.0	9.7	9.6	9.4	9.3	8.9	8.8	8.8	8.9
Transport⁷	13.6	14.5	13.9	13.5	13.7	13.0	13.0	13.0	13.0
Wales⁹	1.6	2.5	2.6	2.5	2.3	2.3	2.2	2.2	2.2
Other civil departments	31.5	31.3	31.4	31.7	31.3	20.2	20.5	20.4	20.5
Total civil departments	486.9	485.3	484.6	465.1	460.0	449.4	443.0	442.3	440.0
Royal Ordnance Factories	22.8	22.9	23.0	21.8	20.8	19.4	18.5	18.5	18.5
Defence	235.9	227.5	224.7	218.0	208.8	197.5	193.5	191.7	190.3
Total all departments¹⁰	745.6	735.7	732.3	704.9	689.6	666.4	655.0	652.5	648.9
of which:									
Non-industrials	571.1	567.3	565.8	547.5	539.9	528.0	521.1	520.3	518.3
Industrials	174.4	168.4	166.5	157.4	149.7	138.4	133.9	132.2	130.4

1. The figures include non-industrial staff but exclude casual or seasonal staff (normally recruited for a short period only and not more than 12 months) and employees of the Northern Ireland Government.

2. Part-time employees are counted as half units.

3. The responsibility for the Paymaster General's Office transferred from the Chancellor of the Exchequer's Departments to 'other civil departments' on 1 July 1979 (868 staff) and are now included with other civil departments. The Treasury Solicitor was reclassified to 'other civil departments' on 1 April 1981 (448 staff).

4. Work on efficiency and personnel management was transferred to the newly formed Management and Personnel Office (MPO) with 1,378 staff from the Civil Service Department on its closure. Certain other divisions from the CSD were transferred to the Treasury and responsibility for CISCO, HMSO, COI and the Government Actuary's Department were transferred to the Chancellor of the Exchequer (9,873 staff in all) on 2 December 1981.

5. Includes Department of Employment: Health and Safety Executive: Advisory Conciliation and Arbitration Service: Manpower Services Commission and (from 1976) Employment Service Agency and Training Services Agency.

6. From 1 October 1980, certain staff in PSA (1276 involved) have been excluded from the manpower count.

7. With effect from 1 April 1986, some 765 non-industrials environment transport common services staff employed on work for the Department of Transport and previously counted in the Department of the Environment were instead included in the former's figures.

8. Departments of the Secretary of State for Scotland and the Lord Advocate.

9. Welsh Office

10. There were 396,300 Males and 270,100 Females in the Civil Service on 1 April 1982, the latest date for which information is available.

Source: HM Treasury and Civil Service Department returns.

TABLE 3   Staff of Central Government Departments
Departmental Analysis

Ministerial responsibilities and departments	Staff Numbers* 1983/84 Supply Estimates 1 April 1983	1 April 1984
Agriculture, Fisheries and Food		
Ministry of Agriculture, Fisheries and Food	12,050	11,494
Intervention Board for Agricultural Produce	600	596
Chancellor of the Exchequer		
Treasury (including Civil Service Catering Organization)	3,959	3,879
Customs and Excise	25,439	25,150
Central Office of Information	979	949
Government Actuary	60	65
Inland Revenue	73,110	69,850
Department for National Savings	8,332	8,100
National Investment and Loans Office	55	52
Registry of Friendly Societies	114	129
Royal Mint	1,061	1,050
HM Stationery Office	4,361	4,000
Education and Science		
Department of Education and Science	2,406	2,455
Victoria and Albert Museum	615	—
Science Museum	468	—
Employment		
Department of Employment	30,955	31,596
Health and Safety Commission/Executive	3,593	3,733
Manpower Services Commission (including its Divisions)	22,687	22,179
Advisory, Conciliation and Arbitration Service	665	649
Energy		
Department of Energy	1,105	1,111
Environment		
Department of the Environment	7,813	6,717
Property Services Agency	26,650	25,536
Supplies Division (Property Services Agency)	1,981	1,970
Ordnance Survey	2,964	2,815
Foreign and Commonwealth		
Foreign and Commonwealth Office	9,261	9,426
Overseas Development Administration	1,849	1,794
Home Office		
Home Office	35,072	36,060
Industry		
Department of Industry	7,746	7,317

*Part time staff are counted as half-units

TABLE 3 continued

Staff Numbers*
1983/84 Supply Estimates

Lord Chancellor		
Lord Chancellor's Department (including Public Trustee Office)	10,224	10,125
Land Registry	5,818	6,725
Public Record Office	397	406
Lord Privy Seal		
Management and Personnel Office (including Parliamentary Counsel)	1,242	1,197
Northern Ireland		
Northern Ireland Office	197	200
Paymaster General		
Paymaster General's Office	869	872
Scotland		
Scottish Office (including Royal Scottish Museum)	10,285	9,800
Scottish Courts Administration	893	879
General Register Office, Scotland	290	283
Registers of Scotland	611	761
Scottish Record Office	127	132
Social Services		
Department of Health and Social Security	94,101	90,709
Office of Population, Censuses and Surveys	2,200	2,130
Trade		
Department of Trade	6,753	6,700
Export Credits Guarantee Department	1,814	1,814
Office of Fair Trading	296	320
Transport		
Department of Transport	12,974	11,667
Wales		
Welsh Office	2,217	2,195
Small Departments		
Cabinet Office	546	527
Charity Commission	327	325
Crown Estate Office	109	114
Director of Public Prosecutions	227	238
Law Officers' Department	20	22
Lord Advocate's Department	20	20
Privy Council Office	30	33
Crown Office and Procurator Fiscal Service	927	966
Treasury Solicitor	422	458
Defence		
Ministry of Defence	190,334	181,073
Royal Ordnance Factories	18,547	18,927
Total (Civil and Defence Departments)	648,912	628,316

Source: Figures supplied by HM Treasury.

TABLE 4   Source of Civil Service Savings, April 1980-81 and April 1981-82

Total posts saved	*−15,301*	*−23,240*
Change in workloads (including revised economic assumptions) increases	+8,403.5	+5,895
decreases	−1,746.5	−3,845
Significantly more efficient work methods	−3,966.5	−4,640
General streamlining (including lower standards of service) and other minor changes	−12,188	−8,526
Major new activities	+3,156	+2,114
Dropping or materially curtailing a function	−6,787.5	−7,184
Privatization, including contracting out	−1,571	−6,046
Hiving off to new or existing public body	−601	−1,008

Source: Figures supplied by HM Treasury

TABLE 5   Changes on Staff in Post* (April dates)

	1974-79	*1979-82*
General category and related grades#		
Assistant secretary level	+69	−111
Senior principal level	+151	−141
Principal level	+848	−611
Senior executive officer level	+1,381	−577
Higher executive officer level	+4,662	−2,072
AT/HEO(D) levels	+155	−216
Executive officer level	+10,934	−3,072
Clerical officer level	+18,237	−9,494
Clerical assistant level	+7,611	−7,848
Science category		
Higher grades	+27	−30
Principal scientific officer	+181	−174
Senior scientific officer	+5	−313
Higher scientific officer	−144	−322
Scientific officer	−14	−167
Assistant scientific officer	−604	−500
Professional and technology category		
Higher grade	−46	−366
PPTO	+196	−156
PTOI	+30	−383
PTOII	+285	−722
PTOIII	+195	−1,359
PTOIV	−1,128	−1,697
Secretarial category	+2,079	−1,941
Other non-industrial groups and grades	+8,844	−5,573
Industrial civil servants	−13,723	−28,068
Total Civil Service	+40,226	−65,913

Source: Civil Service Department and Her Majestys Treasury Staff in Post records quoted in
H.C.Deb, Written Answers, col.98, 1 March 1983.

Notes: *Staff in post changes have been calculated on a full-time equivalent basis.
Includes the administration, economist, statistician, librarian and information
officers groups. Inland Revenue grades and DHSS local officer grades are also included.

One cannot discuss reductions in civil service manpower without
making some reference to the decision in November 1981 to abolish the
Civil Service Department; this closure was not, of course, unique as some
31 other departments have suffered a similar fate since 1960. The
immediate background to this decision was the twenty-one week long civil
service strike in 1981, although well before this time the Prime Minister
undoubtedly held the view that the civil service department was '... an
agency which would defend the position and rights of civil servants instead
of reshaping the machinery of government on the lines she preferred'.[3]
The CSD's responsibilities for manpower matters and negotiations on pay
and conditions of service have been transferred to the Treasury.

A question of further interest has to do with the particular grades of
staff affected most (or least) by the cuts. The available figures for 1979-82,
together with those for 1974-79, are set out in Table 5.

On the basis of the above figures, we examined the possibility that the
major (least) reductions in 1979-82 were in the particular grades of staff
that had grown the most (least) in the period 1974-79. Spearman (rank)
correlation coefficients were computed and the hypothesis was strongly
confirmed in the case of the general category and related grades; exactly
the opposite relationship existed, however, in the cases of the science and
professional and technology categories. The latest figures on reduction by
grade level are set out in Table 6.

TABLE 6 Non-industrial Home Civil Service Staff in Post by Grade Level as at 1 January of each year

Grade Level	Jan 79	Jan 83
Clerical officer and below	318,300	289,300
Executive Officer up to Senior Executive Officer	216,700	202,300
Principal and Senior Principal	18,000	17,200
Assistant Secretary	5,200	4,600
Open Structure	814	695

*All grades have been allocated to their equivalent levels in the Administrative group.

Notes

(a) Figures are for full-time equivalents, i.e. part time staff are counted as half units.

(b) Numbers are rounded to the nearest 100, except for the Open Structure.

(c) All non-industrial grades have been allocated to their equivalent levels in the Administrative group.

Source: HM Treasury Staff in Post Records.

The relevant percentage reductions were as follows: 9.1% for clerical officer and below; 6.6% for executive officer; 4.4% for principal and senior principal; 11.5% for assistant secretary and 14.65 for open structure. In short, these figures seem to suggest that the middle level grades have borne a less than proportionate share of the reductions; over the same time period the industrial grades declined by some 21%.

To round off this section, we now consider the position of the national health service, which with some 1 million employees is the largest single component of central government manpower. In the period 1979-82 employment in the national health service actually increased by some 90,000 or 7.5%; a rate of increase considerably in excess of any other in the public sector. Some more detailed figures for recent years were as follows:

+ 36,000 (2.9 per cent)	: 1980-81
+ 23,000 (1.8 per cent)	: 1981-82

The increase in 1981-82 was virtually the only one that occurred in the public sector; admittedly health and social services and the police achieved increases in this year, but only of the order of 0.6 and 0.5% respectively. Some recent figures provided by the DHSS indicate the extent of growth by staff categories in the NHS in England (only) over the period 1979-82.[4] The relevant percentage figures were as follows:

Doctors and Dentists	:	+6.3%
Nurses and midwives	:	+10.8%
Professional and technical	:	+11.7%
Ancillary	:	−0.8%
Ambulance	:	+6.8%
Works	:	+8.8%
Maintenance	:	+4.4%
Administrative and clerical	:	+5.7%

The above indicates that only the ancillary grades have declined even slightly, while the major growth categories have been professional and technical staff, followed by nurses and midwives.

The seemingly guaranteed increase in NHS employment has, however, been called into question by the public expenditure cuts announced in July 1983. These involve a £140 million reduction for the health service, a figure which has led the TUC health services committee to predict the loss of some 20,000 jobs in the future.[5] Moreover, the Government's total public sector manpower target for 1983-84 is 4,120,000, but a recent CBI document[6] has urged a figure of 3,857,000; the latter would involve something like a 82,000 reduction in the national health service. The decision, which was announced in September 1983, to cut 1,800 jobs by March 1984 in three regional health authorities in the South-East of

TABLE 7 Joint Manpower Watch Statistics on Local Authority Employment

Date	England			Scotland			Wales		
	FT	PT	FTE	FT	PT	FTE	FT	PT	FTE
June 1979	1,626,372	886,232	1,975,156	221,729	76,362	256,704	109,699	48,296	128,924
September 1979	1,624,491	838,163	1,963,924	224,203	75,493	258,850	109,908	46,042	128,513
December 1979	1,616,964	886,725	1,963,415	224,252	76,732	259,407	108,388	49,767	128,219
March 1980	1,613,213	883,548	1,959,449	223,622	76,726	258,706	108,596	48,637	127,957
June 1980	1,609,391	865,358	1,951,159	225,702	76,473	260,680	108,231	48,397	127,564
September 1980	1,599,470	816,033	1,931,284	226,224	75,903	261,020	107,135	46,646	126,133
December 1980	1,588,911	861,674	1,927,930	224,004	76,352	259,054	106,086	48,478	125,428
March 1981	1,583,020	856,365	1,921,108	222,541	75,290	257,109	105,625	48,524	125,067
June 1981	1,576,709	844,075	1,913,990	225,281	75,499	259,960	104,866	47,686	124,113
September 1981	1,565,050	788,647	1,891,327	224,438	74,106	258,531	104,222	45,577	122,963
December 1981	1,544,239	850,190	1,889,736	221,819	73,969	255,902	103,225	48,532	122,543
March 1982	1,553,279	856,514	1,891,267	221,097	74,109	255,134	103,196	48,506	122,635
June 1982	1,552,004	840,023	1,887,010	221,572	73,737	255,460	103,965	48,016	123,265
September 1982	1,548,638	788,610	1,873,874	220,496	72,813	254,001	103,519	46,439	122,590
December 1982	1,542,991	859,151	1,880,025	217,727	74,447	251,953	103,069	50,087	122,997

Source: relevant issues of the *Department of Employment Gazette*

England constitutes the first NHS manpower cuts for 30 years.[7] On-going negotiations with other authorities have already raised this figure to over 3.5 thousand jobs, although individual authorities appear to be losing rather less than was originally proposed by the DHSS.

Local Government Manpower

Turning now to the local authorities, I set out in Table 7 figures from the joint manpower watch for the period June 1979 - December 1982.

If I take the two end points of the series then the following picture emerges:

	Full-Time	*Part-Time*	*Full-Time* Equivalent
England	−83,381 (5.1%)	−27,081 (3.1%)	−95,131 (4.8%)
Scotland	−4,002 (1.8%)	−1915 (2.5%)	−4,751 (1.9%)
Wales	−6,630 (6.0%)	+1,791 (3.7%)	−5,927 (4.6%)

The interesting part here has to do with the differences between the regions. The largest percentage fall for full-time staff has been in Wales, where there has been an actual increase for part-time staff; this increase is only due, however, to the big increase in part-time employment between September and December 1982. In England, the reduction for part-time staff is less than that for full-time, although this again is due to the big increase in part-time employment between September and December 1982. The very small reduction for full-time staff in Scotland is particularly noticeable; here the part-time reduction exceeds that for full-time staff. The reference to the large increase in part-time staff between September and December 1982 is a useful caution when considering the above figures. The fact of the matter is that the size of the reduction calculated, particularly for part-time staff, may be highly sensitive to the particular quarter which constitutes the end point of the series.

In commenting on the position in local government *The Economist* claimed:[8]

> Local authority manpower has been cut over the past four years by only 4%. The lower-paid manual workers have been squeezed out, while the pen-pushers have stayed up, automatically moving up salary scales as they dig themselves in. As a result, current spending, largely salary bills, has drifted upwards. The standard of some services has dropped, so productivity per pen-pusher has probably gone down.

This claim is difficult to fully examine on a systematic basis due to the absence of detailed occupational data for local authority employees. However, some perspective on the matter can perhaps be obtained by examining the individual services breakdown in the joint manpower watch figures. Accordingly, for illustrative purposes, Table 8 presents the percentage changes in certain individual services between June 1979 and December 1982. This is done for England only.

Table 8   Joint Manpower Watch Figures, for England, by Individual Services

	Full Time	Part Time	Full Time Equivalent
Education - lecturers and teachers	−5.1%	+3.4%	−4.7%
Construction	−13.5%	−9.9%	−13.4%
Transport	−11.8%	−7.1%	−11.8%
Social services	+1.5%	+5.0%	+2.8%
Recreation, parks and baths	−10.0%	−1.2%	−8.9%
Refuse collection and disposal	−12.7%	+13.6%	−12.7%
Housing	+8.0%	+6.5%	+7.9%
Fire service - regular	+1.3%	−42.9%	+1.3%
Miscellaneous services	−5.6%	−7.7%	−5.7%
Police services - police (all ranks)	+8.2%	★	+8.2%

Source: Relevant issues of the *Department of Employment Gazette*

There are 29 figures in the Table with 17 showing decreases and the remainder increases. The largest increases are for police and housing with a lesser sized one for social services. In contrast the largest sized decreases are in the predominantly manual services of construction, transport, refuse collection (except for part-timers) and miscellaneous services. In short, there would appear to be some evidence here in support of the claim put forward in *The Economist*.

Finally, to round off this section, it is worth highlighting one or two relevant findings from a recent survey of local government collective bargaining. This survey, which was financed by the ssrc Central-Local panel and conducted by Glasgow University, obtained questionnaire responses from some 235 local authorities throughout Britain. Over two-thirds of the authorities reported that they had made some people redundant in both manual and APTC groups; this was the case even in Labour controlled councils, although significantly less so with smaller sized districts. The vast majority of these situations, however, will have been *voluntary* redundancies or at least induced redundancies. Although we had no direct measure of this fact, it seemed highly likely given that almost two-thirds of the authorities had a declared policy on the avoidance of compulsory redundancy. Compulsory redundancies may well increase in the future, however, as moves are made towards the privatization of services. A recent newspaper report, for example, noted that redundancy notices had been sent out to 1,200 school cleaners in Cambridgeshire who are being replaced by private contractors from the next term.[9] Such examples may become increasingly common in the future.

TABLE 9   Manpower in the Nationalized Industries, 1979–1982, by category

Corporation	STAFF NUMBERS 1979	1982	Percentage change 1979-82 (staff numbers)	MANUAL 1979	1982	Percentage change 1979-82 (blue collar)	NON-MANUAL 1979	1982	Percentage change 1979-82 (white collar)
British Aerospace[1]	73,410	—	—	—	—	—	—	—	—
British Airports Authority	7,298	7,120	−2.43	5,866	5,851	−0.25	1,432	1,269	−11.38
British Airways Board	57,741	43,221	−25.14						
British Gas Corporation	102,900	104,748	+1.79	41,500	43,300	+4.33	61,400	61,400	0
British National Oil Corporation[2]	1,423	108	−92.41						
British Railways Board	244,084	212,722	−12.84	176,384	154,164	−12.59	67,700	58,558	−13.50
British Shipbuilders	85,700	66,600	−22.28						
British Steel Corporation	186,000	103,700	−44.24						
British Telecom	233,447	245,882	+5.32	158,199	167,907	+6.13	75,248	77,981	+3.63
British Transport Docks Board[3]	11,533	9,569	−17.02						
British Waterways Board	3,185	3,184	−0.03	2,355	2,281	−3.14	830	903	+8.79
Civil Aviation Authority	7,741	7,433	−0.50						
Electricity Council[4]	159,825	146,655	−8.24	82,881	76,643	−7.52	76,944	70,012	−9.0
London Transport Executive	60,449	58,072	−3.93						
National Bus Company	63,429	51,951	−18.09	48,992	40,579	−17.17	14,437	12,084	−16.29
National Coal Board	297,359	279,161	−6.11	265,850	249,176	−6.27	31,509	29,985	−4.83
National Freight Corporation[5]	34,549	—	—	25,922	—	—	8,627	—	—
National Water Council	63,696	59,645	−6.35	32,975	30,036	−8.91	30,721	29,606	−3.26
North of Scotland Hydro-Electric Board	4,059	4,005	−1.33	2,153	2,144	−0.41	1,906	1,986	−2.36
Post Office[6]	195,194	198,870	+1.88						
Scottish Transport Group	12,800	10,200	—						
South of Scotland Electricity Board	13,739	13,005	−5.34	7,863	7,453	−5.21	5,876	5,552	−5.51
UK Atomic Energy Authority	13,575	14,350	+5.70	4,502	4,694	+4.26	9,073	9,656	+6.42

Notes
1. British Aerospace privatized in January 1981
2. BRITOIL hived off from BNOC in November 1982
3. Associated British Ports (alias British Transport Docks Board) 'privatized' in February 1983
4. Figures for Central Electricity Generating Board are included with the Electricity Council
5. National Freight Corporation privatized in October 1980
6. Post Office figures included sub-postmasters and National Giro employees.

Source: Figures supplied by the Nationalized Industries Chairmens Group

Manpower in the Nationalized Industries

In 1979 total employment in the nationalized industries was 1.81 million, 1.78 million in 1980, 1.71 million in 1981 and 1.63 million in 1982. That is, employment fell by some 180,000 over the period 1979-82. The figures for the individual corporations, broken down into manual and non-manual grades are set out below in Table 9.

An increase in employment over this period is very much an exception in this sector; only British Telecom and the Atomic Energy Authority figure in this regard. Turning to the more common case of decreased employment, one is struck by the considerable size variation apparent. If, for example, one takes two of the most discussed of the nationalized industries, the National Coal Board and the British Steel Corporation, the decline in employment is 6% and 44% respectively. Although a manual and non-manual division of the workforce is not always relevant or available, it is apparent, from the figures that are included in the table, that the decline in nationalized industries employment is not uniquely, or even overwhelmingly, a manual phenomenon. The extensive shedding of manpower in the nationalized industries has certainly not originated in the 1979-82 period, nor will it end there. The new five year plan announced by British Rail, for instance, envisages a further cutback of 17,000 jobs.[10]

Finally, we need to note that employment in the public corporations is largely, but not exclusively, that of the nationalized industries. As Table 1 indicates, employment in public corporations (other than the nationalized industries) was 290,000 in 1976 and 288,000 in 1979, a figure that had fallen to 272,000 by 1982. The reduction in 1981-82 largely stemmed from Cable and Wireless and the National Freight Corporation being reclassified to the private sector in October 1981 and February 1982 respectively.

The Wages Record of the Public Sector

Before considering the movement in public sector wages under the present Government, it is important to recall the basic nature of public-private sector wage movements throughout the 1970s. In essence, the decade of the seventies saw wages move quite strongly in favour of the public sector in the early 1970s, with the opposite tendency being apparent from the mid 1970s.[11] Accordingly, against this background, I set out below in Table 10 the respective wage movements for public and private sector male employees in the period 1979-80 to 1981-82.

For the first two years the public sector does relatively well, whereas in 1981-82 it is the private sector male employee who does better than his public sector counterpart. The table also reveals considerable variation within the public sector itself in any one year. In 1980-81, for example, the increase in average earnings was greatest in local government. This fact largely reflected the timing of the teachers' settlements whereby both the 1980 and 1981 settlements, together with the final stage of the 1979 comparability award, came into payment between the two New Earnings Surveys in April of each year. The final stages of some 1978-79 comparability awards were also reflected in the 1980-81 pay settlements for national health service employees.

TABLE 10   Percentage Increase in Average Gross Weekly Earnings, Male Employees, 1979-80 to 1981-82.

	1979-80		1980-81		1981-82	
	Manual	Non-Manual	Manual	Non-Manual	Manual	Non-Manual
Public sector	23.5	27.0	11.1	17.5	9.7	6.7
Central government	*	*	7.6	7.9	9.5	3.9
Local government	*	*	8.4	21.7	5.5	5.8
Public services (central and local government)	30.4	28.1	8.0	17.1	6.6	5.2
Public corporations	21.0	24.2	12.4	18.2	11.2	10.9
Private sector	18.4	22.8	8.6	13.9	10.3	11.4

Source: Table 1, part A of relevant *New Earnings Survey Reports*.

In Table 11 below the relevant wage information is set out for women employees over the same period of time:

TABLE 11   Percentage Increase in Average Gross Weekly Earnings, Women Employees, 1979-80 to 1981-82

	1979-80		1980-81		1981-82	
	Manual	Non-Manual	Manual	Non-Manual	Manual	Non-Manual
Public sector	29.6	26.1	11.1	18.4	6.6	6.2
Central government	*	*	7.0	9.4	5.6	7.5
Local government	*	*	13.3	27.3	8.3	4.6
Public services (central and local government)	29.0	26.4	10.1	18.5	7.1	5.4
Public corporations	31.2	24.1	12.6	18.6	7.5	11.8
Private sector	20.2	23.6	9.9	15.8	8.3	11.2

Source: Table 1, part A of relevant *New Earnings Survey Reports*.

The picture is very much the same as in the previous table, namely the public sector does relatively well in 1979-80 and 1980-81, whereas the opposite is the case in 1981-82. Again local government non-manuals and public corporation non-manuals do particularly well compared to the public sector average in 1980-81 and 1981-82 respectively.

What happened in the period 1982-83? The New Earnings Survey results for 1983 were not available at the time of writing so that I had to turn to alternative sources of wage information. One such source was the table of settlements and negotiations in the public sector compiled by Incomes Data Services that is set out in Table 12.

TABLE 12   Selected Public Sector Settlements and Negotiations 1982-83

Pay Review Date	Group	Settlement/Negotiations
1982 September	Police	6% increase on basic rate 10.3% agreed. Salaries up 6.6% net of pension contribution increase.
	British Rail	6% deferred from April; withheld for productivity negotiations.
October	UKAEA	4.75% agreed.
November	Fire Service	7.5% agreed.
	Coal mining	7.2% agreed.
	Local authority manual	4.8-5.1% agreed.
	Local authority engineering craftsmen	4.3% agreed.
	Local authority building craftsmen	4.3% rejected.
December	Water service manual	7.3%; 8% (with consolidation) from 27.2.83.
	Water service craft	7.3%; 8% (with consolidation) from 20.2.83.
1983 January	British Airports Authority	4% agreed.
	British steel	Zero national offer disputed, local productivity deals on offer.
	Gas supply manual	4 to 5% offered.
	Municipal buses	5% offered.
	NHS building craftsmen	No offer yet.
February	Electricity Supply engineers	No offer yet.
March	Electricity Supply manual	4.5 to 6.1% agreed.
April	National Health Service	4.5% agreed as second stage of 2-year deals (or equivalent)
	Armed Forces	
	BBC	
	British shipbuilders	Zero offer.
	Civil service non-industrial	
	Teachers	
	Lecturers	
	Teachers, Scotland	3.5% offered.
	British Rail	
	London Transport	
	British Nuclear Fuels staff	

Source: *IDS Report*, 397, March 1983.

This relatively early evidence for the 1982-83 wage round shows quite considerable variation being apparent, ranging from pay pauses to settlements of around 10%. In the extreme case of British Shipbuilders, the zero offer still remains after some 5-6 months discussion between unions and management. At least one union officer I spoke to felt that this offer, or the lack of one, could seriously undermine the existing industry wide bargaining arrangements and intensify the demand for a move to individual company bargaining structures. The bulk of basic rate increases, however, were between 4.5% and 7.5%. A comparison with private sector settlements led to the conclusion that 'throughout 1983 ... most of the public sector has settled lower than the private sector – especially on earnings'.[12] This conclusion is supported by the latest available figures contained in the August 1983 issue of the *National Institute Economic Review*. These figures, which are set out in Table 13, should be placed in the context of the Government's assumptions about cash provisions for central government pay. In October 1982 the Government announced a 'pay factor' of 3.5% to be used in planning for 1983-84, a figure which the *National Institute Economic Review* for November 1982 suggested was too low; a more realistic figure, in their view, was 6.5%. This estimate by the Institute was lowered to 5.5% in February 1983.

TABLE 13   Wage Settlements and Earnings in the 1982-83 Wage Round (Earnings are in parenthesis)

	Settlements in 1982-83 (% increase)
General Government	
Local authority employees	5
Civil service	5
Health	4.5
Education	5
Other workers (mainly police and armed forces)	7.5
Total general government	5.25 (5.75)
Public corporations	6.5 (8)
Private sector manufacturing	6 (8)
Private sector non-manufacturing	6.5 (8)
All sectors	6 (7.5)

Source: *National Institute Economic Review*, August 1983, p.9.

In the 1982-83 wage round (August 1982 – July 1983) settlements in general government averaged 5.25%, while those elsewhere averaged 6-6.5%. The difference was even greater when one considered earnings; 5.75% in general government compared to 8% in the rest of the economy.

The 'pay factors' announced by the Government have fallen over the years; from 14% in 1980-81 to 6% in 1981-82, 4% in 1982-83, 3.5% in 1983-84, and the recently announced 3% for the next year. In practice actual settlements have tended to exceed the 'aggregate provision' by 1.5 to 2% a year since 1980.[13] Some of the constraints and pressures that have led to this divergence are highlighted in a recent case study of the 1981-82 wage round in the local government sector.[14] These constraints and pressures included conflict between central and local government, party political conflict between local authority associations, and interest group conflict within individual associations. The National Institute's predictions for the 1983-84 wage round (August 1983 - July 1984) are as follows:

	%
Local authorities	4
Civil service	4
Health	7.5
Education	4
Others	7
Total general government	5.25 (5.75)
Public corporations	5.5 (6.5)
Private sector manufacturing	5.5 (7.75)
Private sector non-manufacturing	7.75 (8.75)
All sectors	6.25 (7.5)

In short, the expectation is that settlements and earnings in the public sector will again be below those of the private sector, although the Government's announced pay assumptions may again be rather on the low side as regards actual settlements.

Industrial Relations in the Public Sector

A recent review of the country's strike record in 1982 stated that:[15]

> 3 large national rail stoppages and the strike by NHS employees from April to December, together with related sympathy stoppages, accounted for nearly a half of the days lost in 1982. It is estimated that about 3.4 million of the days lost in the year were in the public sector and 1.9 million in the private sector. Between 1975 and 1979, the incidence of days lost through strikes was higher in the private than in the public sector. In the most recent 3 years this position has been reversed.

Under the present Government, the most eye-catching of these strikes have undoubtedly been the four national disputes, whose details are set out in Table 14:

TABLE 14   National Stoppages in the Public Sector, 1980-83

Industry	Duration	Number of workers involved directly	Total working days lost
Steel	13 weeks (1980)	138,000	8,800,000
Civil service	21 weeks (1981)	294,000	867,000
National health service	36 weeks (1982)	400,000	3,441,000
Water supply	5 weeks (1983)	35,000	766,200

Source: relevant issues of the *Department of Employment Gazette*(HMSO)

These four strikes were very much concerned with wage issues and overwhelmingly dominated the strike record in the country as a whole in the relevant years. For example, the steel strike, which accounted for nearly 75% of all working days lost through strikes in Britain in 1980, followed the rejection of a 2% (later 5%) wage offer, and was only called off after a settlement worth some 16% had been awarded by a committee of inquiry. The size of this settlement figure might suggest that the unions had won the steel strike. However, the conclusions of a recent study of this dispute are worth quoting at some length:[16]

> While the strike was in progress, the Employment Act (1980) was being steered through Parliament. Although the legislation was prompted and justified predominantly by the strikes of the winter of 'discontent' (1978-79), the steel strike fuelled public discussions about picketing. The TV coverage of large pickets, seemingly like political demonstrations, gave support to the view that trade unions were too powerful. Furthermore, the notorious Denning judgement ruled that the steel strike was not a trade dispute but a political strike and thus could not be afforded the protection of the law. Although reversed at appeal, a few days later, the point had been made. The definition of a trade dispute became a matter of significance in the first and second Employment Bills (1980 and 1982). The steel strike, then, was a useful background against which the government could gain legitimacy for its legal measures. *In many ways the government, more than either unions or management, were the winners of the strike. (My emphasis)*

As suggested earlier, these four national strikes were only the most dramatic of a number of disputes that have taken place in the public sector under the present Government. Some selected examples of other public sector strikes are set out below in Table 15:

TABLE 15   Selected Examples of Public Sector Strikes

Industry	Date Commenced	Date Finished	Workers Involved	Working days lost
Mining	16.2.81	20.2.81	40,460	124,800
Public administration (Manchester)	17.3.82	17.3.82	15,000	15,000
Public administration (Liverpool)	14.6.82	14.6.82	10,000	10,000
Public administration (London SW)	19.4.82	2.6.82	6,000	17,200
Public administration (Birmingham)	15.9.82	14.1.83	2,000	48,400
Transport and communication	20.10.82	20.10.82	139,000	139,000
Mining (Wales)	21.2.83	11.3.83	18,920	186,500

Source: relevant issues of the *Department of Employment Gazette*, HMSO

These particular strikes were chosen because their major explicit cause was to do with manpower cuts. That is, the two mining disputes were protests against proposed pit closures, the Manchester strike was directed at service cuts and possible redundancies, the Birmingham dispute was for additional staff to cope with increased work levels, while the others in the table were protests against possible privatization. Privatization could be seen as a potent cause of future public sector strike activity. However, the results of one recent opinion poll could be seen to cast some doubt on this possibility. This poll was conducted among British Telecom staff and the results indicated that 56% were opposed to industrial action against privatization, with fully 79% believing that industrial action against privatization would not cause the Government to change its mind but that it would damage BT's commercial prospects and put jobs at risk.[17] The Post Office Engineering Union have, however, questioned the rigour of the poll and hence its accuracy.

Finally, it is worth emphasizing that industrial conflict is a broader notion than simply strike activity. This is particularly so in central and local government where non-strike forms of industrial action, such as work to rules and go-slows, are relatively popular with white collar workers. Certainly the recent SSRC – Department of Employment Workplace Industrial Relations Survey found that non-strike forms of industrial action considerably exceeded strike activity in central and local government in the 12 months to mid-1980.[18]

Industrial relations is, of course, much more than simply strikes and disputes so that we need to look at other important developments, or possible developments, in the public sector under the present Government. In saying this, one must acknowledge that some of these developments or proposals have directly followed in the wake of disputes such as the civil service and national health service ones. One potentially important development is suggested by the contents of a recent Government report which examined 17 arbitration arrangements in the public sector.[19] In fully 11 of the agreements examined, the report recommended that the employers concerned withdraw and renegotiate the relevant arrangements so as to remove the right of *unilateral* reference to arbitration. This recommendation followed on three basic criticisms of unilateral arbitration: (1) it encourages irresponsibility among the parties who have no responsibility for the final agreement and thus tend to hold their original positions in negotiations; (2) it tends to favour the union side; and (3) it is potentially inflationary, with a tendency to undermine incomes policy and cash limits. If such a change occurs then it will bring the nature of public and private sector arbitration arrangements much closer together. Unilateral access to arbitration has been one of the important topics being discussed by the civil service unions and Treasury following the Government's basic acceptance of the Report of the Megaw Committee of Inquiry.

The Megaw Committee of Inquiry, which was set up after the 1981 civil service strike, contained four basic recommendations.[20] First, that market and efficiency considerations should play a more central role in the wage determination process. Secondly, that a Pay Information Board should be established to collect information on pay movements outside the civil service. Third, that the civil service unions and the Treasury would have to conclude a settlement each year within the 'inter-quartile' range of pay movements, i.e. below the top quarter of increases and above the bottom quarter. And finally, every four years, the board would produce a fuller evaluation of whether civil service pay had moved seriously out of line. The initial union reactions to the proposals were somewhat divided. Some unions, like the Institution of Professional Civil Servants, cautiously welcomed them, arguing that they could assist problems associated with internal differentials, whereas the larger clerical unions, such as CPSA, were considerably more critical of them feeling that they could involve a permanent reduction in the relative pay of civil servants. Throughout the summer of 1983 the unions held discussions with the Treasury on matters such as whether they would be able to evaluate and negotiate over the data produced by the Pay Information Board.[21] Whatever the final outcome of such discussions, it is clear that the comparability principle in civil service pay determination is far from dead, as some people seemed to feel when the Government abolished the Clegg Comparability Commission and suspended the operation of the Civil Service Pay Research Unit.

In July 1983 the Prime Minister announced that an independent pay review body would be established for nursing staff, and other professional medical workers, with effect from April 1984. The most controversial aspect of this body is that the Government will reserve the right to exclude from the scope of the recommendations any groups that resort to industrial action.[22] This 'no strike pledge' predictably produced hostile responses from all the unions concerned, except the Royal College of Nursing. This may well be the first in a series of moves in this direction as 'there is an increasingly strong lobby in government circles arguing that industrial action should be limited or abolished in return for guarantees on long-term pay arrangements, possibly linked to prices or average earnings'.[23] Certainly a recent newspaper report indicated that the Employment Secretary would like to discuss with the TUC at some future stage the question of industrial action in essential services.[24]

Finally, one needs to consider the impact of the Government's policies towards the public sector on: (i) the attitudes and behaviour of unions, as organizational entities, and (ii) the attitudes and behaviour of public sector employees, as individuals. On the matter of the impact on union behaviour, there are signs of increased co-operation and coordination among the public sector unions. The local authority manual unions in 1981, for instance, committed themselves to following the TUC Public Services Committee's advocacy of a *common core element* in all claims (a pay increase to protect living standards and a reduction in working hours); a more extensive exchange of information was apparent during the 1981-82 wage round, and there has even been discussion of the potential advantages of moving to a common wage settlement date.[25] Such coordination moves seem likely to continue, or at least be sought by a number of public sector unions. The Post Office Engineering Union, for example, proposed the following motion at the 1983 TUC meeting:[26]

> ... Congress ... instructs the General Council to introduce a co-ordinated campaign ... The campaign would (i) encompass the work of both the Public Services Committee and the Nationalized Industries Committee; (ii) be established with the intention of remaining in existence at least until the next General Election; (iii) act as a focal point for Trade Union opposition to attacks on the public services by providing help, guidance, information and expert analysis to affiliates; (iv) adopt an overall strategy based on the assumption that public opinion has to be re-educated and re-assured as to the benefits of public services rather than private profit; (v) use as many means as possible to influence public opinion drawing on the experience of the campaigning already done by the TUC and individual affiliates.

The strategy outlined here provides a useful indication of the thinking of at least one public sector union. The Government's attitudes and policies also appear to have substantially accelerated, as opposed to caused, fundamental changes in the character of certain public sector unions. This has been perhaps most apparent in the civil service where the General Secretary of the CPSA stated, in a message to the TUC, that 'During that 21 weeks (of the 1981) strike the civil service trade unions came of age ... let no one ever again call civil servants the soft underbelly of the trade union movement.'[27] In short, such bodies are becoming less staff association like, and more trade union like (as the term is traditionally understood) in terms of their attitudes and behaviour.

There have been numerous claims that job satisfaction and employee morale in the public sector have fallen substantially from the early 1970s; a state of affairs that has been seen to have considerably worsened under the present Government. The evidence in support of such claims has typically been highly impressionistic, almost anecdotal in nature. However, a systematic analysis of the job satisfaction questions contained in the 1974 and 1978 General Household Surveys revealed that the number of male employees in central and local government who reported themselves as dissatisfied rose from 5.4% in 1974 to 15.7% in 1978, while for women the rise was from 3.2% to 11%.[28] These figures for central and local government can be put into context by noting that the rise for the rest of the sample was from 6.7 to 12.6% in the case of men, and from 4 to 9% in the case of women. In short, there was a general rise in dissatisfaction over this period of time, but it was sharper in the case of public sector employees. The figures in the 1978 survey are intriguing, not to say disquieting, when used as a basis for speculating about the level of job satisfaction in the public sector at the present time.

Conclusions

A number of the major findings reported in this chapter can be summarized as follows:

(1) The reduction in public sector manpower in the three years to mid-1982 was considerably less than that in the private sector; a 5.5% fall compared to a 10.1% reduction.

(2) Civil service manpower was reduced by some 11.4% from April 1979 to April 1983; a further 3% is needed (and expected) to attain the Government's April 1984 target of a civil service totalling 630,000 persons.

(3) Employment in the national health service actually increased by some 7.5% in the three year period 1979 to mid 1982, but the public expenditure cuts announced in July 1983 make such future growth highly unlikely; indeed the unions are already talking of a 20,000 job loss, and cuts of more than 3.5 thousand have already been agreed for March 1984.

(4) Local authority employment (full time equivalents) fell by 4.8% in England and 4.6% in Wales in the period June 1979 - December 1982; in Scotland the equivalent period reduction was only 1.9%.

(5) The size of the reductions in local authority manpower varied considerably by individual service; in England, the 8% increase for police contrasted strongly with the 13% reduction for construction.

(6) Total employment in the nationalized industries fell by some 10% in the period 1979-82, but considerable variation was apparent between the individual corporations; for example, the 6% decline in the National Coal Board contrasted strongly with the 44% reduction for the British Steel Corporation.

(7) In wage terms, public sector employees, both men and women, did relatively well in the years 1979-80, and 1980-81, as the Clegg comparability awards worked their way through the system. They did less well, however, than their private sector counterparts in 1981-82 and 1982-83.

(8) The public sector settlements in 1982-83 were somewhat in excess of the Government's announced cash limits; the 3.5% 'pay factor' compared with an average settlement figure of 5.25% in general government.

(9) The forecast in the *National Institute Economic Review* for the 1983-84 wage round is that settlements and earnings in the public sector will again be below those of the private sector.

(10) In contrast to 1975-79, the incidence of days lost through strike activity in 1979-82 has been higher in the public than the private sector.

(11) The national pay disputes in steel, the civil service and the national health service very much dominated the strike figures for the country

as a whole in the years concerned, but a number of lesser disputes have also occurred over the issue of manpower reductions.

(12) The 'no strike' pledge associated with the recently announced pay review board for nursing staff could constitute the start of an attempt to restrict the right to strike in certain parts of the public sector.

(13) The Government's policies towards the public sector have produced more centralized, co-ordinated activity among the public sector unions, although, to date, this co-ordination is very largely confined to information sharing.

(14) There is evidence of a considerable reduction in job satisfaction in the public sector prior to the present Government assuming office. And the present Government's policies towards the public sector are hardly likely to have halted this loss of satisfaction.

Postscript

Since the writing of the chapter in late 1983, there have been a number of important occurences and developments in the public sector with regard to employment, wages and industrial relations. Many of these will be familiar to the reader as they received extensive media coverage. The concern of this postscript, however, is with a number of lesser publicized developments, in particular the appearance of certain pieces of information and data not available at the time of writing in late 1983. The most comprehensive set of public sector employment figures are reported in *Economic Trends*. Table 16 below was published in the March 1984 issue and updates (to mid-1983) Table 1 in the text.

The conclusions of the article in the March 1984 issue are worth quoting at some length:

> On the basis of both head-count and full-time equivalent public sector manpower reached its peak in 1979. Since then it has fallen by 7.1% on a head-count basis and 7.6% in full time equivalents. Some of the reduction on either basis stems from privatization of nationalized industries (British Aerospace, Cable and Wireless and the National Freight Corporation); if these are excluded, the reductions are 5.7% head-count, 6.1% full time equivalent. General government employment fell by 2.4% (head-count) and 2.3% (full time equivalent). Despite the overall similarity the two measures show differences at the subsector level. The full time equivalent employment in the national health service rose by 6.5% over the period compared with 5.8% in numbers, signifying partly an increase in the contracted hours of part time staff but partly reflecting the reduction in 1979 of the standard working week of nurses from 40 to 37 hours. In contrast, other central government civilian staff fell by about 10%, slightly more in full time equivalents. Local authority employment fell by a little under 4% on both bases.

The pay findings of the New Earnings Survey for 1983 have been published since October 1983 and the relevant figures are set out below in Table 17.

TABLE 16   UK Public Sector Employment 1977-1983 by Major Categories

Thousands

| | General government | | | | | | | | | | | Public corporations | | | |
| | Central government | | | | Local authorities | | | | | | | | | | |
Mid-year	HM Forces	National health service	Other central government	Total central government	Education services	Health and social services	Construction	Police (incl. civilians)	Other local authorities	Total local authorities	Total general government	Nationalized industries (incl. Post Office)	Other public corporations	Total public corporations	Total public sector
Headcount															
1977	327	1,114	886	2,327	1,506	322	155	172	766	2,921	5,248	1,866	223	2,089	7,337
1978	318	1,136	879	2,333	1,512	334	155	170	761	2,932	5,265	1,844	217	2,061	7,326
1979	314	1,170	871	2,355	1,539	344	156	176	782	2,997	5,352	1,849	216	2,065	7,417
1980	323	1,192	847[3]	2,362[3]	1,501	346	152	181	776	2,956	5,318	1,816	222[3]	2,038[3]	7,356
1981	334	1,226	828	2,388	1,454	350	143	186	766	2,899	5,287	1,657[4]	210	1,867[4]	7,154
1982	324	1,246	801	2,371	1,434	352	132	186	761	2,865	5,236	1,554[5]	202[5]	1,756[5]	6,992
1983[2]	322	1,246	785	2,353	1,434	360	130	187	768	2,879	5,232	1,465	198	1,663[6]	6,895
Full time equivalent															
1977	327	947	866	2,140	1,099	222	152	168	683	2,324	4,464	1,835	224	2,059	6,523
1978	318	961	859	2,138	1,105	228	152	165	675	2,325	4,463	1,843	218	2,061	6,524
1979	314	975	856	2,145	1,110	235	150	172	701	2,368	4,513	1,818	217	2,035	6,548
1980	323	999	832	2,154	1,087	235	146	176	699	2,343	4,497	1,785	223	2,008	6,505
1981	334	1,036	818	2,188	1,058	240	136	180	692	2,306	4,494	1,656	206	1,862	6,356
1982	324	1,045	781	2,150	1,041	241	131	180	681	2,274	4,424	1,538	198	1,736	6,160
1983[2]	322	1,038	769	2,129	1,034	246	130	182	686	2,278	4,407	1,444	197	1,641	6,048

1 Appendix 2 gives details of the definitions and coverage of the sectors and sources of the statistics and major changes in them between 1977 and 1983.

2 Preliminary estimates based upon data covering nearly 95 per cent of the general government sector; these should not be regarded as accurate to the last digit shown.

3 The establishment of HMSO from 1 April 1980 as a trading body implies the transfer of about 6,000 to public corporations.

4 British Aerospace was reclassified to the private sector in February 1981 reducing public corporations' employment by about 73,000.

5 Cable and Wireless was reclassified to the private sector in October 1981 and National Freight Corporation in February 1982, together reducing public corporations by about 28,000.

6 Britoil was reclassified to the private sector in October 1982 and Associated British Ports in February 1983, reducing public corporations by about 14,000.

Source: E. A. Doggett, Employment in the public and private sectors 1977-1983, *Economic Trends*, March 1984, p. 99.

TABLE 17 Percentage Increase in Average Gross Weekly Earnings, 1982-1983

	Male Manual	Male Non-Manual	Female Manual	Female Non-Manual
Pubic sector	6.8	7.8	9.3	9.6
Public services	7.3	7.7	9.6	9.5
Central government	7.3	6.2	9.8	10.8
Local government	7.1	8.5	9.6	8.3
Public corporations	6.7	8.3	9.5	10.3
Private sector	7.4	9.5	9.9	9.4

The figures indicate that the average rate of increase in the private sector exceeded that for the public sector for both categories of male employees and for female manuals; the differences, however, were small, with the possible exception of male non-manuals. In the case of female non-manuals the increase in the public sector was slightly in excess of that for the private sector. These figures generally confirm the expectations in the text, although the public sector does not appear to have done as badly compared to the private sector as in 1981-1982, nor as badly as the Government pay factor might have led one to expect.

Incomes Data Services recently published an interesting comparison of actual public sector wage settlements with the size of the Government's 'pay factor' for such settlements. The results are set out in Table 18.

The contents of Table 18 clearly indicate that many of the actual settlements exceeded the target figure(s). The Government's approach does appear, however, to have had some success in bringing down settlement levels in consecutive years.

Mention was made in the text of a survey of local government collective bargaining conducted at the University of Glasgow. The survey, which produced responses from some 45% of all local authorities, specifically enquired about the incidence of various forms of industrial action (strike and non-strike) that had occurred over *purely local issues* in the period January 1980 – March 1982. An analysis of the responses produced the following results: (1) 21% of authorities reported a local strike involving white collar workers; (2) 9% and 8% of authorities reported an overtime ban by manual and white collar workers respectively; and (3) 15% and 21% of authorities reported a work to rule by manuals and white collar workers respectively. The level of local industrial action tended to be positively associated with the extent of trade union membership and the numerical strength of the Labour Party on the council, although, contrary to expectations, it did not appear to be associated with the number of bonus schemes in operation.

TABLE 18 Percentage Increases On Basic Rates During Each Government 'Pay Provision' Period

	Sept 79-Aug 80 %	Sept 80-Aug 81 %	Sept 81-Aug 82 %	Sept 82-Aug 83 %	Sept 83-Aug 84 %	Comments
PAY PROVISIONS	14	6	4	3.5	3	
PUBLIC SERVICES						
Central government						
Civil service (Non-Industrials)	15.3-27.8	7.5-8.4	4.7-6.3	3.5-4.0*		*plus £70 pa
NHS nurses & midwives	13	6	12.3*	—		*2 yrs: 1982-84
NHS ancillary workers	12.3-12.9	8.4-6.1*	6.4-4.7	4.8-3.6		*15½ months
Armed forces	14.5-20	8-15	4-8.9	3.9-9.9		Review Body
Local government						
Local authority manuals	12.4-13.1	6.7-8.4	6.3-7.8	4.8-5.1	4.1-5.1 (offer)	
Local authority staff	15*	7.3	5.7	4.6-5		*staged
Teachers (E & W)	13	7.5	6	5	3 (offer)	
Police	13.5	21.3	13.2	10.3	8.4	
Fire service	20	18.8*	10.1	7.5	7.8	*staged
PUBLIC CORPORATIONS						
NCB	20*	9.8	8.6	7.2	5.2 (offer)	*staged
Electricity supply manuals	17	11	6.2-7.5	4.5-6.1		
Gas supply	18.8-21.3	9.9-10.7	7.7-8.0	5-6	4.1-4.9 (offer)	
Water industry manuals	13	10.2	9.1	13.5-14.1*		*16 months
British Rail (manual, operating)	20	11*	6**	4.5		*staged **paid late
Post Office operational grades	18	9.5*	7	6*		*staged

NB. Delayed awards from Clegg which were increases relating to 1978-79 are excluded.

Source: *IDS Report*, 421, March 1984.

References

1. W.A. Eltis, Do government manpower cuts correct deficits when the economy is in deep recession?, *Political Quarterly*, 53, 1982, 12-13.
2. Michael Heseltine, Ministers and management in Whitehall, *Management Services in Government*, 35, (2), May 1980, 65-67.
3. Michael Lee, Epitaph for the CSD, *Public Administration*, Spring 1982.
4. *The Times*, 16 September 1983.
5. *The Times*, 12 July 1983.
6. *The Times*, 21 July 1983.

7. *The Guardian*, 23 September 1983.
8. *The Economist*, 23 April 1983, 30.
9. *The Times*, 8 July 1983.
10. *The Times*, 19 August 1983.
11. See, for example, P.B. Beaumont and J.W. Leopold, Public sector industrial relations in Britain: an overview, *Public Administration Bulletin*, (48), December 1982, 12-13. Also Chris Trinder, Pay of employees in the public and private sector, *National Institute Economic Review*, (97), August 1981, 48-56.
12. *IDS Report*, (402), June 1983, 21.
13. *The Times*, 16 September 1983.
14. Ian Kessler and David Winchester, Pay negotiations in local government - the 1981/82 wage round, *Local Government Studies*, 8, (6), November/December 1982.
15. *Department of Employment Gazette*, July 1983, 304.
16. Jean Hartley, John Kelly, and Nigel Nicholson, *Steel Strike*, Batsford, 1983, 166-67.
17. Special edition of *Telecom Today*, August 1983, 4.
18. W.W. Daniel and Neil Millward, *Workplace industrial relations in Britain*, Heinemann, 1983, 228-30.
19. See J.W. Leopold and P.B. Beaumont, Arbitration arrangements in the public sector in Britain, *The Arbitration Journal*, 38, (2), June 1983, 56.
20. This summary is based on David Thomas, Paying for high stakes on public sector pay, *New Society*, 7 July 1983, 14.
21. See *Red Tape*, August 1983, 3.
22. *The Times*, 28 July 1983.
23. *IDS Report*, 400, May 1983, 28.
24. *The Financial Times*, 22 August 1983.
25. See, for example, *Annual Report of the Trades Union Congress*, 1981, 302-33, and for 1982, 279-82.
26. *POEU Journal*, August 1983, 280.
27. Quoted in Chris Painter, Civil service staff militancy: joining the mainstream of trade unionism, *Public Administration Bulletin*, (40), December 1982, 36.
28. P.B. Beaumont and M. Partridge, *Job satisfaction in public administration*, RIPA, 1983.

5

Conservative Industrial Policy 1979-83

Stephen Wilks

Industrial policy under Mrs Thatcher's first government failed to come to grips with the incongruity of attempting to undertake a 'supply side revolution' in the face of the worst recession for forty years. Largely as a result, industrial policy, which in Britain has never been acclaimed as successful, was by 1983 beset by an increasing number of contradictory pressures and continued to offer an incoherent and unsatisfactory response to industrial decline. After a 'scene setting' examination of the industrial economy this chapter outlines the 'philosophy' of Conservative industrial policy and goes on to review the major policy developments. Problems of implementation are then analysed. The conclusion suggests that the philosophy had been retained into 1983 although it had undergone some significant amendments. The discussion excludes the issue of privatization which is dealt with in the chapter by Heald and Steel and, for the sake of manageability, it does not systematically analyse relations with the nationalized industries.

Developments in the Industrial Economy

The dominant feature of the industrial economy from 1979 to 1983 was the acceleration of its structural transformation from a manufacturing to a service orientation, and the associated role of the oil sector in camouflaging that transformation. 'De-industrialization' has been criticized as an imprecise term but it amply describes recent developments. The index of industrial production fell sharply, virtually from the moment the Conservatives entered office in May 1979, and continued a meteoric slide into the second quarter in May 1979, at which point it levelled off giving an overall fall over the life of the Government of 10.2%, as shown in Table 1. This decline in industrial production – its causes, structural composition and the policy response to it – forms the backdrop to any evaluation of industrial policy. As Table 1 shows, the decline was concentrated in manufacturing. Disaggregated figures show that the mechanical engineering, metal manufacture and textile sectors

TABLE 1   Index of Industrial Production, 1979-83

(1975=100)	all industries	excluding oil	manufacturing
2nd quarter 1979	116.6	107.7	107.6
May 1983	104.7	93.1	90.2
decline, 1979-83	10.2%	13.6%	16.2%

Source: *Economic Trends*

declined to a markedly greater extent. It must be regarded as doubtful that industry, while 'leaner', had become significantly 'fitter'. There were undeniably productivity gains but they have been described as 'degenerate productivity gains' in that they resulted from scrapping marginal plant rather than from any broadly based productivity advance. In this process productive capacity has therefore contracted, thus reducing the basic wealth creating physical facilities. Net new investment, the seedcorn of the future, actually turned negative after 1980; 'over the three years to 1982 it has been estimated by the (OECD) Secretariat that net capital stock (in plant and machinery) may have decreased by up to 7 per cent.'[1]

Accompanying the fall in production was a drop in world market share for British industries, which included disturbing increases in import penetration across most manufacturing sectors.[2] There was also a considerable reduction in employment and, throughout 1981 and 1982, the marked increases in labour productivity meant that 'de-manning' continued at a rapid rate even as the absolute level of production stabilized. The consequences for the labour market were clear. Virtually the entire reduction in employment opportunities was concentrated in the industrial, as opposed to the service, sector, as Table 2 illustrates.

TABLE 2   UK Employment, 1979 and 1983

	UK working population ('000)	total	index of production industries	manufacturing industries	service industries
March 1979	26,547	23,356	9,005	7,084	13,124
percentage of working pop.			33.9	26.7	49.4
March 1983	26,264	20,069	7,038	5,412	12,808
percentage of working pop.			26.8	20.6	48.8
percentage fall in numbers, 1979-83			21.8	23.6	2.4

Source: *Department of Employment Gazette*, July 1983, Table 1.2 seasonally adjusted figures, not adjusted for under-recording.

The proportion of the British workforce employed in 'industry' has therefore fallen from one third to just over one quarter and the transition of the economy towards a 'service economy', already widely remarked in 1979, has rapidly gathered pace. For unemployment the consequences have been intractable and appalling. Table 3 shows the comparative unemployment picture and Table 4 gives some idea of the regional impact of the increase. It is familiar, but worth re-emphasizing, that unemployment in the UK increased at internationally exceptional

TABLE 3   Comparative Unemployment, 1979-83

	UK Rate (April) Department of Employment	UK	US	France	W.Germany	Italy	EEC average
					OECD standardized rates		
1979 No. per cent	1,254,000 5.1	(aver) 5.6	5.7	5.9	3.2	7.5	5.5
1981 No. per cent	2,301,000 9.5	(aver) 10.7	7.5	7.3	4.4	8.3	7.7
1983 No. per cent	3,021,000 12.7	(first quarter) 13.5	10.1	8.0	7.1	9.6	9.9

Sources: *Department of Employment Gazette*, UK unemployed excluding school leavers, seasonally adjusted. OECD *Economic Outlook*, July 1983, 33, 169.

TABLE 4   Regional Unemployment Rates, 1979 and 1983

	1979 2nd qtr %	1983 2nd qtr %	increase 1979 to '83 %
Total UK	5.1	12.5	145
three smallest percentage increases:			
Scotland	7.0	14.2	103
N. Ireland	9.9	20.2	104
S. West	5.3	10.9	106
three largest percentage increases:			
W. Midlands	4.9	15.3	212
S. East	3.4	9.2	171
E. Midlands	4.2	11.4	171

Source: *Economic Trends*, July 1983.

rates so that by the first quarter of 1983 only Spain (17.3%) and Belgium (14.1%) among the 15 major OECD countries had rates in excess of those in the UK. Within the UK it can be seen from Table 4 that there has been some inter-regional sharing of the misery and therefore that the rationale for concentrating regional aid in the traditional depressed regions was, on this simple statistical basis, looking increasingly threadbare.

Although the workforce has suffered heavily the fiscal and trade consequences of this industrial decline were masked by the growth in oil production, taxation and export. Petroleum Revenue Duty now accounts for 5% of total public revenue, more than the yield of Corporation tax, while oil now makes a net positive contribution of £3.8 billion to the visible trade balance which in 1982 showed an overall surplus of £2.2 billions.[3] The security provided by oil production in a period of rapidly rising oil prices had a buoyant effect on the exchange rate and therefore helped to reduce the competitiveness of British industry. Setting aside non-price factors (such as design and delivery), competitiveness is dictated by the three factors of the relative exchange rate, the rise in domestic costs (particularly labour costs), and the rate of growth of productivity. Between the autumn of 1979 and the autumn of 1981 British competitiveness declined at an extraordinary pace, due largely to the appreciation in the exchange rate. There can be little doubt that the pressures on manufacturing industry, already intense as a result of the recessionary phase of the cycle, were gravely accentuated by the exchange rate. The fall in production and in employment must be seen in this light. Thus du Cann's draft report for the Treasury and Civil Service Committee, which was published shortly before the 1983 election, pointed out that the real effective exchange rate rose 45% from early 1979 to the peak in January 1981. It quoted the former President of the Bundesbank to the effect that 'this is by far the most excessive overvaluation which any major currency has experienced in recent monetary history',[4] and went on to argue that therefore about half the rise in unemployment could be attributed to the international recession. By implication the balance was attributable to deliberate policy choices, particularly the choice to allow the exchange rate to appreciate. The relationship between macro-economic policy (as seen, for instance, in exchange rate policy), and industrial policy has become increasingly imbalanced in favour of macro-economic considerations; the institutional manifestation of this, in the form of Treasury dominance, is returned to below.

The Conservative industrial policy agenda was therefore confronted by some urgent general industrial issues arising from the decline in the 'real' economy. The general issues included:

(1)   How to respond to the structural shift to a service economy, accompanied by net negative investment in manufacturing. Whether, for instance, to defend manufacturing, to hasten its decline and/or to reorientate policy towards the service sector.

(2)   How to respond to the unemployment crisis. Whether the stress on demanning should be continued; whether increases in productivity would result in increased output; whether and how to encourage

labour intensive development or whether the issue should be handled by labour market rather than industrial policy measures.

(3) What attitude to take to the 'Dutch disease' of oil production and exports producing an unrealistically uncompetitive exchange rate. How to respond to the projected decline of oil earnings in the early 1990s.

(4) How to restructure regional policy to take account of relative unemployment rates; of the need to boost productivity; and of the impracticality of manufacturing offering any short or medium-term solution to the unemployment problem.

(5) What posture to adopt as an intermediary between the needs or demands of industry over various controversial aspects of macro-economic policy (such as exchange rates, national insurance surcharge, interest rates and cuts in capital spending); and the macro-economic policy 'community' in the Treasury and the Bank.

The Conservative 'Manifesto View' of Industrial Policy

The 1979 Conservative Manifesto gave high salience to the problem of economic and industrial decline. 'Our country's relative decline is not inevitable' it declared; 'we in the Conservative Party think we can reverse it'. The two major economic tasks, it said, were first, to control inflation and the unions and second, to restore incentives. For industrial policy as such there were hints and sentiments but no systematic presentation of the role to be played by an industry department. Among the more important points were the assertion that 'we shall reduce government intervention in industry' and 'we shall ensure that selective assistance is not wasted'. The section on industry asserted the importance of profit, accepted that it could be in the national interest to 'help a firm in difficulties' (albeit temporarily) and, in relation to regional policy, 'we do not propose sudden, sharp changes in the measures now in force'. In a separate section on small businesses their importance in creating new jobs was strongly emphasized.

A literal reading of the Manifesto might have led to the conclusion that 'business as usual' would be the motto of the Thatcher industry department; a little less business, but no necessary abrupt truncation of activities. With the exception of the privatization initiatives the theme of business as usual or 'evolutionary change' is quite suitable as a description of the pattern of legislation, spending, ministerial initiatives and administrative processes undertaken within the Industry and Regional departments between 1979 and 1983. Unfortunately, although evolutionary change is a fair description of developments at the administrative level, it gives a misleading impression of first, the course of the political debate and its impact on the all-important 'expectations' about industrial policy; second, of the redefinition of industrial policy to include novel issues and to regard it increasingly as a multi-departmental policy; and third, it underemphasizes the shortcomings of policy as operated in 1979 which, in the absence of reform, was simply less adequate by the spring of 1983.

The Major Policy Developments

As Grant points out, study of industrial policy is complicated by the fact that the Department of Industry (DOI) does not have responsibility for all branches of industry.[5] Industrial policy has always been fragmented institutionally and important ingredients are the responsibility of the Treasury, the regional departments, the Departments of Trade, Employment, Energy and so on. The main focus of this section, however, is on the DOI, which was merged into a new Department of Trade and Industry (DTI) in 1983. The question of inter-departmental coordination is taken up in the section on implementation. The discussion is organized into three broad time periods. The first 18 months when 'doctrinal' policies were dominant; the first nine months of 1981 when crisis after crisis made Sir Keith Joseph an increasingly less dominant industry minister; and third, the period from September 1981 onwards when Patrick Jenkin took over the industry portfolio.

Sir Keith and Conservative 'Doctrinal' Policy, May 1979 to December 1980

The first 18 months or so after the May 1979 election were marked by a strict ideological interpretation of industrial policy on the part of ministers which produced indecisiveness and a reluctance to adapt policy in the face of recession and *ad hoc* crises. The initial indications were, however, of moderation. All the major areas of industrial policy activity were contracted but none were entirely discontinued. Thus the National Enterprise Board was maintained, with reduced powers and a brief to help 'certain high technology companies'.[6] This role was facilitated by the de facto removal of the NEB's two big 'lame ducks', Rolls Royce and BL, after an acrimonious dispute and the resignation of the entire Board (chaired by Sir Leslie Murphy) in November 1979. Later the NEB was merged with the National Research and Development Corporation to form a new British Technology Group, a decision confirmed by Sir Keith in September 1981. Similarly, the tripartite work of the National Economic Development Council was largely maintained, only 7 of the 61 EDC's (Economic Development Councils) and SWP's (Sector Working Parties) were wound up in January 1980, although talk of an 'industrial strategy' ceased. Selective financial assistance (section 8 of the 1972 Industry Act) was maintained with more specific criteria, which provided aid for 'internationally mobile' projects or for investment which would lead to 'very substantial improvements in performance', would be innovative or would increase output.[7] Perhaps more significant than these more selective, but still elastic, criteria was the provision that 'assistance will be given only for projects that would not go ahead as proposed without it, and will be negotiated as the minimum necessary to achieve this'.[8] This rigorous 'additionality' criterion accentuated the discretionary element of bargaining in relations between the Department and corporate applicants. It provided officials with an explicit and paradoxical requirement to negotiate, and made companies more uncertain of their likely success. Finally, regional aid was limited through reduction in the geographical coverage and in some rates of regional development grant. A saving of £233 million was anticipated by 1982-83, rather more than a third of the regional aid budget, but the changes were phased over three years and the basic structure of aid was maintained.

Further indications of an altered but still active and pragmatic role for the DOI came through Sir Keith Joseph's evident interest in public purchasing as a means of promoting industrial efficiency.[9] As Sir Peter Carey, DOI's Permanent Secretary, later remarked, public purchasing 'seems to be a legitimate way in which a non-interventionist government can, in fact, help industry'.[10] The policy was slow in getting underway. One obvious problem was that dilution of a strict cost criterion for evaluating suppliers involved civil servants in judgements about the prospects for products and firms which looked uncomfortably like 'picking winners'. More practical problems emerged in the overwhelming preference of the Treasury, of the Public Accounts Committee, and also of the spending departments, for 'value for money', defined as minimizing immediate cash outflow. DOI civil servants were, however, enthusiastic about the potential for buying British and for amending purchasing procedures to facilitate longer term competitive product development.[11] But the guidelines eventually drawn up by the Treasury in March 1981 indicated a very modest initiative which 'went little further than to lay down what was already regarded as best practice' and DOI control was reduced to a bare minimum. As the guidelines mildly advised, 'in any cases of doubt about individual implications of individual contracts, Departments *might wish to consult* sponsor divisions of the Department of Industry'.[12] Little has subsequently been heard of this initiative.

Initially, therefore, the indications were that the Conservatives intended to pursue their 'supply side revolution' through a judicious gradualism, thus substantiating John Elliott's early conclusion that 'Sir Keith is a pragmatist and a skilful politician as well as a theoretician'.[13] But such reassuring impressions were modified over the following months as gradual administrative changes co-existed increasingly uncomfortably with a ferocious free market rhetoric from Sir Keith. Symbolic of Sir Keith's commitment to a strict doctrinal position was the remarkable reading list which he immediately circulated to senior officials. It provided an annotated introduction to the libertarian position from Smith and

Hayek to Jewkes and Joseph himself.[14] In an interview in June 1979 Joseph went on to declare that Britain's prosperity was wrecked by the six 'poisons' of a politicized trade union movement, excessive government spending, high direct taxes, egalitarianism, excessive nationalization and an anti-enterprise culture. This extreme and controversial rendering of the supply side argument was repeated in a major industrial policy debate almost exactly a year later.[15] Such determined maintenance of a clearly and publicly articulated ideological position made it difficult for him to accept the compromises, bargains and rationalizations which are part of a minister's life in a pragmatic spending department.

The steel industry provided the most potent source of disillusion with attempts to reinforce market discipline. There came huge losses, massive redundancies, the first national steel strike since 1926 and the appointment of Ian McGregor as Chairman of BSC. The agreement and announcement of McGregor's terms of appointment was handled with a disconcerting lack of political awareness which began to do increasing damage to the credibility of industrial policy. The House of Commons listened with incredulity to the prospect of paying up to £1.825 million to Lazard Freres to secure Mr McGregor's services. A month later, in June 1980, Sir Keith also announced a rescue package for BSC involving debt write-offs of £1.1 billion and £400 million of new finance.

Meanwhile other departments were undertaking more radical liberalization. In July 1979 the Price Commission, which under Roy Hattersley's direction had raised so much industrial ire, was abolished by the Trade Secretary, John Nott. The Office of Fair Trading (OFT) was strengthened, in particular by extending its powers to the investigation of nationalized industries, but competition policy in the traditional anti-monopoly sense remained low profile and there have been periodic criticisms of the unpredictability of OFT's references of mergers to the Monopolies and Mergers Commission. In October 1979 the Treasury abolished exchange controls, prompting a surge in overseas portfolio investment which proved, against governmental expectations, not to be a 'once and for all' adjustment but a massive and continuous outflow which raised legitimate fears of export of needed investment capital.[16] Later in the life of the Government liberalization was extended by the Trade Department's shrewdly timed abolition of hire purchase controls in July 1982.

The second half of 1980 saw a *de facto* policy reappraisal which outflanked the Industry Secretary. The pressures for policy change were formidable. Unemployment went through the 2 million mark in August. Conservative 'wet' opinion, still strongly represented in the Cabinet, was genuinely outraged by the monetarist fundamentalism and the CBI was increasingly restive about exchange rate and interest rate policy which seemed totally isolated from consideration of the 'real' economy. Industry felt that the DOI was failing to express industrial needs forcibly within

Whitehall and November saw an outburst from the newly appointed Director-General of the CBI. At the CBI Conference Terence Beckett argued that industry must have lower interest rates, a lower pound and a reduction in the NIS (national insurance surcharge). He declared that 'we have to have a bare knuckle fight on some of the things we have to do', telling his audience that (apropros the Cabinet) 'they don't understand you. They think they do but they don't. They are even suspicious of you and what is worse they don't take you seriously'.[17] Following a familiar pattern of prime ministerial intervention in industrial policy, Mrs Thatcher reacted to pressures of this sort. In July 1980 she announced the long delayed decision to back the NEB's microchip subsidiary INMOS with £25 million to build a new factory in South Wales. In October the first indication emerged that Cabinet Office/ACARD (Advisory Committee on Applied Research and Development) pressure for support of information technology would result in a high profile technology promotion function for the DOI; at the same time the new term 'constructive intervention' reflected Mrs Thatcher's cautious realism and in a contemporary rendering 'means directing money into industries which are considered to have a future'.[18] This was followed by the November Treasury economic statement which allocated a further £52 million for industrial support. In January 1981 the DOI's policy stance was decisively changed in the Cabinet reshuffle which removed several 'wets' but heralded a rather less arid Industry Department.[19]

The Interregnum: January to September 1981

The January reshuffle appointed Norman Tebbitt and Kenneth Baker as Ministers of State giving the DOI a forceful second tier. A neat division of functions made Norman Tebbitt responsible for the declining sectors where his economic liberalism would reinforce market discipline. Kenneth Baker was entrusted with the growing, more technologically orientated sectors which were the areas of approved 'constructive intervention'. As Hugh Young commented, 'In Kenneth Baker, a quite shameless critic of the faith, the Department has at last been given a minister who actually believes in the policy of industrial support'.[20]

On the 'crisis' side of industrial policy, early 1981 was dominated by a series of the set-piece 'rescues' which have traditionally posed such a problem for the industrial policy machine. Each rescue added to the embarrassment of the Industry Secretary and the Prime Minister and Sir Keith himself increasingly appeared to be a 'lame duck' minister. In January 1981 the Cabinet bowed to the inevitable and, in the face of Sir Michael Edwardes' remarkably astute handling of the Government, approved a huge two year package of £990 million in equity funding for BL.[21] In February Mrs Thatcher astonished observers by an immediate back-down in the face of a threatened miner's strike when she and David

Howell (Energy Secretary) relaxed the NCB's EFL (External Financial Limit); postponed the closure of 23 pits and agreed to limit coal imports. Later in the month came the results of the review of BSC's corporate plan which had been submitted in December 1980. MacGregor's plan was largely accepted which involved a capital reconstruction, writing off £3.5 billion in capital and loans, and an injection of £880 million in new funding. The decision was widely regarded as unavoidable but the provision within the new Iron and Steel Bill to allow future denationalization, and promises that the private steelmakers would be safeguarded, were not sufficient to hide the fact that the realities of recession had forced the Government into massive and ideologically indefensible intervention. March brought fresh problems with Sir Keith's very reluctant announcement of a rescue for ICL in the form of a £200 million bank overdraft guarantee[22] and a budget that was very unpopular with industry. Businessmen were appalled by the failure to cut the 3.5% national insurance surcharge which the CBI had insisted, as strongly as possible, should be cut by 2%.[23]

Misadventures on this scale focused the discontent which was widely being expressed about the course of industrial policy. *The Times*, for instance, opined that 'the first need is for a Secretary of State for Industry who can provide a new industrial strategy ... the time has come for (Sir Keith) to hand over this critical task to someone else ... The Government cannot hope to prosper so long as there is this lacuna at the centre of its policy'.[24] In April the NEDO Director General made an outspoken attack on the absence of a 'coherent long term objective' on industrial policy and Conservative backbench criticism became increasingly vociferous. But a change of personnel did not come until September 1981 when Mrs Thatcher's 'bloodiest reconstruction of a Cabinet since Macmillan's night of the long knives',[25] moved Sir Keith to Education, Norman Tebbitt to Employment, brought in Patrick Jenkin from DHSS and promoted Norman Lamont from Parliamentary Under-Secretary at Energy to Minister of State in Tebbitt's place.

When Jenkin arrived, however, he inherited substantial programmes already underway in the areas of small businesses and information technology. The Treasury took the lead on the small business front through a substantial 'enterprise package' in the March 1981 budget. Nigel Lawson, then Financial Secretary, explained that the reasoning was threefold: to facilitate capital mobilization; to give additional tax concessions; and to reduce administrative interference.[26] The most important measures were the introduction of a Loan Guarantee Scheme to be administered by the DOI, with an initial funding limit of £150 million, and a Business Start Up Scheme which allowed investors in small companies to set off up to £10,000 of investment against income tax. Although well conceived both schemes displayed a Micawberish approach. The Loan Guarantee Scheme provided a government guarantee for 80% of bank loans up to £75,000, but it was designed to be self-financing and later there was criticism of bank lending policy. It was said that the failure rate was too high and that banks were not using the scheme to support new lending but as a 'safety net' to cover existing risky lending. All the same, the Scheme proved a great success and in January 1982 the small firms Minister, John MacGregor, was proudly asserting that 'the scheme is going like hot cakes in its present form'.[27] The allocation was doubled in the March 1982 budget to £300 million and again in the 1983 budget to £600 million. Yet the whole small business bandwagon proves difficult to evaluate. There are a range of initiatives at local as well as national level but only impressionistic evidence as to their impact or success. In his valedictory message to Parliament, summing up the achievements of four years, Patrick Jenkin declared that 'the Government have introduced 108 measures for small businesses to stimulate the flow of finance, to improve incentives, stimulate investment, improve the supply of premises, encourage exports, reduce burdens and provide advice and information'.[28] The 108 measures could, however, be said to reflect confusion rather than clarity and many of the assumed benefits are largely a matter of faith.

During 1981 Kenneth Baker launched a spectacular high profile ministerial brief for 'information technology' through his responsibility for the British Telecommunications Bill which split the Post Office into posts and telecommunications. It would be difficult to overestimate the importance of this development. British Telecom employs about 240,000 people and is very profitable; it made £458 million in 1981-82. It provides the basic telecommunications infrastructure which, following reports from Professors Beesley and Littlechild, has been substantially liberalized. The eventual privatization of BT in November 1984 was spectacular. Over 2.4 million shareholders purchased 50.2% of the shares in the world's largest ever flotation. The Government raised £3.9 billion although the shares went to an immediate 90% premium and by the time the 1984-85 profit of £1.48 billion was announced these shares were at double the flotation price. The issue had appeared underpriced, at a considerable loss to the exchequer. Under its Chairman, Sir George Jefferson, BT is operating successfully and as one of the world's largest private corporations its strategies will have a substantial and controversial impact on the national and international information technology market. At the beginning of November 1981 the DOI raised the level of exhortation through a 'joint initiative with business' which designated 1982 as 'Information Technology Year'. The objective was to persuade companies and the public of the importance of using 'IT' by means of publicity, conferences, demonstrations and so on.

Baker managed to tap into and to exploit a popular media interest in the social and industrial implications of microelectronics and associated technologies. For instance, in the debate about 'cabling' and the establishment of the Hunt Committee to evaluate the broadcasting aspects of a cable system, Baker enthused that cabling and associated services 'could literally change the fabric of the society in which we shall be living ... the revolution that they will bring about will have more far-reaching effects on our society than the Industrial Revolution 200 years ago ... This is the biggest industrial opportunity and the biggest industrial investment programme before our country in the next 15 to 20 year. It is as important as that'.[29] The Hunt Committee reported in October 1982 and recommended a liberal broadcasting regime with minimal regulation but with a new 'oversight' authority. The White Paper giving the Government's preferred options was promised before Christmas but held up by novel inter-departmental disputes between the Home Office and the DOI over the level of regulatory control. The cabling White Paper was published in April 1983[30] and proposed: a cabling authority which would license cable operators; more extensive restrictions on programme content; but little dictation of network technology; both 'start' and 'tree and branch' configurations are acceptable in either fibre optics or co-axial cable. By Spring 1983, however, some of the glitter had faded. On the basis of American experience, cable networks were seen to be less lucrative than had been imagined, the potential for 'interactive' services to be very much latent and the DOI, BT and potential operators were displaying considerable caution. A modest stable of eleven operators were eventually licensed in November 1983.

During 1981 it also became increasingly obvious that regional policy as traditionally operated was becoming indefensible. A report from the Public Accounts Committee pointed out the shortcomings. It emphasized the DOI's tentative conclusion that 'it seems highly probable that regional policies have had a positive effect', although the effect was more marked prior to 1971, and argued that 'the need for greater flexibility ... should be considered'.[31] Further, the policy was expensive. It concentrated on capital subsidy to manufacturing whilst the new jobs were in services; it bore increasingly less relation to the regional distribution of unemployment, and it was too crude to cope with the urgent concern with inner-city unemployment, so amply dramatized by the urban riots of May/June 1981. The policy review was, however, slow to bear fruit. It was not until November 1984 that Norman Lamont announced a new regional aid regime that abolished Special Development Areas, cut overall grant by £300 million by 1987-88 and extended the area covered embracing, in particular, large parts of the West Midlands. The main revision before the 1983 election was the appointment in March 1983 of John Butcher as Minister with special responsibility for the West Midlands. His role was reminiscent of Michael Heseltine's 'Minister for Merseyside' brief and his new powers were equally modest. It was a case of 'too little too late' (see Table 4 above) and West Midlands industrial opinion was sceptical of the worth of the initiative.[32]

Patrick Jenkin and the 'Managerialist' Approach: October 1981 to May 1983

Industry policy and the Industry Department under Patrick Jenkin took on a less crisis-laden, more down-to-earth tone. In part this was due to the stablization of industrial activity; and while industrial production improved only marginally during 1982 at least the major crisis of steel, BL and shipbuilding had been coped with in some fashion. There was also good news. The Treasury at last felt able to reduce the NIS which had become for the CBI a symbol of irrational prejudice against industry. It was reduced from 3.5% to 2.5% in the March 1982 budget which also signalled a more sympathetic and flexible view of the overvalued exchange rate and of monetary targets. In the Autumn statement NIS was reduced to 1.5% and brought down to 1% in the March 1983 budget, thus, overall reducing the industrial 'burden' by £2 billion. In part also the moderate policy style reflected the more pragmatic approach of the new Secretary of State and his preference for giving coherence to existing activities rather than for rhetorical prescriptions for an ideal industrial economy.

In December 1981 Jenkin signalled the acceptance of a more activist industrial policy with the announcement of a £22 million aid scheme to assist in the rationalization of private sector steel firms. This was the first 'section 8' sectoral aid scheme introduced since the election although, in the event, the scheme proved unattractive and take-up was low.[33] Of more significance was Jenkin's public defence of activities and existence of the DOI. He argued that the Department had a constructive role to play; he set up a central policy unit and initiated a review of industrial 'strategy', a word that rapidly became acceptable once more. Jenkin was quoted as characterizing the Department as 'steaming into the night without any lights', which struck many as an accurate description.

The results of Jenkin's policy review were made public in November 1982. If the motivation had been simple departmental or ministerial aggrandisement, then the outcome seemed successful. Jenkin unveiled a 'management system' which was favourably compared with the MINIS management information system which Heseltine had introduced into the DOE. The initiative set the context for some important and overdue re-evaluation of the role of the Industry Department. In particular Jenkin stressed first, that the DOI was too capital orientated and gave insufficient attention to 'human skills' as a way to improve performance. This heralded a fresh emphasis on technical training and by implication on the unduly low profile Engineering Council established in November 1981 as a result of the Finniston Report; it also pointed to the importance of managerial competence. Second, he redeveloped the well worn theme of funding skewed to the support of declining sectors, with an implicit bid not only to cut the 'lame duck' budget, but also to boost substantially the funding for 'sunrise' high technology sectors. In concrete terms the management system seemed both revealing and functional. At the top tier

14 'strategic aims' were identified, including neutral topics such as 'elimination of trade barriers to UK industry'; controversial political issues such as privatization; and the equally controversial, because avowedly interventionist, aim of 'selective financial instruments to assist in increasing output and improved company performance'. These aims were broken down into 150 policy objectives and over 1,000 operational targets. For instance, the target for the loan guarantee scheme was to turn round applications in three weeks and to pay out on failures within two weeks.[34] Within and outside the DOI there was some enthusiasm for the setting of objectives by reference to which the Department's work could be evaluated.

Two other major initiatives during 1982 were the launch of another sectoral scheme, SEFIS (small engineering firms investment scheme) launched in March, and the Alvey initiative. SEFIS was designed to promote investment in new tooling for firms employing under 200 people. It proved highly successful and an additional £100 million was provided in the 1983 budget. The Alvey initiative was more profound in its implications. In April 1982 the DOI established a study group headed by John Alvey of BT to explore a research strategy for a British version of the fifth generation 'user friendly' computer. This was a direct response to Japanese and American collaborative research efforts. The Alvey team reported within five months, but the Government's response took another eight months to emerge, in April 1983. As suggested by Alvey, the DOI set up a directorate to 'network' research spread between universities, industrial companies and software houses. £200 million of government research funding was earmarked (out of existing budgets of the DOI, DES and Defence) but industrial research was to be 50% supported rather than Alvey's preferred 90%. This model represents potentially an important departure. It amounts to state led inter-firm collaboration on the Japanese model, working to a long term strategic objective. It indicates a substantial government commitment to technological innovation which goes well beyond setting the climate or even providing incentives.

On 5 May 1983 Patrick Jenkin listed in a written answer 'the principal achievements ... within his Department's responsibility since 1979'.[35] As an end of term report it was interesting in three respects. First, the dogma of the early Joseph days was almost entirely absent. There was no reference to the 'climate' or 'incentive frameworks' of earlier statements. Second, a list of familiar expenditure items was given, such as £282 million for national selective assistance and special support schemes, without apology for their interventionist implications. Third, the list represented a set of 'inputs', a list of major spending items with no attempt to evaluate their impact in terms of productivity gains, employment, investment or other criteria. This third point illustrates a problem with any analysis of industrial policy measures. The overall results are intangible, causation is multiple and it is impossible to establish clear links between favourable (or unfavourable) outcomes. Policy, like industry itself, is subject to the vagaries of the market; unlike programmes such as education or social security there is little homogenous, measurable output and evaluation is therefore peculiarly qualitative.

Problems of Implementation

The problems of implementation can conveniently be broken down into six groupings, of which three are problems of 'policy design' and three are more strictly administrative issues. First, and totally dominant for the first two and a half years of the Government, was the chasm between manifesto policy sustained by Sir Keith Joseph, and the existing pattern of activity within the DOI. As I have argued elsewhere,[36] industrial policy is particularly vulnerable to the disease of 'doctrical policy making'. Governments have been apt, in other words, to adopt an ideologically purist model of the desirable relationship between the state and industry, to incorporate it into their manifestos and to attempt to implement it despite the reality of complex interdependence between government and industry. This produces a divorce between the rhetoric of ministers and the administrative continuity of their departments and is apt to produce the 'U-turns' beloved of journalists when 'doctrinal policy' is eventually modified, as industrial policy was partially modified by Patrick Jenkin after December 1981. The implementation problem was thus that the market orientated 'supply side' definition of policy espoused with great honesty by Sir Keith Joseph gave no guidance for the industrial support activities which his Department undertook; indeed, policy required that such activities should cease. This made Sir Keith a weak minister within a departmental and Cabinet system which places a premium on a minister's single minded departmental partisanship. He found difficulty in imparting a sense of purpose to his Department (and was widely believed to have wanted to merge it into Trade); he found it difficult to argue industry's case in Whitehall and therefore was regarded by industry in an unsympathetic light; and when obliged by the strength of the argument to approve industrial support (as with steel and BL) he found it difficult to exploit the substantial merits of the cases.

It would, of course, be entirely unreasonable to place the burden of failure to adapt policy on Sir Keith's shoulders alone. He was appointed by the Prime Minister and sustained in his commitment to liberating market forces by the equally intransigent monetarist position which centred on the axis between the Prime Minister and the Chancellor. Indeed, Sir Keith perhaps performed an unusual and useful function in not attempting to hide or avoid the sharp dilemmas and conflicts between theory and reluctant practice. His public reluctance to accept the interventions and budget expansion forced upon him revealed clearly the shortcomings of the theory itself. In any case, a deep seam of 'doctrinal' influence was maintained by Patrick Jenkin, especially as concerns privatization. This issue is discussed elsewhere in this collection but it was clearly pursued vigorously as an ideological policy goal which detracted from a more pragmatic concern with industrial performance. For instance, Sir Michael Edwardes fought an acrimonious and eventually successful battle with Jenkin to avoid the precipitate privatization of BL. Edwardes' memoirs are critical of Jenkin, whom he agrees was pragmatic, but who had 'very little concept of, or even interest in, the strategic framework of the Government's relationship with a high-calibre Board', Jenkin was therefore prone to 'intervene in our affairs'.[37]

A second implementation problem lay in the increased distance between the industrial policy makers in Whitehall and their natural constituency. A heated debate continues on whether Britain has, has had or should have, some form of corporatist relationship between the state and the major producer groupings. Whether or not corporatism, in one of its multiple guises, is functional for some or all of the interests in society is a question beyond the scope of this chapter. One might, however, suggest that there should be some form of relationship involving the exchange of views, of information and of suggestions for policy change between the groups representing capital, management and labour on the one hand, and the state on the other. But dialogue was constrained by the Government's greatly reduced interest in tripartism as a principle for policy development and by the demonology of anti-unionism which soured relations with organized labour. In addition, both the unions and the business organizations were unusually divided. The unions were divided by left/right struggles within the Labour Party, by flirtation with the SDP, by the rise in white collar unionism and by the weak leadership of the two big but declining manual unions, the Transport and General Workers Union (TGWU) and the Amalgamated Union of Engineering Workers (AUEW). Business also suffered divisions between the increasingly influential Institute of Directors and the CBI, within the CBI between Thatcherites and technocrats, and between the hard pressed manufacturing membership and the more complacent service and retailing interests.

The danger of giving a lower priority to good relations with producer groups lay in accentuating the existing 'insularity' of industrial and economic policy making. The insularity of a closed policy-making system had two clear drawbacks. Most obviously, limited information about, and understanding of, the particular impact of general measures may produce inflexible and over generalized policies. This specific problem was tackled with some success by the Labour industrial strategy attempt to summarize NEDC working party discussions for input into the Treasury budgetary process. Second, reduction in contact can produce a vicious circle of distrust whereby industry tends to blame government without looking to its own shortcomings, and government officials develop a 'laager mentality' which leads to the dogmatic defence of flawed policy.

A third grouping of policy design implementation problems was posed by the depth and rapid onset of the recession. The acute industrial decline outlined at the outset of the chapter was not anticipated by the incoming Government and constituted a qualitative change in the environment within which policy operated. The recession threw up a series of 'crises', especially in steel and BL, which forced the Government into either/or decisions about state intervention. It also dramatized the assumptions on which policy was based. While a philosophy of increasing incentives and liberating market forces had credibility in a period of economic optimism, it appeared a cruel parody at a time when unemployment was rising through 2 million and market forces were in the destructive recessionary phase of eliminating firms and productive capacity. The state seemed to be providing a push from the edge of the cliff rather than a supportive cushion. In particular, the abrupt structural changes in the economy, in declining manufacturing employment and oil affluence for instance, appeared to be receiving little serious analysis from ministers.

Turning to more strictly administrative concerns, a fourth group of problems has lain in the fragmentation of responsibility for industrial policy. The DOI was created out of the Board of Trade via MinTech (1964-70) and the DTI (1970-74) and has always had a tenuous departmental 'personality'. The DOI's responsibility for industrial policy has depended, however, on its ability to 'carry' other departments. Relevant activities are divided functionally across a range of 'sponsoring' departments (for instance, the DHSS 'sponsors' the pharmaceutical industry), and geographically across the 'national' departments, such as the Scottish Office, who have their own development agencies and substantial control over important aspects of regional policy, as well as automatic membership of the key inter-departmental Whitehall committees. Micro-economic policy has therefore never enjoyed the focus, the coherence or the sheer power within Whitehall that the Treasury network gives to macro-economic policy. This general problem of a weak institutional base for industrial policy leadership thus handicapped new initiatives, such as public purchasing, and sustained the compartmentalized nature of continuing activities. A further source of fragmentation has become increasingly important in the shape of European Community oversight and the need to comply with the principles and regulations of the Community. In subsidy cases, such as the BL and BSC rescues, in the case of regional policy, and in relation to regulative issues such as car prices or information to workers, the policies of the Community and the oversight of the Commission provides an increasing constraint. In general, however, this reduction in economic sovereignty promises to be more irksome for a future interventionist Labour Government than for a market-orientated Conservative one.

The fifth grouping of problems reflects the pre-existing fragmentation of industrial policy responsibilities which became much more marked under the Conservatives. Fragmentation verged on disintegration as the market philosophy meant that the DOI was constantly being pre-empted by initiatives from other departments. When a new merged Department of Trade and Industry (DTI) was created in June 1983 it was a natural reflection of a DOI which had shrunk in status, salience and budget since 1979. Both on issues of supply side orthodoxy and of 'constructive interventionist' pragmatism the DOI was outflanked. On the supply side the major acts of liberalization and the relaxation in the tax and regulative environment were undertaken by the Treasury and the Department of Trade. Similarly one of the more experimental liberalization measures, the creation of 'enterprise zones', first announced in the March 1980 budget, was a Treasury initiative. In the constructive intervention area of promotion for research and innovation the lead came from the centre. The Cabinet's ACARD (Advisory Committee on Applied Research and Development), the CPRS and the Chief Scientist (based in the Cabinet office) all had a hand in advocating the support of information technology and therefore the upgrading of Kenneth Baker's post. The Prime Minister formally holds the Government's science and technology brief and has taken a close interest in this area, symbolized by the PM's 'advisory panel on information technology', a powerful inter-departmental mechanism established late in 1981 of which other industrial interests are understandably jealous.

Further challenges to the DOI's definition of the industrial policy problem area came from the Department of the Environment and the Department of Employment. The DOE began to build up a significant portfolio of economic development initiatives under the umbrellas of 'enterprise trusts' and of the urban programme. The DOE under Michael Heseltine, with his Minister for Merseyside responsibility, was picking up much of the debris of industrial decline, particularly in the inner cities. The DE and MSC (Manpower Services Commission) meanwhile were presiding over a massive expansion in employment programmes, which indicated a sea change in policy priorities away from industrial policy as a means of alleviating social dislocation towards a new concern with the labour market. The sea change can best be illustrated with spending figures. In 1979-80 the DOE outturn spending was £1,055 million and that of the DE and MSC £1,236 million; in the 1983-84 plans the DOI budget was set at £1,148 million, hardly any increase in cash terms and a substantial reduction in real terms, while the DE and MSC budget had risen almost threefold to £3,021 million.[38]

The final group of implementation problems concerns the morale and competence of the DOI itself. Given the range of problems outlined above it is hardly surprising that morale should suffer, but there are also legitimate questions to be raised about the suitability of the administrative machine at regional and national level. The DOI (now DTI) civil servant walks a difficult tightrope between the sensibilities of businessmen, the ideological preferences of his minister and the need simply to secure value for money. The job is made difficult by its ambiguity, but it could be made easier by the confidence that civil servants might acquire from a greater degree of business experience; certainly it would enhance their standing in the eyes of business people. The DOI 'buy' advice from industrialists, merchant bankers, accountants and management consultants and they increasingly appoint acclaimed managers to run firms such as BL, ICL or BSC, but they are not themselves managers. As a problem this is neither new nor peculiar to the DOI but both in its relations with industry and in its internal management a more technocratic, less defensive, bias might be thought desirable. The Department recently experienced the Jenkin management review, an internal review by Coopers and Lybrand and a 'Rayner scrutiny' of value for money and aid criteria. These perhaps indicate a certain internal concern with improving performance.

Conclusions

As far as the politics of industrial policy is concerned, the policy developed under the influence of three, not always compatible, forces. There was first the pressure for administrative continuity which was reflected in the manifesto and led to a cautious approach to the redesign or abandonment of existing legislation, institutions and programmes. The activities of the DOI in May 1983 were quite recognizably similar to those in May 1979. Second, there was a modest development of policy in the tradition of incremental policy change which took place from late 1980 under the banner of 'constructive intervention'. The concern with new technologies and the sponsorship of research was hardly novel; it evoked echoes of the Ministry of Technology from 1964-70 and it should be remembered that the main micro-electronics support programmes were set in train under Messrs Callaghan and Varley in 1977-78. Nevertheless, the Conservatives' enthusiasm for the 'sunrise industries', for fifth generation computing and new generic technologies (from robotics to bio-technology) was a significant departure from anti-interventionism and defined an important role for the DOI which looked increasingly like a presumptive technology ministry. Third, however, was the overall ideological posture of the Government which changed the system of norms and expectations within which industrial policy operated. The monetarist, libertarian approach, which Mrs Thatcher espoused, embodied a supply side philosophy which involved a minimalist industrial policy but which suggested a strong framework of law, tax incentives, union regulations and competition provisions, including privatization, which would create an appropriate 'climate' for enterprise. As Sir Keith Joseph reiterated late in 1980 'the Government's prime job ... is above all and first and foremost to get the framework (right)'.[39] Thus, curiously, a major obstacle to the implementation of Conservative industrial policy was the entrenched programmes operated by the Industry Department itself. Supply-side industrial policy was defined as basic to the Conservative approach to government and therefore as multi-departmental. The guardians of the new industrial policy were the Treasury and the Departments of Trade and Employment. The traditional role of the DOI, to 'improve industrial performance' was defined as beyond the scope of government.

There continued, under the Conservatives to be a deep ambiguity running through industrial policy which recalled the John Davies period in 1970-72 or the Tony Benn period during 1974-75. The ambiguity consisted of a gap between the professed policy of the Government and the reality of continued, arms length, industrial support. It could be argued that the ambiguity had been resolved through the 'U-turn' over constructive interventionism and Jenkin's subsequent defence of active industrial policy. But the 'U-turns' were partial and lukewarm and with the commitment to privatization, the breathing space provided by the modest 1983 recovery and Mrs Thatcher's re-election it seems probable that the Conservatives will succeed in achieving a more complete disengagement from industry than had previously seemed feasible. Such a disengagement has no parallel in the industrial policies of the other major industrialized nations. It will prove extremely difficult to sustain in the face of further industrial crises and unless the supply side revolution proves a massive and historically exceptional productive success, this policy is likely to create profound problems for the future.

References

1. OECD Economic Survey, *United Kingdom*, February 1983, 44.
2. See, for instance, the various NEDC studies such as *Report to the NEDC on the Sector Assessments*, NEDC (83) 18, March 1983, chart 5.
3. *National Institute Economic Review*, August 1983, 75.
4. Second Report from the Treasury and Civil Service Committee, *International monetary arrangements*, 1982-83, HC 385, xx, xxi.
5. Wyn Grant, 'Industrial policy', in P. Jackson (ed), *Government policy initiatives 1979-80*, RIPA, 1981, 63.
6. Industry and Trade Committee, Minutes of Evidence, 1979-80, HC 367iiY, para.45.
7. H.C. Deb., 970, col.1308, 17 July 1979.
8. *Ibid.*
9. See, for instance, *The Economist*, 23 June 1979.
10. Third Report from the Committee of Public Accounts, *Introduction of a new general policy for public purchasing*, 1981-82, HC 29, 5.
11. See the positive assessment by John Elliott, Sir Keith looks for winners, *Financial Times*, 6 January 1981.
12. Third Report from the Committee of Public Accounts, *op. cit.*, 9 (emphasis added).
13. *Financial Times*, 21 July 1979.
14. *The Economist*, 19 May 1979 and Nick Bosanquet, Sir Keith's reading list, *Political Quarterly*, July-September 1981.
15. H.C. Deb., 998, cols. 983-84, 10 July 1980.
16. For an analysis of the effects of abolition of controls see *Bank of England Quarterly Bulletin*, January 1983; and Chapter 2 of this volume.

17. *Financial Times*, 12 November 1980.
18. M. Rutherford, Mrs Thatcher's new name for intervention, *Financial Times*, 17 October 1980.
19. For an analysis of the Cabinet reshuffle see M. Burch, Mrs Thatcher's approach to leadership in Government, *Parliamentary Affairs*, 36, (4), Autumn 1983, 404.
20. *Sunday Times*, 11 January 1981.
21. See S. Wilks, *Industrial policy and the motor industry*, Manchester University Press, 1984, chapter 8.
22. See K. Dyson and S. Wilks (eds), *Industrial crisis: a comparative study of the state and industry*, Martin Robertson, 1983, 148-55.
23. See *The will to win*, CBI, March 1981.
24. *The Times*, leader, 20 February 1981.
25. Adam Raphael, *Observer*, 20 September 1981.
26. HM Treasury, *Economic Progress Report*, 132, April 1981.
27. H.C. Deb., 16, col. 599, 15 January 1982.
28. H.C. Deb., written answer, 5 May 1983.
29. H.C. Deb., 22, cols. 230-31, 20 April 1982.
30. *The development of cable systems and services*, Cmnd. 8866, HMSO, April 1983.
31. Fifth Report from the Committee of Public Accounts, *Measuring the effectiveness of regional industrial policy*, 1980-81, HC 206, 4 and x.
32. See, for instance, *Financial Times*, 23 March 1983.
33. See *Guardian*, 31 July 1982, by which time only £2.2 million had been paid out.
34. *Financial Times*, 16 November 1982, see also *British Business*, 26 November 1982.
35. H.C. Deb., written answer, 5 May 1982.
36. S. Wilks, (1984), *op. cit.*, chapter 3.
37. M. Edwardes, *Back from the brink*, Collins, 1983, 245.
38. See W. Grant and S. Wilks, Continuity and change in industrial support, *Public Money*, 3 (2), September 1983, 63-67.
39. Keith Joseph, 'At least make the framework sensible ...', in RIPA, *Allies or adversaries? Perspectives on government and industry in Britain*, 10.

6

The Changing Pattern of Central-Local Fiscal Relations 1979-83

Justin Meadows

The first term of office of the present administration was characterized by a fundamental restructuring of the relations between central and local government. Early promises of greater freedom for local authorities stemming from greater local accountability were not realized. Instead the Government introduced successive measures designed ostensibly to control those authorities which did not respond 'sufficiently responsibly' to their new-found freedom, but which had the effect, in practice, of reducing the autonomy of all authorities. It became rapidly apparent as these measures were introduced, that any freedom to be afforded to local government was to be constrained within tightly specified limits, whilst the authorities themselves were to have relatively little say in precisely where these limits were to be set. In many cases the limits themselves became progressively tighter as the Government's term of office proceeded.

Whilst the implications of these policy initiatives may have come as a shock to local government, the policies themselves should not have done. The attitude of the Government towards local government was made clear both in opposition and in their 1979 election manifesto. Essentially local government was seen as a part of the public sector and was, therefore, to be reduced in size along with general public expenditure cutbacks and made more competitive and more responsive to the requirements of the private sector. It is these three themes which recurred throughout the policy initiatives pursued by the Government during the course of its first term, and it is under these headings that I consider the policies towards local government which have been pursued.

Before considering these initiatives in detail it is helpful to consider the nature of the legislation enacted in relation to local government. The major piece of legislation affecting local government during the first term was the Local Government, Planning and Land Act 1980. Not only was its subject matter wide-ranging but so also was its effect on the structure of central-local relations. The important feature of the Act was the fact that it was largely enabling in nature. In other words, it did not contain specific and rigid details to be applied to local authorities but rather afforded the Secretary of State for the Environment considerable discretion to make such regulations, orders and directions as he considers necessary. It has been the initiatives, pursued under these enabling provisions, which have been largely responsible for the increasingly tight limits placed on local authorities.

In contrast the other major piece of leglislation relating to local government, the Local Government Finance Act 1982, did contain some specific and rigid details regarding supplementary rates and the establishment of the Audit Commission. However, a significant part of this Act (that relating to the establishment of targets for individual authorities and the introduction of penalties for those authorities overspending them) again comprised largely enabling provisions. We shall consider all of these measures in greater detail below.

In the following section I consider those policy initiatives which have been pursued with the objective of reducing the level of public expenditure. It is not my intention here to become involved in a debate as to whether or not the concern of the Government with local authority spending is justified,[1] but rather to examine the nature of the policies which have been adopted in the pursuance of the achievement of this objective and whether or not they have been successful. The majority of developments in central-local relations can be considered under this heading. In Section 3 I consider those initiatives which have been pursued in connection with introducing a greater degree of competition into local authority activities with a view to securing improved value for money in the provision of services. Policy initiatives relating to facilitating the activities of the private sector are discussed in Section 4 and general conclusions are presented in Section 5.

Reducing Public Expenditure

The desire of the Government to ensure that local government made its proper contribution to achieving a reduction in the level of public spending was demonstrated almost immediately after the 1979 election. In the same month as the election the Secretary of State for the Environment, Michael Heseltine, called for a review of all manpower requirements of local government and a temporary curtailment of recruitment. In July a circular[2] was issued in connection with reductions in the level of planned local authority spending which also stressed the importance which the Government attached to measures designed to effect reductions in the manpower requirements of local government. However, despite this and a considerable number of further ministerial exhortations during the early months of the new administration, this concern with staffing levels *per se* was not sustained throughout the first term but rather gave way to a more explicit concern with local government spending, initially perhaps with a view to achieving manpower reductions through the imposition of financial constraints. Whatever the reason, there was a rapid shift in the focus of the debate surrounding local government away from questions of staffing levels and towards an explicit consideration of local authority spending.

The concern of the Government with the spending levels of local government continued to develop from this early stage and was the motivating force behind many of the initiatives pursued during its first term of office. The initial concern was to secure a rapid and substantial reduction in the level of local authorities current spending. To this end the circular[3] referred to above was issued in July 1979 requiring an immediate reduction of 3% in local authority budgets for 1979/80. The following year, 1980/81, authorities were requested to plan on the basis of a reduction of 5% on the plans for current expenditure included in the previous Government's White Paper.[4] It is not my intention here to present a blow by blow account of changes in the Government's expenditure plans during the course of its first term. As far as local government is concerned this information has already been presented and extensively discussed.[5] The important feature of these plans is that local authorities were initially required to make a rapid and substantial reduction in their budgets,[6] and, thereafter to sustain a more modest reduction in real expenditures. It should also be noted that these reductions followed on from an 11.2% reduction in real expenditure by local authorities between 1974/75 and 1978/79.[7]

It is, perhaps, not surprising that the desire of the Government to achieve such significant reductions in local government expenditure in such a short time meant that they were obliged to re-examine the system of control over local authority spending. The first task was to see whether the existing system of control could be tightened up sufficiently to afford the degree of control which they considered would be necessary to achieve the reductions in spending levels which were being sought. In the event the Government considered that the existing rate support grant system did not offer the possibility of maintaining sufficient control over local authority spending and they were, therefore, obliged to consider alternative systems of grant distribution. That the Government was able to act so quickly on this decision was due to the fact that the new block grant system which was proposed in the Local Government Planning and Land (No. 2) Bill, and subsequently incorporated with minor, purely cosmetic amendments in the 1980 Act, was modelled on the unitary grant proposals which had been considered, and rejected, by the previous Labour administration.

It is not appropriate here to present a detailed discussion of the mechanics of the block grant system.[8] It is, however, helpful to outline the basic elements of the new system with a view to identifying those characteristics which were designed to ensure greater central control over local authority spending, and how the system has been developed over time to meet this requirement.

The objectives of the new block grant system introduced in the Local Government, Planning and Land Act 1980 were essentially the same as those associated with the previous system, together with one important addition. These objectives can be briefly stated as follows:

(1) to compensate authorities for differences in their spending needs;
(2) to compensate authorities for differences in their local taxable resources;
(3) to reduce the burden which would otherwise fall on local taxpayers;
(4) to influence the total, composition and distribution of local authority spending generally and of high spending authorities in particular.

Whilst the new system was intended to improve the equalization objectives set out as (1) and (2) above, it was objective (4) which the introduction of block grant was primarily designed to achieve.

Under the new system the grant entitlement of an authority was calculated on the basis of the following formula:

Block Grant = Total Expenditure − (Grant Related Poundage × Rateable Value × Multiplier)

All of these terms are defined and explained in the rate support grant reports,[9] but there are two elements of the formula which merit further consideration in connection with the Government's desire to control the spending of local authorities generally and high spending authorities in particular. The first element of interest is the Grant Related Poundage (GRP). The importance of the GRP lies in the fact that the local income from rates taken into account in determining the grant entitlement is calculated by multiplying the authority's own rateable value by its GRP (and multiplier, if any). In order to understand the nature and significance of the GRP more fully, it is necessary to examine in some detail precisely how it is derived.[10]

For each local authority there is a central assessment of its costs of providing normal average standards of service after taking account of its own particular circumstances. The figures thus produced are termed Grant Related Expenditures (GRE) and are unique to individual authorities. However, although they are intended to reflect the cost of providing comparable levels of service, it was stressed when they were introduced that they are not intended to be prescribed levels of spending since local authorities should be free to determine expenditure appropriate to their own view of local conditions. I do not propose to present here a detailed examination of the GRE methodology [11] but, as far as grant entitlements are concerned, the significance of the central assessment of the GRE for each authority is two-fold. In the first instance, it provides the link to a GRP schedule and, furthermore, it allows the Government to determine a point beyond which the rate of grant is tapered. We shall discuss each of these considerations in turn.

The equalization objective of the grant system requires that all authorities providing the same range of services should levy the same rate for spending in line with the centrally assesses GRE. It should also be the case that they face the same change in rate poundages for equal changes in spending per capita above or below their GRE. The GRP schedule is based on these two features, and provides the link between the different levels of spending and the rate levy to be assumed in calculating an authority's grant entitlement. The Secretary of State sets a schedule of GRPs which increase as an authority's total expenditure increases. The rate at which these GRPs increase determines the rate poundage cost to authorities of increases in expenditure by defining the tariff for each increment of spending. There are separate schedules for each tier of authority, based on the same tariff, which take account of the different mixes of functions. The separate schedules applying to the tiers in each area do, however, add up to the same overall schedule.

The major innovation of the block grant system was the tapering of grant support for additional expenditure above a predetermined level. It is this part of the block grant system which is designed to achieve the objective of providing a disincentive to high spending by requiring a higher contribution from the local ratepayer for increasing expenditure above the threshold level. When introducing this arrangement into the new system the Government recognized that the centrally assessed levels of spending need (GREs) could not be accepted as perfect measures of the costs of comparable standards of service. It was, therefore, accepted that the grant taper could not be reasonably be introduced immediately expenditure exceeded GRE, and the threshold for each authority was set at the level of their own GRE plus their class share of 10% of the national GRE. Above this point the GRP schedule increases at a faster rate. Since the introduction of the new system the taper has been consistently set at 25% and has the effect of increasing the amount of income deemed to have been raised from rates in the grant calculation. It is this feature which was intended to provide the disincentive to high spending by authorities.

Before going on to consider further developments of the grant system it is useful to briefly examine whether the introduction of the block grant system did lead to the achievement of the equalization objectives and disincentive to high spending which the Government had hoped for. As far as the equalization of local taxable resources is concerned, it is argued that, under the new system, this equalization can be more clearly and fully achieved. Previously the resources element only brought local authorities up to the national standard. With block grant those authorities with resource bases higher than the national standard can now be levelled down, thus permitting full resource equalization at a lower Exchequer cost than under the separate Needs and Resources elements.

As far as compensating for differences in the spending needs of authorities is concerned, the following observation about the GRE system of needs assessment is illustrative of a significant body of opinion:

> GREs are calculated on a service by service basis by a series of complicated statistical formulae using a wide range of data. There remains a great deal of disagreement about how best to calculate GREs... The essential point is that GREs are not, and never can be an objective measurement of need in a particular area.[12]

The concern of the Government with high spending authorities was twofold. Under the old rate support grant system the open-endedness of the Resources Element provided a positive incentive to high spending and enabled high spending authorities to pre-empt grant from those with lower levels of expenditure. The open-endedness of the system was certainly reduced by the introduction of a taper in the GRP schedule which led to a reduction in the marginal grant rates for high spending authorities. This led to certain benefits for the low spending authorities which were given any grant removed from the high spenders. However, for most authorities extra grant was still available for additional spending even if it did attract a lower rate of grant. As far as providing a disincentive to high spending was concerned one commentator described the effects of introducing reduced marginal grant rates for high spenders and the new system of assessing spending need in the following way:

> There is no evidence that these changes have led to a reduction in spending by local authorities, or that the grant incentives in the new system are measureably different from those of the one it replaced.[13]

Clearly the Government agreed with this analysis and at the time of the 1981/82 settlement the Secretary of State was expressing concern at what was regarded as persistent and deliberate 'overspending' by a small number of high spending authorities. It was not surprising, therefore, when, in January 1981, the Government announced that it was to introduce expenditure targets for individual local authorities. These targets were completely separate from the GRE figures for each authority, being based on their actual current expenditure in previous years rather than on any assessment of their need to spend. There were two principal reasons for this. In the first instance it had always been stressed that GREs were simply a measure of the costs to an authority of providing a standard level of service and not a prescribed level of spending. In other words, it was in no sense intended to be a target. Furthermore, the budgets of some authorities were so far above their GREs that the latter figure could not possibly be used with any credibility as a realistic expenditure target for those authorities.

It was argued that these targets were designed so as to focus attention on the reduction needed from each authority in order to meet the Government's overall expenditure plans for local government. The targets implied an overall reduction in the volume of local authority net current expenditure of about 3% below target expenditure in 1980/81, equivalent to 5.6% below outturn in 1978/79. In his January statement the Secretary of State indicated that, if the anticipated general overspending did make it necessary for him to propose a reduction in the overall level of grant, then all those authorities which had achieved their individual targets would be protected from any effects of these measures.

By June 1981 it had become clear from the returns of local authority budgets that there was the prospect of a significant overspend and local authorities were requested to revise their budgets. These were submitted in July and August and still indicated a substantial overspend. On 3 September 1981 the Secretary of State announced that he would be proposing to submit to Parliament a supplementary report to reduce the amount of grant available for distribution in 1981/82. At the same time he announced certain revisions to his earlier proposals, including an exemption from the effects of the proposed reduction for authorities spending at or below their GRE. However, when the supplementary report was laid before Parliament in January 1982, it did not implement this grant reduction, but rather gave warning that a second supplementary report would be issued to reduce the total of block grant and give effect to the proposed exemptions if the Local Government Finance (No 2) Bill was approved by Parliament. Part 2 of this Bill contained provisions giving the Secretary of State specific power to adjust the block grant payable to an authority according to its performance in relation to any expenditure guidance he may issue.

Following the passing of the Local Government Finance Act 1982 in July of that year, a further supplementary report was laid before Parliament which gave effect to proposed grant reductions for 1981/82. The nature of the grant abatement scheme proposed was such that the maximum penalty across all tiers was just over 9p in the £ and would be incurred if expenditure at outturn was more than 4% above target. The penalties were expressed in terms of pence in the £ and the actual loss in grant to an authority could be calculated by multiplying this figure by the rateable value of the authority. In effect, it could be thought of as making the slope of the GRP schedule even steeper for spending above the level of expenditure target. It, therefore, increased the amount which the authority is deemed to raise from its rates in order to finance this level of spending.

By the time the issue of grant abatement was resolved in July 1982 the second year of settlements under the block grant system was well under way. Local authorities had been provided with provisional expenditure guidance figures in December 1981 and these were confirmed at the time of settlement in February 1982 with a warning that a grant abatement scheme would operate if the relevant (No 2) Bill was enacted. In addition to the threat of grant abatement there were two further developments between the 1981/82 and 1982/83 settlements designed to encourage reduced levels of spending. The first of these was the reduction in the rate of grant support from 59.1% of relevant expenditure in 1981/82 to 56.1% in 1982/83. The second measure concerned the exclusion from the calculation of safety net multipliers, any losses of grant arising purely from an authority's own decisions about its expenditures. In other words the effects of the losses of grant due to the lower marginal rate of grant support for expenditure beyond the threshold were no longer to be moderated as had been the case in 1981/82.

As noted above, the Local Government Finance Act received Royal assent on 13 July 1982 and, subsequent to this in December of the same year, a supplementary report was issued which gave effect to the threats of grant abatement included in the original main report. In view of the lack of success of the previous year's grant abatement scheme the penalties proposed in the supplementary report were more severe than in the previous year, involving additions to GRP of 3p in the £ for each 1% spending above target up to a maximum of 15p in the £ across all tiers at a level of spending 5% above the expenditure guidance figure.

The Local Government Finance Act 1982 set out the context in which expenditure guidance figures or targets and the grant penalties associated with them could be issued in future years. Following representations made in response to the original Bill, the provisions of the 1982 Act required that the targets and associated penalties must be announced before the start of the financial year to which they related and could not be adjusted subsequently to make the penalties any harsher than those specified before the beginning of the year. The 1983/84 settlement was the first settlement to be announced on these principles/

Given the Government's concern that the supposed disincentives to high spending included in the block grant system were not having the desired effect it was not surprising that the 1983/84 settlement contained further measures to encourage reductions in local authority spending levels. The rate of grant was again reduced from 56.1% in the 1982/83 settlement to 52.8% in the 1983/84 settlement. The grant abatement scheme included in this settlement was also more severe, with the first 2% of spending above target attracting a penalty of 1p in the £ and each subsequent 1% of additional spending resulting in a 5p in the £ increase in GRP until the authority had no grant left. In addition the exemption from penalties of those authorities which spent above their targets but at or below their GRE, which had operated in the previous two years, was discontinued. This was consistent with the statements made when the block grant system was being introduced, namely that GREs were in no sense intended to represent a prescribed level of spending.

The 1982/83 settlement was also significant in that, during the course of the negotiations leading up to the settlement, there was an admission by the Government that they had so far failed to realize their expenditure plans for local government. At a meeting of the Consultative Council on Local Government Finance on 27 July 1982 the Government announced a £900 million increase in the current expenditure provision for local government set out in the Expenditure White Paper (Cmnd. 8494).[14] The interesting point about this additional sum is that only £200 million of the total was allocated between the various service heads whilst the remaining £700 million remained unallocated. In a statement to the July meeting of the Consultative Council the Secretary of State provided the reason why the £700 million had not been allocated between the various local authority services:

> It will be a global sum needed to recognize the fact that local authorities are going to be spending more in 1983/84 than the Government believes to be desirable.[15]

In addition to providing the legislative basis for the system of targets and penalties, the provisions of the Local Government Finance Act 1982 also related to the power of local authorities to raise supplementary rates or precepts. The Government became increasingly concerned that any pressure on an authority to cut its spending, arising from harsher rate support grant settlements was reduced by the ability of these authorities to raise supplementary rates or precepts. The Government initially attempted to overcome this problem by including provisions in the Local Government Finance Bill to set a limit to the overall rate which could be raised by an authority. Authorities would be allowed to raise any number of supplementary rates or precepts up to this level but could only exceed it after subjecting their expenditure proposals to a local referendum. If they obtained sufficient support from this they could then make the necessary supplementary rate to cover the proposals. No further supplementary rates could then be raised. Following considerable opposition to these proposals from all quarters, including the Government's own back-benchers, the Bill was dropped and replaced by the (No. 2) Bill which contained the proposals which were subsequently enacted.

The provisions contained within Part I of the 1982 Act removed the power of authorities to levy supplementary rates or precepts during the course of a financial year. Under the provisions of the Act, authorities could, however, make a substitute rate or issue a substitute precept providing the estimated product of the substituted rate or precept did not exceed the estimated product of the original rate or precept.

This concern with the rates being levied by local authorities was a recurrent theme in the justifications being advanced for the ever more stringent controls being placed on local government spending. It was also the motivating force, in December 1981, behind the publication by the Government of a Green Paper entitled *Alternatives to Domestic Rates*

(Cmnd. 8449).[16] The Green Paper was concerned primarily with discussing the requirements of a system of local taxation and the extent to which alternative sources of local revenues met these requirements. Comments were invited from interested parties which were required to be submitted by 31 March 1982. After receiving these representations and after a lengthy period of deliberation, it became clear that the Government was not prepared at this time to undertake any major review of the rating system. This did not surprise a number of commentators who felt that the Green Paper had been misconceived in the first instance.

> At a time when local government finance is in crisis, when central-local relations are a major constitutional question and when there is a widespread agreement that a fundamental solution is required, a Green Paper is produced which focusses on Domestic Rates, which constitute less than 20% of the income of local authorities.[17]

Once the Government had reached a decision that it could not effect any significant improvements to the rating system in the immediate future, there appeared to be a strengthening of the resolve to ensure that future increases facing local authority ratepayers should not be unacceptably large. It also became clear that this would be enforced through increased controls if the Government considered this to be necessary.

As far as local government capital spending is concerned, the situation has been rather different. Prior to the publication of the Local Government, Planning and Land (No 2) Bill, a consultation document on proposed controls on local authority capital spending was circulated to the authorities and associations. At this stage it would be divided into five blocks, housing, transport, education, personal social services and other items, and that authorities would make bids and receive authorization for capital expenditure up to a prescribed limit on each of these blocks. The authorities and their associations did not react well to the prospects of such a system and, following their representations, the provisions included in the (No 2) Bill, and subsequently in the 1980 Act, were modified to allow authorities freedom to combine all five blocks and to spend up to the prescribed limit on whatever service or services they considered appropriate on the basis of their own locally determined priorities. Authorities were also allowed to carry over up to 10% of proposed capital expenditure from one year to the next, and to transfer part of the entitlement from one year to the next and between counties and their constituent districts.

The control of capital expenditure provisions, which were included in the 1980 Act, represented a significant departure from the system of controls which had existed previously. The key difference lay in the fact that the control was now on local authority spending rather than borrowing. Prior to this local authorities had been able to finance some capital expenditure through revenue contributions and through the sale of capital assets, free from any control by central government. In the initial discussion paper referred to above, it was envisaged that both these potential sources of funds for capital expenditures would be brought under the control of central government. However, again following representations from the authorities and their associations, some concessions were made by the Government in the provisions which were ultimately incorporated in the 1980 Act. These concessions related to the exemption of certain items from classification as prescribed expenditure, the eligibility of certain items as capital receipts, and the proportion of receipts which may be used to supplement capital expenditure allocations. Each year any changes in these entitlements were to be included in a new set of Local Government (Prescribed Expenditure) Regulations[18] which are made under Part VIII of the 1980 Act. In April or March of each year a circular[19] is also issued which describes and provides guidance on any changes in this year's regulations and updates the previous year's circular.

It is difficult to assess the degree of success in controlling and directing the capital spending of authorities which has followed from the implementation of these provisions in the 1980 Act. Presumably, the Government itself was reasonably satisfied with the way the controls were operating, as the year on year changes which were included in successive regulations have been marginal in nature, and the level of capital spending was certainly substantially reduced below that which was obtained when the Government was first elected. In fact, this reduction was so dramatic, that by October 1982, it appeared likely that there would be £1 billion capital underspend by local authorities during 1982/83. In response to the concern expressed by the construction industry at such a turn of events the Secretary of State sent a letter to local authorities on 29 October 1982 announcing that two administrative steps were to be taken to assist authorities to increase their levels of capital spending. The first of these initiatives was a stated willingness of all government departments to consider applications for additional capital allocations in order to facilitate new capital investment during the remainder of the year. The second measure announced in the letter was the granting of freedom to housing authorities to spend as much as they wished during the remaining part of the year on home improvement grants.

However, it is difficult to assess if it was these new capital controls which were responsible for the reduction in capital spending. This is due to the fact that there were two other factors which exerted a major influence on the levels of capital spending undertaken by local authorities during this period. In the first instance, the squeeze on local authority current spending, and the uncertainty surrounding the introduction of a new grant system, meant that authorities were unwilling to commit themselves to major new capital projects which would necessitate incurring additional debt burden that would have to be serviced in future years from the already hard-pressed revenue account. Furthermore, the fact that interest rates were extremely high throughout much of this period meant that the cost of borrowing was extremely high, particularly if authorities were obliged to accept fixed rate loans such as those which were being offered by the Public Works Loan Board at the time. It appears more likely that these two factors were primarily responsible for any trends in local authority capital spending over the period.

A further, relatively minor initiative in connection with the Government's desire to achieve a reduction in the level of net public spending was the introduction of fees for applications and deemed applications for planning permission made under the town and country planning legislation. Section 87 of the Local Government Planning and Land Act 1980 empowered the Secretary of State to introduce fees for most types of application made under the planning legislation. In March 1981 the Town and Country Planning (Fees Applications and Deemed Applications) Regulations 1981 (SI 1981/369) were issued requiring local planning authorities to charge prescribed fees for planning or advertisement applications made on or after 1 April 1981. In May 1982 these regulations were amended[20] and a new scale of fees introduced. The stated aim of this measure[21] was to effect a reduction in the cost to the public sector of operating a development control system. There has clearly been a measure of success in this area, although it has been suggested that the Government overestimated the income which would be received from this source by £18 million in the first year of operation.[22]

Improved Value for Money

In addition to the desire to reduce directly the claim on available resources of the public sector in general and local government in particular, the Government has consistently expressed a wish to introduce a greater element of competition into the activities of local government. This was undoubtedly inspired in part by a recognition that any move in this direction would almost inevitably result in the transfer of certain activities to the private sector which had hitherto been provided by public sector agencies such as local government service departments. Ostensibly, however, the initiatives introduced under this heading, both in terms of new legislation and in terms of guidance issued to authorities, were undertaken in pursuit of improved value for money in the provision of local government services.

In September 1979, the Government issued a White Paper[23] which contained a list of nearly 300 central controls over local authorities which it proposed to relax. Furthermore, it stated that

> The Government's objective is to provide councils with greater local discretion and autonomy and help them to achieve better value for money.[24]

Following consultations, Part I of the Local Government Planning and

Land Act 1980 proposed the relaxation of the ministerial controls set out in Schedules 1 to 7 of the Act. The intention behind these relaxations was a desire to free local government from a number of unnecessary controls, and, thereby, increase both the discretion and autonomy of authorities and the speed and efficiency of local authority action in certain areas. However, whilst significant in number, these particular controls were not significant as far as the structure of central-local relations was concerned, and represented the relaxation of only a number of minor administrative constraints on local authorities. In fact, the 1980 Act also introduced over 100 new central controls on local authorities, many of which were considerably more significant to the future of central-local relations than those which were abolished. This particular initiative provides a good illustration of the fact that the Government was prepared to see greater freedom afforded to local authorities, provided that those freedoms were constrained within tightly specified limits.

In October 1979 a consultation document, based on earlier work by CIPFA and SOLACE, was issued in connection with the publication of financial and other information by local authorities. After consultations with local authorities and their associations a draft code of practice was issued in July 1980. In September of the same year a circular[25] was issued in connection with the publication of financial and other information by local authorities. This was produced in anticipation of the enactment of Part II of the 1980 Act and outlined the following three areas in which the Government wished to see developments in the publication of information:

(1)   information to be circulated to the public at the same time as rate demands are issued;
(2)   annual reports by local authorities;
(3)   certain key performance indicators, such as levels of manpower, which might be published more frequently.[26]

Accompanying this circular was the code of practice[27] relating to the first of these areas, based on the earlier consultation paper and draft code. Although issued before the relevant legislation had been passed it called upon authorities to accompany their April 1981 rate demands with the approved information. Legislative backing for this initiative was provided with the passing of the 1980 Act in November.

In February 1981 the code of practice[28] relating to the second area of interest of the Government was published. The code covered all the main local authority services and Annex A to the code contained a list of basic statistics to be published by the authorities, normally in comparison with figures from similar authorities and with the average for the same class of authority. Authorities were also encouraged to provide any supplementary information which they considered to be appropriate. In August 1981 a code of practice[29] relating to the third area of interest was published as an annex to Circular 24/81.[30] The code of practice related specifically to the publication of manpower information and recommended that local authorities should publish information about their manpower each quarter in a form compatible with their Joint Manpower Watch returns. This code of practice remained unchanged throughout 1982 but Circular 3/83[31] published in January 1983 a revised code.[32] The major changes introduced were in the following areas;

(1)   the form in which information was to be presented was specified in order to ensure a consistent approach from all authorities;
(2)   the range of comparative information was extended to include comparisons of the change in numbers employed by an authority with the change in those employed by all authorities of the same kind;
(3)   the period between the survey date and publication was reduced to two months.

The circular also contained the following advanced warning for local authorities:

> Having regard to the fact that a number of authorities either refused to publish information, or are not publishing quarterly manpower information in accordance with the code of practice, the Secretary of State is of the opinion that it is necessary to exercise the powers conferred on him by Section 3 of the Local Government Planning and Land Act 1980 to make regulations in order to ensure that authorities in England publish manpower information and in the manner and form specified.[33]

The Local Government (Publication of Manpower Information) (England) Regulations 1983[34] were issued subsequently in March 1983.

A series of further initiatives, also pursued in the desire to secure improved value for money in the provision of local authority services, were those relating to local authority direct labour organizations (DLOs). The start of these initiatives came in August 1979 when the Government issued a consultation paper[35] detailing potential improvements in the running of DLOs. After the completion of consultations the Government's proposals were incorporated into Part III of the 1980 Act and represented a considerable change in the legislative framework within which local authority DLOs were expected to operate. There are four particular areas in which this legislation has had significant implications for authorities: accounting provisions, tendering requirements, rate of return requirements and requirements to publish information:

The provisions of the 1980 Act required local authorities to maintain separate revenue accounts for each of four categories of work:

(1)   general highways work;
(2)   works of new construction other than highways with a value in excess of £50,000;

(3) works of new construction other than highways with a value of £50,000 or less;

(4) works of maintenance other than highways maintenance.

The purpose of maintaining these separate accounts was to ensure that there was no cross-subsidization between the work of the separate sections of the DLO. The remaining provisions of the 1980 Act relating to DLOs such as those requiring a certain rate of return, were based on the maintenance of these separate accounts.

On 5 March 1981 regulations[36] were made under Sections 7(2) and (4) and Section 9(3) of the 1980 Act specifying that for each of four areas of work - highways, sewerage, new construction and maintenance - schemes above a certain value have to be put out to tender. The first set of regulations imposed the following requirements on local authorities:

(1) general highways work - all jobs over £100,000 had to be put out to tender, but there was no requirement below this level. Winter maintenance work was also exempt;

(2) sewerage works - all sewerage works above £50,000 whether new works or maintenance, must be put out to tender;

(3) New construction - all schemes whose values exceed £50,000 must be put out to tender, and below that figure one third of the previous year's turnover must be put out to tender;

(4) maintenance - all schemes with a value of more than £10,000 must be put out to tender.

Successive sets of regulations[37] have increased the obligations of local authorities in this area; particularly in relation to the requirement to put out to tender a certain proportion of work whose value is below the threshold. The reasons for these moves were set out in the 1983 Regulations issued on 5 May 1983:

> The Secretaries of State recognize that many authorities awarded a substantial proportion of their work to contractors, but they also noted that little of the work awarded to DLOs had been subjected to competition and that there could, therefore, have been insufficient testing of the efficiency and cost effectiveness of such DLOs.[38]

This statement made it clear that the Government was not satisfied with having transferred a certain amount of activity from the public to private sectors, but was adamant that the work should only remain with DLOs if they could be shown to be competitive with the private sector.

This attitude was also prevalent in the third set of initiatives in connection with DLOs, those relating to rates of return. The provisions of the 1980 Act empowered the Secretary of State to make directions regarding the rate of return on capital which local authority DLOs were obliged to make. The first set of directions[39] in 1981, and subsequent pronouncements,[40] required local authorities to make a 5% rate of return on capital employed within each of the four categories of work for which separate accounts were maintained. The rate of return must be calculated on a current cost accounting basis rather than on the historical value of capital. The provisions of the 1980 Act also required that if the required rate of return is not met in any year then the Secretary of State must be informed. If the required rate is not met for three consecutive years for the same category of work, then a report must be prepared for consideration by the authority itself and by the Secretary of State who may remove the power of local authorities to undertake this work.

Section 18(2) of the 1980 Act placed a duty on local authorities to prepare a report by 30 September in the financial year following that to which it related and include such information as the Secretary of State may direct. The 1982 Directions[41] made under this section required any local authority or development body which undertakes construction or maintenance work from 1 April 1982 to include a specified list of items to be included in the report prepared in accordance with this section of the Act. Section 13 of the Act also required the preparation of a balance sheet, revenue account and statement of rate of return which must also be open to public scrutiny.

A further set of initiatives relating to the pursuit of improved value for money in the provision of local authority services are those relating to the establishment of the Audit Commission.

In July 1981 the Government issued a consultation paper[42] in relation to the establishment of the Audit Commission which stated that:

> It is necessary to ensure that the expertise and experience of auditors, in both the public and private sectors, are more fully and effectively brought to bear on the cost effectiveness of the provision of local authority services.[43]

After proposing the establishment of an Audit Commission the paper stated that it would:

(a) be responsible for securing the audit of local authorities in England and Wales;
(b) promote and undertake more value for money auditing including comparative studies of performance;
(c) widen the range of expertise used in local government audit work by bringing about a more even balance between private and public sector audit effort.[44]

Following discussions with the authorities and their representatives the provisions relating to the establishment of the Audit Commission were included in Part II of the Local Government Finance Act 1982. In addition to establishing the Commission these provisions also gave it some extensive powers in relation to local government audit activities and allied areas. The Commission was empowered to appoint auditors to each local authority, who were no longer allowed to make their own choice in this area. The Commission was also required to produce and update a code of audit practice as well as establishing a prescribed scale or scales of audit fees. The auditors themselves were required not only to certify the accounts but also to issue a statement of their opinion regarding the performance of the authority. The Secretary of State was also empowered to make regulations regarding what information should be presented in the audited accounts, how it should be presented, where the accounts should be deposited and to whom they should be made available. Of perhaps potentially more significance to local authorities, at least in the longer run, were the miscellaneous provisions contained in this part of the Act which empowered the Commission to undertake studies designed to secure an improvement in the economy, efficiency and effectiveness in the provision of local authority services and to prepare reports on the impact of statutory provisions.

One final initiative in relation to securing improved value for money was the issuing in April 1983 of Circular 12/83[45] in connection with housing maintenance. The contents of this circular were concerned with drawing local authorities' attention to the importance of value for money in the housing maintenance field and the ways in which the contracting out of certain activities might help to secure improvements in value for money in this area. The circular was not so much important for its particular contents but as an indicator of one possible area of development of future policy initiatives towards local government. Indeed, if the Government had not become involved in other, fundamental and highly contentious, issues after the publication of this circular it is likely that it would have travelled a good deal further down the path of encouraging the contracting out of major local authority services.

Facilitating Private Sector Activity

In opposition, its 1979 manifesto and in its early months in office, the Government expressed its concern that the public sector generally, and local government in particular, could represent a serious constraint to the activities of the private sector. Given this concern it came as no surprise that Parts IV to XVIII of the Local Government, Planning and Land Act 1980 were concerned with planning and planning-related matters designed to remove unnecessary barriers to private sector activity. It is not appropriate here to discuss all these provisions in detail but it is helpful to identify the ethos which underlies these proposals, and those measures which are likely to have the most significant consequences for local government.

As with the other parts of the Act, many of the planning-related provisions were essentially enabling in nature, empowering the Secretary of State to make directions, regulations and orders as he thought necessary. Specific provisions were included in the Act, among them the redistribution of planning functions between planning authorities. The intention here was to decrease the number of county matters so that more applications could be dealt with directly by the district and hence reduce unnecessary delays in the system. The provisions to allow local plans to be adopted in advance of the approval of a structure plan were similarly intended to speed up the planning process. The Act also contained provisions for the Secretary of State to require a local authority to produce a register of its land holdings and, where he was satisfied that the land was not being used sufficiently or at all, to require the authority to dispose of this surplus land. Other provisions related to powers to reduce the designated areas of new towns and dispose of surplus land, the extension of powers to make grants for the reclamation of derelict land, the repeal of the Community Land Act and the establishment of the Land Authority for Wales. Of particular significance for local government were the proposals to establish enterprise zones, with their special provisions regarding planning requirements and rate payments, and urban development corporations where the responsibility of the local authorities was removed altogether.

The obvious intention behind these initiatives was to remove any unnecessary hindrance to the private sector, such as through the retention by local authorities of land that was in practice surplus to requirements, and to give a direct incentive to the private sector through the kind of inducements included in the legislation relating to enterprise zones and urban development corporations.

The basic planning ethos of the Government was set out in Circular 22/80[46] published in November 1980 which contained the following statements.

> Unnecessary delays in the development control system can result in wasted capital, delayed production, postponed employment, income, rates and taxes and lower profitability. They can create a poor environment for future investment ... This circular is concerned with planning applications. It has two aims: the first is to secure a general speeding up of the system. The second is to ensure that development is only prevented or restricted when this serves a clear planning purpose and the economic effects have been taken into account ... Applications should be dealt with quickly and efficiently. The presumption should always be to grant permission unless there are overwhelming reasons why not.[47]

The circular also stated that the Government's priorities had changed, and instead of giving priority to housing and industrial applications authorities should now deal first with those applications which would contribute most to national and local economic activity.

This initiative was backed up by the publication of two further circulars[48] dealing with the changes in the system of development plans and in the system of planning and enforcement appeals. This latter circular stressed that the importance of a speedy and efficient development control system applied as much to appeals as to applications. The Town and Country Planning General Development (Amendment) Order 1981 also removed detailed planning controls over a number of minor developments.

Conclusions

> Democratically elected local authorities are wholly responsible bodies who must be free to get on with the tasks entrusted to them by Parliament without constant interference in matters of detail by the Government of the day. On the other hand, there are certain national policies which it is in the Government's duty to pursue even though they may be administered locally; for example where by statute responsibilities are shared between central and local government or where the Government of the day may have secured a particular mandate at a general election. It would be inappropriate, therefore, to abandon all control over local government; to do so would be an abdication of the Government's proper role.[48]

This particular passage sums up quite neatly the Government's attitude towards local government. Local authorities should be free to pursue their own policies to the extent that these do not conflict either with the national interest or with policies which the Government believes it has received a mandate to pursue in a general election. Presumably the Government would normally argue that any policy initiative falling into the latter category would also be in the former. It is not appropriate here to discuss whether or not we actually have a mandated government in this country, although there is considerable room for doubt. Nor do I wish to become involved in a debate as to whether specific policy initiatives which were pursued during the first term of office were in the national interest. What is interesting is the way in which this perception of the relationship between central and local government determined the nature and extent of the policy initiatives which the Government chose to pursue.

It is clear that the Government believed that it had a strong mandate to roll back the frontiers of the state, reducing the size of the public sector's claim on available resources, both financial and manpower. It is equally clear that the Government believed that local government should play its part in this process but would be unlikely to do so in the absence of strong controls over local authorities. It is for this reason that the Government moved swiftly when it came to power in order to prepare the ground for the Local Government Planning and Land Act 1980. It was noted in the introductory section that the nature of this legislation was essentially enabling rather than directive. It could be argued that this represented a hope by Government that local authorities would accept the 'reality' of the situation and would voluntarily adopt the measures which the

Government believed to be necessary to achieve the objectives which it was pursuing in the national interest. Alternatively, it could be argued that the Government knew very well that if it made explicit the requirements which it intended to impose on local authorities under the powers granted by the Act, then it would be likely to face considerable opposition to its proposals from all areas, including members of its own back-benches.

It appears likely, therefore, that legislation, which was to some extent sold to potential opponents on the grounds that it would only be used if local authorities refused to behave 'responsibly', actually represented a roundabout and stealthy way of providing the Government with the rather draconian powers to control local government which it was seeking. The Government knew very well that local government would strongly resist any attempts to restrict its activities and did not wish to have to enact new legislation each time local authorities refused to comply with central guidance. It also became very clear after the 1980 Act was passed that the Government was prepared to, and intended to, use the powers given by the Act to ensure that local government conformed to its wishes.

This was particularly true in the case of the Government's desire to reduce the level of local authority spending. The Government wasted no time in introducing the block grant to the rate support grant system and, when this did not appear to be producing the desired effect in terms of reducing the level of local authorities spending, the Government showed no reluctance to pass new legislation which gave it additional powers to secure this control. It is clear that this legislation has been at the heart of the restructuring of the relationship between central and local government. For the first time the Government has gone beyond a concern with the totality of local government spending to a concern with the expenditures of individual local authorities.

The first step along this path was the introduction of centrally assessed measures of spending needs (GREs) as a important element in the new grant system. By varying the indicators and weightings used in the construction of GREs the Government can influence the distribution of grant between both individual authorities and classes of authority. Furthermore, the introduction of expenditure guidance figures are targets and the grant abatement system under the provisions of the Local Government Finance Act 1980 means that individual local authorities are now given prescribed levels of spending which if they exceed will result in a loss of grant.

The Government has always claimed that these proposals are entirely reasonable because local authorities are free to raise from their own rateable resources the sum they believe is necessary to bridge the gap between their grant receipts and their own assessment of their expenditure need. The fact that the Government attempted to remove this power under the provisions contained in the original Local Government Finance Bill, and is again attempting to do so, is sometimes conveniently forgotten in this debate. The removal of the power of an authority to raise whatever rate it considered appropriate to finance its spending need would represent the complete demise of local democracy in this country.

The history of the Government's attempts to reduce the level of local government spending has been one of abject failure.[50] Whilst some progress has been made towards securing a greater degree of compliance with the Government's overall spending plans this has, to some extent, been due to the fact that more recent plans have not required the drastic cuts in local government spending which were such a feature of the Government's early pronouncements in this area. The attempts of the Government to restrict what it regards as excessive spending by certain individual local authorities has met with an even greater lack of success, as evidenced by the fact that the grant abatement schemes included in successive settlements have been even more severe in an effort to secure greater compliance in this area. One commentator has even gone so far as to suggest that failure is actually built into the block grant system.[51]

The success or failure of other initiatives introduced in the Government's first term is in many cases difficult to assess at this stage. It has already been suggested that prevailing economic conditions during the course of the first term makes it difficult to assess the effects of the new controls over capital spending which were introduced in the 1980 Act.

As far as the value for money initiatives are concerned it is not yet clear what effects the relaxation of certain ministerial controls and publication of financial and other information have had on local authorities. It should be recognized that these measures are not ends in themselves but rather are means to the end of securing improved value for money in the provision of local authority services, and must be judged in these terms. The DLO legislation has had far reaching consequences for many local authorities, resulting in a significant increase in the amount of work being put out to tender and some drastic reductions in the DLO workforces of some authorities. Although there has been significant resistance to these measures from many authorities with very active DLOs the Government does appear to have secured its twin objectives of increasing the role of the private sector in these activities and securing improvements in value for money to a significant extent.

The Audit Commission is only just beginning its work and no conclusions can yet be drawn as to its likely impact on the future of local government.

The planning initiatives designed to facilitate the activities of the private sector have undoubtedly had some effect in terms of the relationship between local planning authorities and applicants for planning permission. Whether or not this has led to any fundamental improvements in the state of the economy as was envisaged in Circular 22/80 must remain a matter for speculation. The establishment of urban development corporations and enterprise zones have resulted in actual developments on the ground, although the appropriateness of these developments and the suitability of these measures have been called into question. There has not yet been sufficient research undertaken to draw any firm conclusions in all the areas, although a series of reports monitoring the enterprise zones have recently been produced.[52]

The future direction of policy initiatives towards local government appears clear. The planning system will continue to be under pressure to facilitate the activities of the private sector. Further value for money initiatives will be introduced which may well include increased pressure on local authorities to consider contracting out some major and support services in line with the initiatives being pursued in connection with certain support services in the national health service. Finally, the Government's attempts to control the spending of local authorities, both individually and in aggregate, will continue. The proposals to abolish the metropolitan councils and introduce rate capping are already known. Although it is stressed that this latter measure is designed to be applied to only 12-15 'irresponsible' authorities, the history of the grant abatement scheme should sound a warning note. When this set of measures was first discussed soon after the Government came to power, it was stressed that they were to be used to penalize 14 'overspending' authorities. By the time the Rate Support Grant Supplementary Report (England) (No 2) 1983/84 was published, it revealed that 161 local authorities were being penalized under the grant abatement scheme. The future for local government appears very bleak indeed.

Notes and References

1. For a discussion of the issues involved see: P.M. Jackson, The realignment of central-local fiscal relations in the UK: the macro-economic perspective, Research Report to ESRC; PSERC Monograph, 1984; R. Jackman, Does central government need to control the total of local government spending? *Local Government Studies*, 8, 3, May/June 1982. For a clear statement of the Government's views see the text of the speech given by Leon Brittan, the then Chief Secretary to the Treasury, to the Society of Local Authority Chief Executives (SOLACE) in York on Friday, 16 July 1982.
2. *Local Authority Expenditure in 1979-80*, Circular 21/79, HMSO, 1979.
3. *Ibid.*
4. *The Government's expenditure plans*, Cmnd. 7439, HMSO, 1979.
5. See for example, the annual reports presented in *Local Government Studies* and CIPFA, *A general guide to the block grant system in England 1983/84*, 1983.
6. The Association of Metropolitan Authorities argued that the expenditure figures given at the time of the 1981/82 rate support grant settlement implied a cut in spending of 16% when compared with the expenditure plans of the previous administration. See AMA, *Block grant and the rate support grant settlement 1981/82*, 1981.
7. *The Government's expenditure plans 1980/81 to 1983/84*, Cmnd. 7841, HMSO, 1980.
8. For a general introduction to the mechanics of the block grant system see CIPFA, *op cit.*, for a more detailed examination see the annual report on the rate support grant settlement in England produced by the local authority associations and GLC.

9. A rate support grant report is produced annually at the time of the settlement. These are referred to as the main reports. One or more supplementary reports may be issued at a later date in order to give effect to any close-ending arrangements or grant abatement schemes. They are all available from HMSO.

10. The following discussion on GRES and the GRP schedule draws heavily on a paper prepared in relation to 1981/82 settlement by the Financial Advisers to the Association of County Councils. It is commended for its simplicity and clarity.

11. For a gentle introduction to the world of GRES see: E.M. Davies, *GREAs: Where they came from and where they are going*, CIPFA and INLOGOV, 1983. For a more rigorous analysis of the GRE system see the two documents published each year by the Department of the Environment: *Grant related expenditure: how the expenditure needs of local authorities are assessed for block grant* (known as the GRE blue book) and the *Technical handbook of grant related expenditure*.

12. See section 2.2. of AMA, *The RSG settlement 1983/84 – a guide*, 1982.

13. T. Travers, Block grant: origins, objects and use, *Fiscal Studies*, 3 (1), March 1982.

14. *The Government's expenditure plans 1982/83 to 1984/85*, Cmnd. 8494, HMSO, 1981.

15. Quoted in AMA, *The RSG settlement 1983/84 – a guide*.

16. *Alternatives to domestic rates*, Cmnd. 8449, HMSO, 1981.

17. G. Jones, J. Stewart, T. Travers, *The way ahead for local government finance: a response to the Green Paper, alternative to domestic rates, Cmnd. 8449*.

18. Prescribed expenditure regulations have been issued in 1981 (SI 1981/348), 1982 (SI 1983/302) and 1983 (SI 1983/296).

19. DOE, *Capital programmes*, Circular 14/81, HMSO, 1981; DOE, *Capital programmes*, Circular 7/82, HMSO, 1982; DOE, *Capital programmes*, Circular 9/83, HMSO, 1983;

20. Tne Town and Country Planning (Fees for Applications and Deemed Applications) (Amendment) Regulations 1982 (SI 1982/716).

21. DOE Consultation paper on the introduction of fees for planning applications, 1980.

22. Article in *Municipal Times*, 52, 622, February 1982.

23. *Central government controls over local authorities*, Cmnd. 7634, HMSO, 1979.

24. *Ibid.*

25. DOE, *Publication of rate demands and supporting information by local authorities*, Circular 14/80, HMSO, 1980.

26. *Ibid.*

27. DOE, *Explaining the local authority rate bill*, HMSO, 1980.

28. DOE, *Local authority annual reports*, HMSO, 1981.

29. *Code of Practice 'Publications of Manpower Information by Local Authorities'*, Annex to Circular 24/81.

30. DOE, *Publication by local authorities of information about manpower and about the employment of disabled people*, Circular 24/81, HMSO, 1981.

31. DOE, *Publication by local authorities in England of information about manpower*, Circular 3/83, HMSO, 1983.

32. *The Local Government (Publication of Manpower Information) (England) Code 1983*, HMSO 1983.

33. DOE, Circular 3/83.

34. *The Local Government (Publication of Manpower Information) (England) Regulations 1983*, (SI 1983/8), HMSO 1983.

35. DOE, *Local Authority direct labour: consultation paper*, 1979.

36. *The Local Government (Direct Labour Organizations) (Competition) Regulations 1981*, (SI 1981/340), HMSO, 1981.

37. *The Local Government (Direct Labour Organizations) (Competition) (Amendment) Regulations 1982*, (SI 1982/1030), HMSO, 1982; *The Local Government (Direct Labour Organizations (Competition) Regulations 1983*, (SI 1983/685), HMSO, 1983.

38. 1983 Competition Regulations.

39. *The Direct Labour Organizations (rate of return on capital) Directions 1981*, HMSO, 1981.

40. DOE *Local Government Planning and Land Act 1980, Direct labour organizations; year 2 (1982/83)*, HMSO, 1982.
41. *The local government (direct labour organizations) (annual reports) directions 1982*, HMSO, 1982.
42. DOE, *Proposals for an Audit Commission for local authorities in England and Wales: consultation paper*, 1981.
43. *Ibid.*
44. *Ibid.*
45. DOE, *Housing maintenance: value for money and contracting out*, Circular 12/83, HMSO, 1983.
46. DOE, *Development control - policy and practice*, Circular 22/80, HMSO, 1980.
47. *Ibid.*
48. DOE, *Local Government Planning and Land Act 1980, Town and country planning: development plans*, Circular 23/81, HMSO, 1981.
49. DOE, Planning and enforcement appeals, Circular 38/81, HMSO, 1981. *Central government controls over local authorities*, Cmnd. 7634, HMSO, 1981.
50. See, for example, A. Harrison with G. Lee, Local authority budgets 1981, *Public Money*, 1, (2), September 1981; J. Gretton with P. Gilder, Local authority budgets 1982: responding to incentives, *Public Money*, 2 (3), December 1982 and P. Smith, Local authority budgets 1983: no reduction of services, *Public Money*, (3 (2). The annual reviews provided by *Local Government Studies* are also a useful reference.
51. J. Gibson, Local 'overspending': why the Government have only themselves to blame, *Public Money*, 3 (3), December 1983.
52. See *Monitoring the enterprise zones: Year 1 Year 2* and *Year 3* produced by Roger Tym and Partners for the Department of the Environment.

7

What the Country Can Afford? Housing Under the Conservatives 1979-83

Alan Murie

The Conservative Government of 1979-83 may well be regarded in future as marking a watershed in policy and policy debate in the housing field. The Government not only introduced major new legislation but presided through a period which saw a decline in local authority new building to its lowest peacetime level since 1925; saw an actual decline in the availability of council housing to rent for the first time since 1919; saw a dramatic fall in exchequer subsidies to housing costs and the replacement of general subsidies benefiting all council tenants by individual means tested subsidy; and saw a real increase in rents to a level greater than at any time since 1945 with consequences for the household budgets of all those paying rent. The support for owner occupation was consistently maintained and, indeed, enhanced by these and other measures. In the Government's own terms, these policies were successful and they entered the 1983 general election promising more of the same. More significantly, the confusion in the ranks of pressure groups and opposition parties was evident, especially in post electoral agonizing over how to combat the apparent success and electoral appeal of these policies. Criticisms of the Government's housing policy in terms of impact on housing need and housing conditions have been widely voiced but the Government has consistently disregarded this conventional basis for evaluation of housing policy. Its actions in housing form part of a taxation and public expenditure policy and have been led by these considerations and concern to provide people with what they want (owner occupation). While this has partly been pursued through privatization of housing, it has not meant a disengagement of government from housing. Indeed, in some respects government has become more deeply enmeshed in the owner-occupied housing market. A plethora of special policies, as well as continuation of existing measures to assist owner occupation, signify a shift in the nature, direction and methods of state intervention in housing rather than a simple withdrawal or abandonment of the tradition of state intervention in housing through the general provision of council housing.

The Disposition of Government

The Conservative Manifesto 1979 had placed considerable emphasis on housing issues. The manifesto referred to housing under the heading 'Helping the Family' and devoted one and a half pages to housing - more than to social security, or education, or health and welfare or the elderly and disabled. Helping people to become home owners was designed to support family life. At the same time, the manifesto's view that 'unlike Labour, we want more people to have the security and satisfaction of owning property' was expressed in the context of creating a more prosperous country and giving more incentives.

It is appropriate for this paper to quote the major manifesto passages concerned with housing. Thus:

HOMES OF OUR OWN

To most people ownership means first and foremost a home of their own.

Many find it difficult today to raise the deposit for a mortgage. Our tax cuts will help them. We shall encourage shared purchase schemes which will enable people to buy a house or flat on mortgage, on the basis initially of a part payment which they complete later when their incomes are high enough. We should like in time to improve on existing legislation with a realistic grants scheme to assist first time buyers of cheaper homes. As it costs about three times as much to subsidize a new council house as it does to give tax relief to a home buyer, there could well be a substantial saving to the tax and ratepayer.

The prospect of very high mortgage interest rates deters some people from buying their homes and the reality can cause acute difficulties to those who have done so. Mortgage rates have risen steeply because of the Government's financial mismanagement. Our plans for cutting government spending and borrowing will lower them.

THE SALE OF COUNCIL HOUSES

Many families who live on council estates and in new towns would like to buy their own homes but either cannot afford to or are prevented by the local authority or the Labour government. The time has come to end these restrictions. In the first session of the next Parliament we shall therefore give council and new town tenants the legal right to buy their homes, while recognizing the special circumstances of rural areas and sheltered housing for the elderly. Subject to safeguards over resale, the terms we propose would allow a discount on market values reflecting the fact that council tenants effectively have security of tenure. Our discounts will range from 33% after three years, rising with length of tenancy to a maximum of 50% after twenty years. We shall also ensure that 100% mortgages are available for the purchase of council and new town houses. We shall introduce a right for these tenants to obtain limited term options on their homes so that they know in advance the price at which they can buy, while they save the money to do so.

As far as possible, we will extend these rights to housing association tenants. At the very least, we shall give these associations the power to sell to their tenants.

Those council house tenants who do not wish to buy their homes will be given new rights and responsibilities under our Tenants' Charter.

REVIVING THE PRIVATE RENTED SECTOR

As well as giving new impetus to the movement towards home ownership, we must make better use of our existing stock of houses. Between 1973 and 1977 no fewer than 400,000 dwellings were withdrawn from private rental. There are now hundreds of thousands of empty properties in Britain which are not let because the owners are deterred by legislation. We intend to introduce a new system of short hold tenure which will allow short fixed term lettings of these properties free of the most discouraging conditions of the present law. This provision will not, of course, affect the position of existing tenants. There should also be flexible arrangements covering accommodation for students. At the same time, we must try to achieve a greater take-up in rent allowances for poorer tenants.[1]

Following its election to office, the Government were clearly convinced of the importance of their housing promises. For example, the Prime Minister in the debate on the Queen's Speech in May 1979 stated:

Thousands of people in council houses and new towns came out to support us for the first time because they wanted a chance to buy their own homes. We will give to every council tenant the right to purchase his own home at a substantial discount on the market price and with 100% mortgages for those who need them. This will be a giant stride towards making a reality of Anthony Eden's dream of a property owning democracy. It will do something else – it will give to more of our people that prospect of handing something on to their children and grandchildren which owner occupation provides.[2]

The Secretary of State for the Environment, two days later, outlined some of the intentions for housing policy:

We intend to provide as far as possible the housing policies that the British people want ... We propose to create a climate in which those who are able can prosper, choose their own priorities and seek the rewards and satisfactions that relate to themselves, their families and their communities. We shall concentrate the resources of the community increasingly on the members of the community who are not able to help themselves.

In terms of housing policy, our priority of putting people first must mean more home ownership, greater freedom of choice of home and tenure, greater personal independence, whether as a home owner or tenant, and a greater priority of public resources for those with obvious and urgent need.

We believe that our economic policies in general will create conditions in which it will be possible for more and better quality homes to be provided by new building, conversion and rehabilitation.

As for specific policies, I have announced the direction of policies to combat the land shortage. We want to speed up and simplify the planning system. We shall repeal the Community Land Act. We shall also be talking to the building society leaders on the subject of mortgage funds for house purchase. We will be looking at a new subsidy system for public sector housing which will direct help where it is most needed. We certainly intend to ensure that local authorities are able to build homes for those in the greatest need – and I have in mind especially the elderly in need for sheltered accommodation and the handicapped.[3]

When electoral success is partly attributed to the appeal of particular policies and when the general inclination of the Government is to repudiate consensus, to reduce the role of government, to cut public expenditure, and to encourage the private sector such promises are important. The single minded concentration on expanding owner occupation and encouraging the private sector and the lack of direct concern with homelessness or housing need have remained marked throughout the period in office. The encouragement of owner occupation could be achieved through privatization and was a means of achieving other goals concerned with public expenditure, market processes, incentives, choices, and self help.

The counterpart of a policy of privatization in housing is one where policies towards new investment, as well as the sale of council, new town and housing association dwellings, offer a limited continuing role for publicly provided housing. This role is largely concerned with meeting the needs of a residual population who cannot fend for themselves in the owner occupied market and cannot obtain adequate housing in the privately rented sector. The tendency to see public housing as only *necessary* for the elderly, the poor and certain groups with special needs is apparent. It is fully consistent with a view that public resources should be channelled towards those in 'real need'. What is anomalous in such a proposition is the relationship with policies which in order to encourage private ownership channel resources towards those with higher incomes, more wealth and better housing.

Policy Change

The characteristics of the housing service have major implications for a government concerned to change the direction of policy. The high cost and durability of housing and the size of the existing stock relative to the volume of new construction in any year mean that attempts to change direction through new investment have a slow impact. Thus, for example, shifting the balance of building activity away from the public sector and towards owner occupation would be a very slow mechanism for realizing a property owning democracy. Indeed in 1979-80 even if higher rates of building had been achieved this mechanism would not have sustained the rate of growth of home ownership experienced in recent years. That rate of growth has been substantially achieved through sales of previously privately rented properties to owner occupiers. As the privately rented sector has declined that method of increasing owner occupation has become less capable of sustaining growth. In this way a government concerned to encourage rapid growth in owner occupation must look to other mechanisms than new investment.

At the same time the housing service is one in which the public sector is in far from a dominant position. Publicly owned dwellings account for one third of the housing stock in England and Wales. The production of housing in public and private sectors is almost wholly carried out by private companies. Direct Labour Organizations are usually preoccupied with repairs and maintenance. There is a financially sound, substantial organizational basis for the operation of the private housing market, from providers of finance (especially building societies) to builders, to exchange professionals (estate agents, lawyers, brokers etc). Private resources for housing financing and investment exceed those of the public sector by an enormous margin.

In this respect a government concerned to enhance market processes does not have to start by creating market based organizations and mechanisms. The existing organization of the housing service enables a government to pursue a policy of privatization with relative ease.

If the framework of private institutions already existed in 1979, so did many of the mechanisms for changing public policy. The previous government had introduced a system of cash limits. Housing Strategies and Investment Programmes had been introduced as a means to control all local housing capital expenditure and implement cash limits.[4] The Conservative Government inherited a mechanism to control and reduce new capital expenditure and did not have to introduce ad hoc controls over particular programmes. The reduction of HIP allocation in mid year in July 1979 (by £294 million) largely eliminated the then predicted underspend. However it was not just a cosmetic exercise. The limits on switching between expenditure areas (virement) meant that some authorities had to halt expenditure on particular programmes. Nevertheless this reduction was insignificant compared with the allocations made for 1980/81. These allocations were announced much later than effective local planning required (at the end of February 1980) and involved reductions of one third of the previous year's spending. The amount allocated represented only half of what local authorities had asked for. Various local authorities reduced, froze, suspended or severely restricted one or more elements in their capital programmes as a result of these reductions.

With a mechanism of this type it could be expected that the Secretary of State would not again have to make mid year adjustments. However in October 1980 a moratorium on new local authority housing capital projects was introduced. It is possible to argue that the decision to introduce a moratorium was designed to gear activity down in preparation for further cuts in 1981/82 or to lead to an underspend on HIPs to offset an overspend on subsidy, arising from higher interest rates than had been planned for in arriving at the division of housing cash limits between investment and subsidy. The moratorium and cuts in expenditure did not only apply to local authorities but have also affected housing associations and new towns. HIP allocations were reduced by a further 15% in 1981/82. Under new arrangements for the treatment of capital receipts, an estimated 20% of this total was not allocated through HIP but was to be available to authorities according to the capital receipts they obtained from the sale of land and dwellings. A similar procedure affected some 25% of the permitted spending for 1982/83 which otherwise was broadly maintained at the previous year's level. This incentive to sale involved a relaxation of attempts to steer capital spending towards those areas with the greatest housing need. It has resulted in a considerable redistribution of permitted capital spending away from London and inner city areas and towards areas not generally recognized as having housing stress.[5] The 1982/83 HIP process involved local authority submissions referring to council housing vacancies and to low cost home ownership – major concerns of government policy – and substantial additional resources were made available for spending on improvement grants. By 1982/83 the HIP process had evolved from a broad and forward looking planning process concerned with local strategies and needs to a more narrow function covering a limited range of centrally determined needs and concerned with informing on progress in implementing government policies. 'The local autonomy and planning objectives of the system have become almost fully subservient to central decisions on the distribution of resources, strong encouragement to follow national policy initiatives and a tightly controlled and uncertain financial climate.[6]

These changes in capital expenditure formed one mechanism for implementing the housing public expenditure plans of the Government. The other major mechanism available to the Government in achieving this was the new subsidy system introduced under the Housing Act 1980, and the leverage this provided in respect of rent levels. The new subsidy system was that devised by the previous Labour Government and involved a deficit subsidy system. The Exchequer subsidy relates to deficits on notional local authority Housing Revenue Accounts (HRAs) after making assumptions about local contributions (including rents) and costs. Where authorities are in deficit, failure to raise rents in line with these assumptions would create a problem in balancing the HRA or involve increased rate fund contributions. The Secretary of State used his powers to double rents from what was the lowest post war level in 1979 to a level in 1982 higher than at any time since 1945. Initially, while most local authorities were in deficit and increased rate contribution risked penalties under the Local Government Planning and Land Act, it enabled the Secretary of State to lay down rent increases. However as local authority HRAs moved into surplus, so local discretion over further rent increases re-emerged. The local authority associations appear to have persuaded the Secretary of State not to clawback notional surpluses on HRAs through block grant funding and so established this discretion. The impact of these rent rises and of capital receipts from sales of council housing and land facilitated reductions in public expenditure. However time lags meant that initially investment was severely cut. It was more difficult to cut subsidy quickly as the new system had to be established and rent increases, although severe, had to be phased. In an environment where every penny that goes towards subsidies is a penny off housing investment,[7] investment was sacrificed until subsidy could be reduced. What was not open to adjustment was the overall level of expenditure.

This overall level of expenditure had not been arrived at by converting needs-related housing investment and subsidy targets into cash figures. The process has been the other way round - the cash figure is what is left after other claims have been made within the Government's overall financial and monetary targets.[8] What this level of expenditure has paid for in terms of housing depends on inflation and interest rates as well as on factors such as rents and revenue from council house sales and the Government consistently refused to indicate what it expected to result. What the outcome in terms of housing was, was not critical to future decisions. In 1980 the Secretary of State for the Environment explained that the figures for housing public expenditure were arrived at 'based on a range of discussions which took place between myself and the Treasury as to, broadly, what the country can afford, broadly what money is available for housing in the context of the public expenditure constraint which the Government has to introduce ...'[9] Not only did these negotiations not start with calculations of what expenditure was needed, but because of local discretion over spending, it was not possible to do more than speculate over what this level of expenditure would produce in terms of housing. The two broad questions for government were 'what could the Government afford to devote to this field of social policy' and whether 'it was best to enable those authorities that were responsible for spending the money in the main to continue ... to make their decision'.[10]

One year later, the Secretary of State elaborated on the circumstances in which discussion about housing expenditure occurred: 'I would be starting from a situation where the Treasury would know, ... , that we have the largest crude surplus of housing stock in our history'. This put him at a 'slight disadvantage with the Secretary of State for Defence' and the different urgency about the scale of allocation of priorities would lead the Treasury to propose a reduction in spending. In addition he had to consider 'whether I actually want to increase that crude surplus or whether I want to get better use of money'.[11]

The levels of expenditure which emerged from this process relegated the housing programme from a major to a minor spending programme. The planned reductions in housing public expenditure from 1980/81 to 1983/84 amounted to 48% and accounted for 75% of the planned reduction in total public expenditure plus contingency reserve. In 1974/75 housing had accounted for 10% of public expenditure programmes. Its share had fallen to 7% by 1979/80 and it was planned to fall to only just over 4% by 1983/84.[12]

The extent of the planned cut was markedly greater than had occurred in the past or than was being planned for any other programme area. The planned rate of reduction in expenditure was considerably greater (at £645 million a year for four years) than the average of £475 million a year between 1974/75 and 1979/79. The proposed reduction for the period 1980/81 to 1983/84 was 48% compared with 25% in the earlier and longer period referred to.[13] The actual spending levels achieved matched what was planned. In contrast to other policy areas, a major shift in spending was achieved. Referring to this O'Higgins states:

> Housing is not only the welfare programme suffering the largest cuts. It is also the only programme where cuts have been overachieved: by 1981/82 the estimated out turn cut was one and a half times the size the government had planned in 1980.[14]

While housing had accounted for 7% of public expenditure in Great Britain in 1978/79, by 1982/83 it had declined to 4%. *Cash* expenditure stood at almost exactly the same level in 1982/83 as it had four years earlier. This was in spite of the volume of housing capital receipts, and in spite of the explosion of improvement and repairs grant expenditure in 1982/83.

As has been suggested, these levels of expenditure were not devised from housing investment and subsidy targets. What it has resulted in, in terms of investment and subsidy, can be briefly summarized.[15] Public sector dwelling starts in England had fallen from 69,400 in 1979 to 43,186 in 1982. In the same period, public sector dwelling completions had fallen from 91,100 to 41,874; public sector improvement work completed had declined from 93,200 to 74,993. Only private sector improvement grants saw an increase from 65,400 dwellings in 1979 to 104,000.

In considering these figures, it is important to note other factors. First the encouragement of improvement activity through higher rates of improvement grants, first announced in the 1982 budget, did involve placing an emphasis on investment – albeit by increasing the assistance available to owner occupiers. Second and linked with this, it was only by the end of the Government's period in office that the reductions in subsidy necessary to release resources for investment (within the overall limits on housing expenditure) had been achieved. The public expenditure White Paper published in 1983, referred to 'a level of gross housing investment in 1983/84 ... Some 11% higher than the expected outturn for 1982/83'.[16] Third, the reduction in general assistance subsidy for council housing and in housing capital expenditure generally has been partly achieved by switching housing subsidy expenditure into the social security budget. As rents have risen, so the costs of means tested assistance with housing costs has increased. The cash cost of rent rebates was two and a half times as great in 1981/82 as in 1978/79 – a rate of expenditure increase more than twice as great as that for social security benefits generally. Taken in conjunction with the increasing proportion of supplementary benefit recipients who are council tenants, this amounts to a significant switch in method of subsidy and does not involve as substantial a reduction in subsidy as appears. It is also relevant to bear in mind that the structure of tax relief and other 'subsidies' to owner occupiers have not been reviewed. Discounts for council house sales involved a new set of subsidies (with a new set of inequities) and meant 'giving away' some £1,782 million by December 1982.[17] Pre-election intentions were to raise the limit on mortgages qualifying for tax relief (at a cost of some £60 million in revenue foregone). These were presumably subsidies the country could afford, because they are not counted as public expenditure, and do not enter into the good housekeeping calculus. In contrast changes to the system of assistance with housing costs for tenants with the lowest incomes had to be made at nil extra cost. As a consequence, the new housing benefit system involved a loss of benefit for some and a perpetuation of key benefit problems. Some of the administrative problems which left this scheme with the appearance of the Government's worst managed piece of 'reform', imposing the burdens of this on the poorest sections of the population, are also attributable to these cost constraints.[18]

Parliamentary answers in 1983 showed that, leaving aside income maintenance subsidies, the average owner with a mortgage was subsidized to the tune of £370 per household, compared with £142 for each council tenant.[19]

Both housing and other expenditure plans were significantly affected by capital receipts. It is worth noting the scale of receipts from the sale of council housing. In public expenditure terms, council house sales have been considerably more important than any other act of privatization. The interest associated with sales of housing and housing land was, by 1983/4 the most rapidly growing source of Housing Revenue Account income and was as important as rate fund contributions in the HRA.[20] This (unexpected) phenomenon is associated with an 'underspending' of capital receipts and a situation in which housing investment *net of receipts* fell below £600 million in 1982/3. Some two thirds of expenditure was offset by receipts.

Thus the introduction, promotion and success of the Right to Buy do not just relate to housing policy aspirations or broader ideological and political views, but also to fundamental economic and financial goals. Enhanced discounts for houses sold under a new general consent for the sale of council houses issued in May 1979, did result in an increased rate of sale. However, there were time lags involved in the policy and the peak for sales (RTB and discretionary) was not reached until 1982.[21] Other dimensions were not within the direct control of government. Most importantly, the level of capital receipts from sales is considerably enhanced if private sector funds are substantially used to finance purchase. While building societies initially expressed hesitation and even caution about their contribution to such financing,[22] their investment situation meant that in practice they made a considerably greater contribution, in 1982 in particular, than had been anticipated. While this kind of 'bonus' assisted government, it otherwise consistently pressed the sales policy. The Housing Act 1980 introduced a Right to Buy and removed local powers to decide whether or not to sell in relation to the bulk of their properties. A substantial advertising campaign was used to inform potential purchasers of their new rights.[23] Local authorities were offered various incentives (reinvestment of receipts) and subjected to monitoring and scrutiny of their sales progress. Some authorities in England were put on a 'black list' and detailed central-local negotiations so far broke down as to result in litigation.[24] In the words of the then Master of the Rolls, the legislation contained 'a most unusual power', enabling the central government 'to interfere with a high hand over local authorities'.[25] The notice of intervention served on Norwich City Council in 1981 resulted in the Secretary of State's representative taking responsibility for the administration of the Right to Buy from a council which had not refused to operate the law but rather was reacting too slowly in the Minister's view. But this represents the tip of the iceberg in a situation where in December 1983 about 200 local authorities were being scrutinized in relation to the Right to Buy. Such scrutiny was not only a departure from normal practice but represented an uneven development of policy. No such scrutiny developed to check whether local authorities were carrying out other housing duties (say in relation to the homeless or badly housed) with sufficient diligence.

Again, while a central government could not prevent time lags and delays, it did have the powers necessary to pursue its aims. It was also willing to augment those powers by revising statutory instruments issued under the Housing Act 1980 to broaden the right to buy, by providing protection to some householders making bad buys under the Act, by increasing discounts under discretionary sales and by introducing new legislation to increase discounts and reduce local authority discretion in relation to the Right to Buy and provide a Right to Buy for housing association tenants.[26] Council house sales have generated substantial capital receipts and local authorities have been able to reinvest (part of) these receipts. The ability to augment HIP allocations with capital receipts was a major theme in the Government's presentation of policy. However, by 1983, the Government was concerned at substantial underspending largely associated with these receipts. Various factors account for this underspend, but it has been argued that one of these is that the distribution of capital receipts bears no relation to housing need, capacity to invest or will to invest. In addition the volume of receipts is not easily estimated in advance. The procedures adopted contribute to underspend, to a wasteful, incremental and unplanned style of local policy and to an allocation of powers to spend which does not relate to ideas of channelling resources to areas of greatest need.[27]

Cash limits, a new subsidy system and the sale of council houses were not the only mechanisms used to implement policy. The Local Government (Planning and Land) Act included measures to restrict the activities of Direct Labour Departments and subject them to market processes and to abolish the Community Land Act (See Chapter 6 above). At the same time changes in planning legislation and procedures were designed to remove constraints on the private sector. Registers of unused or underused land in public ownership, powers for the Secretary of State to direct release of registered land and detailed measures to streamline development control and appeals procedures were all designed to create the climate for private development. Sales of land by new town development corporations, the PSA and the Housing Corporation, a reduction in the rate of Development Land Tax and proposals to relax green belt restrictions were all designed to the same end. The existing mechanism of control over housing associations (through the Housing Corporation) and the new towns enabled the latter programme to be terminated. The increased role given to housing associations can be attributed to their greater malleability and responsiveness in comparison with local authorities. The replacement of the cost yardstick procedure in project approval and subsidy arrangements with a market related value for money formula and abandonment of insistence on Parker Morris standards in public housing developments were also designed to relax central controls. The encouragement of owner occupation involved other policy mechanisms as well as the sale of council houses. In April 1981 a six part plan for low cost home ownership was introduced.

But the total impact of these schemes over the life of the Government[28] is small compared with council house sales or independent private sector activity. And the most productive elements – those arising from the sale of land – are those over which there is least scope to achieve policy objectives concerned with client groups (or, inevitably, the older stock) and where 'displacement' of other activity may have substantially reduced real impact.[29] This issue is more significant in view of the failure of the private sector to fill the gap left by reduced public investment and to respond to the 'favourable climate' created by the Government. In 1981 private sector dwelling completions were 112,960 – the lowest level since 1954 and, although completions rose 121,000 in 1982, this is still only half the level achieved in 1964.[30] Nor had the private rented sector been revived by the measures in the Housing Act 1980. Only some 5,000 short-hold tenancies had been created and there was no evidence to suggest any reduction in the rate of decline of the sector.[31]

The Housing Act 1980 did not include proposals for a mandatory mobility scheme (although the previous Labour Government's Housing Bill had done so). However it did provide powers for the Secretary of State to contribute towards the cost of transfers and exchanges between local authorities. A voluntary scheme worked out through the local authority associations came into operation in 1981 to assist mobility. It appears likely to remain a minor scheme linked to labour market policies, rather than a substantial contribution to increased mobility and choice for council tenants.

It has been widely argued that the right to buy and some other measures to encourage owner occupation will exacerbate the problems of tenants who do not buy and of potential tenants. At the same time measures have been introduced which derive from concern at the absence of legally based rights for council tenants who often had better dwellings than private tenants but have not had equivalent security of tenure. The local authority as landlord could obtain possession of property without having to justify this in a way comparable to the private landlord. The tenants' charter introduced in the Housing Act 1980, while not as radical as the proposals contained in the Labour Government's Housing Bill in 1979 (especially in respect of tenant involvement in management and of mobility) does change the conditions and rights associated with public sector tenancies. The principal development in the tenants' charter is to place tenancies in the public sector within a precise legal framework. This includes definition of security of tenure and procedures and grounds for obtaining possession. Rights of succession for widows, widowers or members of the family who have been resident in the property are laid down. Rights to take lodgers or to sublet, to carry out improvements (subject to a landlord's permission) and apply for improvement grants and rights to consultation and provision of information are laid down. In addition to these rights for tenants the wider public is given rights to information concerning the rules and procedures on housing allocations and transfers; rights to information on consultation procedures and rights to check details which they have provided in making application for housing.

While it is an important development to clarify and back these areas by the law, the tenants' charter often does not require significant changes in local practice. In some localities where management practice has been less enlightened policy changes will be more significant. In certain respects the tenants' charter will change the way policy is carried out, but will not change the substance of policies. The local authority is still able to gain possession in a wide range of circumstances, although the process and justification for possession is changed. Other rights in the tenants' charter are circumscribed by the need to obtain permission or the council's concern over issues of overcrowding. The rights involved do not involve crucial areas of rents or mobility and transfer opportunities. Indeed in most of these cases developments occurring at the same time may highlight the lack of self determination and choice. The tenants' charter will not fundamentally alter the position of the council tenant and remedy problems of 'serfdom' associated with the tenure. Nor has central government been as concerned to monitor and scrutinize how these rights are enforced as it is over the Right to Buy.

Potential and Actual Constraints on Policy Change

The changes introduced by the Government of 1979-83 are important and strategic. The housing market is substantially different as a result — and will be even more noticeably so in ten years' time. In general, the Government has disproved the view that the constraints on a government are such that changes are more likely to be of rhetoric than of importance to individual households. Certain potential constraints have proved less significant than suggested by analyses which seek to explain why policy has so often been marked by continuity. Some of these potential and actual constraints on policy can be considered briefly:

The Actions of Previous Governments

The actions of previous governments could be expected to constrain policy change in two ways. Firstly successive governments have encouraged and preferred owner occupation and facilitated a major growth in recent years. Secondly, public expenditure on housing had been substantially cut before 1979. But a view which would regard these factors as constraints on further change clearly underestimates the political and ideological commitment to policy change. Perhaps more importantly, it assumes some 'housing' related constraints on policy. However, conventional views of the housing problem or of the consequences of reduced investment in housing have not proved constraints on policy. Changes in policy which have been calculated to leave considerable problems of housing shortage and disrepair are indicative of lack of consensus over the nature of housing problems or the best ways of tackling them. The Secretary of State in his evidence to the Environment Select Committee quite explicitly rejected planning and projection techniques.[32] The determinants of policy were what the country could afford but in any case it was desirable to reduce public intervention and encourage the private sector. Views that there is a needs or politically related level below which state provision cannot fall may not have been disproved. But the level of provision is considerably lower than suggested in analyses which presented the existing pattern of provision as necessary to maintenance of the political and economic system. The Secretary of State has variously described housing policy as a 'seamless robe'[33] and housing need as a 'moving target'.[34]

Parliamentary Processes

New legislation has been basic to the Government's housing strategy. With a substantial parliamentary majority it would not be expected that events within Parliament would seriously affect the Government. However the situation is slightly more complex. The progress of the Housing Bill in Standing Committee was an opportunity for filibuster and ritual conflict.[35] Forty-six sittings of this Committee produced only minimal changes. Only one opposition amendment was accepted by the Government and it was a minor drafting amendment. Discussions elsewhere had more effect. A number of amendments were introduced in the House of Lords and the most obvious concession made by the Government was the exclusion from the Right to Buy of accommodation designed or specially adapted for the elderly which it was the practice of the landlord to let to the elderly. The Government wanted the legislation to be passed before the summer recess, and shortage of time virtually obliged it to accept the amendment. In the Commons a dispute over business in the last few days before the recess was resolved through an agreement between the Secretary of State and his shadow Roy Hattersley, over the wording of an agreement. However, the amendments introduced in the House of Lords were significant, were opposed by the Government, led to a considerable dispute in the House of Commons, disruption of business and finally acceptance by the Government of the compromise amendment on the sale of elderly persons' dwellings. The Housing Act and the Right to Buy were amended in the parliamentary process and the lobbying of the local authority associations had some effect.[36] The lack of real political conflict over the subsidy system is best explained by its inclusion in Labour's 1979 Bill. In the case of housing benefits, the legislation was general and did not itself embody the most controversial details on rates of benefit. Other than over amendments to the Right to Buy, the major parliamentary conflict arose in connection with rent increases and the Housing and Building Control Bill 1983. This Bill, which fell with the general election, had been successfully amended as a result of a vigorous housing association lobby – leading to a House of Lords defeat of government proposals to introduce the Right to Buy throughout this part of the housing market.

Local Government

The most apparent obstacle to a substantial change in housing policy was the nature of political control and policies of many local authorities and attitudes towards local autonomy. For most non-metropolitan districts housing is the major local authority service and in many London boroughs and many provincial cities it is politically the most important policy area. Not only Labour controlled authorities regarded aspects of the Government's programme as damaging and objected to restrictions on their autonomy. The experience of the Housing Finance Act 1972 and local opposition to its implementation did not inhibit the Government. Nor did any principle of local autonomy or the fact that some local councils had been elected on the same day as the Government on a platform which included opposition to the sale of council houses. The Right to Buy in the Housing Act 1980 includes powers for the Secretary of

State to intervene, implement and charge for sales. It explicitly rejects any claims that local authorities should have discretion which could significantly limit sales. Although the local authority lobby had some impact on the Housing Act, their appeals in relation to expenditure and other issues had no impact: the Government's stance was to attach greater importance to the need to cut public expenditure and expand private ownership than to public investment or local autonomy. Although the Government has claimed to be concerned with autonomy and to be removing detailed controls and interventions its record on the major areas of rents, housing investment, sale of council houses and direct labour departments does not support the claim. In relation to the Right to Buy, monitoring, blacklisting and progress chasing were detailed and extensive and followed through with legal action. The dispute with Norwich City Council in this area led to litigation and the successful introduction of a representative to take over the council's responsibilities. Norwich's view that this was essentially a constitutional issue about the relationship between central and local government is at least a powerful one.

Interest and Pressure Groups

If the Government has largely disregarded opposition from local government it is not surprising that other interest and pressure groups have had little effect. In general, in the past, housing pressure groups have had little impact on housing policy. However, the Housing (Homeless Persons) Act 1977 and the operation of various committees including the Central Housing Advisory Committee can be quoted against this. In 1979/80 neither professional nor housing pressure groups had had significant impact.[37] The groups most affected by developments – council tenants and potential tenants – are not organized and arguably are divided by the nature of policy developments.

Economic Climate

The final factor potentially constraining policy development is the economic climate. In general, it may be assumed that a policy of expenditure cuts and privatization is consistent with general economic policy. Indeed, the strategy was dominated by consideration of what the country can afford. However, there are other aspects of this. Firstly, the implications of policy are to generally increase householders' expenditure on housing - most immediately among public sector tenants. Previous governments concerned with problems of inflation have in the past frozen rents in similar circumstances. Secondly, the savings in the policy package are not as great as is immediately apparent. Rising rents will reduce housing subsidy but increase income maintenance expenditures. Increasing owner occupation and more immediately high interest rates, implies substantial tax relief. While the Government did consider the position of tax relief on mortgage interest early in its term of office, it took no action. By the end of its term it was increasing tax relief. The disparity between levels of support for council tenants and owner occupiers increased consistently. While the country could not afford public investment, general subsidy to council housing or a 'no losers' introduction of housing benefits, it could afford a rising level of tax relief associated with housing. Thirdly, the appraisal of the financial or economic effects of housing policies has aroused considerable discussion. The financial appraisal of the effects of council house sales published by the Department of the Environment[38] came to substantially different conclusions from the internal document produced by the previous government. Both documents made substantial assumptions and can be shown to be misleading. Longer-term assessments of the implications of policy have not been constraints on policy. Beyond these elements, the broader economic climate has affected the capacity of both banks and building societies to lend for house purchase. As the scarcity of funds relaxed in 1982, increased private financing of council house sales had consequences for the level of capital receipts and for public expenditure which represented a 'windfall' gain not within the control of the Government. By 1983, a much more common theme in housing debate was the failure of owner occupation, problems of marginal owners, of under maintenance and of mortgage arrears. These problems are essential elements of owner occupation but are severely affected by economic recession.

But just as these 'problems' relate to issues beyond the housing service, so has the Government's perspective on housing moved beyond a bricks and mortar approach. The emphasis on the redistribution of wealth or on encouraging labour mobility has been greater than emphasis on homelessness, overcrowding or problems of house condition. In this sense, there has been a re-definition of the terms of the debate about housing. In essence, the Government is beginning to treat housing as a commodity best provided through the market and with little justification for state intervention. Housing is arguably the most likely case among the 'social services' for such treatment. How far such an approach will go and with what consequences remains to be seen.

Conclusions

The actions of the Conservative Government in 1979-83 were marked by the pursuit of a clear set of linked objectives: the expansion of owner occupation and reductions in direct public expenditure on housing. None of the potential limits or constraints on these policies have been effective. The Government has been willing to breach major areas of local autonomy and to ignore the conventional planning and forecasting assumptions rather than to compromise its primary goals. The early difficulties for the Government in achieving its aims involved the unwillingness of building societies to earmark funds for council house sales, but in its last two years of office economic circumstances changed this. Emerging concern about housing conditions were deflected by an increased housing improvement policy. This extension of policy as well as extensions to the Right to Buy coincided with the pre-election period but were consistent with the overall direction of policy to assist private owners.

By the time of the general election of 1983, housing had declined from a major to a minor capital programme; the council housing sector had declined in proportionate and absolute terms; council house sales had formed the largest element in the Government's privatization programme. Investment and subsidy had been slashed and rents dramatically increased. While social security, health and social service expenditure grew in real terms, there was more public debate on real and threatened cuts in these services than there was in housing, which had much more marked cuts in total expenditure. It may be argued that the most important issue is why housing proved so easy to cut; why issues of need and welfare were so easily bypassed; why pressure groups were so ineffective; why new and increased inequalities were so easily introduced. 'Technical' arguments may be advanced showing that it is easier to cut capital programmes or that demographic or economic (unemployment) factors lead expenditure in other policy areas more than in housing. It may also be argued that council housing had less public support than other areas of the welfare state. There are other factors which are at least equally worthy of reference. Cuts in housing investment do not have an immediate or easily identifiable impact on a particular group. There are time lags in when the reduction in housing supply will be felt and there are turnover and other processes affecting who experiences changes and when. In addition the development of a dual tenure system may have divided or confused political opposition to cuts in public expenditure and to privatization. What is apparent is that the single mindedness, thoroughness and consistency in housing policy has not involved a rigorous attempt to either channel resources where they are most needed or to apply consistent criteria of what the country can afford to such different areas as housing benefits, discounts on sales, improvement and repair grants, or tax reliefs. Nor has it involved any response to the Environment Committee's view that 'if a proper judgement is to be made as to how much the country can afford, it is important that careful consideration be given to the impact on employment levels and the social effects of a given level of expenditure and that there should be adequate public debate regarding the claims which housing has compared with other programme areas'.[39]

Notes and References

1. *Conservative Manifesto 1979*, Conservative Central Office, April 1979.
2. H.C. Deb., 967, cols. 79-80, 15 May 1979.
3. *Ibid.* col. 407.
4. See G. Bramley, P. Leather and A. Murie, *Housing strategies and investment programmes*, Working Paper 7, School for Advanced Urban Studies, University of Bristol, 1980.
5. P. Leather, Housing need and housing investment, *Housing Review*, November - December 1983, 202-204; P. Leather, Housing underspending - the problem of capital receipts, *Municipal Journal*, 7 October 1983.
6. P. Leather, Housing (dis?) investment programmes, *Policy and Politics*, II, (2) 1983, 215-229.
7. H.C. Deb., 28, cols. 386-7, 21 July 1982, (Sir George Young).
8. See the evidence given to the House of Commons Environment Committee published with First Report from the Environment Committee Session 1979-80, *Enquiry into implications of the government's expenditure plans 1980-81 to 1983-84 for the housing policies of the Department of the Environment*, HC 714, HMSO, 1980.
9. *Ibid.* 3, col. 2.
10. *Ibid.* 1, col. 2.
11. House of Commons, Third Report from the Environment Committee, Session 1980-84, DOE's *housing policies: enquiry into Government's expenditure plans 1981/82 to 1983/84 and the updating of the Committee's first report for the session 1979/80*, HMSO, 1981.
12. First Report from the Environment Committee, *op. cit.*, v.
13. *Ibid.*
14. M. O'Higgins, 'Rolling back the Welfare State: the rhetoric and reality of public expenditure and social policy under the Conservative Government' in C. Jones and J. Stevenson (Eds) *The Year Book of social policy in Britain 1982*, Routledge and Kegan Paul, 1983.
15. For fuller details see A. Murie, 'Housing: a thoroughly residual policy', in D. Bull and P. Wilding, *Thatcherism and the poor*, Child Poverty Action Group, 1983.
16. *The Government's expenditure plans*, Cmnd. 8789 II, HMSO, 1983, 34.
17. By December 1982 262,000 RTB completed sales at an average discount of £6,800 per dwelling (41%). H.C. Deb., col. 201, 9 May 1983.
18. For a discussion of the introduction of Housing Benefit see M. Hill, *Housing benefit implementation: from unified ideal to complex reality*, School for Advanced Urban Studies, 1983.
19. H.C. Deb., 31 March 1983 and 18 April 1983.
20. See CIPFA, *HRA statistics*, 1982-83 Estimates and 1983-84 Estimates.
21. DOE, *Housing and constructive statistics*, HMSO.
22. House of Commons, Environment Committee, Evidence given by the Building Societies Association, *Council house sales: minutes of evidence*, HC 535 - VI, 1979-80, HMSO, 1980.
23. Between 1980 and 1983 almost £1 million was spent on advertisements telling public sector tenants of the Right to Buy – in some cases along with other information. H.C. Deb., 11 May, 1982 col. 244.
24. R. Forrest and A. Murie, *An unreasonable Act? Central-local government conflict and the Housing Act 1980*, School for Advanced Urban Studies, University of Bristol, 1985.
25. Norwich City Council v. The Secretary of State for the Environment, Transcript of Judgement.
26. Under the Housing and Building Control Bill, 1983 which did not complete its passage through Parliament before the General Election.
27. See P. Leather, *Municipal Journal, op cit.*
28. Some early details are provided in the Third Report from the Environment Committee, *op cit.* A fuller account is in R. Forrest et al, *Low cost home ownership*, SHAC/SAUS, 1984.
29. *Ibid.*
30. *Ibid.* and See *Housing and constructive statistics*, HMSO.

31. See the evidence and discussion in House of Commons, First Report from the Environment Committee, Session 1981-82, *The private rented housing sector*, HC 40 and especially vol. 1 report, chapter 7. By January 1983 approval had been given to 38 bodies to carry out new building for rent for letting as assured tenancies. H.C. Deb., cols. 250-252, 21 January, 1983.

32. House of Commons, First Report from the Environment Committee 1979-80, *op cit.*, 6, passim.

33. *Ibid.* 5, col. 2.

34. Evidence presented in Third Report from the Environment Committee, *op cit.*, 48, col. 2.

35. M. Ferman, The tragicomedy of the Housing Bill, *New Statesman*, 21 November 1980.

36. D. McCulloch, How the AMA fought – and improved – the Housing Bill, *Municipal Review*, October 1980.

37. For example a report in the *Guardian*, 10 August 1983 (J. Carvel, Rented homes still caught in arrears) stated ... 'the housing pressure groups ... have assembled analyses of the housing problems with suggestions for more equitable subsidy systems and a re-invigoration of the rented housing programme. The crisis that they are facing is that no one in Government appears to be listening ... In the last administration ... the ministers responsible for housing policy, refused to discuss the wider issues of shortages and their impact on the poorest tier of society. The housing movement got little help from the Labour opposition ... The media also gave them short shrift ...'

38. Department of the Environment, *Appraisal of the financial effects of council house sales*, 1980.

39. First Report from the Environment Committee, *op cit.*

8

Health policy, 1979 to 1983: the Retreat from Ideology?

Rudolf Klein

The Conservative Government elected in 1979 took office committed to a clear ideological platform. The time had come, as its election manifesto had proclaimed,[1] to cut back the role of the state and to 'restore the balance of power in favour of the people'. The ideological rhetoric was that of self-help and self-reliance. What really mattered was not what the state did for the people, but what the people did for themselves. For the first time since 1945 Britain actually had a Government which took pride in stressing how little it could do, instead of emphasizing how much it would do. Economic crisis had created a minimalist political ideology in its own image, just as economic growth had created a maximalist political ideology in its own image. In this respect, at any rate, the Administration of Mrs Margaret Thatcher marked a sharp break not only with the preceding Labour Government but with all post-war Conservative Governments.

The big drums of ideological rhetoric were, however, somewhat muted when it came to the Conservative Government's specific manifesto commitments on health policy. These were conspicuously cautious. 'It is not our intention to reduce spending on the Health Service; indeed, we intend to make better use of what resources are available. So we will simplify and decentralize the service and cut back bureaucracy', the manifesto stated. Further more, it went on, 'when resources are so tightly stretched it is folly to turn good money away from the NHS and to discourage people from doing more for themselves. We shall therefore allow pay-beds to be provided where there is demand for them; end Labour's vendetta against the private health sector; and restore tax relief on employer-employee medical insurance schemes'. Lastly, it raised the possibility – no more – of examining the scope for 'NHS funding on the insurance principle' – once the Royal Commission on the Health Service had reported.

The ideological rhetoric of the manifesto section on health policy was, despite the studied vagueness of the actual commitments, consistent with the overall stance of the Thatcher Administration in its stress on cutting the role of central government, reducing bureaucracy, encouraging people to do more for themselves and promoting the private sector. So in this chapter we shall examine the extent to which ideological bias was reflected in the policies pursued. The NHS, as created in 1948, was very much a monument to faith in social equity and social engineering: its structure and ethos reflected confidence in the ability of the professionals and planners to distribute health care according to need rather than according to demand.[2] Its collectivist and paternalistic principles repudiated the philosophy of the economic market place expounded by the economists and political theorists from whom the ideological rhetoric of the Thatcher Administration was drawn.[3] The Conservative Government's policies towards the NHS thus represent a specially piquant case study of the relationship between the reality of politics and the rhetoric of ideology: the conflict between reality judgements and value judgements, in the terminology of Sir Geoffrey Vickers.[4]

The conflict, as this chapter will seek to demonstrate, was resolved by the victory of reality judgements although (as we shall also see) the retreat was camouflaged by a smoke screen of ideological rhetoric. At the end of its first term in office, the Conservative Government was congratulating itself on its success in sustaining the NHS rather than changing it. 'We have more than matched our pledge to maintain spending on the National Health Service and secure proper value for money. Even after allowing for price rises, the nation is spending substantially more on health, and getting even better health care', the 1983 election manifesto proclaimed.[5] The number of nurses and doctors working in the NHS had gone up; the capital spending programme had been increased. Resources would continue to be steered towards the most deprived parts of the country and client groups like the elderly, mentally ill and handicapped.

Not that the ideological rhetoric was entirely abandoned. The virtues of the private market, and of the forces of competition, were not neglected. 'We are asking health authorities to make the maximum possible savings by putting services like laundry, catering and hospital cleaning out to competitive tender', the manifesto stressed. Furthermore, 'we welcome the growth in private health insurance in recent years. This had both made more health care available, and lightened the load of the NHS, particularly for non-urgent operations. We shall continue to encourage this valuable supplement to state care. We shall promote closer partnership between the State and the private sectors in the exchange of facilities and of ideas in the interests of all patients'.

But perhaps the most significant aspect of the 1983 manifesto was what it did not say. It contained no mention whatsoever of the possibility – raised in 1979 – of re-examining the financial basis of health care provision in Britain. The Conservative Government had settled for a policy of incremental change at the margin, edging towards a mixed economy of health, but firmly anchored on the central and dominating role of the NHS.

From Expanding Budgets to Increasing Efficiency

> The economic situation has affected all parts of the Health Service, and the constant pre-occupation of all concerned with its administration has been how to use existing resources in staff, materials and equipment, accommodation and finance to the greatest advantage of the Service as a whole. This task must remain with the National Health Service until such time as either a greater share of the national resources can be allotted to it, or the success of preventive measures relieves the strain.

The above quotation aptly sums up the financial strategy of the 1979 to 1983 Conservative Government towards the NHS. It was a strategy which, increasingly over the four years, switched the emphasis from expanding budgets to squeezing more value for money out of the existing resources: a predictable and unsurprising policy given the combination of the country's disastrous economic performance during this period and the Government's own commitment to limiting the public sector borrowing requirement *and* reducing the tax burden. However, the quotation comes from the foreward of Iain Macleod, a Conservative Minister of Health, to the *1953* annual report of the Ministry of Health:[7] a warning against seeking to explain the explanation for the policies of the 1979 to 1983 Government entirely in either its special brand of ideology or in the particular circumstances of the period – as well as a reminder that both the problems and the solutions adopted in the NHS have tended to follow a cyclical path during its entire history.[7]

In fact, the claim of the 1983 Conservative manifesto to have 'more than matched our pledge to maintain spending on the National Health Service' is born out by the expenditure figures. Table 1, taken from evidence given to the Social Services Committee by the Department of Health and Social Security (DHSS), sets out these figures.[8] In contrast to recent Public Expenditure White Papers it provides not only the cash spending figures but also the inflation rates, thus allowing the 'growth in resources', or what used to be known as the growth in volume terms, to be calculated. Thus it can be seen that, taking the four years from 1979-80 to 1982-83, the resources devoted to the hospital and community services increased by 4.4%, while those devoted to the family practitioner services rose by 6.9%.

The figures in Table 1 underline the importance of what might be called the politics of cash limits. In theory, throughout this period the resources available to the NHS were supposed to be regulated by the cash limits system: i.e. the setting, at the beginning of the financial year, of cash limits with built-in assumptions about the rises in pay (which accounts for about 70% of the NHS's total budget) and prices. If pay or prices rose faster than expected, then it should have followed that the volume input of resources should have been reduced proportionately: indeed, this was

TABLE 1   Trends in Actual and Planned Expenditure on the Health Services, 1978-79 to 1985-86

	£ million cash, gross expenditure					
	1978-79	*1979-80*	*1980-81*	*1981-82*	*1982-83*	*1983-84*
Hospital and Community Health Services Current	4,421	5,333	6,886	7,631	8,201	8,708
Cash increase	—	20.6%	29.1%	10.8%	7.5%	6.2%
Inflation etc	—	20.5%	28.0%	8.1%	6.5%	5.0%
Growth in resources	—	0.1%	0.9%	2.5%	0.9%	1.1%
Efficiency savings	—	—	—	0.2%	0.5%	0.5%
Growth in services	—	0.1%	0.9%	2.7%	1.4%	1.6%
Family Practitioner Services current	1,434	1,684	2,114	2,440	2,845	2,913
Cash increase	—	17.4%	25.6%	15.4%	16.6%	2.4%
Inflation etc	—	17.0%	25.5%	13.1%	11.7%	5.1%
Change in resources	—	0.3%	0.1%	2.1%	4.4%	−2.6%
Centrally Financed Services Health Current	236	288	364	413	478	530
Cash increase	—	22.4%	26.3%	13.4%	15.7%	11.0%
Inflation etc	—	16.8%	20.0%	9.6%	7.3%	5.1%
Growth in resources	—	4.8%	5.2%	3.4%	7.9%	5.6%
NHS Capital	365	407	552	673	705	722
Cash increase	—	11.6%	35.6%	21.9%	4.7%	2.4%
Inflation etc	—	20.7%	25.7%	3.6%	2.6%	5.5%
Change in resources	—	−7.5%	7.8%	17.7%	2.1%	−2.9%

Source: Table 1 in Social Services Committee, Minutes of Evidence, Session 1982-83, *Public expenditure on the social services.*

precisely the Government's public posture in its attempt to engineer a deceleration of pay claims by the NHS's 1,000,000 employees.

In practice, of course, the process has proved to be far less automatic and far more complicated – and politicized – than the doctrine underlying cash limits would suggest. The initial cash limits for 1979-80 assumed a rise of 5.0% for pay and 8.0% for prices. In the outcome, the rises turned out to be 20.8% and 20.1% respectively. The initial cash limits for 1980-81 assumed a rise of 14.0% for both elements, and in the outcome they proved to be 31.1% and 18.9% respectively (largely because the Government had committed itself to implementing the Clegg pay award to nurses and midwives). In both cases, however, the Government largely – though not wholly – cushioned the impact of what would have been a savage cash limits squeeze by infusing extra money during the course of the financial year: £360 million in 1979-1980 alone. The result, in 1979-80, was that spending in volume terms was £160 million less than planned in the Public Expenditure of the out-going Labour Government,[9] while in the 1980-81 volume spending was £25 million less than planned in the Conservative's White Paper.[10]

In the subsequent two years, the picture changed somewhat. In 1981-82, the actual pay increases (7.0%) only slightly exceeded the cash limits figure (6.0%). And in 1982-83 – the year of the ancillary workers' strike – a cash limits provision of 4.7% turned into an actual pay increase of 5.7% which was met partly by an extra infusion of funds and partly out of the existing budgets of health authorities. In this case, then, cash limits were used – as intended – as a political weapon in the Government's battle with the public sector trade unions: to an extent, at least, the threat that breaking through the cash limits figures would put jobs in peril was carried out. However, the effect was mitigated by the fact that the price of goods bought by the NHS went up less fast than provided for – by 8.7% instead of 10.3% – so yielding a £30 million bonus to the health authorities.

Apart from the use of cash limits, inherited from the Labour Government, the Conservative Administration introduced a further innovation. This was the notion of 'efficiency savings': i.e. the idea that volume growth in the NHS should be self-financed out of increased efficiency. In 1981-82 these were expected to yield a growth in resources of 0.2%, as shown in Table 1, and in the following years the figure was raised to 0.5%. Conceptually, this posed an intriguing question. Conventionally, the relative price effect is calculated on the assumption that productivity in the public sector does not change, yet the whole notion of 'efficiency savings' assumes that productivity can be increased. So there would seem to be some case for re-examining the assumptions built into the calculations of the relative price effect. Practically, too, the notion of 'efficiency savings' posed some problems. How, in fact, could they be measured in a service like the NHS where it is easy enough to measure the inputs but extraordinarily difficult to measure the outputs since the main 'product' – i.e. the number of patients treated – is heterogenous in its composition and conditions?

The problem of discovering whether, and how, 'efficiency savings' had been made preoccupied the Social Services Committee of the House of Commons. But, so far at any rate, it has been unable to elicit a satisfactory answer from the DHSS. In its 1981 report it noted:[11]

> We are also worried about a basic ambiguity in the evidence currently used to assess efficiency. In the case of the acute services, the presumption is that a fall in costs (per case) is a sign of improved efficiency. In the case of the services for the chronically ill, the presumption is that a rise in costs is a sign of improved quality. There is no necessary contradiction here. But the contrast does indicate a need for caution. One way of increasing efficiency, in terms of shortening lengths of stay and cutting costs per case, might be to reduce quality: another way might be to transfer some of the costs to other services, such as the domiciliary services of the Personal Social Services.

In its 1982 report, the Social Services Committee[12] still remained sceptical. It concluded that 'There is some suspicion that "efficiency savings" are becoming a regular euphemism for "expenditure cuts". When assessing the overall effects of the Conservatives' expenditure policies towards the NHS (see below), it may therefore be as well to discount the contribution of 'efficiency savings' – all the more so since they beg the question of whether or not there may have been an underlying trend towards greater productivity in previous years, before the notion of 'efficiency savings' had been invented.

The figures in Table 1 also draw attention to a further problem in the NHS. This emerges from the contrast between the figures for the hospital and community services (which are cash limited) and those for the family practitioner services (which are not, since much of the demand – e.g. for prescriptions – is open ended). In fact, the picture is mixed. In two of the four years, the family practitioner services grew less in real resources than the hospital and community services; in the other two, they increased faster. However, the contrast does help to explain why the Conservative Administration – and the Treasury in particular – became increasingly interested in the issue of applying cash limits to family practitioner services: an intention which, though leaked in the press, was never carried out – presumably because it implies limiting the freedom of general practitioners, represented by that vociferous and aggressive lobby, the British Medical Association. Once again we find the techniques of public expenditure management being subordinated to political expediency, therefore.

Interpreting the overall impact of the Conservative Government's expenditure policies is not easy. In terms of inputs, the NHS clearly expanded under the Conservatives. For example, the number of hospital doctors in England rose from 37,000 in 1979 to 40,000 in 1982; over the same period, the number of nurses rose from 358,000 to 392,000 – although against this must be partly offset by a reduction in working hours.[13] In terms of activity too, the NHS expanded, with the number of in-patients treated rising by 2.0% a year and that of out-patients by 1.6%. What is impossible to assess, on the available evidence, is whether there was any loss or gain in terms of adequacy: i.e. the relationship between the services provided and need (howsoever defined) and the quality of the services themselves.

The conventional wisdom, enshrined in successive Public Expenditure White Papers, is that an annual increase of 0.7% is required simply to cope with the growing needs of an ageing population, while a further 0.5% is needed to cope with the consequences of technological change. Accepting these figures, and remaining agnostic about the 'efficiency savings', would suggest that the NHS marginally failed to keep up with the increasing demands during the first Conservative period in office. However, these notional percentage increases simply represent extrapolations of past trends: i.e. multiplying the costs of treating elderly people in the past. And since the policy of successive governments has been to *change* the way in which the elderly are treated – to move from expensive hospitalization to what is, hopefully, thought to be cheaper community care – this may not be an adequate measure of changing 'need' since it assumes unchanging patterns of care and treatment.

Taking a needs perspective – i.e. assuming that the NHS exists to provide those services deemed necessary and appropriate by the professional providers, notably doctors – would therefore suggest an agnostic conclusion about the performance of the NHS under the Conservatives. Taking a demand perspective – i.e. assuming that the NHS exists to respond to what consumers want – suggests a rather more severe verdict. This, however, is discussed further in the section of this chapter dealing with the private sector – see below – which examines how far the growth of demands in this sector can be used as a measure of the NHS's performance. The section which follows immediately addresses a somewhat different question: the relationship between the Government's expenditure policies and its policies for the administration of the NHS.

Towards Decentralization – and Back Again

> We are determined to see that as many decisions as possible are taken at the local level – in the hospital and in the community. We are determined to have more local health authorities, whose members will be encouraged to manage the Service, with the minimum of interference by any central authority, whether at region or in central government departments. We ask that our proposals should be judged by whether they achieve these aims ... [14]

It was in these terms that Mr Patrick Jenkin, Secretary of State for Social Services, set forth his plans for reorganizing the NHS in line with the manifesto commitment to 'decentralize the service and cut back bureaucracy'. The main feature of the proposals, as set out in *Patients First*, and subsequently translated into legislation, was the decision to cut out the middle tier in the NHS's hierarchy of administration: the 90 area health authorities. Instead primary responsibility 'for the planning, development and management of health services' would be devolved to district health authorities, which would 'be established for the smallest geographical areas within which it is possible to carry out the integrated planning, provision and development of primary care and other community health services, together with those services normally associated with a district general hospital', to quote the circular subsequently issued to explain the new structure of the NHS.[15] In the event, 192 DHAs were set up, most of whose populations are in the 200,000 to 500,000 range. Eliminating the area tier, it was further argued, would not only simplify the administrative structure. It would also make it possible to cut the costs of administration by 10%, and indeed the new authorities were required to reduce their spending on administration accordingly.

The reorganization of the NHS, which was carried into effect in 1982, may have been in line with the new Conservative ideology. It certainly represented a deliberate repudiation of the philosophy underlying the 1974 reorganization of the NHS carried out by the previous Conservative Government: a reorganization inspired by the desire to have a 'more systematic and comprehensive planning process' and to establish 'closer and more regular contact' between the DHSS and health authorities.[16]

But it would be a mistake to interpret the 1982 reorganization merely as a reflection of the new Conservative ideology. Rather, it represented a wider and more general shift in opinion: a reaction against the 'public philosophy' of the 'sixties and early 'seventies which equated efficiency with large size, and which was grounded in a strong faith in managerial techniques. It was this 'public philosophy' which had shaped not only the reorganization of the NHS but also that of local government. Indeed the 1982 reorganization reflected not so much Conservative ideology as a new consensus. The view that the structure of the NHS was too complex and required simplification was general and had, furthermore, been endorsed by the 1979 report of the Royal Commission on the NHS. [17]

The new 'public philosophy', as enshrined in the 1982 reorganization, rested on a belief in the virtues of localism: the intention was to transfer power to the periphery. That, at any rate, was the theme running through ministerial and departmental pronouncements. 'The thrust of our policy', Sir George Younger, Under-Secretary for Health and Social Security, told the Standing Committee considering the legislation, 'is to have decisions taken as near to the point of delivery of services as is possible'.[18] 'I remain firmly convinced that the National Health Service is a noble concept but we can make it work a great deal better', Mr Patrick Jenkin argued; 'First and foremost, I believe that we must see the NHS, not as a single organization, but as it is perceived by those who use it and those who work in it at the local level – as a series of local services run by local government, responsible to local needs and with a strong involvement from the local community'.[19]

The theme emerged fortissimo in the Government's document, *Care in Action*,[20] setting out its policies and priorities for the health services. In it, the Secretary of State addressed the chairmen and members of the new authorities:

> The handbook sets out the main policies and priorities which Ministers will look to you to follow in running the services for which you are responsible. We want to give you as much freedom as possible to decide how to pursue these policies and priorities in your own localities. Local initiatives, local decisions, and local responsibility are what we want to encourage. This is the main purpose of the current reorganization of the structure and management of the National Health Service. You have therefore a wider opportunity than your predecessors to plan and develop services in the light of *local* needs and circumstances.

Consistent with this emphasis on localism, *Care in Action* – in sharp contrast to the two previous DHSS documents on priorities published by the preceding Labour Government – did not set out its aims in terms of specific norms or targets, whether of levels of provision or financial allocations.[21] While the policies and the priorities themselves did not change – in so far as they were to favour the traditionally deprived groups, like the elderly and the mentally ill and handicapped – they now appeared to be purely hortatory. There were, in effect, no benchmarks against which to measure progress towards the achievement of the policies and priorities of the Government.

This new approach to the implementation of public policies had both conceptual and political logic. One of the characteristics of the NHS is precisely that it is possible to use different mixes of services and skills to achieve intended effects: there is largely scope for the substitution of different kinds of provision. To this extent, expressing priorities in terms of norms of input – so many day places per 1,000 elderly or so many acute beds per 1,000 population – risks reinforcing rigidity and preventing experiment. Given uncertainty about the precise relationship between inputs and outputs, there may be a case for a 'bottom-up' approach to policy making, i.e. giving the greatest possible scope to the service providers.[22]

Political logic further reinforces the argument for devolving responsibility. Expressing priorities in terms of desirable norms of provision assumes budgetary growth: i.e. it is based on the expectation that extra resources will become available and so make it possible to move towards a more generous level of service provision. It is therefore a strategy which reflects the optimism of the period of economic growth. In a period of pessimism and budgetary cut-backs, however, such a strategy simply means that governments are creating a rod for their own backs. To set norms which assume growth is to invite inevitable disillusion. No wonder, then, that *Care in Action* fell back on a vaguely incantatory strategy. If governments seek to centralize credit in good times – to claim responsibility for the dividends of growth – equally, they have every incentive to diffuse blame when times are bad: to this extent, localism is the natural language of a period of economic stagnation.

The 1982 reorganization should thus have introduced a new era of decentralization in the NHS. In fact, it marked the beginning of a new period of centralization. By the end of the first Thatcher Government, the language of localism had sunk to a *diminuendo*. Instead (uncannily echoing the rhetoric of the 1974 reorganization), the emphasis was all on more rigorous accountability to central government and better management. The transformation might appear both paradoxical and perverse, yet it springs from a basic tension within the NHS which has dogged all attempts to achieve a stable balance in centre-periphery relationships during its entire history: the fact that the NHS delivers *local services* but is a *nationally funded* organization. Given that the Secretary of State is accountable to

Parliament for the money spent by the NHS, how can this be squared with the devolution of responsibility to the periphery? The issues raised by this question – fundamental to the way in which the NHS is operated – can, perhaps, be best illustrated by the dialogue between the Secretary of State and Parliamentary committees during the period of the Conservative Administration: a period remarkable precisely because of the interest taken by House of Commons Committees in the NHS.

In a highly critical report in 1980, the Social Services Committee savaged the DHSS's inability to provide evidence about the impact of spending plans on services to patients in the NHS. Furthermore, it drew attention to the danger (as it saw it) that the Government's intention of devolving responsibility might undermine accountability to Parliament:

> We share the Department's anxiety to devolve managerial responsibility and to avoid collecting unnecessary information. But the NHS – unlike education or the personal social services – is a central government responsibility. We would greatly deplore any change which would limit the ability of individual MPs to ask questions or of Parliament collectively to inquire into the operations of the NHS.[23]

The Government's reply[24] to the Committee's report took up the challenge:

> As the Government have stressed in the Consultative Paper 'Patients First' it is at *local* level that patients' needs and the impact of policies are usually best assessed. The Government have accordingly made clear their determination to increase decentralization and strengthen local autonomy within the constraints of national economic policy. This was the health service policy on which the Conservative Party fought the last election and the Government intend to adhere to it. The Committee's view of Ministers' responsibility for detailed local decisions appears to be in direct conflict with this policy. Ministers will certainly answer for the major policy decisions of, for instance, a health authority, if questioned in the House or in correspondence. But they ought not be expected to agree with and to defend each and every decision of that authority. That would inevitably imply a level of intervention by Whitehall in local decisions which would be unacceptable and unbureaucratic.

The passage has been cited at length since it demonstrates so clearly both the DHSS's extreme sensitivity on this point and the collision of views. Interestingly, the Government's defence of its new policy rested on a curious misreading of the Committee's report. As the Committee pointed out the following year [25] it had criticized the DHSS's failure to inform itself – and therefore Parliament – about the overall performance of health authorities and the impact of national policies, and it had not been concerned about the willingness of the Secretary of State to defend 'each and every decision'.

The following year parliamentary pressure on the DHSS was reinforced by the prestigious Public Accounts Committee. In particular, the

Committee's 1981 report criticized the failure of the DHSS to plan manpower – the NHS's biggest input – or even to analyse the very different manning levels found in hospitals up and down the country. 'We are surprised that the DHSS disclaimed responsibility for making comparisons between regions in England, particularly as the regions find difficulty in making such comparisons themselves. We consider this reflects an absence of proper control', the Committee remarked. More generally, the Committee argued:

> ... DHSS have told us that they leave detailed monitoring of a number of aspects to the regions, for example on manpower comparisons, hospital food costs generally and the impact of developments ... We have indicated that we do not find this satisfactory. We accept that DHSS should not carry out detailed monitoring of all the proposed 190 district health authorities. But as the Department accept responsibility for moving in and putting things right at the regional level should things go wrong, they must clearly maintain an awareness of financial performance in the delivery of health care. The broad control of cash limits, the allocation of resources between regions related to objective measures of their needs, and annual discussion of strategic plans clearly have an important part to play, but there remains an essential need for DHSS to ensure ... the means to monitor key indicators of performance by the regions.[26]

Parliamentary pressure had its effects, if only by reinforcing internal pressures within the DHSS. By the time that the Public Accounts Committee looked at the NHS again, in 1982,[27] the DHSS was able to pre-empt criticism by announcing its plans for an annual review system. Each year the Secretary of State would review with each regional chairman and his officers the deployment of resources, the progress towards achieving plans, the standards and efficiency of the services provided and the progress being made towards increasing efficiency and productivity. In turn, each regional chairman would then conduct a similar review with all his district health authority chairmen and their officers. So a Government committed to less central control ended up by introducing machinery which, for the first time in the history of the NHS, provided for the systematic review of the performance of all health authorities and their progress towards the achievement of the DHSS's policies and priorities[28] – although it remains to be seen just how rigorous, and effective, the reviews will turn out to be in practice.

At the same time, the DHSS announced the development of what were called 'performance indicators' for use in the annual reviews. Again, the significance of this development lies less in the instrument chosen than in the evidence it provides of a department committed to a more active involvement in the affairs of the NHS. The performance indicators themselves consisted mainly of routinely collected statistics which had been available for decades:[29] for example average cost per in-patient case, average length of stay, throughput per bed, and so on. They could have been re-christened 'performance indicators' at any time, but it took the

changed atmosphere of the 'eighties – as well as parliamentary criticism –
to persuade the DHSS to use them as a tool of management. Indeed when
the first volume of performance indicators was published in 1983,[30] they
were prefaced by an apologetic introduction, stressing that 'substantial
development work is required to produce a more robust and
comprehensive set of PIs'. And as Sir Kenneth Stowe, the DHSS's
Permanent Secretary told the Public Accounts Committee:

> We have now got a range of indicators which we think will be a relevant base
> for enabling the regions to ask the districts and for us to ask the regions
> relevant questions about their performance. But the point that we want to
> stress is that they will not of themselves take you much beyond the stage of
> asking questions. They will be pointers rather than definitive judgements.[31]

The quotation underlines one of the central dilemmas of accountability in
a service like the NHS. Given the DHSS's inability to define with precision
the aims of health care policy – in terms of measurable outcomes – the
Department is inevitably driven to use statistics which raise rather than
answer questions. In short, there is no policy paradigm to give meaning to
the data.[32] In turn, this inability to assess *overall* performance inevitably
drives the Department into taking a closer interest in detail, for it is only at
the point of service delivery that the statistics can be given real
significance. If success or failure is to be assessed in terms of local
organizational processes – and, in an important sense, process is *the* output
of the NHS – then central government cannot for long detach itself from
what is happening at the periphery.

Again, as the four years went by, less and less was heard of
strengthening the responsiveness of health authorities to the local
community. In 1981 the DHSS told the Public Accounts Committee that it
was 'studying the possibility of districts having an informal accountability
towards the local community by publishing more information about their
performance for consideration by the Community Health Councils'. No
more was to be heard of this proposal, as the balance swung from localism
back to centralism. No more was heard, either, of the proposal – floated in
1979 in *Patients First* – of a review of the role of regional health authorities,
with the implication that this might be diminished. In the system as it had
evolved by 1983, the RHAs appeared to be playing a more important role
than ever, the crucial link in the chain of accountability and a central cog
in the review machinery.

Above all, the end of the first Thatcher Administration marked a return
to the emphasis on good management, as the key to stretching limited
resources, which had marked the 1974 reorganization. Back in fashion
were improved tools of management: thus the 1983 DHSS/NHS Audit
Working Group recommended the institutionalization of value for money
audit units in all health authorities.[33] And, most revolutionary of all, the
report of the NHS Management Inquiry team, led by Mr Roy Griffiths of

Sainsbury's – set up before the 1983 election, although it reported after it – recommended radical changes in the managerial style both of the NHS and of the DHSS itself.[34]

In 1979 *Patients First* explicitly rejected the proposition - first put forward in Kenneth Robinson's 1968 Green Paper – that each health authority should appoint a chief executive. Instead, it defended the principle of consensus management by a multi-disciplinary team. The Griffiths report, in contrast, embraced whole-hog the principle of chief executives or general managers at all levels in the NHS – and, for good measure, recommended the creation of a national NHS Management Board to be headed by a chairman who 'would initially almost certainly have to come from outside the NHS and the Civil Service'. Only by giving power and clear-cut responsibilities to managers, argued the Griffiths report, would the NHS be able to overcome what it diagnosed as the main weakness of the service: its 'institutionalized stagnation' – reflecting 'labyrinthine' processes of consultation and rights of veto by different interest groups – which inhibited change. Only so, furthermore, could management decisions be pushed down the line.

It remains to be seen to what extent the Griffiths recommendations – which have implications far beyond those discussed here – will be implemented. The importance of the report for the present discussion is, however, the clue it provides for explaining the drift back to centralization after 1979. If the desire to diffuse blame in hard times explains the initial appeal of a policy of decentralizing responsibility, it is the need for central government to force change through in a period of resource scarcity which helps to explain the move in the reverse direction.

For the 1979 to 1983 Conservative Government remained committed to policy aims – notably, as noted earlier, extra resources for deprived geographical parts of the country and client groups – which, when they were framed in the early or mid 'seventies – could be painlessly financed by a strategy of differential growth. Or so, at least, it was assumed. In times of low budgetary growth, however, changing the pattern of services inevitably meant attacking the garrison – of doctors, nurses and other NHS employees – defending the *status quo:* i.e. their jobs and the existing pattern of services. Thus, at one and the same time, change became more threatening (to the professional providers) and more necessary (to the policy makers). If the Government was not to abandon its policy aims, it was therefore forced to involve itself ever more in the NHS in order to push for the implementation of its policies.

Privatization: Strategy or Safety Valve

If one clear cut distinction can be drawn between the ideological bias in health care of the 1979 to 1983 Conservative Government, and that of the preceding Labour Administration, it is in the policy stance towards the private provision of health care. For the Labour Party, private practice is at best a necessary evil: something which may have to be tolerated in society at large (though Labour Party conferences tend to pass resolutions calling for its total abolition) but which has to be exorcised from the NHS itself. In the mid 'seventies, the Labour Government carried out precisely such a ceremony of exorcism which, however, ended in a compromise with the medical profession that provided only for the gradual elimination of pay beds in NHS hospitals under the supervision of a specially created Health Services Board.[35] In contrast, the new Conservative Government came to office explicitly committed in its manifesto – as already noted – to ending Labour's 'vendetta' against the private sector and indeed to encouraging its growth.

It is a commitment which the new Government actively pursued. The Health Services Board was axed by the 1980 Health Services Act; the policy of phasing out 'pay beds' from the NHS was abandoned. The power to control – i.e. to licence – new developments in the private sector was transferred from the Board to the new DHAs, although it was limited in its scope: while the Labour legislation had included in its scope all new private hospital developments with more than 75 beds (100 in London), the new legislation raised the limit to 120 – a limit which, in fact, has allowed most of the subsequent new developments to go unchallenged. Equally, while relaxing the restrictions on new developments, the Conservative Governments increased the incentives – if only marginally – to its growth. In the first place, the consultants were offered in 1979 a new contract which allowed all of them to engage in private practice. No longer was the right to earn private fees limited to those consultants who held part-time contracts, and so sacrificed a part of their NHS salary. Now all consultants could treat private patients, although full-timers were restricted to keeping their earnings from this source down to 10% of the NHS salary (although it is far from clear that this can be effectively enforced). In the second place, tax-relief was offered to employers who took out private health insurance for those of their employees earning less than £8,500 a year at a total cost, in terms of revenue foregone, of £6 million a year.

On the face of it, the Government's policy was remarkably successful. The number of people covered by private insurance schemes shot up from 2,765,000 to 3,577,000 between 1979 and 1980 alone, and has since topped the 4,000,000 mark.[36] The number of private hospitals also started to rise, with American commercial for-profit operators moving into a market which had hitherto been dominated by British non-profit organizations like the Nuffield Nursing Homes Trust. While in 1979 there had been only about 3,000 acute – mainly surgical – beds in the private sector, by the early 'eighties the number was rapidly nearing 4,000.[37] And although no up to date overall figures are available of total expenditure on private health care, it would seem reasonable to assume that the incentives given to consultants to encourage demands for their own services is likely to have increased the total size of the market.

But while the direction of Conservative policy is clear, as is its immediate impact, its ultimate destination is far from self-evident. Not all the growth in the private sector can, in any event, be attributed to Conservative policies: the rise in the number of people covered by private insurance policies had started, ironically enough, under the Labour Government – whose battle with the medical profession gave greater visibility to private practice and thus, perversely, stimulated its expansion. For example, the phasing out of NHS 'pay beds' gave a direct stimulus to the building of private hospitals who were assured of customers displaced from NHS facilities. Moreover, there is some evidence that the boom in private medicine may be self-limiting to the extent that costs of insurance go up as more people (with greater health risks) are recruited into insurance schemes. Certainly it seems to have slowed down by 1982.[38] And after its initial tax concession to private insurance schemes, the Conservative Government showed no disposition to repeat or enlarge on its first, generous gesture. Indeed, given the central role of the PSBR in Conservative economic strategy, tax spending on health care is in direct competition with public expenditure on the NHS – and, significantly, perhaps, successive Secretaries of State at the DHSS have appeared to have given primacy to the claims of the national service.   So perhaps the most significant aspect of the private sector of health care, after four years of Conservative Government, is that it remains extremely small. Total private spending care still accounts for less than five per cent of the national expenditure on health care. It is precisely the small starting base of the private sector which explains its dramatic growth – and the fact that this growth has done so little to change the general landscape of health care provision in Britain. This conclusion holds, even if account is taken of the 30,000 or so beds in private nursing homes in addition to the 4,000 beds in private acute hospitals noted above.

The case of nursing homes has special interest because of the example it provides of inadvertent or unintentional policy creep: the Government, in effect, subsidized the private nursing home industry (as well as private residential homes) through the Supplementary Benefits budget.[39] Potentially these cross–sector payments within the DHSS budget, switching resources from social security to health, could significantly encourage the growth of private provision. However, there is no evidence that this represents a deliberate or explicit policy decision, as distinct from an accidental side-effect of social security programmes framed with totally different purposes in mind.

Overall, the Government's policies towards the private sector can perhaps be best interpreted not so much as a move towards trying to establish a new pattern or system of health care – with the NHS becoming a second-class service for those who cannot afford to pay for themselves, either directly or through insurance – but as a political strategy for defusing discontent in a period of resource scarcity. The private sector offers an opportunity for exit to those consumers who might otherwise exert voice within the NHS.[40] In short, it acts as a political safety valve – easing the pressures for more spending on the NHS. Even in good times, the NHS rations health care – as previously noted – according to need as defined by the professional providers, as distinct from meeting the demands of consumers. In other words, there is always bound to be a gap between needs as defined by professionals and demands as articulated by consumers – which is then accentuated, though it is not created, by hard times. The private sector, in contrast, exists to meet consumer demands. It therefore provides those services which rate high on the demand scale of consumers and low on the need scale of the professional providers: notably, those elective operations – for varicose veins, hernias or hip replacements – which may impose considerable social or economic costs on the patient but which are not seen as being in any sense life or health threatening. If the private sector did not exist, it would therefore be more difficult for governments – of whatever political persuasion – to put resources into those parts of the service which provide for medically defined needs as distinct from responding to consumer demands (and to achieve the policy aim of giving priority to vulnerable groups – like the elderly, the mentally ill and handicapped – who combine lack of financial with lack of political resources).

To an extent, therefore, it is as much political expediency as political ideology which helps to explain Conservative policy towards the private sector of health care. The same is true of the Conservative Government's enthusiasm for the privatization of the NHS's 'hotel' services: the insistence that health authorities should put catering, laundry and cleaning services out to tender (an insistence which, once again, runs counter to the original aim of leaving decision making to local health authorities). Here, of course, the policies of the DHSS simply echo those of the Government as a whole rather than reflecting any particular stance in health policy as such. Clearly, these policies do express an ideological bias: they are grounded in a faith in the ability of the competitive private market to deliver 'efficiency'. But they can also be seen as an attempt – reflecting less ideology than sheer desperation – to overcome the rigidities of the NHS and the difficulties of getting change in a highly unionized, segmented organization. From this perspective, the privatization policy can be seen as an explosive charge designed to shake up the organization: as part of the general strategy, discussed in the previous section, of thrusting a new management style on the NHS in the endeavour to achieve more 'value for money'.

Conclusion: the Reality Judgement

In an interim assessment of Conservative policy, written half way through the Government's first term of office, I concluded: 'If hypocrisy is the tribute vice pays to virtue, symbolic action is the tribute political necessity pays to party ideology'.[41] It is a conclusion which needs some modification but which still applies when trying to draw up a balance sheet of the Government's health policy record between 1979 and 1983. The ideological bias of the Conservative party was indeed mirrored in its health care policies. Many of these were, however, largely symbolic in their effect, if not in their intent: for example, the repudiation of the previous Labour Government's stance on 'pay beds' in the NHS had little practical impact but obvious ideological reverberations. And of those ideologically inspired policies which were more than symbolic, most were marginal and minor in character: they were carried into effect precisely because they did not affect the structure of the NHS. For instance, the tax concessions for private insurance schemes might well be put into this category. Lastly, as we have shown, the Government actually performed an ideological somersault when it came to organizational politics: far from power being diffused to the periphery, it was concentrated at the centre and the invocation of localism was replaced by the celebration of managerialism.

The implicit reality judgements which shaped this approach reflect the political, economic and organizational inhibitions on the free exercise of ideological bias in the health care policy arena. First, the NHS is extremely popular. Survey data consistently shows a high degree of public support for the NHS – next to the monarchy, it is probably Britain's most favoured institution – and hostility to spending cuts.[42] Second, and reinforcing the risks involved in challenging the existing health care system, the NHS is Britain's largest employer. Its 1,000,000 employees are, furthermore, highly unionized. Once again, therefore, there is a strong constituency for the *status quo*; as argued earlier.

The irony in all this is that, the organizational inertia of the NHS forces governments into an active stance even if they wish to pursue a more *laisser faire* policy. Not only does society generate new demands on the NHS, notably when the population is ageing. But the NHS itself is an institution for generating new demands: health care professionals are a permanent lobby pressing for more resources to allow them to do more things for more people. If a Government is either denied (or denies itself, because of its own ideology of economic management) the opportunity of meeting these demands by expanding the budget of the NHS, it must inevitably adopt a more interventionist stance if it is to try to squeeze more output out of the available inputs. As in the case of local government, therefore, the Conservative Administration's concern with trying to contain public expenditure has therefore lead it into a reversal of policies in the NHS, contradicting its original ideological position.

References

1. *The Conservative Manifesto, 1979*, Conservative Central Office, 1979.
2. Rudolf Klein, *The Politics of the NHS*, Longmans, 1983.
3. Nick Bosanquet, Sir Keith's reading list, *Political Quarterly*, 52 (3), July/September 1981.
4. Sir Geoffrey Vickers, *The art of judgement*, Chapman and Hall, 1965.
5. *The Conservative Manifesto, 1983*, Conservative Central Office, 1983.
6. Ministry of Health, *Report for the year ended 31st December 1952*, Cmnd. 8933, HMSO, 1983.
7. Rudolf Klein, *op. cit.*
8. Social Services Committee, Session 1982-83, *Public expenditure on the social services: minutes of evidence*, HC 321, HMSO, 1983.
9. Social Services Committee, Third Report, Session 1979-80, *The Government's White Paper on public expenditure: the social services*, HC 702, HMSO, 1980.
10. Social Services Committee, Third Report, Session 1980-81, *Public expenditure on the social services*, HC 324, HMSO, 1981.
11. *Ibid.* para. 40.
12. Social Services Committee, Second Report, Session 1981-82, *1982 White Paper: Public expenditure on the social services*, HC 306, HMSO, 1982.
13. Chancellor of the Exchequer, *The Government's expenditure plans*, Vol. 2, Cmnd. 8789, HMSO, 1983, Table 2.11.4.
14. Department of Health and Social Security, *Patients first*, HMSO, 1979.
15. *Health service development: structure and management*, Health Circular HC (80) 8, DHSS, July 1980.
16. Secretary of State for Social Services, *National health service reorganization: England*, Cmnd. 5055, HMSO, 1979.
17. Royal Commission on the National Health Service (Chairman: Sir Alec Merrison), *Report*, Cmnd. 7615, HMSO, 1979.
18. Parl. Deb., Standing Committee G: Health Services Bill, First Sitting, col. 46, Thursday 7 February 1980.
19. Patrick Jenkin, Speech at the Annual General Meeting of the National Association of Health Authorities, 27 June 1980.
20. Department of Health and Social Security, *Care in Action*, HMSO, 1981.
21. Rudolf Klein, The strategy behind the Jenkin non-strategy, *British Medical Journal*, 28 March 1981, 1089-1091.
22. David Hunter, Centre-periphery relations in the National Health Service in Ken Young (ed.), *National interests and local government*, Heinemann, 1983.
23. Social Services Committee, 1980, *op. cit.*, para. 25.
24. Department of Health and Social Security, *Reply by the Government to the Third Report from the Social Services Committee*, Session 1979-80, Cmnd. 8086, HMSO, 1980.
25. Social Services Committee, 1981, *op. cit.*, para. 48.
26. Committee of Public Accounts, Seventeenth Report, Session 1980-81, *Financial control and accountability in the national health service*, HC 255, HMSO, 1981, para 55.
27. Committee of Public Accounts, Seventeenth Report, Session 1980-81, *Financial control and accountability in the national health service*, HC 375, HMSO, 1982.
28. David E. Allen, Annual reviews or no annual reviews: the balance of power between the DHSS and health authorities, *British Medical Journal*, 28 August 1982, 665-667.
29. Rudolf Klein, Performance evaluation of the NHS, *Public Administration*, 60, (4), Winter 1982.
30. Department of Health and Social Security, *Performance indicators: national summary for 1981*, DHSS, 1983.
31. Committee of Public Accounts, 1981, *op. cit.*, Q.1634.
32. Aaron Wildavsky and Ellen Tenenbaum, *The politics of mistrust*, Beverley Hills: Sage, 1981.

33. Department of Health and Social Security, *Report of the DHSS/NHS Audit working group* (Chairman: Patrick Salmon), DHSS, 1983.
34. Department of Health and Social Security, *NHS Management Inquiry Report* (Chairman: Roy Griffiths), DHSS, 1983; Patricia Day and Rudolf Klein, The utilization of consent versus the management of conflict: decoding the Griffiths report, *British Medical Journal*, 10 December 1983.
35. Rudolf Klein, Ideology, class and the national health service, *Journal of Health Politics, Policy and Law*, 4 (3), Fall 1979.
36. *Provident scheme statistics*, Provident Associations, 1983.
37. Alan Maynard, 'The private health care sector in Britain' in Gordon McLachlan and Alan Maynard (eds.), *The public/private mix for health*, The Nuffield Provincial Hospitals Trust, 1982.
38. Derek Damerrall of the British United Provident Association, *The Times*, February 1982, quoted in Maynard, *op. cit.*, 142.
39. Linda Challis, Patricia Day and Rudolf Klein, Residential care on demand, *New Society*, 5 April 1984.
40. Rudolf Klein, Models of man and models of policy: reflections on exit, voice and loyalty, *Milbank Memorial Fund Quarterly*, 58 (3), Summer 1980.
41. Rudolf Klein, 'Health Services' in P.M. Jackson (ed.) *Government policy initiatives 1979-1980*, Royal Institute of Public Administration, 1981.
42. See, for example, the MORI poll, *Sunday Times*, 13 November 1983.

9

Monitoring Policy Initiatives: The Personal Social Services 1979-83

Adrian Webb and Gerald Wistow

Issues and hypotheses

Four years ago[1] we proposed two hypotheses to be tested during the life of the Conservative Government which came to office in 1979. The first was that attitudes towards the role of the state and public expenditure were so dominant as virtually to preclude the development of specific policies for the state sector of the Personal Social Services (PSS) – or even the active maintenance of the policy inheritance. The second was that the minimalist approach taken to the role of government would inhibit the implementation of any policies which did emerge. While the government was self consciously radical, our underlying argument was that, in the PSS, there was a lack of precision and of detailed thought about policies – and not a few contradictions. The present task is to re-examine these impressions and predictions in the light of events up to the end of the first Thatcher Administration in June 1983.

Our starting point must be the Administration's inheritance. The PSS had emerged from obscurity only in the late 'sixties and early 'seventies. One sign of this emergence was a rash of policies, programmes and legislative developments in respect of particular client groups: the elderly, the mentally handicapped, mentally ill, chronically sick and disabled, families and children, the homeless. No client group was totally ignored and for most the advances in thinking or in specified objectives and targets were considerable. The other sign was that budgetary famine was replaced by an historically rapid rate of growth. However, this growth was sharply reduced – but not excised – in the retrenchment of the mid-seventies. A minimum of 2% real growth per annum was seen as essential, even in straightened circumstances, for two reasons.[2] The first was the scale of unmet and growing need among these client groups and the consequent political and administrative problems of bringing the short-lived and long-awaited period of growth to a premature end. The most vulnerable members of society were seen to need protection. The second was that the equally long-expressed desire to transfer 'long-stay' patients (e.g. the mentally handicapped, mentally ill and elderly) from the NHS to the PSS depended on additions to local authority services. The assumption was, and largely remains, that community based care would be more acceptable and less expensive than hospital care.[3]

Apart from policies towards particular client groups, therefore, there was an overarching objective of shifting the centre of gravity of care for socially dependent people from the NHS to the PSS – from a central government service to local government services. To this was added, in the late 'seventies, a drive to strengthen the role of the family and neighbourhood as a source of informal care and a growing interest and belief in the work of voluntary organizations – which had long been valued in practice but virtually disregarded in principle.[4]

It was against this background that we developed our hypotheses and subsequently refined and modified them.[5] Our starting point was a particular view of policy. The 'sixties and 'seventies had been characterized by a real, though often frustrated, attempt to produce a coherent and integrated approach to PSS. Stated objectives and the flow of resources did not always correspond in the short term, but the chosen mechanism for coordinating them in the long term was that of forward planning. The remit of the DHSS allowed it to foster planning systems which reflected the desire to transfer demand from the NHS to the PSS. The inheritance, therefore, made it possible to speak of policy as if it were an unproblematic and coherent whole. By way of contrast, we suggested that it is more generally appropriate to think not of a body of coherent policies, but of distinct streams of policy relating to: service objectives; resources and the role of the state and the style of government. Such streams of policy are not inherently complementary, especially if they arise from different divisions or departments of government and if they are based upon different ideologies or value systems. Compared with the previous struggle to create some coherence between them, the first year of the new Tory Government suggested that major contradictions were beginning to appear between these policy streams.

A determination to constrain public expenditure and to effect a decisive shift away from reliance on state services was clearly underlined, in 1979 and 1980, not only by the Cabinet but also by the then Secretary of State for Social Services – Patrick Jenkin.[6] Even if one accepted the Government's premises and objectives, problems arose. First, while achieving long-term cost effectiveness across health and social services depended upon a development of local authority services, expenditure constraint implied squeezing these services particularly fiercely because other areas of DHSS expenditure had been the subject of election promises and safeguards (the NHS) or were extremely difficult to control in the short run (Social Security). Second, the minimalist philosophy of government made it difficult actively to implement a shift in gravity away from the state towards family and neighbourhood care, voluntary organizations, and private provision. Even the latter might not develop readily without some governmental action.

To think in terms of contradictions, however, is to retain the mental set of the earlier period. If the real objective was to move away from state social service provision, would not a sharp squeeze on expenditure – combined with an emphasis on the social obligations of family life and self care – be a coherent policy? We certainly suggested that it might.[7] However, such a strategy would mean abandoning any idea of government protection for the most vulnerable members of society and questioning the role of community care as a route to cost effectiveness in the health services. If DHSS sought to retain these well developed policy stances, therefore, the contradictions would presumably remain – and might emerge as overt conflicts.

Several areas of policy will be examined in turn as a means of exploring the issues raised. The first, and most fundamental, is that of public expenditure trends and their implications. The second is that of specific policies towards client groups. The third concerns the relationship between the health and personal social services, and the fourth is that of the projected move towards alternatives to state provision.

Expenditure Policies: Trends in Inputs and Outputs

The internal politics of the DHSS determined the detail of expenditure policy in 1979 and 1980; the politics of central-local relations and the overall pressure on local government expenditure became the dominant factor thereafter. Let us consider the early period first. Expenditure on the PSS was earmarked for 'cuts' in June 1979 and again in November. Indeed, the White Paper of November 1979 sought to impose a cut in the PSS which exceeded that applied to local government generally. Such a marked break with the recent past practice of favouring the PSS apparently arose from the difficulties which DHSS experienced in taking its 'share' of cuts. The PSS suffered on paper to the short-term benefit of health and social security. That it was essentially a paper exercise arose from the fact that local authorities generally continued with their own past practice of supporting the PSS. Actual expenditure in 1979-80 proved to be 1.4% higher than that allowed for by the previous Labour Government and local authority plans implied a continued willingness to maintain a modest rate of growth.[8]

The ability of local government to circumvent centrally planned restraint had been vital to the PSS from the late 'seventies onwards. Not least, it was vital to the success of Joint Finance. Joint Finance was introduced in 1976 as a means of supporting developments in community services from NHS monies – providing such developments brought clear benefit to the NHS. Joint finance is, in principle, a trenchant statement of belief in the cost effectiveness of community care. In practice its contribution to cost effectiveness depends on how productively the monies are used. As local authorities have, eventually, to pick up the cost of long-term projects primed through Joint Finance, tight budgeting in local government would tend to favour short-term or one-off spending and the selection of projects high on the list of PSS priorities. Conversely, room for growth would favour the adoption of projects with longer-term financial implications, and the productive use of Joint Finance necessitates a fair proportion of such long-term projects.

In some areas, local authorities may have supported PSS growth because they were being led by the nose by Joint Finance rather than because they freely chose this order of priorities. But whatever the motives and causes, the ability of local government during the 'seventies to protect growth in the PSS made it more likely that Joint Finance would be used effectively. It is, however, an ability which has been steadily undercut by government policies.

The fundamental limitations of examining government expenditure plans are well illustrated by the example of Joint Finance. Expenditure plans reveal little or nothing about outputs. Consequently, the whole discussion of 'cuts', we have argued, has been basically unsound and unhelpful.[9] The older practice of producing figures in 'constant price' terms merely concealed the effects of actual, as opposed to estimated, levels of inflation. The current practice of producing figures in cash terms reveals nothing at all about trends in outputs; its only merit is that it does not imply such trends. But nature abhors a political vacuum as much as any other and claims and counter-claims about the reality and consequences of cuts have flooded in to fill the gaps in our understanding.[10]

Given the central role of public expenditure trends, it is essential to by-pass the rhetoric and to establish an authoritative answer to the question: have there been cuts? The answer in terms of expenditure inputs is that government plans have involved cuts relative to the previous Labour Government's plans for the early 'eighties. Nevertheless, the period 1979-1984, taken as a whole, has been one of apparently real growth: 1983/84 local authority budgets for the PSS showed an increase of 12.5% in constant price terms compared with 1978/79.[11] If a radical shift away from the state was intended and was to be effected through cuts in state expenditure, it seems not to have been implemented.

If a cut is defined differently, however, the picture is completely changed. We have argued that a cut, in service terms, is any reduction below a constant level of service output.[12] This means allowing fully for changes in need and for the actual costs of producing services of a given quality. The problem is that of measuring outputs. Two proxies are available. The first is the well established DHSS assumption that real growth of 2% is needed in the PSS merely to cope with increasing needs. The second is trends in the levels of services made available to clients. Neither are satisfactory, but both are better than nothing.

The 2% real growth commitment was first made in the mid-seventies and it is not clear how far it takes into account the impact of, for example, mass unemployment on families and the handicapped. Nevertheless, an unequivocal message emerges if expenditure trends are measured against this benchmark. Growth exceeded this minimal level throughout the second half of the 'seventies and into the early 'eighties, with the exception of two years: 1977/8 and 1981/2. But while this is true of the nation as a whole, local experience varied greatly. In 1978/9 some 27% of local authorities in England and Wales failed to achieve 2% growth in PSS expenditure; by 1981/2 the figure had climbed to 67%.[13] This was, in fact, the first (and only) year in which current spending on the PSS fell in real terms. The issue for the future must be whether controls on 'high spending' authorities (whose expenditure has helped sustain the national aggregate total) will lead to a repetition of the 1981/82 experience.

Trends in some specific services tell the same story. For example, small reductions in *absolute* levels of provision have occurred in certain services for the elderly in some years. However, reductions *relative to need* (as measured by changes in the elderly population) have affected all services for the elderly except day care and they have progressively deepened since the mid-seventies.[14] The implication seems to be clear: service provision for the elderly was declining even while growth in expenditure inputs was relatively high. Growth has since been cut back very firmly and local government's ability to protect the PSS is being further reduced. The real squeeze on state services has, therefore, been much harsher than would at first appear.

The output consequences of pressure on inputs is actually less than certain in terms of detail. For example, the divergence between input trends and outputs in services for the elderly have been the product of several factors. Local priorities have certainly been important and, to an extent, the elderly have been 'sacrificed' in order to support other client groups – notably the mentally handicapped. In addition, we have already indicated that need is almost certainly rising faster than is officially assumed. Our own analysis also suggests that rising unit costs have been crucial in the past and may continue to be so even in the face of lower inflation rates, since it is the actual inflation faced by social services departments which matters. These forces are not immutable and the elderly may fare better in the future, but the basic issue cannot be avoided: even steady expenditure growth seems to have been insufficient to meet all forms of officially recognized need in the past, and even the minimum 2% growth has been achieved by decreasing numbers of authorities.

There is, however, little evidence that the Government actively sought to obtain real and long-term cuts specifically in the PSS between 1979 and

1984. The pressure was the more general one to reduce local government expenditure as a whole to offset increases in central government expenditure. Implementing that policy has been less than straightforward. On the other hand, we have shown that cuts in service outputs have been real and may well have been severe. The availability of public services to clients, most noticeably to the elderly and the physically handicapped, has been declining steadily as a result of pressure on resources. These cuts have almost certainly contributed to a transfer of demand away from state provision. In some localities, for example, social workers actively seek to place old people in private homes because of the long waiting lists for places in local authority homes; in other localities there is virtually no need for local authority homes because private provision has grown so rapidly. More generally, some hitherto unmet needs may have been provided for through voluntary organizations and some may have been absorbed by families – though many families caring for dependents must themselves figure strongly in any calculus of unmet need.[15]

Downward trends in service outputs may, therefore, have contributed significantly to the shift in the centre of gravity away from the state. However, if this is the case, our analysis suggests that the previous Labour Government helped to create the preconditions. It was during the late 'seventies that rapidly rising unit costs began to undermine service outputs and the squeeze on inputs was at times as great as during the subsequent period of Conservative Government.

Specific Policies

Given the expenditure background, our suggestion that this would be a government of little or no progress in client group policies seems to have been a safe bet. In fact, we may go further and look for a withdrawing from inherited commitments. In practice, of course, the latter could prove to be politically embarrassing – and it has been totally unnecessary. The DHSS has always expressed a strong belief in the desirability of local autonomy in establishing priorities and implementing policies; the policy role of the centre is that of establishing a framework of broad objectives. The problem of matching ambitious goals to shrinking resources is thus decentralized. The danger is not that central government will withdraw from policy commitments, but that it will fail to recognize or admit that they have become redundant by becoming unattainable.

The general paucity of white papers and circulars during the early 'eighties seems to support our hypothesis – as well as to remind us of the declared objective of cutting down on the level of central intervention. On closer inspection the picture is slightly more complicated. In the case of the elderly, for example, the Government inherited a consultation process on the whole policy approach. The questions and issues were posed in *A Happier Old Age*, published in 1978.[16] The response was presented in a

White Paper entitled *Growing Older*, published in 1981.[17] Comment is almost superfluous when such titles are juxtaposed. The White Paper contains no targets, no hostages to fortune. Faced by well documented need, it confirms the emphasis to be placed on informal care:

> Significant numbers of elderly people have no immediate family; and of those who do, some live far away. In such circumstances they should be able to look for support to friends, neighbours and the wider community. Informal help of this kind is already available. Regular callers such as milkmen and postmen keep an eye on elderly people, especially those living alone ... [18]

Despite the availability claimed for informal help, the evidence of loneliness and isolation suggests that there is a need for a sharply focused review of the problem – if not a policy. The White Paper simply provides an appendix containing the names of helpful voluntary organizations. A minimalist view of the role of the state and a lack of room for manoeuvre in the face of resource scarcity duly produced a white paper largely innocent of policy. However, while the previous Labour Government might have increased expenditure if returned to power in 1979, we have indicated that room for manoeuvre has been lacking for some years. The record contains considerable evidence of continuity as well as change. Ideology may have decreed difference, but resource trends have decreed a considerable degree of similarity.

Policies in relation to other client groups suggest that our hypothesis needs to be modified, but not abandoned. The political and economic environment has constrained the overall levels of development, but it has also shaped the pattern of initiatives. Comparatively inexpensive changes have fared best. In the case of child care and mental health, for example, clients' rights and the legal framework have attracted attention. The Mental Health Act 1973 was the culmination of a long period of debate concerning the protection of patients; parental access to children in care has raised analogous issues. Other changes in these fields – such as the appointment of designated social workers under the 1983 Act, or the investment in Intermediate Treatment as an alternative to institutional regimes for young offenders – have attracted limited additional expenditures. In the latter case modest sums have been channelled into the voluntary sector rather than local authorities.

Some specific policies have found favour precisely because they are seen to imply greater cost effectiveness in the use of public money. A case in point is the advocacy of adoption and fostering as alternatives to residential child care, on which the Audit Commission has recently focused attention.[19] Other fields in which the development of services and long-term cost effectiveness could possibly go hand-in-hand have changed less rapidly because of the need for pump-priming investment. For example, the review of services for the mentally handicapped in England[20] did not advocate the radical shift towards 'normalization' which eventually emerged across the border in the All Wales Strategy.[21] We consider in the next section the more limited initiative which has taken shape in England.

A Shift in the Centre of Gravity: From NHS to PSS

The clearest exception to our thesis that there have been no service policies was embodied in *Care in the Community*.[22] Issued as a consultative document in 1981, it outlined ways in which Joint Finance might be both developed and complemented as a means of extending care in the community. By the end of the 1970s Joint Finance had settled into a recognizable role: it seemed to contribute to keeping people out of hospitals but not to getting long-stay patients out of them and into the community.[23] The new proposals centred around methods of transferring resources permanently, or on a long-term basis, from the NHS to the PSS. The resources would come from savings achieved by closing long-stay wards, or whole hospitals. The basic issue had been jointly identified by local authorities and the DHSS. The outstanding questions were: how best to make such transfers; what changes in regulations and legislation were required to permit such developments, and how might Joint Finance contribute to the new objectives?

Although the proposals seemed to go dead for a while and a loss of political support was feared when ministers were shuffled, the consultations ultimately bore fruit. A substantial extension was conceded in the time period under which Joint Finance could be made available to local authorities, but only in respect of expenditures which permitted patient transfers to be effected. Health authorities were also permitted to make grants from their main budgets and without time limit, in respect of such expenditures.[24] Thus there does seem to have been a steady stream of ministerial support for the rehabilitation of hospitalized mentally handicapped people in particular and for the general objective of shifting the boundaries of social care. It is one of those issues which appears to have thrived at the junior minister level and to have bobbed to the surface despite the undertow of expenditure constraint. But has it?

As we have indicated, the productivity of Joint Finance depends crucially on the budgetary context of local government; resource transfers are similarly dependent – but they also rely upon the willingness and capacity of the NHS to create specific savings in the first place. Local authorities have few incentives for fulfilling their part of the bargain: an increasing orientation towards meeting the needs of the NHS exposes them to accusations of neglecting community based need. The NHS has few incentives to close wards or hospitals unless the savings to be made are sufficient to permit some resource transfer and some 'profit'. Health authorities also face the disincentives of staff and union concern at closures. They do close facilities, they have no real incentive to transfer the savings to local authorities and every incentive to retain the patients within the health services so as to retain the resources associated with them.

The success of the *Care in the Community* initiative remains to be seen. In the meantime it represents one of the few attempts actively to maintain and build upon the policy inheritance and to provide succour to the long-standing but fading policy of community care. It may yet prove that a drive for long-term cost effectiveness, which is what it represents, can survive the intense pressures of public expenditure cuts; it may equally prove the opposite.

Shifting the Centre of Gravity: From State to Non-Statutory Provision

The rehabilitation of non-statutory welfare was not initiated by the first Thatcher Administration, as least so far as the voluntary sector is concerned. It was the Heath Government which in 1972 established the Voluntary Services Unit (VSU) in the Home Office to act as the voluntary sector's 'friend at court'.[25] The following year saw the creation of the Volunteer Centre, funded by VSU, to operate as a national focus for the development of information and good practice in volunteering. The Labour Administration of 1974-79 was scarcely less interested in the voluntary sector. As Secretaries of State for Social Services, both Barbara Castle and David Ennals stressed the importance of developing and sustaining family and neighbourhood care, the 'Good Neighbour Campaign' of 1977 being one concrete expression of interest in this field. It was the same Administration which helped to promote discussion of the role of formal voluntary organizations through its publication of a consultative document[26] in response to the privately sponsored Wolfenden Report[27] on the future of voluntary organizations. Meanwhile, local voluntary action was benefiting in more tangible terms through the expansion of the Urban Programme, the initiation of MSC job creation schemes, and the introduction of Joint Finance. Perhaps more surprisingly, the Callaghan Government was also responsible for a working group on Volunteers and Paid Workers, chaired by the Minister of Social Security.[28] This met through the 'winter of discontent' of 1978-79 and led to David Ennals' appeal for volunteers to help cope with industrial disruption in the NHS.

Thus, there was a substantial policy inheritance for the Thatcher Administration in terms of the endorsement of, and practical support for, the organized voluntary sector, informal care and volunteering. What, if anything was added to that base during the period 1979-83? Was the repeated advocacy of non-state welfare, to which we drew attention in our previous report,[29] more a difference in presentation than substance? To address these issues fully, we need to distinguish between the rhetoric of ministerial intent and the reality of administrative action. In other words, we need to address ourselves to the issue of how far ministerial preferences have been carried through into practice. This, in turn highlights further questions about the capacity of this Administration in particular, and central government in general, to stimulate change in the balance between statutory and non-statutory contributions to social care.

Let us begin with the declared intentions of the first Thatcher Government. These may be distinguished from previous administrations' expressions of support for non-statutory welfare in three respects: the cumulative weight of ministerial support; the primacy of the role accorded to the voluntary sector and most particularly to informal care; and the emergence of political endorsement for private care as a significant element in the non-statutory sector. We consider each of these developments below.

While previous administrations had accorded increasing recognition to the actual and potential role of the voluntary sector, they had done so in somewhat limited terms. The new government immediately placed its endorsement of the voluntary sector at the centre of the policy stage and it became an ever-present theme in ministerial statements and official documents. It seemed that no minister could address himself to the PSS field without indulging in something approaching the 'beatification' of voluntary provision.[30] A comparison of the content of official documents also reveals a new and consistent emphasis on the need to support and extend all kinds of voluntary and informal care.[31] Even more significant than the constant repetition of the voluntary refrain, however, was the reworking of the traditional logic. Ministers were not simply proposing a new point of balance between statutory and non-statutory welfare: they were wholeheartedly adopting the Wolfenden Committee's argument that the relationship which had been established between the two sectors in the post-war period should, in effect, be stood on its head.[32] Thus the Prime Minister, herself, expressed the belief that 'the statutory services are the supportive ones, underpinning where necessary, filling the gaps and helping the helpers.[33] In the post-war welfare consensus it was the voluntary sector which had been allocated this supplementary, gap filling role. Patrick Jenkin, as Social Services Secretary, advanced a similar view, making it clear that the pivotal position was occupied neither by the statutory services, nor even the organized voluntary sector. Rather, it was his view that the informal sector lay 'at the centre' with other forms of care providing 'back up, expertise and support'.[34]

The Growth of Private Care

The pre-eminence accorded to informal care was accompanied by a new emphasis upon private care. As Challis[35] argues, while the Labour Government's policy documents show it to be aware of the voluntary sector's contribution to the care of the elderly, they made almost no mention at all of private provision. By contrast, Conservative Government documents demonstrate an intention to place the support of private action firmly alongside that of voluntary action, with the state acting in a largely residual role. Thus the degree of continuity which we identified in the generalized support for the voluntary sector is not paralleled in the case of private care, nor in the centrality accorded to informal care by friends and neighbours. Such a development would, if translated into practice, represent a major shift in the emphasis of PSS provision, so much so that no administration might reasonably expect to achieve it during a single term. However, if we should not expect to find the situation in general transformed during the period under review, we might nonetheless explore how far ministerial rhetoric has been translated into practical programmes for action and whether trends are emerging in the field consistent with ministerial emphases.

There are major difficulties in constructing comprehensive time series based on reliable and up-to-date data on voluntary, informal and private care. Nonetheless, in the case of private residential provision, the overall trend is strikingly clear, and particularly so in respect of the elderly. Thus, Johnson notes that there has been an 'unprecedented rate of growth'[36] in private provision during the first Thatcher Government which resulted in the scale of private care outstripping that of the voluntary sector. Taken together, private and voluntary provision appear to have grown, he suggests, from 40% of total residential provision for the elderly in 1980 to about half of all registered places by 1983. While much of this growth took place in traditional retirement areas (for example, the number of homes in Devon, Cornwall and Norfolk doubled in 1981-82), it is now widespread and appears to be taking place in all but depressed city areas.[37] With the private sector moving more recently into the provision of high dependency sheltered housing,[38] there is a real possibility that the private sector will become the leading provider of residential accommodation for the elderly within a relatively short time. Similar trends are evident in residential provision for other client groups, though they are less well charted.

On the face of it, therefore, the Thatcher Administration appears to have secured a substantial and continuing shift in the balance of provision. Yet, on further examination, one of the more notable features of this phenomenon is the relative absence of a direct link to governmental action. It has arisen, Johnson argues, 'not out of the more usual processes of policy formulation, consultation and promotion, but by default'.[39] Certainly it is difficult to detect anything like a coherent or developed programme which goes beyond the level of rhetoric. What actions the Government has taken have been essentially regulatory, reactive or indirect. Thus legislation has been enacted to regulate registration and inspection procedures, while changes in the social security field have had the effect of increasing support to the residents of private homes and prolonging their ability to pay for care. Both of these developments, however, were primarily a response to changes already taking place in the pattern of provision and to problems subsequently identified rather than part of programmes which actively sought to initiate the expansion of private care.

The inability of social service departments (SDDs) to maintain levels of residential services relative to growing numbers may also have been of some consequence for the growth of private provision. Yet, the relationship between the supply of public services and demand for private care is by no means clear or direct. Indeed, the most important factor in the expansion of private care is arguably neither the relative decrease in public sector provision nor public support for private provision. Rather, it is the capacity of individuals to buy care for themselves or for their families. This, in turn, is related more to the consequences of long-standing policies and trends outside the PSS field than to premeditated actions within it. Thus the growth of occupational pensions and the spread of home ownership seem likely to have contributed fundamentally to the expansion of private care. Indeed, the growth of private sector sheltered housing, if it takes place, will directly utilize the capital values of homes, now too large for personal needs, in order to purchase more modest accommodation and personal care as this becomes necessary.

The extension of private care must be seen, therefore, as a phenomenon which has been concurrent with the coming to power of an administration favourable to that development rather than as being the consequence of its policies. Government has been swimming with a spontaneously swelling tide and its policies, so far, seem destined to enable the tide to flow a little further up the beach than might otherwise have been the case. This does not mean that the necessary role of government has been adequately fulfilled. Considerable concern exists about the consequences of allowing such a shift in the balance of provision to take place by default. This revolves around, *inter alia*: the consequences if a two-tier system of care emerges ,n which local authority provision is offered only to the poor; the ability of SSDs to register and monitor satisfactory standards of care, particularly in the light of pressures on their own staff and variations in the level and quality of private care;[40] the allocation of public subsidies through social security on the basis of inability to pay fees rather than an assessed need for residential provision; and the fact that an uncontrolled boom in private care could lead to a repetition of the scandal and exploitation which swept America when individuals became entitled to state aid for residential care in nursing homes.[41] We may conclude, therefore, by noting first that the 1979 Administration appears to have supported a substantial expansion of private care but not to have initiated it. Second, that as this development has occurred largely by default of government, even the traditional minimalist functions have remained under-developed, particularly the monitoring and regulatory functions.

Voluntary and Informal Provision

In our analysis of the initial period of the Thatcher Government,[42] we identified two principal limits on its ability to implement a shift in the roles of, and balance between, statutory and voluntary care: the lack of levers to pull, coupled with an ideological inclination to disengage from detailed involvement in local decisions; and the absence of a fully developed alternative strategy for securing such shifts. As with private care, government intentions appeared to exist at no greater depth than that of ministerial exhortation. We need to examine, therefore, how far government policies towards the organized voluntary sector and informal care developed after 1981 and then review the means adopted for their implementation. Two things are immediately clear: first that the whole tenor of public statements about voluntarism moderated towards the end of Patrick Jenkin's period at DHSS and the essential role and contribution of the statutory sector was re-emphasized. This, in turn, reflected the influence of concern inside and outside the voluntary sector that government policy appeared to be based both upon unrealistic expectations of what voluntary action could achieve and also that, in the process, relationships with statutory authorities were being undermined.[43] Westland powerfully highlighted the implications of this situation:

> Uncritical praise for the voluntary sector juxtaposed with the maximum vilification of local government does not make it easy for the praised and the damned to live and work together, sharing similar objectives, acknowledging their interdependence.[44]

That the Government took on board these reservations is evident in a new emphasis which began to appear in ministerial statements. Thus, for example, in a speech to Age Concern in 1981, Jenkin's successor, Norman Fowler, was careful to start by recognizing 'the marvellous job' done by statutory services (meals on wheels, home help and community nursing) in supporting both the elderly and their supporters. While noting that it was these carers who enabled elderly people to remain at home, he also argued that 'the best way of easing the pressure' which this placed upon them was to 'share the burden (with) central government, local government, health authorities, voluntary bodies and, not least, employers and the general public'.[45] As this emphasis on 'shared care' reveals, ministerial rhetoric had shifted somewhat since the early period of Conservative rule. The secondary role for statutory services identified by Jenkin had been replaced by an approach which, as Wolfenden had done, stressed the importance of partnership in planning and service delivery with the organized voluntary sector and also a partnership in caring with families of socially dependent people.

How was this revised approach to be implemented? Did it, in fact, amount to a coherent strategy? A number of observers have continued to doubt not only whether, as Deakin expressed it, the 'Government can get its act together, but whether there is an act at all, in the sense of anything more than a general disposition to favour voluntary action when circumstances permit'.[46] From positions within the voluntary sector Morgan[47] has made a similar point about the absence of strategy, while Stubbings[48] has produced compelling evidence to question whether the Government has had a coherent policy towards volunteering. He concludes that policy making has tended to be *ad hoc* and has used volunteers to serve other ends, most notably in the employment field. We similarly commented on the apparent lack of policy at other than a most generalized level and suggested that even a government which sought to disengage from detailed local involvement might, nevertheless, have developed and more systematically pursued a coherent programme in this field.[49] We also argued that, while the opportunities open for implementing such an approach were limited, three preconditions could be identified for securing the expansion and strengthening of local voluntary action: creating a supportive, philosophical environment; stimulating innovation within the voluntary sector; and expanding voluntary agency funds.

By 1983 it was still difficult to argue that there was a detailed and consistent policy towards voluntary action as a whole, or that the means used to strengthen it amounted to a coherent package, particularly when viewed alongside policies being pursued simultaneously in the local authority sector. Nevertheless, a number of developments had taken place which bear directly upon our three preconditions. The continuing, albeit moderated, advocacy of non-statutory welfare has undoubtedly helped create a supportive policy climate in which statutory agencies are more likely to give regard to the potential role and views of organized and informal voluntary action. By 1983 the voluntary sector was more firmly on the policy agenda of local statutory agencies than in 1979. Arguably, however, this owed less to government rhetoric than to government funding initiatives through which, *inter alia*, central government sought to promote innovation and develop the resource base of the voluntary sector locally. Included among such initiatives are not only those parented by DHSS (e.g. for Intermediate Treatment, mentally handicapped children in hospital and the Opportunities for Volunteering programme), but also the greatly expanded MSC employment creation programmes, a not insignificant proportion of which appears to benefit voluntary agencies in the personal social services field. The established Joint Finance and Urban Programmes have also explicitly accorded greater priority to the voluntary sector.

Two features of these initiatives are noteworthy. First, they are all short-term pump priming exercises, very largely dependent upon local authority resources for the continuation of projects funded under them. As such they are potential victims of the tightening control on overall local government expenditure. There is thus an apparently fundamental inconsistency in the Government's approach to the financial support of the two sectors and one which, as the local government expenditure tap is turned off, could result in a contraction in the organized voluntary sector as rapid as the expansion which central funding has certainly brought about. A second feature common to these initiatives is that they are all examples of direct funding by central government of local projects: they by-pass local government and thereby expose one of the centre's fundamental dilemmas in securing the implementation of policies for the voluntary sector. Both the overall control of local government expenditure and the non-hypothetical nature of rate support grant require the earmarking of central funds for the promotion of specific action locally. These devices have, of course, been utilized to direct resources at local level into both the statutory and non-statutory sectors and in principle could be designed to promote joint bids for resources. Nonetheless, to the extent that they encourage local voluntary agencies to bid for funds in isolation from their statutory counterparts, they tend to undermine the concept and reality of the inter-sector partnership in planning and service delivery which the Government is apparently anxious to encourage.[50] Such a consequence, the possibility of which was most recently voiced by the Association of Metropolitan Authorities,[51] would not only work against the grain of government intentions, but could also serve to counteract the government blessed action of the NCVO and the local authority associations themselves in seeking to promote good practice in statutory/voluntary partnerships.[52]

At the same time, however, we should retain a sense of perspective. The total value of centrally funded DHSS initiatives amount to under 1% of PSS spending.[53] They represent change at the margins therefore, rather than at the heart of the local personal social services – though the significance of such change is heightened as the margins get tighter in local government. Equally, it would be wrong to imply that such central funds represent a coherent approach to the voluntary sector. Sceptics see them as a substitute for a sense of direction,[54] though they could equally be seen as a relatively systematic attempt to 'bend' established spending programmes and new initiatives towards the organized voluntary sector. Nonetheless, it remained true, in 1983 as in 1979, that the precise dimensions of the role expected of the organized voluntary sector – whether as a partner in service delivery or as an innovative gap filler – remained unclear and, in consequence, a coherent implementation programme was largely lacking.

By contrast, however, the beginnings of a somewhat more coherent approach to informal care could be detected and one which appeared to be emphasizing an unusual approach to implementation. The problems for any government seeking to develop informal care may be simply stated. First, there is a need to secure change in the attitudes and behaviours of innumerable individuals. Second, there is a need to counteract established social trends, such as social and geographical mobility and the increasing participation of women in the workforce, which might weaken family and community ties. Third, many of the 'levers' which government might in principle pull to affect levels of informal caring (such as social security and income tax arrangements) are outside the remit of the personal social services. Fourth, changes are required in procedures for service allocation and in the methods of working adopted by frontline fieldworkers. However, it would be wrong to misconstrue the task by under-estimating either the number of persons providing family and neighbourhood care or the volume of the care they provide.[55] The present challenge for the statutory services is not so much the declining capacity of the community to care, as the need to focus support on the most hard-pressed among the vast army of informal carers and to mobilize the full potential of such care where it remains undeveloped.

Yet these are tasks which the statutory services have been historically ill-equipped to perform. Formal services do not seem to mesh well with informal care. Indeed, they may undermine it by taking little account of it, or by treating the availability of informal care as, in effect, a disqualification for receipt of scarce services. Thus, a decade ago, Bayley[46] highlighted the tendency of professionalized services to supplant, rather than supplement and support, family and neighbourhood care. More recently, studies have shown that the formal services are slow to provide assistance for dependent persons with access to other sources of support. For example, Levin et al,[57] concluded that, while relatives were usually 'available, willing and able' to make a key contribution to the care of the elderly mentally confused, they were 'often worn down by the care they provided'. A major reason for this was the underprovision of community services to elderly people living with carers. The elderly living alone were more likely to receive home help and meals services. At the same time, however, the research suggested that community services could be effective in reducing the build up of strain on carers. Other work also appears to show that where the formal services adopt a preventative and locally based approach, which explicitly seeks to stimulate and support informal care, the demand for statutory services may be reduced.[58] A key barrier to change has been the orientation in social work training and practice towards casework or counselling: working with individuals rather than mobilizing community resources. Social workers have not, in the main, been equipped to 'interweave' formal services and informal care. Given its preference for 'care by the community', how did the first Thatcher Administration tackle these barriers to change?

One problem – the need to target services so that they support informal carers – has been neglected. Indeed, support services have been more thinly spread as a result of expenditure cuts. The desire to cut 'bureaucracy' may also have reduced the likelihood of more careful targetting in future: effective management requires time and resources. However, the problem of developing a preventative, community based approach in social work was tackled indirectly. The Government's support for the establishment of the Barclay Committee, which reviewed the nature and future of social work, represented a desire to influence social work objectives and attitudes. The report said most of the things the Government hoped for, but it also said altogether too many other things with too many voices. The call for community based social work was obscured by the muddied waters of rhetorical debate. Despite the ensuing confusion and the lack of incisive DHSS follow up, however, attitudes have been changing rapidly. The tide has been flowing in the Government's direction even without direct intervention or control.

The success of an indirect approach to implementing change is necessarily difficult to assess, but the possibility that indirect influence may have carried the day must be taken seriously in this case. Ministers have repeatedly called for support for informal carers, the terms 'supporting the supporters' and 'caring for the carers' having increasingly entered the vocabulary of community care. The rhetoric was backed up by financial support to the newly formed Association of Carers and by a Social Work Service exercise aimed at promoting a 'national debate' on the subject. The latter was particularly interesting in that it represented an unusually systematic attempt – through national, regional and local conferences – to build on the policy climate created by ministerial speeches and to place the issue on the active agenda of agencies in both the statutory and voluntary sectors. Chairmen of health authorities, local authority committees, chief officers, local leaders of voluntary organizations, and carers were all involved in an attempt to extend the debate from the centre to the locality, and to identify the nature of the problem and disseminate models of good practice. It may be seen, therefore, as an example of the 'indirect' approach to implementation which we advocated earlier.[59] As it emerged only at the very end of the period under review (June 1983), an assessment of its effectiveness would be premature. There are, however, indications that the SWS project has been used to stimulate a broadly based debate in at least some localities. The question is whether it can thrive in the absence of resources specifically channelled into supporting informal care. As Levin et al point out, it requires an investment in formal services to ensure the essential back up that carers require.[60] As we indicated above, far from that investment having been made, services have been spread more thinly.

We are, therefore, back in the by now familiar situation of a government with clear policy preferences, but with few means of direct implementation and faced with the consequences of its own resource policies for local government. The SWS initiative was an attempt to confront such limitations and was an unusual attempt to develop policy thinking and to disseminate models of good practice at the interface between voluntary and statutory services. Nonetheless, it was still open to the criticism that, at best, the Government was failing to orchestrate the full range of measures which might promote informal care (ranging from the social security and tax systems through to subsidized public transport). At worst, it was open to the charge of tokenism and of placing unsupportable burdens on families – particularly their female members – in order to reduce public expenditure rather than increase its long-term cost effectiveness.

Conclusions

Looking back over the full period of the first Thatcher Administration, it is the contradictions of government and the, not unrelated, limitations on the DHSS to affect preferred patterns of change locally that stand out most clearly. At one level, there has been a fundamental contradiction between resource policies and those for community care. Whether pursued as an alternative to NHS long-stay services, or to statutory provision more generally, community care has long been favoured as a route to cost effectiveness. In neither case, however, is this a costless policy, especially in the short term. This has been the crux of the issue. At a second level, however, there is the apparent contradiction between intent and actuality in resource policy. While stressing the over-riding imperative of constraint, the Government has been quietly failing to achieve, and has indeed been raising, its 'targets' for the PPS. This contradiction has been 'explained' in terms of local government autonomy in the determination of spending priorities. Nonetheless, even growth at levels above those initially intended has been insufficient to maintain constant levels of service and the overall approach to local government expenditure implies yet more limited growth in the future. Social need has been relegated to a secondary place on the political agenda. The 'nanny state' and central planning have been on the retreat in the Elephant and Castle, but centralization has reigned supreme in Marsham Street.

If, at first glance, the PSS looked very similar in 1983 to 1979, that reflected the limited room for manoeuvre and for direct influence from DHSS. But beneath the surface there had already been much change and the indirect influence of new philosophies, and of public expenditure constraint, had been considerable. The real issue is what a continuation of these trends will mean for the future. They could ossify the statutory services in their traditional heartland and their traditional modes of working. On the other hand, they might stimulate real change and further shift the balance between statutory and non-statutory agencies. Out of such a process, a new definition of their respective roles might ultimately emerge. Either way, the impact of Government policies is likely to continue to be indirect and subject to contradictions. The outcome at local level remains uncertain and particularly dependent on how far local government is able to continue channelling additional resources into the personal social services.

References

1. A.L. Webb and G. Wistow 'The personal social services' in P.M. Jackson (ed.), *Government policy initiatives 1974-80: some case studies in public administration*, RIPA, 1981.
2. DHSS, *Priorities in the health and personal social services*, HMSO, 1976.
3. DHSS, *Report of a study on community care*, 1981.
4. See Wolfenden Committee, *The future of voluntary organizations*, Croom Helm, 1978; S. Hatch, *Outside the state*, Croom Helm, 1980; F. Gladstone, *Voluntary action in a changing world*, Bedford Square Press, 1979.
5. A.L. Webb and G. Wistow, *Whither state welfare? policy and implementation in the personal social services 1979-80*, RIPA, 1982.
6. See below, 13-14.
7. Webb and Wistow, *op. cit.*, (reference 5).
8. *Ibid.*
9. A.L. Webb and G. Wistow, Public expenditure and policy implementation: the case of community care, *Public Administration*, Spring 1983, 21-44.
10. See Webb and Wistow, *op. cit.*, (references 1 and 5).
11. H.C. Deb., col. 886, 22 February 1984.
12. Webb and Wistow, *op. cit.*, (reference 9).
13. *Ibid.*
14. *Ibid.* table 4, p. 33.
15. M. Nissel and L. Bonnerjea, *Family care of the handicapped elderly - who pays?*, Policies Studies Institute, 1982.
16. DHSS, *A Happier old age*, 1978.
17. DHSS, *Growing older*, 1981.
18. *Ibid.* para. 6.12.
19. See, for example, Consultants to judge SSDs performance, *Community Care*, 1 March, 1984, 3.
20. DHSS, *Mental handicap: progress, problems and priorities*, 1980.
21. Welsh Office, *All Wales strategy for the development of services for mentally handicapped people*, 1983.
22. DHSS, *Care in the community: a consultative document on moving resources for care in England*, 1981.
23. G. Wistow, Joint finance and care in the community: have the incentives worked?, *Public Money*, 3, (2), 1983, 33-37.
24. DHSS, *Health service development: care in the community and joint finance*, Circular HC (83)6/LAC (83)5, 1983.
25. Lord Windlesham, *Politics in practice*, Jonathan Cape, 1975.
26. Home Office, *The Government and the voluntary sector*, 1981.
27. Wolfenden Committee, *op. cit.*, (reference 4).
28. P. Stubbings, *Central government policy towards volunteers*, M.Sc. Dissertation, Cranfield Institute of Technology, 1983.
29. Webb and Wistow, *op. cit.*, (reference 1).
30. P. Westland, The year of the voluntary organization, *Community Care*, 19 November 1981, 14-15.
31. L. Challis, *Private and voluntary residential provision for the elderly*, Centre for the Analysis of Social Policy, University of Bath, 1982.
32. Stubbings, *op. cit.*, (reference 25).
33. M. Thatcher, Speech to WRVS Conference, 1981.
34. P. Jenkin, Speech to ADSS Conference, 1980.
35. Challis, *op. cit.*, (reference 27).
36. M. Johnson, Controlling the cottage industry, *Community Care*, 25 August 1983, 16-18.
37. *Ibid.*
38. R. Bessell, In defence of the private sector, *Community Care*, 29 September, 1983.

39. Johnson, *op. cit.*, (reference 32).
40. Challis, *op. cit.*, (reference 27).
41. J. Lawrence, Is big business moving into caring, *New Society*, 10 February 1983, 211-214.
42. Webb and Wistow, *op. cit.*, (references 1 and 5).
43. See, for example, P. Westland, *op. cit.* (reference 26) and N. Deakin, *The voluntary sector in the eighties*, Birmingham Settlement, 1982.
44. P. Westland, *op. cit.* (reference 26).
45. N. Fowler, Speech to Age Concern, 1981.
46. N. Deakin, Providing an ambulance wagon is not what we're here for, *Voluntary Action*, Autumn 1982, 16-17.
47. A. Morgan, Foreword, *Annual Report 1982*, National Association of Councils for Voluntary Service, 1982.
48. Stubbings, *op. cit.*, (reference 25).
49. Webb and Wistow, *op. cit.*, (references 1 and 5).
    50. See for example, DHSS, *op. cit.*, (reference 21).
51. Association of Metropolitan Authorities, *Working together - partnership in local social service: report of a follow-up study*, Social Services Circular No. 27/1983, AMA, 1983.
52. AMA/NCVO/ACC, *Working together - partnership in local social service*, Bedford Square Press, 1981.
53. P. Westland, No sense of direction, *Community Care*, 17 November 1983, 15-18.
    54. *Ibid.*
55. See, for example, Equal Opportunities Commission, *Caring for the elderly and handicapped*, EOC, 1982; S. Humble, *Voluntary action in the 1980s*, Volunteer Centre, 1982.
56. M. Bayley, *Mental handicap and community care*, Routledge and Kegan Paul, 1973.
57. E. Levin, I. Sinclair, P. Gorback, *The supporters of confused elderly persons at home*, National Institute for Social Work, 1983, typescript.
58. See, for example, M. Bayley, 'Helping care to happen in the community', in A. Walker, *Community Care*, Blackwell and Robertson, 1982; D. Challis and R. Luckett, A new life at home, *Community Care*, 24 March 1983.
59. Webb and Wistow, *op. cit.*, (reference 5).
60. Levin et al, *op. cit.*, (reference 57).

10

Making Sense of Social Security? Initiatives and Implementation 1979-83*

Susanne MacGregor

'Our social security system is now so complicated that even some Ministry officials do not understand it', said the Conservative Party Manifesto in 1979.[1] This was, however, a kinder view of the British income-maintenance system than that of Bruce Page who in the previous year had commented that it 'often gives the impression of having been assembled by Franz Kafka on a gloomy Sunday'.[2] Or than that of Adam Raphael who described the present tax and social security system 'under which the State acts like a vast octopus handing out more than 40 means-tested benefits while simultaneously sucking in large amounts of tax and national insurance from the low paid as a monster that not even Frankenstein could have created'.[3]

Such criticisms are familiar to those attempting to manage social security. Sir Geoffrey Otton, (Permanent Secretary at DHSS), has pointed out the increasingly complicated institutional relationships involved in income maintenance in this country.[4] In addition to the 500 local offices and 260 subsidiary offices manned by 67,000 field staff of DHSS, the Inland Revenue has been involved in collecting contributions through PAYE since 1975, the Department of Employment pays unemployment benefit through its local offices for DHSS and growing provision for job training has been hived off to the Manpower Services Commission. The British system is characterized by its relatively low level of benefits but also by its large and comprehensive scheme. Twenty-five million separate claims and one billion payments for social security are made each year but in spite of this the cost of administration accounts for less than 5% of the total budget.[5] The complexity of the system derives very largely from the substantial role played by means tested benefits and these account for much of the work of local office staff, half of whom are involved in administering supplementary benefit.

In post-war years, the lack of a coherent long-term strategy for income maintenance has often been noted by observers of British social policy. In the post-1976 context of attempts to cut public expenditure and a squeeze on manpower in the administration of social security, it was not surprising to find that a siege mentality or *ad hoc* form of decision making developed. Expenditure projections and assumptions about the social security programme, depending to a large extent on assumptions about employment patterns and levels of economic growth, had been seen as unrealistic and ill-informed. The Social Services Committee of 1980 were struck by 'the apparent lack of strategic policy making at the DHSS: the failure to examine the overall impact of changes in the social environment across the various services and programmes for which the Department is responsible'.[6] (Others, however, have argued that this *ad hoc* and confused response hides a more deliberate and conscious encouragement of the hidden welfare state of occupational benefits and tax allowances.)

Should 'priorities pick themselves' in social security or was it possible for a firm government to seize control of this octopus-like monster and knock it into shape, as part of the attempt to restructure economic and social life and re-orient popular culture towards the values of hard work, thrift and competition?

Policy Objectives

The formal objectives of the Conservative Government in 1979 were stated initially in its manifesto. Over the course of the next four years, public statements by ministers clarified what priority would be given to each of these and spelt out in more detail the assumptions behind this choice of objectives and the manner in which implementation would be attempted.

The detailed proposals and targets for social security must be understood within the framework of the 'banner goals' or over-riding objectives of the new Government from which they derive. Indeed the consistency and clear integration between middle range and immediate policy objectives and these banner goals is a striking feature of the radical Right's ideology. A stress on values is one hallmark, especially relevant here being that on 'self-reliance'.[7] The primary goal was 'to rebuild our economy and re-unite a divided and disillusioned people' and to this end five tasks were set out. Three refer to the attack on inflation and controlling the trade union movement, upholding the importance of Parliament and the rule of law and improving defence. Two relate directly to social security provision:

> to restore incentives so that hard work pays, success is rewarded and genuine new jobs are created in an expanding economy ...

and

> to support family life, by helping people to become home-owners, raising the standards of their children's education and concentrating welfare services on the effective support of the old, the sick, the disabled and those who are in real need:[8]

So far then, we can see the *simplification* of the system (cf. Appendix) increasing the *differentiation* in income between the 'hard working' and 'successful' and those who are unemployed, failures or lazy, and the concentration of resources on the *deserving poor* as key objectives within the specific area of social security and taxation. However, the predominant goal of the new Government was to conquer inflation and it is clear that the pursuit of this would have had implications for the institutions (principles and practices) of social security: 'the state takes too much of the nation's income; its share must be steadily reduced. When it spends and borrows too much, taxes, interest rates, prices and unemployment rise so that in the long term there is less wealth with which to improve our standard of living and our social services'.[9] Thus substantial economies would have to be made by government through 'the reduction of waste, bureaucracy and over-government' and 'we shall look for economies in the cost of running our tax and social security system'.[10] This would take the form in particular of a reduction in the civil service.

Here it is interesting to note that the total size of the budget for social security marks it out as a prime target for cuts. But being a demand-led service, cash limits cannot be used to control spending since the volume of provision is based on entitlement to benefit. Changes, apart from attempting reductions in the cost of administration, would have to be made either by cutting the *level* of benefits (mainly through de-indexing) or by altering the rules governing entitlement to benefit (the right to claim). Both methods were in time to be adopted by the Government but with little impact on the overall size of the budget, given the increasing demands placed on social security as a result of rising unemployment and increases in the number of old people and of single-parent families.

To cut income tax and to tackle the poverty trap were other goals set out clearly in the manifesto, mainly to reward hard work, responsibility and success. 'It is especially important to cut the absurdly high marginal rates of tax both at the bottom and top of the income scale. It must pay a man or women significantly more to be in rather than out of work. Raising tax thresholds will let the low paid out of the tax net altogether and unemployment and short-term sickness benefits must be brought into the computation of annual income.[11] In this area, as we shall see, some success was achieved at the top of the income scale but for family men it became much more difficult to escape from both the poverty trap and the unemployment trap.

But both the stick and the carrot were to be used to attack the 'why work' syndrome. While the carrot was little in evidence, the stick of acting more vigorously against fraud and abuse received greater publicity, although its effects too were open to dispute.

To a remarkable extent these remained the objectives of the Thatcher Administration throughout the four years of government. The 'why work' problem was to be tackled by the taxation of unemployment benefit (scheduled for April 1982) and an increase in the role of special investigators.[12] Reducing public expenditure remained an over-riding goal: 'the primary purpose of the (Social Security (No. 2) Bill) is to achieve public expenditure savings amounting to £270 million in 1981-82, rising to £480 million in 1982-3.[13] The Government took the view that increased expenditure on social security over recent years had come about 'not through any conscious decision but because the level and scope of benefits have been improved in anticipation of a growth in output which has not been achieved ... Any effort to curb the growth of public spending must therefore, include this programme' (Sir Geoffrey Howe in his Budget Speech of 1980).[14]

Spending on social security would be subordinate to the primary objective of building a healthier, more productive economy. Only when success was achieved in this area could improvement in welfare be envisaged. Patrick Jenkin, Secretary of State for Social Services said 'if we are going to look after the young, the old, the sick and the poor, we cannot afford to do this properly if as a nation we fail to pay our way'[15]: 'what we can afford for our social services has to be paid for by our economic performance ... No one stands more to gain from this than the old, the sick, the handicapped and the deprived.[16]

Context

In setting out these objectives the Government was facing up to a considerable challenge. The sheer cost of maintaining welfare programmes at a time of little or no economic growth is a problem for all the countries of northern Europe. Independent observers continue to stress that influenced by demographic pressures, if no welfare changes are made and economic growth is sluggish, the share of Gross Domestic Product devoted to state spending will shoot up in the years to the end of the century, producing a 'crisis in social security'.[17] The similar reaction of western governments to a common problem is indicated in France, where the socialist government agreed to a severe programme of cuts because the annual deficit on the social security fund was running at £2.4 billion per year. In West Germany, rises in pensions were delayed and student grants converted into loans. Holland recognized the need to thoroughly revise its social security system and in Belgium drastic pruning has been introduced. Denmark too has embarked on radical changes.[18]

Framework of analysis

The context in which the Conservative Government initiated changes, and within which the success or failure of its attempts to implement these should be assessed, is that of 'economic crisis', especially the requirement to cut public expenditure, (social consumption in particular) if investment and economic restructuring were to be achieved. The key question regarding social security is to what extent the system proved to be either amenable or resistant to cuts and restructuring.

Social security could be said to be relatively vulnerable to cuts compared to other areas of social consumption because of the political weakness of its client group (the poor, the deprived, the old, sick, disabled, unpopular). It lacks a powerful group able to oppose attempts to introduce changes. Other institutional areas are characterized either by stronger client groups or by alternative power bases, as in the local authorities where supporters of local socialism have tried to oppose central government directives or, as in the NHS, or universities, where well-organized professional interests can deflect the direction of government attempts at restructuring. This lack of strong vested interests is encouraged by the institutional practices of the tax and social security system which, in its individualized treatment of the contributor or beneficiary, reduces the likelihood of collective oppositional action. These factors tend to argue for the vulnerability of social security relative to other programmes in a situation where reductions in public expenditure are the order of the day. Moreover, this is encouraged by public opinion! Public acquiescence towards rising unemployment and support for attacks on those 'who do not play their full part' could be said to have been indicated in the re-election of the Thatcher Government in 1983. However, some softening of attitudes between 1976 and 1983 appears to be evident from a comparison of surveys conducted in those years.[19] In a 1980 MORI survey, 44% of respondents had singled benefits out for cuts but by 1983 only 23% favoured such cuts. Significantly, in this later survey, 36% said they or someone in their family had received supplementary benefit and one in three had either been unemployed or someone in their family had been unemployed in the past year. Experience of hardship seems to have had some impact although ambivalence remains. By 1983 62% still agreed that many people on SB are on the fiddle and 57% agreed that 'Britain's welfare system removes the incentive for people to help themselves'. There were signs also in these survey findings that people accepted unemployment and poverty fatalistically, as things that cannot, or cannot easily, be changed.

Yet by 1983, in spite of fears (or hopes) engendered by rhetoric and leaks, the character of the social security system remained much as described in our introductory paragraph. What countervailing pressures intervened to restrict the extent to which the Government initiated new policies? The main factors to which we should look are firstly that of the civil service, both managers and unions and, secondly, given the sheer size of the organization, the time required to effect radical change. In addition, pressure groups played a part, particularly where able to influence media presentation or to influence strategic groups within the Conservative Party itself. Insofar as the 'wets' or the 'centre' seemed likely to influence voting within the Cabinet or the Commons, policy decisions had to take this into account. As Mrs Thatcher gained increasing pre-eminence within the Party and tightened her grip on the Cabinet, this source of opposition diminished. Such barriers to policy change rest on the values of 'paternalism' which mute the extent to which a more radical attack on the 'why work' syndrome and reductions in the standard of living of the dependent population could be carried through. Added to this was the fear of disorder which, especially as it found its source in the young of the inner cities in the riots of 1981, also moderated the disciplinary function of social security. The backcloth to the whole process is the steady growth of an underclass, those outside or on the margins of the labour force, together with the lack of any coherent strategy for managing the relationship between these groups and those more closely integrated into both the economy and the polity. Restructuring of social security to take account of this would need to be coordinated with a restructuring of manpower planning, industrial policy, taxation policy and education and training. Effecting such coordination would clearly require longer than one term of office.

Key Objectives and Policy Implementation

To assess how far the Conservative Government was successful in achieving its objectives, we shall concentrate selectively on five areas taken as key illustrations, considering how policies were formulated and the problems faced in the attempt to implement these between 1979 and 1983. These key areas are: the total size of the social security budget; the issue of fraud and abuse; the simplification of the system; the poverty and unemployment traps; and housing and fuel benefits.

The Size of the Social Security Budget

In almost all areas of social security, Britain has fallen behind her closest neighbours; for example, retirement pensions are lower than in most other EEC countries. In 1979, when the Government took office, the most recent available figure for UK expenditure on social security as a proportion of GDP was 8.8%, compared for example to 18.7% in the Netherlands (the highest proportion) and 9.2% in Eire (the next lowest). Expenditure on health and social security in the UK was 13.6% of GDP compared, for example, to 19.4% in West Germany and 19.1% in France.[20]

At the same time, in a 1978 review of the proportion of GDP going in tax in a number of industrial countries, Britain came eleventh out of 18. Over the 1970s, when social security contributions were calculated, the total tax burden actually fell. Britain's place in the world league table dropped from fourth to ninth in 1977. In 1978, the proportion of GDP paid in tax revenues in the UK was 35.2% (only Italy and Ireland paid a smaller proportion among EEC countries). But significantly only 6% of tax revenues in 1977 came from tax on corporate income. The rest was paid from household income (36%) expenditure (39%) and social security contributions (19%).

In spite of this, in 1980, direct taxation was cut by £4,500 million. Families, however, gained nothing. If families had gained their share of tax cuts – that is if child benefit had been raised in proportion to what would have been gained under the previous system of child tax allowances – child benefit would have had to have risen to about £8 per week. This would have helped the poverty and unemployment traps, to be discussed more fully below.

The 'black economy' features here too, estimated variously as between 10% and 20% of total economic activity. The tax loss here could be about £11.1 billion, insofar as a perceived high burden of total direct tax (including social security contributions) encourages such evasion.

In the early years of the Administration, it was estimated that social security expenditure (for 1979-80) would be £15,835 million.[21] The largest item by far was for retirement pensions, (£7,609 million) with supplementary benefit accounting for £2,000 million and child benefit for £1,834 million (net when the abolition of child tax allowances was taken into account). Unemployment benefit accounted for £648 million. Increases in the social security budget were due mainly to the increased number of retirement pensioners, the increasing number of unemployed, the number of new benefits introduced during the 'seventies (especially for the disabled) and the increasing value of long-term benefits (note however that the unemployment on supplementary benefit (SB) never graduate to the longer-term rates, worth about £10 per week for a couple). In 1978, the number dependent on SB was 4,598,000 (the number unemployed in May 1979 was 1,239,000). At the end of their term of office in 1983, the number dependent on SB was 7.1 million people, nearly one in seven of the population and a rise of 60% since 1979. Of these 7 million, 2 million were children. (The worst conditions were found in Northern Ireland where poverty is 50% higher than in the rest of the UK.) Most of the increase was accounted for by a sharp rise in the number of unemployed claimants, from 566,000 in 1979 to 1.7 million in 1983, constituting 40% of SB claimants, reflecting the rising rate of long-term unemployment (the total number of registered unemployed being over 3 million). To attempt to reduce the total size of the social security budget under these circumstances would clearly have been a herculean task.

Yet, over the four years of the first Thatcher Administration, the Government did succeed in deducting £2,000 million from the level of social security benefits. Child benefits dropped in mid-term to a thirty year low; earnings-related sickness and unemployment benefits were abolished in 1982; support for children in families of the sick, disabled, and unemployed on national insurance benefits was cut by up to 23% over these four years; SB payable to strikers' families was cut by £12. The changes introduced in 1980 saved £480 million through cuts in the levels of benefit and entitlement to claim; £400 million was gained by taxing short-term benefits and longer-term invalidity pensions from 1983; and £250 million was saved by not raising child benefit in line with prices. These were the first serious cuts in the real value of social security benefits since the 1930s (and cuts then had coincided with falling, not as in the 1980s, rising prices). The Government argued, however, that it had kept to the terms of its manifesto objectives. It is important to note here that the aim had been explicitly to concentrate support on the 'old, the sick, the disabled and those who are in real need'. The unemployed and the long-term unemployed were conspicuously absent from all these statements. Geoffrey Howe felt able to claim that the cuts were not done in a way that bore unfairly on the 'most vulnerable' members of society. (This of course presupposes a particular definition of 'real need' and ignores the vulnerability of a much neglected group among the 'deserving poor', that of the low paid workers and their families.) But benefits for these 'most vulnerable' groups kept in line with prices, although the link with earnings was abolished. Whilst the value of child benefits was eroded in the first fourteen months of the Government's term, later pressure from liberal backbench Tories and the Women's National Advisory Committee of the Conservative Party secured protection against inflation in 1980 and a substantial increase was promised for November 1983.

The most vigorous action seems to have been taken in the first two years of office. Rising unemployment reduced the scope for action later and added to the demands placed on the system. Indeed, expenditure on the administration of social security might have risen more if staffing in DHSS local offices had kept pace with the increased demand. A four month dispute in Birmingham during the winter of 1982-83 and a fourteen week strike in Oxford, for example, indicated the stress being placed on staff. In Birmingham the unions claimed that the number claiming SB had increased by 21.5% during the same period in which staffing had fallen by 2.5%, and the ratio of staff to clients had worsened from 1:52 to 1:91 in under three years. Staffing is now at its lowest level for six years.

Another demographic and social change which constrained the Government's attempts to reduce the number dependent on social security was the increase in the number of children living with one parent, an increase of 6% per year throughout the 'seventies. One in eight children are now being brought up mainly living with one parent and 40% of one parent families receive SB.[22]

Overall then the attack on public expenditure through social security was largely unsuccessful. In spite of a shift from capital to current spending, public expenditure was not effectively reduced, mainly because of the increase in 'current grants to persons', almost all being social security payments. In 1983, the social security budget was calculated to have increased by £1.5 billion over the previous year to a high of £35 billion, almost one-third of all public expenditure. The Government then decided that increases in benefit would be fixed by the annual rate of inflation actually applying in the Spring, rather than on the basis of the forecast rise for the cost of living for the future years. This was as near to adopting good housekeeping practices in social security as compatible with a demand-led service (when volume planning was being buried in other departments). Both tendencies reflect disillusion with the poor results of planning and estimating that had characterized the 'seventies in the field of public expenditure. Compared to 1980 the social security budget for 1983 increased benefits by 16.5% and the rise in the basic retirement pension was described by Patrick Jenkin, Social Services Secretary, as the biggest increase ever. The Government was continuing to give relatively more protection to pensioners, widows, disabled and others 'in real need'. Unemployment benefits on the other hand had been reduced in real terms and their value compared to average earnings declined. Different principles were being applied to different categories of claimants, separating the deserving from the undeserving – but this has long been the case in British social security. (However, the 5% abatement to short-term benefits of 1980 would be made good in November 1983.)

The Attack on Fraud and Abuse

Two main routes were followed in implementing this policy, investigations of those drawing unemployment benefit (UB) and investigations of those claiming supplementary benefits.

In September 1983, Norman Tebbitt, the Employment Secretary, argued that up to £1 million ought to have been saved in benefit payments by using the Regional Benefit Investigation Team (nicknamed the 'Rabbit Squad' by local officers) to persuade people to stop drawing unemployment benefit. The Department of Employment found that 869 people in the West Midlands, North-West, and South-East of England had been persuaded to stop claiming. If each of these then avoids claiming benefit for half a year approximately £503,000 could be saved. If each ceased to draw unemployment benefit for a full year, the savings would rise to £1,314, 019. The object of the exercise was to persuade people not to claim and the costs of the exercise would be balanced by savings if all suspected claimants were deterred from claiming for ten weeks. The trial exercise cost more than £307,000; the average claim per day for expenses by these Regional Officers being about £18. The civil service unions argued however that such estimates of benefit savings depend on the assumption that people are deterred from claiming for a long period and there is little evidence to support this. The effect may be to encourage single people in particular to move around, looking for work perhaps, and changing their address, who then shortly claim unemployment benefit again through a different local office. There are also, of course, important questions raised here about 'fair practice' and the inevitable increase in the likelihood of arbitrary treatment which such a system encourages.

Reg Prentice, the then Minister for Social Security, had earlier in the period of the Conservative Administration announced a major drive against fraud and abuse within the SB system. The main form of 'fraud' specified was that of working while drawing supplementary benefit (as with UB) and making false claims. 'Abuse' has mainly to do with voluntary unemployment, remaining on benefit when jobs are available. To tackle this, an extra 1,050 officers were employed and it was expected that they would save £50 million in 1980-81. The 'why work' syndrome continued to be identified as a major problem by the Conservative Administration in spite of over 3 million being unemployed. Local Conservative party members also continued to argue that people should be forced to work. However, in current conditions, it is more plausible to see the 'why work' syndrome as largely a myth, used to justify keeping benefits paid to unemployed family men at an especially low level.

The key problem in assessing the effectiveness of the implementation of policy in the field of social security is the difficulty of knowing what actually happens in practice, especially at the periphery after decisions have been taken at the centre. Some research has been carried out (for example that at the Policy Studies Institute) which may help to answer this question. Otherwise one is left with claims and counter claims. Some evidence of maladministration has appeared. For example, the Government has admitted underpayment to some unemployed people and mistakes in decisions about payment of SB to some disabled people. Other indicators are strikes at local offices and the evidence of confusion surrounding the introduction of the new housing benefit. With the issue of the attack on fraud abuse, evidence is even harder to adduce with certainty. What actually happens in the interview between the local investigating officer and the suspected claimant who is persuaded or deterred from continuing to claim? Evidence here is patchy, although concerned pressure groups have documented cases of harassment.

Another group identified for special investigation was that of single mothers. Of single mothers' benefit claims, 1,009 were investigated and 'irregularities' were found in 507, in a special enquiry in one region conducted between February 1980 and 1981. In 1980, in the nation as a whole, 794 single mothers were prosecuted for fraudulent claims in connection with the 'living together' rules. The main forms of abuse identified here were claiming while living together with a man; claiming desertion when this had not occurred; and working while claiming benefit. The Social Security Bill 1981 increased the penalties for social security fraud to a maximum fine of £1,000 and six months in jail. The attack on abuse was initiated with vigour in the early years of the Administration but it is important to note that this was not a new priority for government. It had been a key concern of all governments since the mid-seventies. Prosecutions for fraud increased steadily through the 'seventies, so that the later years saw four times as many prosecutions as in the earlier years of the decade. The one thousand plus additional anti-fraud officers announced by Reg Prentice and the new tactics of mobile regional squads, taking the initiative in selected areas rather than awaiting referral from the local level, may prove to be more effective in reducing the number of claims. The work-shy rules date from 1968 and these, together with the four week rule and the anti-fraud campaigns, indicate the continuing inspectorial and disciplining functions of the social security system. There are indications that this aspect has tightened up in recent years and one element in this has been the effect of revised forms of staff performance review operated at the local level, where efficiency is defined in terms of the number of cases cleared and the number of claimants on the books. Staff time spent on being helpful or considerate to claimants is not itemized as a factor in these efficiency measures.

Although the effectiveness of the fraud and abuse campaign in making savings is difficult to estimate and has been the subject of intense disagreement, the publicity given to this policy may have produced effects other than direct savings in public expenditure. Again there are few hard facts to settle the debate. Some may indeed have been deterred but numbers claiming rose dramatically over the four years, as we have already seen. Some influence however may have been exercised on the public image of the welfare recipient. This has been an unfavourable one for most of this century and particularly since the anti-scrounger campaigns of the mid-seventies. One well publicized event which occurred recently was that at Oxford. On 2 September 1982, police and SB investigators sprang a trap planned for two months to arrest 283 people on the biggest operation yet in the clamp down on alleged social security fraud. A bogus DHSS office was set up in a disused school opposite Oxford police HQ (to which '283 of Oxford's poorest citizens were directed' and 'where under the gaze of closed circuit television they were arrested, imprisoned and later tried in special courts'.[23] Claimants given cheques for weekly accommodation and living expenses were arrested and held for questioning on suspicion of obtaining payments of £67 a week by giving false bed and breakfast addresses. More than 100 police took part. (At the time with no permanent address an applicant for benefit would receive £18.62 per week, but with an address at lodgings in Oxford he could claim up to £42 for rent and personal allowances plus £25.50 for other expenses.) This swoop was publicized nationally as a major attack on fraud. In the event, Operation Major turned out not to be a major attack on big sharks, but a dubious method of netting petty minnows. The main outcome was the harassment of homeless single men and a further ostracizing of welfare claimants.

The main issues raised by this operation, which are still the subject of debate, can be summarized: how far did local benefit officers in effect act as *agent provocateurs* in continuing to pay out fraudulent claims while preparations for the swoop went on? How far was the aim of the exercise to get a great deal of publicity for a big fraud success? Was the attack planned to be on the landlords or on the larger number of claimants whose fraudulent claims were not always deliberately dishonest? Were claimants wrongly advised to plead guilty and did they receive their due rights in the process of arrest and trial?[24]

Leading up to these activities was a concerted attack on fraud and abuse by the Government. In 1981, Patrick Jenkin had claimed that £40 million had been saved through the campaign against welfare fraud. However, some of the decisions to disallow claims at an early stage were later overturned on appeal. And the Rayner Report had indicated that one in twelve claimants, over 200,000 people, might be obtaining social security benefits by fraud. These estimates were based on a sample survey of social security offices which, the report argued, showed that 8% of claimants were receiving UB or SB while working. (The main problem relates to part-time working, but this aspect of the hidden economy is, in part, the direct product of an inflexible social security system which discourages the unemployed from improving their living standard and maintaining the habit of work by the restrictions placed on the ability to earn money over and above the minimum benefits received. There are strong arguments for revising these regulations, particularly for people with young children in the present economic circumstances. Although this issue is not of direct relevance to the present essay, it is worth bearing in mind when discussing the actual definition of fraud and abuse used in these campaigns.) What is certain, however, is that the value of most of these estimates is open to serious question, since the data used are collected in a variety of circumstances by a variety of people using different criteria and with varying motives. Social researchers have criticized these estimates for the quality of the information and analyses on which they are based.[25] The main effect of these guesstimates and of the campaign, however, has been to produce a climate of opinion suspicious of those claiming benefit (while at the same time investigations of tax evasions were cut back).

The cumulative effect of changes in the administration of social security and in the parallel re-organization of the employment service has arguably been to encourage a 'sedimentation' of an 'underclass' consisting of the long-term unemployed who have become paupers outside society, ostracized and condemned. Furthermore, civil liberties have been undermined in some key areas of practice. These relational effects are equally, if not more important, than any saving that might be produced.

The way in which these investigations are conducted encourages this, especially since the emphasis has moved from prosecuting cases in court to withdrawing benefit on the basis of evidence that the investigators know may not stand up in court. In spite of the claims made when the Social Security Acts were introduced at the beginning of the 'eighties, the administration of social security seems, in fact, to be moving further away from adherence to a principle of justice than when there was a greater element of discretion built in formally to the system: now that operates informally and unseen. (The role of the Specialist Claims Control Team, for example, with their special fraud drives against unemployed people and single mothers include 'checks on other departments' records, discreet enquiries of employers, business associates or neighbours, or, if time allows, approved special investigation methods such as observation, shadowing, liaison with police and checking of vehicle numbers.)

Yet it has to be noted that less than 3% of the total staff of DHSS are engaged on fraud work. It might be argued that the new methods used by the 'flying squads' are 'rational' in deciding to monitor 'at risk' groups, those from experience found to be most likely to include cases of fraud. However, this is something like a self-fulfilling prophecy, which can lead to prejudice and discrimination against *all* members of such categories. Parallels with the debate on police methods of monitoring 'mugging' and the identification of 'young blacks' as an 'at risk' group may be obvious here, and carry similar implications and cautions. (To some extent police have responded to these cautions, but social security seems not yet to have learned the same lesson.) In November 1981, Specialist Claims Control, having been tried out locally was introduced nationally. Teams were established in each region which moved into local offices on a cyclical basis. Cases were to be looked at on the basis of set criteria. Grounds for suspicion were such as having been on benefit for over one year without applying for a lump sum grant: or having high fuel direct payments while appearing to live above one's means. These were subject to special review and the main objective was to have a deterrent effect. 'The cessation of a claim might be regarded in appropriate cases as the most cost effective way of dealing with the matter' rather than prosecution. Cost effectiveness would be the main criterion of success, that is 'getting people off the books'. At interview, an officer would state the reasons for suspecting fraud and the claimant might then decide to withdraw the claim. This procedure worries the Society of Civil and Public Servants: 'investigators are being asked to conduct interviews with the aim of persuading the person concerned to withdraw their claim'. One man was said to have been told 'unless he shows proof of having looked for work his money would be cut off again'. The power to withdraw benefit is actually invested, however, only in certain officers under the Social Security Act of 1980 (EOs, UROs and Liable Relative Officers have this power, but not Special Investigators (26)). The Government pressed on with this campaign however in the hope that the teams might achieve benefit savings of about £15 million at a cost of less than £3 million.

All this serves to demonstrate the primary obsession with abuse in the debate on social security, which feeds through to the atmosphere surrounding the apparatus of welfare administration, encouraging the misery that generates hate. This is especially important as the means-tested element in the social security system, already significantly greater than in other European countries, continues to expand. This led the Social Security Advisory Committee in March 1982 to comment in its *First Report* 'We are concerned that this major shift from contributory to means tested non-contributory benefit appears to be taking place without public debate on its implications ... There is greater need than ever to scrutinize the conditions which the Supplementary Benefit scheme contains for unemployed claimants'. (cf. Appendix)

The Simplification of The System

This objective followed directly from the growing importance of Supplementary Benefit within the overall social security system, which has been referred to above. The situation inherited by the new Conservative Administration was one where the exercise of discretion was producing anomalies. Conservative Central Office did not produce its own proposals independently but awaited the results of the internal enquiry, published as Social Assistance in 1978, and the responses to it from concerned groups. The reforms of the Social Security Acts of the early years of the new Administration aimed mainly to reduce the number of discretionary payments. Streamlining changes included such changes as: the five SB child rates were reduced to three; the Supplementary Benefits Commission (SBC) was abolished and some of its functions taken over by the Social Security Advisory Committee; and it was arranged to pay child benefit monthly rather than weekly (cf. Appendix).

But the changes introduced in the payment of SB, although limiting discretion, replaced the previous system with volumes of case law; so that it is open to question how far simplification was, in fact, achieved. The main function of the SB reforms of 1980 was to fit it to cope with its *mass role* of dealing with increasing numbers of claimants. This it was certainly called upon to do in the following years. Increasing numbers are now dependent on SB, especially important being the growing number of long-term unemployed. Implicit in these changes is a continuing devaluation of the National Insurance (NI) system, with cuts in certain benefits and pensions and the abolition of earnings related supplements in 1982. The unemployment insurance system has virtually collapsed during the recession and is now supporting less than half of those out of work. (Nearly three out of four unemployed men now rely on SB or receive no benefit at all). In February 1982, over 1.4 million unemployed men and women relied wholly or in part on SB (compared to the corresponding figures of 46% and 43% in November 1980 and 27% and 25% in 1966); 430,000 unemployed people in February 1982 received neither NI or SB, so even SB is hardly a safety net if so many fall through it. The cost to the National Insurance Fund of each increase of 100,000 in the unemployed is about £180 million in extra benefit and lost contributions. While NI benefits are awarded by right, with the key test for the unemployed being that they are available for work, SB are means-tested benefits, the effects of which are to confuse, deter and stigmatize those needing help. The key issues in assessing the effects of the Social Security Acts of 1980 are whether making the regulations public made the decision of officers more predictable and easier to contest and whether the system became more or less responsive to changing human needs and circumstances. Given the cuts in the civil service, the signs are that it became less so. This area is one requiring further study and more hard evidence. But the problem of individualized justice remains inherent in a means-tested system, even though the decisions of local SB appeal tribunals may now be referred to appeal to Social Security Commissioners on a point of law. The decisions of the Commissioners set precedents for the future but there has been some delay in reaching decisions, so it will take a longer time before the principles at work become clear. (These procedures were revised in 1982 and have been somewhat improved.) On the whole, the price of replacing discretion by detailed obligations imposed by regulations has been complexity rather than simplification. So although the key objective of the Social Security Bill No. 1 (Dec. 1979) was said to be simplification, and although headquarters' officials worked hard on setting out a mass of regulations to transform the legal basis of the new scheme, to train staff and tribunal chairmen to implement it, and train 400 special care officers to deal with cases of special difficulty, in the end no radical simplification was achieved and the fundamental bias of the system against the unemployed remained unaltered.

Planned computerization of records and access to VDUs in local offices or welfare rights offices may in the future simplify administration although it is unlikely to increase the claimant's understanding of the way the system works. £1.6 billion has been invested in this technological innovation, the aim being comprehensive records, based on a 'whole person' approach. However, if this new system cannot be linked with computerization of tax records, an opportunity to rationalize the interface of tax and social security may be missed.

Another attempt at simplification was the drive to improve forms; that forms should be easy to understand and to fill in and that there should be no more forms than are actually needed. 12,000 types of forms are presently used by DHSS nationally. The implementation of this policy is just getting under way and its effects are to be monitored.

The administration of sick pay was another area where simplification or streamlining was attempted. The growth of occupational sick pay schemes formed the background here. By the mid-seventies, 80% of all workers were covered by such schemes and half would get full pay during the initial period: the great majority no longer relied on national insurance during short-term sickness. However, DHSS was processing 10 million claims per annum for sickness benefit, a costly duplication of work by employers and the state. Also these benefits were not taxed. The aims of the reforms here were stated to be to end wasteful administration, bring sick pay into taxation, reduce unnecessary public expenditure and reduce the size of the civil service. Legislation was postponed until February 1981 to consider certain objections raised to proposals, mainly from small employers and industries with higher than average employee sickness records. 230 representations were received by the Government to the consultative document, and meetings took place between the Government and the CBI, the Engineering Employers' Federation and representatives of small businesses and others. In this case, we see a good example of modifications introduced and constraints on policy implementation raised by questions of workability: that is, for the scheme to work the cooperation of other groups was required and so the Government changed its position and accepted the 100% scheme (whereby the employer would deduct the full amount of the statutory sick payment made from the monthly NI payments). Therefore, every payment of sick pay made by an employer is now deducted from NI payments, so the savings obtained are not as large as the Government originally conceived and it is necessary to check employers' assessments. But the Government could claim some savings in the number of staff employed in the administration of sick pay and argued significantly that this development demonstrated a 'new balance between state and private elements in our welfare system'.[27]

The Poverty and Unemployment Traps

The Conservative Administration's view was that it is clearly unacceptable that some people are better off unemployed than they would be in work, in spite of evidence from DHSS research on a cohort of unemployed that this situation applies to very few people indeed. This belief was used however partly to justify the reduction in income tax from 33% to 30% and the taxing of UB introduced early in the life of the Administration. Consideration was given early as to whether UB should be linked to prices or whether it should be de-indexed. It was argued that this would ease the 'why work' problem and reduce public expenditure, although it was recognized that the position of the poorest unemployed families on SB might require special consideration.

The Government's attitude to child benefits (well recognized by experts as the most effective direct means of relieving the poverty and unemployment traps) was ambivalent. Child benefit was not raised in November 1979 but after representations from, among others, their own party's Women's National Advisory Committee, they altered their policy decision in later budgets. This vacillation however further tightened the poverty trap. Although attacking the 'why work' syndrome and reducing the poverty trap were key objectives stated in the manifesto and in speeches, by the end of their term of office the situation had not improved and there was some evidence of deterioration.[28] In 1982, a family man who doubled his weekly earnings from £60 to £120 would be better off by just £4.39 when loss of means-tested benefits and payment of income tax and national insurance were taken into account. In 1950, the two child family on average earnings paid less than 4% of income in income tax and national insurance. By 1981, this had risen to 26%. In the autumn budget of 1982, NI contributions rose to 9% of incomes from 6.5% in 1979-80, making the poverty trap worse. Over recent years the situation for the low income family has worsened and the incentive to work, arguably, been reduced (only however in 'economic man' models of behaviour because much other evidence of social research indicates that the desire to work is prompted by a range of other considerations in addition to purely financial calculation). The 25% rate of income tax on the first £750 of taxable income was abolished in 1980 and in 1981 personal tax allowances were not raised in line with inflation. After budget changes in 1982, at three-quarters of average earnings (£7,000 p.a. in 1981) a model 'family with two children' would have found tax payments of all kinds increased by 17% after allowing for inflation. However, a two child family on five times the national average would pay 6% less tax in real terms. In addition, price rises for the poor increased by 4% more than prices in general because the poor are estimated to spend proportionately more on food, housing, transport and fuel.

Other evidence of the continuing problem of the 'poverty trap' came from the Study Commission on the Family who found that the value of state support for children had fallen since the war while tax burdens had grown heavier. The purchasing power of child benefits was lower in 1981 than in 1960. Since 1978-9, child benefit for a two child family had fallen by £1.10 in real terms.[29]

Research on the likely impact of the introduction of housing benefit (to be discussed below) concluded that after April 1983 there would be a more rapid withdrawal of assistance as income rises above the needs-allowance level, equivalent to an increase in the marginal rate of tax on income over the relevant range. There would be some worsening of the unemployment trap (constraints on return to work) especially for a family man earning between £60 and £100 per week: over £100 per week the effect would begin to tail off.[30]

In 1980, the differential for a three child family earning £70 and another earning £110 was estimated to be only £6.25. A man with three children earning £81 per week was estimated to be worse off than someone in the same position earning £20 a week less. This was because the higher wage earner lost both 'family income supplement' (FIS) and free school meals.[31] The solution clearly lies with higher child benefits, but no progress has been made on this front and indeed at the beginning of the Conservative Party's second term of office in the 'eighties, debates are going on about possible cuts in benefits. Child benefits in Britain are among the lowest in Europe but neither the Government nor the trade unions seem to be either aware of or to care very much in practice about the problem of the unemployment and poverty traps. In effect, though the manifesto and early speeches by Patrick Jenkin claimed to be interested in 'reducing the poverty trap' the number of poor families caught by this actually doubled between 1978 and 1982. Official evidence to the Treasury and Civil Service Sub-COmmittee Inquiry into the Interaction of Taxes and Benefits indicated that 120,000 families who were poor enough to receive FIS were also paying tax and national insurance contributions. Out of every £1 extra earned, families caught at this point in the overlap of the social security and taxation systems lost 80p.[32] To add to the problem, the number claiming FIS is less than that of those entitled to it. Data from the Family Finance Survey (Sept. 1978 - Sept. 1979) indicated a take-up rate of only 51% (previously it had been assumed that 75% of eligible parents received FIS). Reasons for this low take up are generally ignorance of the regulations about entitlement and anxiety about the hassle involved in claiming. In 1980-81, £357,000 was spent on publicity for FIS to try to improve take up.

The Select Committee referred to above, chaired by Michael Meacher, investigated the interaction of taxes and benefits. Its task was to investigate the effects of personal direct taxation and income support on the distribution of income and on the incentive to work and to explore the administrative problems associated with the present system and possible alternatives. In looking at its findings it is worth noting that the issue of the poverty trap concerns not only *incentives*, as emphasized by this Conservative Administration, but also that of *equity*. In practice, the social security system, heavily dominated by means-tested benefits, fails to deliver. Low take up rates, as evidenced in the DHSS cohort study of the unemployed, exacerbate the hardship suffered, especially by the families of long-term unemployed. But while the emphasis is on incentives rather than equity a substantial, rather than rhetorical, attack on the poverty and unemployment traps seems unlikely. 'If you believe economic salvation can only be achieved by rewarding success and the national income is not increasing then you have no alternative but to make the unsuccessful poorer',[33] and this was effectively done by pushing more people into the poverty trap.

The malign interaction of the tax and social security system acts as a disincentive to the low paid family man: but, with three million unemployed is there really much point in increasing this incentive? A solution would lie in raising tax thresholds and child benefit, abolishing the married man's allowance and unifying the tax and social security systems. The Conservative belief, however, is that these developments must wait until resources permit change. The revitalizing of the economy through cutting public expenditure remains their first priority and plans such as those outlined above would run directly counter to this policy.

Housing Benefit and Fuel Benefit

Special 'tabbed' benefits can have the effect of increasing the dependency and pauper-like status of recipients and increase the tightness of the poverty trap. Some had argued that there was a need for a comprehensive fuel benefit, especially given the rapid increase in fuel costs encouraged by changes in government policy towards the nationalized industries. Patrick Jenkin, however, rejected the idea of a fuel rebate as too complicated to administer and because it encouraged the poverty trap. In respect of fuel debts, action remained with the industries and their operation of a code of practice. Berthoud however concluded that the code had failed to protect the poor from disconnection.[34]

However, with increases in council rents (with the move towards economic rents which began in the early 'seventies) and with the squeeze on local authority expenditure and increases in poverty and unemployment, rent arrears are now at an all time high. £80 million is owed councils, mainly in the big cities. The Social Security and Housing Benefit Act (November 1982) was a key weapon to curb future debts by increasing the extent of direct payment of rent costs from DHSS to the local authorities. Already in Birmingham, 65% of council tenants had their rent paid direct by DHSS, 53% in Coventry and 36% in Liverpool. In London alone, £40 million was owed in rent and the administrative costs involved in collecting rent arrears were high and expensive because personal casework was often involved. It was estimated that 60% of London's 750,000 council tenants live on or below the poverty line; 46% of Islington's and 54% of Camden's tenants owe arrears of rent.

For local authorities, the housing benefit scheme thus proved attractive in offering the possibility, through direct payment of rent, of cutting back on rent arrears. For central government, the attraction was that of reducing the number of civil servants and thus central government's contribution to public expenditure (although increases in local government employees could be anticipated). In March 1981, the Government issued a consultative document, *Assistance with Housing Costs*, which proposed changes in the ways in which low income householders would be helped with their rent and rates. The Social Security and Housing Benefit Bill followed from this. In mid-1981, it was estimated that 2.9 million householders received amounts towards housing costs through SB. The average benefit received was £11.90 per week. After the changes (to be effected from November 1982 for local authority tenants and from April 1983 for the remainder) it was estimated that 1,050,000 pensioner households would gain (60% of gainers being tenants) and 2 million would lose from the new formula.[35] When introduced, there was much criticism of the administration of the housing benefit scheme, with private tenants in particular being caught in the transition. The new system proved to be highly complex and produced severe problems for local authorities. In addition, the tapers were altered from those originally proposed and later changes proposing reductions in entitlement looked set to cut the income of pensioners and poor families, so that even the 'deserving poor' seemed to be targets for government cuts. Unease and discomfort with these policies gained strength among traditional Conservative supporters.

Conclusion

From this necessarily condensed review of developments in social security in five key areas over the years of the first Thatcher Administration, we can discern some consistent trends and make an assessment of the effectiveness of the Government's attempts to pursue its stated objectives.

The major goals of the Government on taking office were to cut public expenditure and eliminate wasteful bureaucracy, thus to reduce the social security budget. The administrative structures were to be knocked into shape, streamlined and procedures simplified. To restore dynamism in society and in economic life, competition would be encouraged, through increasing incentives and, thereby, social differentiation. Scarce resources would be concentrated on those in 'real need'. The social security budget in 1983 was indeed less than it would have been had policies existing in 1979 continued: but social security expenditure still grew dramatically. The Government had little room for manoeuvre, given social and demographic trends. Yet the most significant pressure increasing the budget resulted from the Government's own pursuit of objectives in other policy areas, most notably in economic policy, which contributed to rapidly rising unemployment and, within that, to the increasing proportion of long-term unemployed.

Administration was cut to its lowest level for several years while increasing demands were being placed on local offices. Strikes indicated the point where the cuts seemed to have gone too far, as unions resisted. Other less overt resistance came from top management within DHSS. And sections within DHSS itself and external pressure groups and local authorities sometimes acted to increase demand by encouraging increases in the take up of benefits.

The aim to simplify and thus cut the cost of administering the system met its greatest countervailing pressure, however, from within the structure itself; increasing reliance on means-tested benefits and the virtual collapse of the national insurance system[36] led to high costs of administration (because of the requirement for individual assessment of need). If the administration is cheap, this may indicate that the costs have been shifted on to the claimant, not only through mistakes but in waiting-time, anxiety and so on: a study of what happens in the process of claiming might elucidate this. There is, in fact, a built-in contradiction between the aims on the one hand to simplify and end the poverty trap and on the other to encourage a means-tested system for 'those in real need'. 'Real need' is an ambiguous concept which operates on subjective assessment and definitions of standards which must be constructed within a political and moral setting. Given that the prevailing ethos remains one in which people in 'real need' should not suffer, the only practicable way to reduce the demands on the system is to deter those who are not in 'real need' from claiming. Thus the emphasis on rooting out fraud and abuse and the increasing differentiation between the conditions provided for the long-term unemployed, especially those with children, and those with other forms of dependency. The increasing role played by supplementary benefits and means tests in protecting the poor is crucial here, and it is important to note that this is a legacy of the 'new initiatives' in social security of the Conservative Government of the early 'seventies, quite different in conception from the hoped for universalism of the legislation of the 1940s. In addition, increasing inequality and social differentiation resulting from recent changes in earnings and taxation has exacerbated the poverty and unemployment traps. Those who lost out were the families of the long-term unemployed and of low wage earners. The ideological effects of these deterrent practices increased the stigmatization and stereotyping of those on social security. Although public attitudes were slightly less condemnatory than in the late 'seventies, these poor were still seen as inadequate and as losers who were paying the price of failing in a harsh, competitive world. The costs of increasing dynamism in the economy and in social life by cutting public expenditure were shifted on to a particular social strata, the unemployed and the working poor. Others who continued in employment, while suffering some anxiety, did not see such a drastic cut in their living standards, if any at all. In this the Government could be seen to be pursuing policies begun under the previous Labour Administration but with notably more determination and vigour.

The shift from the more visible direct to the less visible indirect taxation may partly have contributed to the weakening of the welfare backlash (the political uproar about social security expenditure which had marked the late 'seventies and from which the Conservative Party had benefited. The long-term unemployed and the low wage earner with children bore the brunt of the attack on pre-existing expectations and structures. Whether a revival of the economy will result from this, time will tell.

Although throughout this discussion we have used the term 'objectives' in the sense used in 'policy studies', the term can be misleading. It implies a coherence and cogency in policy making which is largely absent in practice, and especially so in this area of social security. Critics of the

Government would argue that the incoherence of policy and the increasing complexity, confusion and inequality of treatment and receipt of social benefit, which have been evidenced in recent years, indicate the underlying purpose of specific interest groups acting on and through the state. These are to increase inequality and inequity and restrict the rights of citizenship, and that these conditions reflect the changed balance of class forces. Even critics who would not take such a radical 'capitalist' state view, have pointed out that social security policy in the years 1978-83 was inconsistent. For these 'social democrats' hoping for a rational, planned social policy, the policies and practices fostered in these years seem not to reflect a clear underlying social philosophy but to be simply hasty, ill-conceived and random products of the desire to cut the number of DHSS staff and restrain public expenditure. There were few central ideas guiding these policies, they would argue. Rather they reflected the need to meet short-term objectives, particularly with regard to staffing. The latest spending and staffing targets produced annually led to a series of *ad hoc* cuts and adaptive policies. It is interesting to note here the lack of public complaint about such cuts. Apart from the resistance of the unions and workers in local offices, public concern has been absent, a notable contrast with the situation regarding the NHS (where the Labour Party has taken up the protection of jobs and services as a key oppositional issue.)

The main impact of these years has been on the tone of the administration rather than on its structure. This must have something to do with the fact that the structure of social security contains very little of the 'welfare state ethos' of social justice, universalism and collectivism, found to a greater extent in education and health. To this Government, the structure of social security is not fundamentally disagreeable. The unemployed are already discriminated against and means-testing has a principle place in the system of allocation, a great deal of this being the inheritance of the 1970-74 Conservative Government. To a large extent it was this Government which created the 'monster octopus' of social security, with the shift in direction brought about by the new benefits introduced when Sir Keith Joseph was Secretary of State.

The over-riding objective then for the Government was that of cutting back on the welfare state. Cuts in expenditure and reductions in staffing were the prime goals. Thereafter it mattered less how these cuts were to be effected, and here it was left very much to officials to devise particular schemes within the constraints set. Officials within DHSS have on the whole attempted, within these severe restraints, to pursue an equitable and efficient policy but they have publicly admitted that the effect of these cuts has been to reduce the standard of living of those receiving benefit to one which is clearly inadequate. They are also concerned at the reduced coverage of the system, many of those eligible not being reached and at the abysmal quality of the service offered. 'Never mind what it is, lets have less of it' seemed to be the order of the day.

The Thatcher Government was indeed relatively successful in the circumstances in cutting social security expenditure, reducing the costs of administration and concentrating help on those defined as in 'real need'. The administration was shaken up and, after the Rayner review and other attempts at introducing more effective practices, some innovations had been set in motion. The incentive to escape from reliance on social security was increased, not through cash inducements but by increasing the deterrent effect of the stigma and discomfort attached to claiming. But while the poverty and unemployment traps tightened, people with family responsibilities found they had little choice but to put up with this discomfort. The basic problem of the system's increasing reliance on means-tested supplementary benefit produced effects which counter-acted the pursuit of other key objectives. And, policies pursued in other areas, which ranked higher in priority than social security, impacted strongly on the total demand for social security and reduced the possibility of attacking the poverty trap.

The most important effect of these four years was arguably not that on material standards of living for those dependent on social security. Although numbers claiming increased and the NI and unemployment benefit was cut, the actual level of supplementary benefits did not fall as dramatically as some had perhaps feared. Although the discrimination against the long-term unemployed remained, the effect was rather on social relations and values. The myth of social security was exposed and the system revealed as a residual service catering for a large and growing under-class, distinct from other social strata. Although benefit levels could not be significantly reduced nor entitlement to claim severely restricted without challenging the philosophy of caring for those in real need, the discomfort and stigma connected with claiming, built in since the nineteenth-century Poor Law, could serve to deter all but the hopeless from relying for too long on that system. Thirty-five years after the Poor Law was thought to have been finally abolished, the principle of 'less eligibility' remains at the heart of our social security system, a fitting tribute to the strength and vigour of the New Poor Law, which appropriately in 1984 celebrated its 150th anniversary.

Appendix

1. The Conservative Party Manifesto of 1979 argued under the heading 'Making sense of social security':

> Our social security system is now so complicated that even some Ministry officials do not understand it. Income tax starts at such a low level that many poor people are being taxed to pay for their own benefits. All too often they are little or no better off at work than they are on social security.
>
> This was one of our principal reasons for proposing a tax credit scheme. Child benefits are a step in the right direction. Further progress will be very difficult in the next few years, both for reasons of cost and because of technical problems involved in the switch to computers. We shall wish to move towards the fulfilment of our original tax credit objectives as and when resources become available. Meanwhile we shall do all we can to find other ways to simplify the system, restore the incentive to work, reduce the poverty trap and bring more effective help to those in greatest need.
>
> Restoring the will to work means, above all, cutting income tax. It also involves bringing unemployment and short term sickness benefit within the tax system - an objective fully shared by Labour Ministers. The rules about the unemployed accepting available jobs will be reinforced and we shall act more vigorously against fraud and abuse.
>
> We welcomed the new Child Benefit as the first stage of our tax credit scheme. One-parent families face much hardship so we will maintain the special addition for them. (Conservative Party 1979, p.27).

2. For a more detailed discussion of the situation inherited by the new Conservative Government in 1979 and the debate about *Social Assistance*, see Susanne MacGregor, 'Social security' in *Government policy initiatives 1979-80*, (ed.) Peter Jackson, RIPA, 1981.

3. In the late 'seventies, over 30,000 staff were employed on SB work alone, more than half the total number of staff in local offices but paying out only 14.5% of the total budget.

4. *Social Security Expenditure 1979-80*

Pensioners £ million

	£ million
Retirement pensions	7,609
Widows' pensions, industrial death benefits	471
War pensions, old persons' pensions, Xmas Bonus	361

Disabled

Invalidity benefits	947
Attendance allowance, invalid care allowance and mobility allowance	272
Industrial disablement benefit	218

Family

Child benefit*   1,834
Family income supplement   26

Remainder

Supplementary benefits   2,000
Sickness/injury benefits and maternity allowance   761
Unemployment benefit   648
Administration and miscellaneous services   638
Other   50

£15,835

Net Exchequer cost taking account of abolition of child tax allowances.

(Source: Cmnd. 7439)

5.   *The Social Security Act 1980*

The Social Security Act 1980 received the Royal Assent in May 1980. The reformed scheme came into operation on 24 November 1980. The changes fell into two main areas – legal and administrative changes and changes in the structure of the benefits themselves.

Legal and Administrative Changes

(a)   A revised legal structure involved the setting out of entitlement and assessment in the Act. These would be explained in layman's language in a revised version of the SB handbook. For the first time therefore, it was claimed, all the rules of the SB scheme would be published in full.

(b)   Individual claims would be decided by local SB officers. These officers took the place of the SBC as the determining authority. These decisions would be subject to the right of appeal to SB appeal tribunals and, on matters of law, from tribunals to a Social Security Commissioner.

(c)   A Social Security Advisory Committee was established taking the place of the SBC which was abolished (together with the NI Advisory Committee). The value of this new committee was that it would be able to give advice across the whole field of social security benefits, both contributory and non-contributory.

(d)   Claimants would receive written notices of how their benefit was assessed.

(e)   Special officers were established to help with cases of special difficulty.

Benefit Changes

(a)   The qualifying period for long-term scale rates was reduced. Where previously claimants under pension age (other than the unemployed) could qualify for the higher long-term rate after they had been receiving benefit continuously for two years, this period is now reduced to one year.
(b)   The number of scale rates for children of different ages was reduced. The previous five were collapsed into three, giving new bands of 0-10, 11-15 and 16-17 years.
(c)   The long-term rate of SB was brought into line with the NI rates.
(d)   Contributions towards housing costs from non-dependents were standardized.
(e)   Changes were made in the treatment of resources. If a claimant had more than £2,000 capital he would not be eligible for SB. (Insurance policies are classed as capital.) There will be a standard disregard of £4 of the earnings of claimants and spouses. Lone parents would be able to retain more of their earnings - half their earnings between £4 and £20 per week. Other changes covered occupational pensions, and war widows' pensions and sick pay from an employer.
(g)   Men and women would be treated equally as regards the right to claim benefit where a couple lived together. (This followed from an EEC directive to establish equality in social security provision for men and women.)
(h)   As part of the move towards clear published rules, the regulations would set out what expenses would be covered by the scale rates, what additional expenses would be provided for and the circumstances in which discretionary payments would be allowed. (This attempt to codify the administration of what had previously been discretionary payment opened up a labyrinth of complexity and pendantry likely eventually to fill volumes.)
(i)   Other changes refer to liability for sponsored relatives under the Immigration Act 1971, the extension of the over-80s rate to married couples, special rates for the blind and laundry additions.

6.   *Social Security (No. 2) Bill*

The Social Security (No. 2) Bill covered the following changes: short-term social security benefits and invalidity pensions could be increased by up to 5% less than full price protection; the retirement pension earnings limit would be frozen; the linking period used for incapacity and unemployment benefits would be shortened, and benefit would not be paid for spells of incapacity of less than four days; the earnings-related supplement to short-term benefits would be reduced in 1981 and abolished in 1982; unemployment benefit would be reduced for those who had retired on a substantial occupational pension; and supplementary benefit for strikers' families would be reduced by £12.

7. The Rayner Study Plan

The Rayner study plan pointed out that about 26,500 man-years are now involved in the administration of unemployment and supplementary benefits for unemployed people, in the DOE and DHSS, while another 500 staff are employed on registration and related work in the Employment Services Division. The total cost of these staff in the three organizations in 1978-9 was about £200 million. The amount paid out in benefits for the unemployed in that year was £1,300 million. The Rayner Team point out that this multiplicity of benefits and organizations, each having its own network of local offices, leads inevitably to travelling between offices by unemployed people and to major flows of paper and information. Some significant changes have taken place in recent years - the computerization of UBS, the introduction of fortnightly attendance and payment for the unemployed; the physical separation of job centres and unemployment benefit offices; higher levels of unemployment and increasing recourse to SB; and greater concern about fraud and abuse. 'In the light of these considerations it was thought desirable to review the complex of inter-acting systems which have developed and consider whether they could be made more effective'.

8. The Long-Term Unemployed and Social Security

In their 1983 report, the Social Security Advisory Committee recommended that the long-term unemployed should receive the long-term rate of supplementary benefit. They pointed out that at present married couples would be better off separating and claiming benefits in their own right. Sir Arthur Armitage, the chairman, said the proposal would cost about £395 million.

In evidence to the House of Commons Social Services Select Committee, in 1982, DHSS civil servants forecast a big increase in the numbers claiming over the following three years. Between 1982 and 1984, the proportion of unemployed people living on supplementary benefit was expected to rise by a fifth. A greater proportion of unemployed people rely on SB than on UB at present, and this proportion will rise until 1984-5 when over half the unemployed will be living on the poverty-line of SB.

The seven million people (one eighth of the population) depending on SB in 1983, represent a 50% increase since 1979. Most of this increase was caused by rising unemployment. This inevitably means an increase in the extent of poverty in British society. A further indication is that one-third of households are entitled to receive housing benefit. Poverty and hardship, far from being 'residual pockets' now constitute the hard facts of life for a large and growing social strata. The burden of restructuring the economy has fallen disproportionately on those already worse-off.

9.   Patrick Jenkin issued a statement to justify the claim that the extra 1,050 staff put on social security fraud and abuse work had saved £40 million in 1980-81 (H.C. Deb., 6 May 1981, Vol. 4, col. 79-80).

The extra staff largely concentrated on the unemployed. As a result of this campaign, about 53,500 more unemployed workers had their benefit cut off (out of the total of 102,000 who lost benefit).

Some of the procedures adopted involved checks on particular categories of claimants and certain trades (plumbers and motor mechanics, for example). In more than half the cases selected for detailed scrutiny, it was found that benefit 'should be adjusted or stopped'.

10.   Some other changes implemented during this period may be briefly noted: (more details are available in the useful publication, *Social Security Notes*, issued by DHSS).

(a)   amendments to the November 1980 rules of the SB scheme were introduced in July 1981;
(b)   from Nov. 1981, unemployed SB recipients aged 60 and over would be able to get the higher, long-term rate of benefit after a year at the ordinary rate *provided they chose no longer to register for work*.
(c)   modifications to the regulations concerning part-time study while receiving SB, limiting the 21 hours allowed purely to hours of classroom instruction but also extending a qualifying period of 3 months to people of all ages;
(d)   registration for work at a Jobcentre to cease to be a condition of entitlement to benefit for those unemployed (from October 1982). Availability for work would still be tested at the unemployment benefit offices or local DHSS office.
(e)   from 6 December 1982, SB claims from unemployed people would be by a postal claim form acquired from an UB office and sent to the local social security office.

11.   *The Social Security Advisory Committee*

This replaced the NI, Advisory Committee and the SBC, with the SB reform of 1980. It is a purely advisory body and straddles the divide between contributory and non-contributory benefits. Its duties are to advise the government on social security matters; to watch the quality of service to the public; and to offer its own comments and advice. Its influence is more restrained than that of the SBC under Donnison, which acted to some extent as a pressure-group for claimants. However, less vociferously and confined to debates within the civil service, it has tried to influence thinking on certain key issues: financial support for families; benefits for the long-term unemployed; and benefit for disabled people.

Their first report (1981) was published by HMSO (in March 1982). There it was noted that the changes introduced in the early period of the Administration had 'increased dependence on supplementary benefits and shifted the balance between contributory and means-tested benefits'. The Committee initiated a natural monitoring exercise on the working of the new SB scheme. They noted *seven* areas of concern, while welcoming the reduction in the number of children's scale rates, the reduction from two years to one in the qualifying period for the long-term rate, and the new disregard for lone parents' earnings. The problems noted concerned: *the way the new scheme is being administered in local social security offices* (delays, errors, lack of awareness of the regulations and poor treatment of claimants. Confusion had been produced by the haste with which the scheme was introduced); *Single payments* (that these might be too restrictive, the exclusion of those not receiving SB from entitlement; it was noted that the cost in real terms of single payments had fallen by 16% even though numbers on benefit increased); *capital rules* (that should be raised with inflation); *the new legal structure of regulations and adjudication; urgent need payments* (regulations too complicated); *no benefit for school leavers* (whether this tended to encourage young people to leave school at Easter); *special leaflets.*

They noted the immensity of the social security system – at the same time 23 million benefit payments were made each week (plus 700,000 in N. Ireland) by 121,000 civil servants in DHSS and the Department of Employment. They noted that, although in general speed and efficiency were observed, pressures on staff and claimants 'sometimes thwart the best of intentions'. They recommended an advice and information service within local offices to help claimants, noting that Beveridge had suggested this in 1942.

They reiterated the lack of debate about the shift towards means-testing in the overall social security system and the lack of public debate on its implications. They pointed out that 'the growing band of long-term unemployed has to exist on a basic level of personal benefit which is little more than two-thirds of the minimum the Government has established for others in similar circumstances'. An increase in benefits for families with children should be the first priority.

12.   By 1983, ten of the recommendations in the 1981 SSAC Report had been implemented in whole or in part:

(a) the real value of SB and FIS had been preserved, and the 2% shortfall was restored in Nov. 1982;

(b) the 2% shortfall in child benefit was restored in Nov. 1982. In November 1983, child benefit was restored to its April 1979 value, being the highest ever level in real terms;

(c) the 2% shortfall in short-term contributory benefits was restored;

(d) the SB capital cut off increased to £2,500 in Nov. 1982 and £3,000 in Nov. 1983 and the single payments capital limit was raised to £500;

(e) from June 1983 unemployed men over 60 receive the long-term rate of SB *immediately* and, from Nov. 1983, couples receive the long-term rate where the woman is over 60 but the man is not.

(f) the 5% abatement of UB was restored Nov. 1983.

(g) the 'invalidity trap' removed from Nov. 1983.

(h) pilot advice and information projects started.

In addition, by the end of 1982, 59% of all unemployed claimants relied wholly or in part on SB, emphasizing the shift from contributory to means-tested support for large numbers of people. One-third of those unemployed at the end of 1982 were aged under 25 years. The total number of SB claimants reached over 4 million. (SSAC 2nd Report (1982), HMSO, Nov. 1983).

13.   Although pensioners were protected by the Government during this period, there remained at the end of their term of office a growing concern that the New Pension scheme, due to mature at the end of the century, might be unable to deliver its promises, since the cost might be far greater than estimated. There were signs that the Government would be prepared to consider fundamental changes in the state earnings-related pension scheme. Here the constraint operating on the Government, which conflicts with its commitment to protect the old, is the basic one that it has also to manage the affairs of the country as well as pursue formally stated objectives. In the last twenty years, for example, the number of old people has increased by over one third. By 1986, there will be 25% more people over 75 than in 1982.

14.   In certain local areas, attempts were made by welfare groups and local authorities to increase awareness of benefits and thus take up. In Cardiff, for example, three bureaux of the Citizens' Advice Bureau used mini-computers to assess entitlement to benefit and Strathclyde experimented with a postal campaign to encourage people to claim. A campaign by Cleveland Social Services Department produced take up of £600,000 unclaimed benefit (mainly SB, attendance allowance and housing benefits). This ten week campaign cost the authority £47,000.

References

* Peter Esam and Patrick Hennessy read a draft of this chapter and I should like to thank them for their comments.

1. Conservative Party, *The Conservative Manifesto*. Conservative Central Office, April 1979, p. 27.
2. Bruce Page, *New Statesman*, 7 April 1978, 461.
3. Adam Raphael, *Observer*, 24 October 1982.
4. Sir Geoffrey Otton. Lecture given at RIPA, 15 February 1983.
5. *Ibid*.
6. *Social Services Committee*, 1980.
7. *The Conservative Manifesto 1979*, op. cit., 7.
8. *Ibid*.
9. *The Conservative Manifesto 1979*, op. cit., 8.
10. *op. cit.*, 9.
11. *op. cit.*, 13.
12. *Politics Today*, No. 9, 19 May 1980, 144.
13. *op. cit.*, 148.
14. H.C. Deb., col. 1458, 26 March 1980.
15. Speech by Patrick Jenkin at Oldham, 9 January 1980.
16. Patrick Jenkin in H.C. Deb., col. 651, 14 June 1979.
17. Jean-Jacques Rosa (ed.), *The world crisis in social security*, Transaction Books, 1982.
18. The withering of Europe's welfare states, *The Economist*, 16 October 1982, 65-67.
19. Commission of the European Communities, *The perception of poverty in Europe*, March 1977.
20. H.C. Deb., cols. 86-87, 23 July 1979, WA.
21. Study Commission on the Family, *Family issues and public policy*, 1982.
23. *Fraud and Operation Major – an assessment*, CHAR Occasional Paper, No. 1, 1 October 1983.
24. *Ibid*.
25. W.W. Daniel, In defence of job centres, *New Society*, 16 April 1981.
26. Peter Moore, Scroungermania again at DHSS, *New Society*, 22 January 1981, 138-9.
27. Hugh Rossi, *The Times Health Supplement*, 30 October 1981, 9.
28. Escaping from the poverty trap, *The Economist*, 13-19 November 1982, 46.
29. Study Commission on the Family, *Family incomes since the War*, 1982.
30. G.C. Fiegehen and L. McGwire, Economic Advisers' Office, DHSS, The income and incentive effects of the Housing Benefit Reform, *Social Security Workshop*, 11 June 1982.
31. Study Commission on the family, *Equity and family incomes*, 1980.
32. *New Society*, 27 May 1982, 340.
33. Reg Prentice quoted by David Donnison, *New Society*, 22 January 1981, 153.
34. Richard Berthoud, *Fuel debts and hardship*, Policy Studies Institute, 1981.
35. G.C. Fiegehen and L. McGwire, *op. cit*.
36. *Economic Bulletin for Europe*, September 1983. Quoted in Frances Williams, *The Times*, 24 October 1983, 4.
37. Harold L. Wilensky, *The 'New Corporatism', centralization and the welfare state*, Sage Contemporary Politics Sociology Series, Vol. 2, 1976; Susanne MacGregor, *The politics of poverty*, Longman, 1981.
38. *Social Security operational strategy: a framework for the future*, DHSS, September 1982; *A strategy for social security operations*, DHSS, 1980.

11

The Energy Policies of the 1979-83 Conservative Government

Roger Williams

The Government's overall approach to energy policy was conveniently summarized in the Department of Energy's *Proof of Evidence for the Sizewell 'B' Public Inquiry*[1] in October 1982. Because in the energy sector the concentration of resources and distribution networks in public monopolies left the market 'far from free and competitive', the thrust of policy was said to be the removal where possible of market distortions, the Government's unequivocal and explicit view being that market forces are more efficient regulators of supply and demand than central planning. In furtherance of this policy the Government cited its various attempts to transfer functions from the public to the private sector, its initiatives to reduce the monopoly powers of the nationalized industries, and its efforts to introduce an alternative discipline where full exposure to market forces was not possible. It was said to be 'central to this market-oriented approach' that energy be priced realistically since supply-demand interaction was 'mainly determined by price'. Energy pricing was therefore included, the *Proof* continued, in the formulation of financial targets for the nationalized industries, so that prices might reflect market pressures, where there were reasonably open markets, and supply costs otherwise. Thereafter it was for the consumer to rank his own investment priorities in the light of the prevailing prices. It was stressed that the Government for its part had no wish to 'take to itself the decisions of millions of consumers'. The international nature of the energy market and its instabilities between them meant that there could be no 'set blueprint of energy development', but access to international markets, the Government argued, relaxed the need to match UK energy production exactly to UK demand.

The assumptions and figures in the Labour Government's 1978 Green Paper on *Energy Policy*[2] were initially updated in *Energy Projections 1979*.[3] However, no political change of direction was implied by the new projection, though the figures in the two documents were very different, the estimate of total demand for the year 2000, for instance, being reduced from 450-560 million tons of coal equivalent (mtce) to 445-510 as between the two papers.[4] The 1979 paper itself quickly became out of date but a revised version was not published until 1982, when new figures were produced for the Sizewell inquiry. It was again stressed that the figures in the resulting *Energy Projections 1982*[5] were not to be regarded as forecasts.

The weakening of the world oil market, together with the recession and its impact on the structure of the UK economy, were said in this document to have produced a background 'very different' from that which had obtained in 1979. It was also stated that the methodology used in preparing the projections had itself changed as between 1979 and 1982, the most important change identified being the provision that market prices play an explicit role, along with economic activity, in determining demand in each consuming sector, thereby *inter alia* removing the need for a separate allowance for energy conservation.

Energy Projections 1982 arrived at a very wide spread for possible primary energy demand in the year 2010, mainly because of the 'fundamental uncertainty' attaching to the economy and energy prices, the range for the year 2000 being wider than that contained in *Energy Projections 1979* as a result of a wider spread of GDP growth rates having been considered. The highest and lowest figures for primary energy demand in 2010 were put in the 1982 document at 549 and 327 mtce respectively. The corresponding range for total electricity generating capacity in 2010 was given as 130.8 to 64.1 GW,[6] and for nuclear 106.2 to 31.5 GW (on cost grounds alone and without constraints), and 65.9 to 26.4 GW with such constraints.

These projections and observations apart, the 1979-83 Conservative Government had no 'energy policy' as such but rather policies towards each of the separate energy sectors, and necessarily therefore the rest of this paper reviews these separate policies. It should be noted that there were two Secretaries of State for Energy during this period, Mr Nigel Lawson replacing Mr David Howell in the autumn of 1981.

Coal

The Government's Coal Bill of 1980 contained a sharp policy departure. It offered continuing support for the National Coal Board's ten year capital investment programme, by this time reaching its peak with expenditure of £600 million at 1979 prices scheduled for each of the following four years, and it provided for deferred interest loans, a device which the Energy Secretary suggested could be worth up to £40 million a year. Provision was also made in the Bill for the continuation and enhancement of social grants. However, the contentious aspects of the Bill were its observations in respect of operating grants and profitability.

The Government's position[7] here was that, whereas profitability was the only lasting foundation for any industry, the NCB had last made a profit in 1976/77 and its reliance on government finance had since then been growing. The Government said it had therefore decided that the Board must be set a firm financial target, to return to profit from 1983/84 on an historic cost basis and after interest and social grants. Operating grants, which 'had reached £192 million in 1979/80, would in consequence be phased out, a maximum of £590 million in 1978/79 prices being allocated for the tapering off period. The Government insisted that since operating grants constituted only 4½% of a £4 billion turnover, their loss should have no bearing on pit closures.

The Opposition attacked the coal industry's new financial structure as amounting to a straitjacket, and the coal industry as a whole argued that subsidy to coal producers in Europe was substantially above that being given in the UK, even under existing arrangements. The National Union of Mineworkers was particularly bitter in denouncing the 'blind adherence' to the doctrine of monetarism which it blamed for the Government's policy. This, the NUM claimed, had reduced coal demand by encouraging recession while stimulating imports through allowing a high exchange rate. Some 7 million tons were in fact imported in 1980, most by the Central Electricity Generating Board and the British Steel Corporation, while domestic coal stocks reached 37 million tons. The NUM complained that interest payments to the Treasury already exceeded operating grants, while the surge in interest rates under the Conservatives was increasing these interest charges still further.

The NCB was well known to be unhappy with the 1980 Act and its motives were thus questioned when, in February 1981, in a meeting with the NUM, the possibility emerged of 50 pit closures entailing perhaps 15,000 redundancies over the following five years. Yorkshire miners had already voted to give their leader, Mr Arthur Scargill, the right to call a strike if necessary, and on 17 February an unofficial strike began in South Wales. The Energy Secretary, maintaining that projected closures were lower than the number which had been rumoured, observed that the NCB's worst 10% of pits were losing £190 million a year.[8] By 19 February, however, Mr Howell was indicating a readiness to discuss the financial constraints on the industry 'with an open mind and also with a view to movement', and he undertook additionally to try to reduce imports to an irreducible minimum.[9] In due course the Minister's promise was firmed up, the NCB withdrew its closure proposals, and the NUM urged its members to return to work. The Opposition was naturally delighted with what it saw as an instance of jack-knifing, the media spoke of a 'humiliating retreat' and of miners having thrice in a decade 'stopped a Conservative Government in its tracks'. Many Conservative backbenchers were also critical, some describing the Government's handling of the affair as a 'shambles'.[10] In due course the Government's action also came in for heavy criticism from the Commons Energy Committee,[11] which felt ministers had 'simply handed the money over without troubling to ask too many awkward questions'. The cost for the first year (1981/82) of the Government's concession was put at £231 million.

In 1982 there was a new coal industry bill. With grants to the industry now running at £550 million a year and total external financing at £1100 million – the Prime Minister actually referred at this time to a £1 billion subsidy – the Government remained deeply concerned at the fall in coal demand, despite pluses such as rising productivity, now once again at 1972/73 levels. An oil-to-coal boiler conversion scheme had been introduced in 1981 but the marginal effects of this had to be seen against the background of a 25% fall in industrial demand for coal since 1980.

Following the 1980 Act and the policy reversal entailed in the 1981 concessions, political interest in the coal industry came to focus on the personalities of the new chairman of the NCB in succession to Sir Derek Ezra and of the new leader of the NUM with the retirement of Mr Joe Gormley. As expected, in December 1981 Mr Arthur Scargill was elected president of the NUM with a 70% vote. Thereafter Mr Scargill's determination to confront the Thatcher Government was never in doubt. His first stand came almost immediately. Negotiations with the NCB on pay having broken down, a delegate conference endorsed the NUM executive's unanimous recommendation for a strike 'if necessary'. Miners were balloted on a strike in January 1982, the Coal Board campaigning hard against. Possibly influenced by a newspaper article by the outgoing NUM president, the miners firmly rejected the appeal of their executive. Inevitably, the outcome was regarded as a personal defeat for Mr Scargill.

In mid-1982 it was announced that in succession to Sir Derek Ezra the deputy chairman of the Coal Board, Mr Norman Siddall, was to be appointed chairman for one year, the Government having failed to find a more permanent chairman of the calibre it wanted. There now developed between Mr Scargill and Mr Siddall a running argument as to whether the NCB did or did not have a 'hit list' of pits for closure; Mr Siddall's position being that while no secret list existed, it could not be right for 12% of the NCB's output to attract losses of £250 million, as had happened in 1981. At Mr Scargill's first NUM conference as president, at Inverness in July 1982, delegates voted for industrial action on a series of demands, including a 31% pay rise, a four day week, and no pit closures. With Mr Scargill also lending his support to strikers in the national health service and on the railways, and the miners seeking a 200 million ton output, the NUM's posture after Inverness seemed indeed more one of political action than of industrial negotiation. The NCB's annual report for 1981/82, released at this time, showed that total government grants to the Board were up from £254 million in 1980/81 to £575 million in 1981/82, including a deficit grant increase from £149 million to £428 million, the latter largely being required to cover interest payments of £341 million.

In the autumn of 1982 a coal strike came to seem increasingly likely. On the other hand, coal stocks were near an unprecedented 50 million tons and miners remained near the top of the wages league. Miners were balloted on strike action at the end of October, the ballot paper controversially linking the pay and pit closures issues. Despite a barnstorming campaign by their leader, again the miners rejected their executive's call for a strike – 61% voting to accept an 8-9% increase – and again the outcome was represented as a defeat for the NUM president. But almost immediately Mr Scargill returned to the attack. The NCB confirmed in November 1982 that it planned to close 60 pits by 1991 on grounds of exhaustion but, summoned to appear before the Select Committee on Energy after having initially declined to appear in advance of the NCB, Mr Scargill accused the Board of duplicity in regard to its true closure intentions and demanded its dismissal.[12]

By February 1983 it was being strongly rumoured that the next chairman of the NCB would be Mr Ian MacGregor, in a transfer move from the British Steel Corporation, where, after a highly controversial appointment, he had carried through some severe pruning and rationalization. This was interpreted as indicating that, perhaps encouraged by Mr Scargill's failures in 1982 to mobilize his members, the Government was at last facing up to the need to reorganize the coal industry. As one commentator[13] put it, coal had 'benefited from four years of industrial appeasement ... with levels of state aid unknown in Labour's rule from 1974 to 1979'; Mrs Thatcher's 'political prudence', deriving from memories of the 1972 and 1974 confrontations between the NUM and the Heath Government, having 'hitherto outweighed her ideological economic instincts'.

Late in February 1983 a strike began in South Wales over the proposed closure of the Tymawr-Lewis Colliery. This initially seemed more likely to produce a national dispute than had similar cases in the winter of 1982/83 at Kinneil in Scotland and Snowdon in Kent. Mr Scargill called an emergency meeting of the NUM, indicating that local area decisions could lead effectively to a national strike without a national ballot, and also that an escalation of industrial action beyond the mining industry was possible. In the event however the NUM leadership was forced to accept a ballot, Mr Scargill making it clear in the course of this that the pit closure question, 70 pits and 70,000 jobs on his figures, was closely linked in his mind with the projected appointment of Mr MacGregor as NCB chairman. Thus put to the test, the solidarity Mr Scargill asked for from his members was again not forthcoming, 61% voting against a strike, and even Mr Scargill's own Yorkshire area failing to record the necessary 55% vote. The NCB had naturally opposed Mr Scargill's call for a strike, but the outgoing chairman and his board were reported nevertheless to have reservations about Mr MacGregor's appointment, as also were Tory backbenchers, in particular in regard to the fee the Government was having to pay the New York investment bank, Lazard Freres, for Mr MacGregor's services. Mr

MacGregor's appointment was formally confirmed in late March.

In April 1983 a further sensitive coal issue returned to embarrass the Government. This concerned coal imports by the CEGB. These had been limited to 750,000 tons as part of the Government's concessions of February 1981 and the Government now indicated that this limitation would continue 'for the time being'.[14] The problem was that, the CEGB being contracted to take Australian coal, stocks were piling up at continental ports, at high costs to the Government in compensation payments to the CEGB.

May 1983 found the Energy Secretary insisting that the coal industry was a major problem which was costing the country £1.5 million a day and which had to be sorted out; Mr Siddall urging the NUM to accept that hopeless pits must be abandoned; and Mr Scargill outlining new tactics of attrition to defeat pit closures, including selective strikes, funded by miners still at work, as an alternative to a national strike. The industry's problems were clearly huge, with UK demand at around 110 million tons, some 10 million tons below supply, national stocks above 50 million tons, and large quantities of cheap foreign coal also available. The Government for four difficult years had avoided political defeat at the hands of the miners, but this only at high economic cost and it seemed clear that in the case of coal the next Government would have to find, or endorse, a new balance between politics and economics.

One other major policy issue relating to coal arose during the period of this Government: whether or not to allow mining in the Vale of Belvoir. An inquiry in respect of this opened in October 1979 and closed in April 1980, but the minister's decision did not come until March 1982.[15] The central argument concerned the balance between the national need for Belvoir's coal as against the local environmental and social impacts, the Environment Secretary, Mr Michael Heseltine, coming under great pressure during 1981, in particular from Mr Joe Gormley.

When he eventually announced his decision, Mr Heseltine said he accepted that the Belvoir coalfield would be developed. Had he not been faced with a single planning application he would, he said, have been minded to approve the two of the three proposed mines which were outside the Vale itself, provided acceptable proposals had also been made in respect of spoil heaps. As it was, although the inspector had recommended approval for all three mines and for one of the three proposed spoil heaps, Mr Heseltine said that he found one mine proposal 'environmentally unacceptable', and that he was also concerned about all three spoil heaps. Other disposal methods should therefore be considered. The inspector having concluded that it was 'somewhat more likely than not' that Belvoir would be needed as planned, the Environment Secretary said he had concluded that delay to allow more weight to be given to environmental objections was 'not incompatible' with either the need for Belvoir's coal or the employment possibilities, and he was therefore refusing planning permission for the application as it stood. As and when a new application was submitted, then provided the environmental objections were overcome, he did not anticipate further delay. A first pit was in due course approved by Mr Heseltine's successor, Mr Tom King, in March 1983.[16]

In this connection too, the Commission on Energy and the Environment, which in a sense had grown out of the Royal Commission on Environmental Pollution produced a major report in 1981, *Coal and the Environment*,[17] to which the Government in due course replied. However, in July 1981 the Government announced[18] that this Commission was being allowed to 'fall into abeyance for the time being', on the grounds that there remained no other area comparable to nuclear power and coal significant enough for study by such a high-powered group.

Nuclear Power

Mrs Thatcher's support for nuclear power was well known before the 1979 election and in July 1979 she confirmed her belief that Britain would have to have a larger nuclear programme.[19] She also revealed at this time her hope that the fast reactor inquiry to which the Government was pledged would not be long delayed. The Energy Secretary reiterated this firm support for nuclear power in his address to the Conservative Conference in October 1979. The minutes of a cabinet committee that month on nuclear power were leaked to the press: they referred to the need for a 'low profile' in order to avoid confrontation.[20]

The Government's nuclear policy was eventually set out in a Commons statement of 18 December 1979.[21] Stressing the continuity with the previous Government's policy, Mr David Howell now indicated that the Government wished the next nuclear order to be for a Westinghouse Pressurized Water Reactor. Subject to consents, clearances and a public inquiry, Mr Howell said he looked to a start on site in 1982. He added that the Government intended a 15 gigawatt programme over the decade from 1982, but with the reactor choice for later stations remaining open. The Kenemy report on the American Harrisburg accident of 1979 showed, in Mr Howell's view, that the shortcoming there had been due to human failure rather than to the system itself, and it was wrong for the CEGB to remain cut off from the PWR given the international dominance this reactor had come to enjoy. Mr Tony Benn, Energy Secretary in the previous Government, criticized the new programme as a crash one which would increase public controversy, and the official Opposition spokesman, then Dr David Owen, while stressing his wish for as much bipartisanship as possible over energy, also expressed reservations. Mr Howell committed himself, as his immediate predecessor had done, to the fullest possible release of information to allay the strong feelings he said he knew existed. Mr Howell also announced on this occasion that the three-tier arrangement of the nuclear construction industry (General Electric Company/Nuclear Power Company/National Nuclear Corporation) was to be consolidated into a single structure under a new chairman.

In January 1980 Mr Howell defended his policy before the new Commons Select Committee on Energy.[22] Warning against 'advancing into the future with confidence on any projections whatsoever', Mr Howell described his policy as consistent with a rate of growth of GDP up to 1985 of less than 1%, and with only a slight rise thereafter. There was also, he said, a very strong presumption that nuclear economics were better than those of alternative energy sources.

The Government had confirmed soon after coming into office the outgoing Government's decision to order two more advanced cooled reactor stations. A CEGB cash shortage, reduced demand and a desire if possible to make a cleaner switch to the PWR between them, for a time, put these new AGR orders in jeopardy, but industry pressure, support from the Central Policy Review Staff and the fact that the PWR could not be quickly licensed led to formal approval of the two AGR stations on 14 April 1980.[23]

To speed up the elaboration of the PWR design, which, as expected, the CEGB announced in October 1980 would go on the Sizewell, Suffolk, site, a special task force was set up in 1981 under Dr Walter Marshall, then of the Atomic Energy Authority, later Chairman of the CEGB. It was nevertheless not until January 1982 that the Government was able to announce a firm date for the Sizewell inquiry.[24] It was now scheduled to begin in January 1983, but despite this the new Energy Secretary, Mr Nigel Lawson, continued to maintain that, provided the inquiry result were favourable, a firm PWR order could be placed during the lifetime of the 1979 Parliament. This hope was of course overtaken by the Prime Minister's decision to bring forward to 1983 the date of the next General Election.

The suggestion was widely canvassed that the state should give financial aid to objectors at Sizewell, but the Energy Secretary rejected this proposal at an early stage. However, the preliminary meeting for the Sizewell inquiry, held in June 1982, brought forth renewed requests. As a result, on 18 July the inspector, Sir Frank Layfield, wrote to the Energy Secretary asking him to reconsider this question, though Sir Frank himself made no specific recommendation on the point. Mr Lawson in due course replied, declining to change his original decision.[25] In his letter Mr Lawson rejected the argument that the Sizewell inquiry would be the only opportunity for examining the PWR case. Rather, it would be for an inspector at any future inquiry to decide what evidence he wished to hear. Nor was the Energy Secretary persuaded that making public funds available to objectors at Sizewell would not be regarded as a precedent. Considerable sums had already been spent to safeguard the public interest, including the cost of the inquiry itself, £7 million by the Nuclear Installations Inspectorate on the PWR since 1974 and £2 million a year by the Inspectorate currently. To argue that objectors needed expert assistance to master Central Electricity Generating Board and NII documentation seemed to Mr Lawson to undervalue the contribution which the NII itself would make as a totally independent body. In addition, there was the independence of the inspector himself, as well as of his three assessors.

The Government's nuclear plans were criticized in 1981 by both the Monopolies Commission,[26] in its first examination of a nationalized industry under the 1980 Competition Act, and by the Commons Energy Committee, in its own first report.[27] The Commission in effect implied that the CEGB was deluding itself about the economic advantage enjoyed by the PWR, while the Committee was concerned at the scale of the 15 gigawatt nuclear programme which the Government had announced, and the fact that the two reactor types were still being developed for this. In its reply to the Committee[28] the Government argued that prudence dictated as wide a range of options as possible: a programme which would still leave only 30% of electricity nuclear by 2000, and in which each station was separately justified, was not, as the Government saw it, excessive.

Despite its early hopes the Government was not in the event in a position to announce on the fast reactor until November 1982.[29] Mr Lawson then stated that it was now expected that series ordering of the fast reactor would not begin until after the year 2000, 'and thus on a longer timescale than we have previously envisaged'. Since more time would therefore be needed before construction could begin of a first full scale reactor, Mr Lawson explained that the development programme would be geared to this new appreciation, with further efforts being made in the interim to try to establish a basis for international cooperation. The Government's initial views on research into the disposal of high level nuclear waste were set out in a written statement of 24 July 1979.[30] The Environment Secretary, Mr Michael Heseltine, then stressed that the programme in hand was purely one of research to investigate the feasibility of disposing of vitrified waste. Land disposal was regarded as only one of three possible methods of permanent disposal, but if this method were in the end chosen then the aim, in about ten years, was to narrow down the fifteen possible sites which had been identified as suitable to two or three at which demonstration facilities would then be constructed.

Even at the time of this announcement there was much public opposition to the programme of test drilling necessary if suitable sites were to be proved, and this opposition in due course became much more widespread and significant. This could have left the Government with a serious dilemma, but in mid-1981 an advisory committee suggested[31] that 'at least 50 years' could be allowed before it would be essential to dispose finally of stored nuclear waste. As a result of the public opposition and this opinion together, the Government changed its policy.[32] 'Appropriate provision' would now be made for the surface storage of vitrified waste, research meanwhile being reoriented away from field investigation. The Government said it felt that underground storage had in fact been 'established in principle', but in the new circumstances the intention to build a demonstration plant would be dropped and appeals for planning permission to test drill would be withdrawn. By contrast, there was no opposition to a bill introduced in 1981 to raise British Nuclear Fuel Limited's financial limit from £500 million to £1500 million.

Electricity

The Government made two major announcements in July 1980 in regard to the electricity industry. First, the Energy Secretary announced that he had not been persuaded that any benefits from unifying in one corporate structure the generation and distribution of electricity, as proposed by the Plowden Committee in 1976, would outweigh the 'risk of over-centralization'.[33] And second, the Government confirmed its intention to remove the statutory prohibition on the generation of electricity as a main business by private companies.[34] Despite the Energy Secretary's reference, in making the first of these announcements, to the Electricity Council's Chairman, Sir Francis Tombs, as his 'main policy adviser within the industry', in October 1980 Sir Francis resigned, the Energy Department acknowledging that the job he had been recruited to do was in effect no longer available. Of the second announcement the CEGB Chairman, Mr Glyn England, told the Commons Energy Committee that if the opportunity to generate electricity privately were taken up on any scale then this might well lead to uncertainty in predicting the load on the national grid. A Bill giving effect to the Government's intention in respect of private electricity generation was however introduced in 1982. The prohibition on private generation as a main business was, Mr Lawson said at this time, archaic.[35] This Bill also provided for access to the national grid by private generators, with a provision for any dispute between such generators and the electricity authorities to be referred to the Secretary of State. The Opposition rejected the Bill.

The Government decided in 1982 to translate Sir Walter Marshall from the Chairmanship of the AEA to that of the CEGB. It was understood that this was because Sir Walter had been a firm supporter of the pressurized water reactor while at the AEA and the Government wished to capitalize on his drive and commitment.

Like gas, electricity began to come under pressure in 1980 over its industrial prices, especially from the steel industry. In December 1982 this culminated in a clash at a National Economic Development Council meeting between the CBI and the Energy Secretary, the former being particularly critical of the effect of the Government's coal policy on electricity prices; Mr Lawson defending these prices as not being greatly out of line with continental ones.

Gas

In January 1980[36] the Energy Secretary announced that the British Gas Corporation (BGC) and the electricity supply industry had been set new financial targets which could be expected to lead, over the three years to 1983, to price rises of 10% per annum above the rate of inflation in the case of gas, and of 5% above costs in the case of electricity. Acknowledging that BGC's profits would help reduce the Public Sector Borrowing Requirement Mr Howell insisted that the increases were nevertheless being made on energy grounds. The Government's position was that domestic gas prices had fallen 10% in the previous decade while energy prices in real terms were rising, but it was admitted that BGC itself would have preferred smaller increases.

The Opposition attacked these increases as insensitive, unfair, inflationary, and necessary partly because the Prime Minister had earlier vetoed rises. The Government also met strong criticism from its own backbenchers on the increases, on grounds that they had been badly justified and presented, and that they had not been accompanied by a proper scheme to help those in greatest need (such a scheme was later set up).[37] With BGC having made £360 million in 1979-9, with gas prices being raised to bring them more into line with other energy prices but electricity prices themselves being increased, with a rise having been refused in 1979, and with no satisfactory device immediately to hand for putting increased gas profits at the Government's disposal, the public relations aspect of Mr Howell's announcement clearly did leave something to be desired.

In 1980 industrial energy prices also became the subject of a running argument between the Government and manufacturing industry.[38] Industry, faced with recession, high interest rates and an appreciating currency, saw energy prices above those of foreign competition as the last straw, and between January and July 1980 the Energy Department received well over 100 representations on the subject, with the chemical, steel, paper, aluminium, glass and clay industries, as heavy energy users, in the van. In November 1980 the CBI itself weighed in, asking for the abolition of the duty on fuel oil (originally imposed to protect coal almost two decades before when oil prices were low), as well as a slowing in the rate of gas price increases and steps to ensure that electricity charges did not reflect the price of what the CBI saw as uncompetitive British coal. Despite these various pressures, the Government throughout 1980 held firmly to the line that while some large energy users might have a grievance, the great majority of firms were getting supplies at prices roughly similar to those faced by their overseas competitors, and that anyway, it was easy to overstate the impact of an energy-related differential on competitiveness.[39] This view the CBI equally firmly rejected, and in January 1981 the Government did finally agree that a NEDO task force should establish the facts. NEDO's main finding was that, while gas and electricity prices for over 95% of industrial customers were in line with continental ones, there were important groups of bulk users for whom gas prices were 10-20%, and electricity prices 10-35%, higher than in Europe.

In response to this report the Government introduced a package, said to be worth £168 million, which included a nine month plateau for industrial gas prices, a two-year £50 million grant programme to encourage conversion of industrial boilers from oil to coal, and a promise to review tariffs for large electricity users. But industry remained dissatisfied and in June 1981 the Government agreed to a second NEDO report. The second NEDO report in due course found that the heaviest electricity users were still paying more than their continental competitors but that even for them the disadvantage had narrowed.

Among the points which this dispute on industrial energy prices brought out was that simply establishing the basic facts on an agreed basis was difficult and that the Government had the decisive say in determining prices. It is also worth noting that the 1979 Conservative Government, having adopted as a policy guideline the principle that prices should reflect the estimated cost of replacing existing supplies when energy prices are expected to rise over time, this assumption becomes built into prices as an automatic inflationary pressure. The low price of gas relative to alternative fuels in 1978-9 and the instabilities in the oil market resulting from the Iranian revolution had by 1980 precipitated a sharp increase in gas usage, leaving BGC with difficulties in matching supply and demand at peak. The Government therefore introduced a Bill at the Corporation's request to ease the latter's statutory position.[40] BGC was also by now enjoying windfall profits. These arose from gas purchased from the UK Continental Shelf under very low cost, long-term contracts and sold at prices more than four times higher. This situation led to another Bill imposing a special levy which was expected to transfer £1.3 billion from the Corporation to the Exchequer in the three years to 1983.[41] Some Opposition members criticized this as a gas tax but the Government rejected their arguments on the grounds that BGC would have a revised financial target to allow for it. BGC's profits prior to this had been deposited with the National Loans Fund, allowing the Corporation to earn interest without losing principal.[42]

There were also a number of differences between BGC and the Government in the period 1980-83. The Government announced in June 1980 that it had decided upon an offshore pipeline to gather gas and gas liquids.[43] This, as recommended by a BGC/Mobil study group, was intended to reduce flaring, help gas supplies, encourage exploration, and stimulate petrochemical development, and BGC, Mobil and BP were asked to form an organizing group for a 'private utility transmission company outside the public sector'. The Government said that it wished BGC to have 30% of the equity (the Opposition wanted at least 50% for the

Corporation) and that it hoped that the oil companies, financial institutions and the public would take up the rest. When in 1981 the project ran into difficulties over its financing, BGC was anxious to increase its stake but the financial institutions wanted guarantees, and by allowing BGC to give these the Government would on a strict interpretation have been adding to the PSBR, which it was determined not to do. In October 1981 the project thus collapsed. The oil companies, the Government said,[44] must therefore continue to make their own arrangements, adding, to mitigate the implications of the collapse, that flaring was now down by a half.

In July 1980 the Monopolies and Mergers Commission reported on BGC's gas appliance retailing monopoly, finding it to have operated against the public interest and recommending either that it became a private sector activity or else that BGC be required to account separately for it. A year later the Minister of State for Consumer Affairs, Mrs Sally Oppenheim, announced the Government's decision: BGC would be required to dispose of its 938 showrooms over five years.[45] Immediately gas workers called a one day strike, their first ever, and warned of a prolonged one if the Government failed to change course. By October the Government had decided on a deferral, explaining this as due to a lack of parliamentary time for the legislation on new safety standards which would be necessary with privately manufactured appliances.

Despite encouragement by successive governments, relatively little on-shore oil has actually been found in Britain. Britain's largest onshore field is at Wytch Farm in Dorset which was initially developed jointly by BGC and BP.[46] Directed[47] in 1981 by a Government with which it was already at odds to sell an asset of which it was especially proud and of which it entertained considerable expectations, BGC fought a determined rearguard campaign, the critical formal obstacle in the way of a sale being the gap between the Corporation's valuation of the asset, £450 million, and market assessment at less than half this. This was an issue of great sensitivity given the Government's embarrassing experience during the same period with the sale of Amersham International, the fact that the success of the Wytch Farm field was an unequivocal achievement of public enterprise, the consideration that the sale would be to oil companies and not to the public at large, and the circumstances that there was in 1982-3 a buyer's market in oil. Wytch Farm in the event proved perhaps the most difficult privatization initiative the Government became engaged in between 1979 and 1983, and far from its having been completed by the end of their 1981/2 financial year, it had still not been carried through at the time of the 1983 General Election, though finalization remained then only a matter of time.

The existing Gas Act contained sufficient disposal powers to cover the Wytch Farm case, but in the Oil and Gas (Enterprise) Bill of 1981 the Government sought far wider ones. The Energy Secretary made it plain that the new powers would be used in the first instance to privatize BGC's investment in North Sea oil and directions to this end were subsequently given, though there was insufficient time for the assets concerned to be offered to the private sector before the end of the 1979 Parliament. But another important provision in the 1981 Bill was that relating to the breaking up of BGC's monopsony in regard to the purchase, and monopoly in regard to the supply of gas. BGC's purchasing monopoly had meant, the minister claimed, that there had been little incentive for companies to explore for gas, so that resources were not fully known, while the supply monopoly had meant that many industrialists had not been able to get the gas they wanted. To make the new arrangements effective, private suppliers would be allowed, the minister said, to have access to BGC's pipeline network on terms to be negotiated and with a right of appeal to the department.

Accusing the Government of harbouring a 'bilious prejudice' against the public sector, the Opposition now condemned it for having a 'special hatred' of British Gas. Labour did not accept that BGC had sold the nation short by forcing the multinationals to accept a low price for gas; nor did it believe that the new arrangement would lead to cheaper gas. Rather, its object, as Labour saw it was more to permit gas exports. The Energy Secretary did indeed in 1982 indicate a willingness to consider such exports, though he also pointed out at that time that since existing gas supplies were fully committed for use in Britain, only with future finds would exports be possible.

The BGC's chairman, Sir Denis Rooke, had had his differences with the previous Labour Government, but it was with Mrs Thatcher's Government that he really joined battle. While Mr David Howell was Energy Secretary, Sir Denis enjoyed considerable success but when Mr Howell was replaced by Mr Nigel Lawson friction increased significantly. Thus, the revelation in the Queen's speech of October 1981 that BGC's oil interests would be privatized and its gas monopoly broken led to the BGC board issuing a formal statement opposing these moves. If the Government insisted on introducing private capital, then BGC said its preference was for a BP-type solution rather than the break up of a successfully integrated business. Given the differences of view between the BGC chairman and Mr Lawson as Energy Secretary, and the well known determination of both, there was much speculation in 1982 as to how long Sir Denis would survive, but there was also every evidence that he was not a resigning man and that he would continue to organize the best defence possible of BGC's position. The Wytch Farm case in particular came to be reported as a straight test of wills between the two men, a clash in which the merits or otherwise of privatization became lost.

The precise effect of privatization and the ending of BGC's monopoly remained uncertain in 1983, and it was also by no means clear that the Government would succeed in its objectives of increasing gas exploration and enhancing competition. The restriction on BGC continued with the announcement that the Corporation would not be allowed to explore in the eighth licensing round those areas of the UKCS which were expected to yield oil. To encourage exploration subsequent to the ending of BGC's gas monopoly, this round also contained a number of blocks located in the gas province of the North Sea.

Oil

'Appalling' was how Mr David Howell described the fall which had occurred in exploratory drilling when he revealed the Conservative Government's initial oil policy in July 1979.[48] The British National Oil Corporation, he said, would continue but with a reduced role and changed status. As regards oil trading by the BNOC, the Corporation would retain the right through participation agreements to 51% of British continental shelf oil. This and royalty oil would strengthen the Government's position in circumstances of limited shortage, while the Energy Act of 1976 was available for major shortage conditions. As regards exploration, development and production in the North Sea, BNOC had too many license obligations and privileges vis-a-vis other companies: these would be reduced and the preferential position the Corporation had enjoyed in the fifth and sixth licensing rounds ended. The Chancellor had already indicated that BNOC was to lose its exemption from petroleum revenue tax, and Mr Howell himself had earlier said he would end the policy of giving BNOC first refusal in the North Sea. He now added that the Corporation's special access to government finance through the National Oil Account would also be terminated. In addition, the Corporation's statutory role as adviser to government would be removed. These proposals were furiously attacked by the Opposition, and BNOC's chairman, Lord Kearton, was also critical.[49]   In the seventh North Sea licensing round eighty blocks were eventually offered, [50] and, by contrast with earlier rounds, in this companies were invited to nominate blocks of their own choice in the most explored area of the North Sea, it being understood that up to 20 would be awarded at a £5 million premium per block. Some 125 applications were received from 204 companies in this round and 42 premium licences were announced in December 1980, bringing in £120 million, a further 36 discretionary licenses being awarded in March 1981. BNOC, no longer automatically having 51% of each block on offer, joined consortia to bid.

The eighth round of licensing took place in 1982/3. There were some 60 applications from 100 companies, the Government having said it would award about 85 licenses.[51] Fifteen blocks in the mature northern North Sea were up for auction, bids worth around £30 million being entered for half of them. In this round, British Gas's monopoly powers over offshore gas purchase having been broken and the Corporation having indicated a willingness to pay several times the price it had paid in the sixties, there was substantial interest in the southern North Sea Gas province.

The Government having originally planned to raise £5-600 million by selling shares in BNOC in 1980-81, the Corporation was asked to contribute £400 million in the summer of 1979, a figure later increased to £500 million. However, by selling forward oil the Corporation did even better, providing £622 million, and it repeated the exercise with some £550 million in 1981. The Government was also assisted by BNOC's profits, which increased rapidly at a convenient time, from £77 million in 1979 to £308 million in 1980 and £438 million in 1981.

In office the Conservatives quickly came to appreciate the control of oil supplies which they could exercise through BNOC. It was in principle possible for this to be retained by splitting BNOC, keeping its trading operations under government control and introducing private capital only into its exploration and production activities; but it seemed at first that this arrangement would have complications, in particular that BNOC's agreements with some 62 private companies would require renegotiation. The Opposition had already made clear both that if the Government sought to introduce public equity the normal parliamentary conventions would not be observed, and also that a future Labour Government would renationalize. In this context the Energy Secretary appointed a new BNOC chairman, Mr Philip Shelbourne, a merchant banker known to be strongly in sympathy with the privatization objective, and shortly afterwards Mr Alastair Morton, a key executive at BNOC who might under other circumstances have succeeded Lord Kearton, resigned.[52]

Mr Howell eventually announced his first effort at privatization of BNOC during the Conservative Party Conference in October 1980. Although future legislation would provide for private equity, he said he had decided that in the interim there would be a revenue bond scheme. Predictably, this scheme was described as 'window-dressing to cover the continuation of BNOC unchanged' by the Opposition spokesman, but it was also seen as 'just one more example of the Government's words being braver than their actions' by the Conservative Selsdon Group.[53] Labour had said earlier it did not regard the Government's other initiatives in respect of BNOC, though objectionable, as 'outside the bounds of reasonable bipartisanship'.[54]

A Petroleum and Continental Shelf Bill published in February 1981 did in fact provide for equity sale but this was allowed to lapse the following month and it was left to Mr Nigel Lawson to introduce a new measure later in 1982, in his Oil and Gas (Enterprise) Bill.[55] The Government had now decided that it would indeed transfer the whole of the BNOC's oil producing activities to a subsidiary called Britoil. Initially 51% of Britoil's shares would be sold, and more might be sold later. The Government said it would not intervene in Britoil's subsequent commercial decisions, but would provide in its articles of association that the Government's shares, though less than 50%, would constitute a majority in the case of any attempted take over. Since regulatory controls over the North Sea were not vested in BNOC these would remain exactly the same, and it was this control that mattered, the Government insisted, and not ownership of an oil company responsible for only 7% of output. BNOC would remain as a state trading body dealing mainly in participation oil but its access to the National Oil Account would, as indicated earlier, be ended. Britoil would itself enter into participation agreements with BNOC, and public access would be sought in respect of up to 51% of Britoil's oil from the first four rounds, and perhaps to more in respect of the fifth and sixth rounds where BNOC's equity share, which Britoil would inherit, was a substitute for participation.

The Government saw private shareholding of the kind it was providing for as giving a truer sense of public ownership than that made possible through a state corporation. The Opposition on the other hand saw this as a cruel deception in that it would be institutions and not individual working people who would take up the shares.

With the opposition fighting it line by line, the Oil and Gas (Enterprise) Bill made slow progress through its various stages in 1982. At the same time, the Bill's privatization objective was made still more controversial by several developments. First of these was a fall in oil prices, BNOC taking the lead with a $4 a barrel cut in March 1982. This must, it seemed, knock several hundred million pounds off the value of the BNOC and BGC assets to be sold under the Bill. By the time Britoil came into existence in August 1982 in fact the sum expected to be realized by the sale of 51% of its shares had fallen from around £1000 million to perhaps £600 million, with the latter by no means necessarily a bottom figure. Second was the embarrassment to the Government which resulted from another exercise in privatization by Mr Lawson, the substantial under-pricing in the sale of Amersham International in February 1982, this company's shares being oversubscribed some 23 times. And a third development which cast a shadow over Britoil's projected privatization was the leak of documents demonstrating a heated dispute between Britoil and the Energy Department over the capital structure to be provided for Britoil prior to its flotation. Britoil and its merchant bank adviser were looking for an injection of capital by the Government to give the corporation a debt/equity ratio in line with other oil companies, but this Mr Lawson refused.

That the sale of Britoil's shares proceeded was undoubtedly thanks squarely to the determination of the Energy Secretary. As he saw it, this was an area where state ownership had 'no rational justification whatsoever'.[56] But even those in favour of privatization in general had doubts. *The Times* for instance observed that 'the question is whether selling assets at a discount in a buyer's market (and transferring ownership from twenty million taxpayers to a few hundred thousand shareholders), simply to raise a relatively small amount of money at a time when the

Government is for once overfunded, makes much sense except on grounds of political dogma. The case is not proven'.[57]

In the event, with the Amersham case in mind, the Government decided to have the issue underwritten by six merchant banks, thus guaranteeing its eventual £548 million target. This in turn led to criticism of the fees being earned by the underwriters, but when less than a third of the shares on offer were taken up, this criticism lost much of its point. With 90% of applications coming from small investors, Mr Lawson declared the exercise a successful privatization on eminently fair terms to the taxpayer.[58] The Opposition however dismissed the flotation as a sensational flop and accused the Energy Secretary of having now twice misjudged the market (see Chapter 3 above on 'privatization').

Despite having thus privatized the oil production half of BNOC, in early 1983 the Government found itself under some pressure to abolish BNOC altogether. This arose as a result of BNOC's role in the oil price slide which occurred at that time. The Government had retained BNOC formally to ensure security of supply and to facilitate taxation via its reference price for North Sea oil, but 1983 demonstrated that BNOC's existence also allowed the Government some influence over world oil prices, Britain now being the fifth or sixth largest producer. With OPEC unable for some time to agree a price regime there seemed in January and February 1983 to be a possibility of a price war. BNOC was forced to cut its price in February by £3 to £30.50 and for a time it proved impossible to equalize its buying and selling prices; there was also a threat that Nigeria in particular would undercut. In April however OPEC agreed a cut in the official market price from £34 to £29 and Nigeria decided it could live with North Sea oil at £30. Mr Lawson defended BNOC's actions in this instance by arguing[59] that while only the balance of supply and demand could ultimately determine price, BNOC was well placed to smooth transitions and thus help avoid shocks such as those of 1973 and 1979-80. The government of a temporary oil and gas producer like Britain could not be expected to ignore completely the possibility of smoothing the impact of the various financial, industrial and energy-related effects arising from oil and gas production, or to forgo without consideration the opportunity of maximizing the political and security advantages of indigenous supply. On the other hand, any policy to control depletion of reserves presents its own problems and could even prove to be, taking the long view, counter-productive. Important assurances on depletion having initially been given to oil companies by Labour in 1974, the Conservative Government made its own commitments in July 1980 and June 1982.[60] Depletion policy was also the subject of a major report by the Commons Energy Committee in 1982.[61]

Mr Howell's statement in 1980 continued Labour's assurances but was otherwise low-key, the Minister emphasizing the 'vast uncertainty' attaching to any depletion policy. The Government expected at this time that North Sea production would equal all consumption later in 1980, peak in the mid-eighties, and fall to leave the country again a net importer by 1990, thus permitting a 'significant surplus' taking the '80s as a whole. Having encouraged accelerated exploration in its first months of office, the Government did not see a need, Mr Howell said, to defer some oil production, but there could still be no rigid plan. The Government would continue to demand good oil field recovery practice, would tighten controls on flaring, and would otherwise take decisions on a case by case basis, aiming to blunt the production peak.

In its report on depletion, published in May 1982, the Commons Energy Committee came down firmly against any depletion policy beyond a monitoring role, preferring instead policies designed to emphasize repletion, that is the establishment and exploitation of new reserves. The Committee's opinion was naturally cited by Mr Nigel Lawson when he announced shortly afterwards that, although he was retaining rights to delay development of new fields and to restrict projects which might waste gas produced with oil, there would be no other depletion controls before 1985. Production at this time had reached 100 million tonnes a year and was expected to be between 95 and 130 million tonnes by 1985, while domestic demand, some 75 million tonnes by 1981, was projected to remain largely static over the same period. These production and demand figures were both lower than earlier estimates had predicted, and the lower production figures, and also the Government's need for revenue, will have weighed with the Energy Secretary in his decision to resist depletion controls.

The one instance there had been up to this time of a government-imposed development delay had occurred in 1980 with BNOC's Clyde field. The Energy Committee was assured that this delay had indeed been for reasons of depletion policy but it continued to suspect Treasury influence aimed at holding down the Public Sector Borrowing Requirement.

Although governments have preferred to see it as broadly neutral in its impact on depletion, the fiscal regime applied to the North Sea is obviously important in this connection. This is naturally also of great political moment in its own right. From 1975 to 1979 there was a three-tier tax system for the North Sea comprising first, royalty at $12\frac{1}{2}\%$ on well-head values; this deductible from second, Petroleum Revenue Tax (PRT) levied at 45% on a field by field basis, with capital and oil allowances and safeguard provisions specifically aimed at high cost marginal fields; and both these taxes together deductible from third, corporation tax at 52%. In June 1979 the Conservatives took over a proposal of the outgoing Labour Government and increased PRT from 45 to 60%. At the same time, the allowance of tax free oil was halved from 10 to 5 million tonnes, and the capital expenditure which could be set against PRT was reduced from a generous 175% to 135%. Later in 1979[62] the Government introduced a bill to advance payments of PRT, acknowledging that the move had been triggered by cash flow problems caused by delayed payments of phone bills and VAT. In the Finance Act of 1980 PRT was again increased, to 70%, and a further advanced payments provision was introduced. Then in November 1980 a wholly new tax was announced. This, Supplementary Petroleum Duty (SPD), was a 20% levy on the total value of oil produced, less a one million tones a year tax free allowance. It was provided that the new tax could be offset against PRT and corporation tax, its effect therefore being to bring forward tax revenue on each field, £1 billion extra being anticipated in the year of its introduction. There were bitter criticisms about this tax from the oil companies but in the 1981 Finance Act the various PRT allowances were further tightened. In his budget statement of March 1982 the Chancellor, having invited the views of the oil companies, relented to the extent of declaring an intention to abolish SPD, but he also announced that PRT would be increased to 75% and be payable in advance. The tax take on a large and profitable field was now put at 86-87%, on a marginal one at around 65%, the 1982 budget having eased the theoretical top tax rate only from just over to just under 90%. The oil companies, including BNOC, were more than ever incensed, arguing that the tax burden was much too high, especially on marginal fields, that profits rather than revenue should be the appropriate basis for tax purposes, and that frequent tax changes had damaged confidence and long-term planning. In this context the postponement of several new field developments was announced. However, falling oil prices and difficult geological conditions undoubtedly also contributed to these latter decisions by the oil companies. Some support for the oil companies at this time came from both the Commons Energy Committee and the Comptroller and Auditor General.[63] The Comptroller's conclusion was that the tax structure had become too complex to allow its effects to be reliably predicted, while the Energy Committee doubted that the impact of the fiscal regime was still neutral.

The Treasury had seen its North Sea tax rise rapidly in the late '70s, from less than £100 million in 1976 to £3.8 billion in 1980-81, £6.4 billion in 1981-2 and £8 billion in 1982-3. On the other hand, capital spending by the offshore industry, having reached almost £3 billion in 1981, approximately one fifth of total industrial investment in Britain, had fallen by a fifth in 1982, putting at risk the jobs of several thousand platform building workers in the North East and Scotland. Twenty-six fields were producing or about to produce at this time, but all had reserves upwards of 400 million barrels, and concern was now focused on fields in the 60-80 million barrel class. The Chancellor, Sir Geoffrey Howe, urged by a delegation from the UK Offshore Operators Association to amend his policies, did finally agree in June 1982 that some mitigation was called for, but the modifications he introduced at that time were relatively minor, amounting only to some £60 million over the following two years. The

Treasury's position remained essentially unchanged: oil company returns on North Sea investment were adequate with the existing tax take and this was therefore justified. The United Kingdom Offshore Operations Association however continued to lobby.

Mr Lawson hinted at a reduction in North Sea taxes immediately before the Britoil flotation but action had to await the 1983 budget. By then, with oil prices having fallen, there had been only two fields submitted for development approval since the summer of 1980 and there had been substantial job losses in Scottish offshore construction yards. In his budget the Chancellor offered relief which it was said would save the industry £800 million over four years. The measures included a cut from 20 to 15% in advanced PRT and an undertaking to phase this tax out by 1986; a doubling of tax free oil allowances on future discoveries and a waiving of the 12.5% royalty on them; and more generous relief on pre-development spending. There had been at least ten tax changes affecting the North Sea since the Conservatives took office, making it a highly taxed area by international standards. The relief now offered, the first significant amount since the North Sea tax regime had first been established in 1975, was therefore welcomed by the UK Offshore Operations Association as a stimulus to the development of marginal fields, but it was also noted that the sums involved were less than 2% of the Government's probable oil revenues over the relevant four years.

Renewables and Conservation

Government's spending on renewable energy sources grew steadily from the mid-70s, reaching £13.6 million in 1981/8 and for most of this period wave power, previously an unconsidered technology, enjoyed pride of place, expenditure on it reaching almost £4 million a year. However, in 1982 the prospect for the renewables as a whole darkened considerably. This was because of the advice of the Advisory Council for R & D on Fuel and Power, to the effect that no new work should be funded on wave power or solar heating. In fact, only wind and geothermal energy sources came even reasonably well out of this review by ACORD. The Government, having already said that the funding of the renewables could not be entirely insulated from the public expenditure cuts then being made, readily accepted this advice. Expenditure in 1982/83 it was said would be cut to £11-12 million and the Minister now described wave power as 'one of the less promising options'.[64] Despite this check to the renewables programmes, it remained, in the Government's words, 'an insurance policy for which we are prepared to pay a substantial premium'.

A group under Dr Walter Marshall reported on the prospects for combined heat and power schemes in 1979 and the Government was naturally attracted to the report's suggestion that up to 30 mtce annually might, in theory, be saved by CHP. The Government saw the 'crucial' question as being the relevant economics, together with the associated social disturbance. A first step it thought must be establishing feasibility in particular locations, with a second stage involving further study of one or two of these. The Government said firmly that while it would pay for consultancy fees, all other charges must be covered by local authorities and the electricity boards.

Another committee, with Sir Hermann Bondi as chairman, reported[66] on schemes for a Severn Barrage in 1981, unanimously recommending a further £20 million preliminary design study of a scheme capable in principle of meeting about 6% of 1981 electricity demand at a cost of £5,600 million. However, in May 1983 Mr Lawson announced that he had decided the right way forward in this case was the provision of matching funds up to £250,000 over two years towards a further study by the privately organized Severn Tidal Power Group.

Within a year of coming to office the Government was being attacked by consumer and environmental groups for taking what those groups saw as a less concerned attitude towards conservation than had Labour. The Conservative energy ministers were clear about their philosophy: 'The best incentive for householders to use energy efficiently is realistic pricing of fuels, coupled with a vigorous information and advice campaign ... No one would deny that investment in insulation ... is cost effective. The only question ... is, who is to foot the bill ... the state or the individual? ... Investment comes better from the individual than from the state'.[67] The Government did subsequently introduce financial help for recipients of supplementary benefit, and also increased the funds for home insulation grants by £8 million in the 1982 budget. In addition an Energy Conservation Act was passed in 1981, though this was concerned mainly with setting standards for heat generators and gas appliances, and did not deserve its comprehensive title. But government conservation expenditure fell in real terms by 20% between 1980/81 and 1981/82, from £164 million to £149 million. The resulting situation was reviewed by the Commons Energy Committee in 1981/82.[68]

The Committee was unequivocal. Contrasting expenditure on conservation (£149 million) with the subsidy to the coal industry (£550 million), the AEA vote (£218 million for R & D) and even heating allowances (£240 million), the Committee vigorously attacked Government, referring to 'the lack of political will ... which smothers the efforts of the Department of Energy's Conservation Division', to 'the Government's fundamental disinterest in conservation, especially when public expenditure is involved', and to the requirement that conservation investment satisfy much higher rates of return than supply investment ('a testimony to the irrationality of present energy policy'). The Committee still concluded that the real barrier ultimately was not the Government's own scepticism so much as institutional inertia and the fragmentation of responsibility, and to put this right it asked the Government to consider, urgently, a new arrangement. These criticisms were echoed in a report from a Lords Committee and this too asked for institutional change.[70] But it was in response to a study by the Rayner Efficiency Unit that Mr Lawson eventually moved.[71] The weekend before the general election was called he announced that he was setting up within his department an Energy Efficiency Office. However, it seemed that the staffing level of this would be the same as that of the existing departmental unit, and relationships with other departments, responsible for most government conservation expenditure, also remained to be worked out.

Conclusion

It is apparent that the 1979-83 Conservative Government encountered a number of significant political problems in implementing its various energy related policies. Some of these were extraneous in origin, above all the availability and price of oil, while others followed more or less directly from the Government's own actions, notably the uneasy confrontations with the NUM. Still others were at root technical but acquired a political dimension, the appropriateness of the pressurized water reactor especially. The Government gave itself a clear enough goal in principle, the maximum realization of market forces, yet it can be argued that it underestimated both the distortions being introduced by its own actions, for instance the continued subsidy of nuclear power via the AEA vote, and also the potential for desirable developments achievable in part only through non-market initiatives, for example in the field of conservation. These four years also demonstrated the importance, and the dangers, of ministerial determination in carrying through policies radically different from those in place. The final conclusion must be that despite the various difficulties which arose between 1979 and 1983, Britain's present energy abundance goes a long way towards protecting policy makers from their failures, whether of commission or of omission.

References

1. DEn/P/1.
2. Cmnd. 7101.
3. Department of Energy (mimeo).
4. For comparison, total UK inland consumption of primary fuels for energy use in 1980 was 328.0 mtce.
5. DEn/P/1/Annex
6. For comparison, the UK electricity idustry had an output capacity in 1980 of 68.3 Gigawatts (GW = 10^9 watts), of which the nuclear component was 5.7 GW.
7. H.C. Deb, Col., 986, 1 377-1478 (2R); H.C. Deb, col. 989, 813-901 (3R).
8. H.C. Deb, col. 999, 137-48.
9. H.C. Deb, col. 999, 457-61.
10. See for instance *Sunday Times* and *Observer*, 22 February 1981
11. HC 231, 1981-82, The Department of Energy's estimates for 1981-82.

12. H.C. Deb., col. 20, 1096-1105.
13. *Observer* 13 1983 (Robert Taylor)
14. H.C. Deb., col. 41, 110 WA.
15. H.C. Deb., col. 20, 1096-1105.
16. H.C. Deb., col. 39, 235-6 WA.
17. Department of the Environment, 1981
18. H.C. Deb., col. 8, 217-18 WA.
19. H.C. Deb., col.969, 1116-8.
20. *Guardian*, 6 December, 1979.
21. H.C. Deb., col. 976, 287-304.
22. H.C. 397, Session 1979/80.
23. H.C. Deb., col.982, 776.
24. H.C. Deb., col.16, 284-90; see also H.C. Deb., col. 9, 128-9 WA.
25. DEn Press Notice 143, 23 September 1982.
26. The Monopolies and Mergers Commission, *Central Electricity Generating Board*, HC 315, 20 May 1981.
27. HC 114-I, Session 1980-81; H.C. Deb., col. 17,21-102.
28. *Cmnd, 8317.*
29. H.C. Deb., col. 33, 2-3 WA; for earlier statements see H.C. Deb., col. 988, 452, 1980 and H.C. Deb., col. 989,16.
30. H.C. Deb., col. 971, 215-9 WA.
31. 2nd Annual Report of the Radioactive Waste Management Advisory Committee.
32. H.C. Deb., col.15, 171-2 WA.
33. H.C. Deb., col.988, 445 WA.
34. H.C. Deb., col. 989, 61.
35. H.C. Deb., col. 32, 865-943.
36. H.C. Deb., col. 976, 1644-61; H.C. Deb., col. 977, 1029-1106.
37. H.C. Deb., col. 981, 1661-2.
38. See for example Second Report from the Select Committee on Energy, Session 1980-81, *Industrial energy pricing policy* HC 169, 1981-82.
39. H.C. Deb., col. 989, 801-4; H.C. Deb., col. 990, 40 WA.
40. H.C. Deb., col. 984, 1596-1654.
41. H.C. Deb., col. 984, 191-2 WA.
42. H.C. Deb., col. 983, 113 WA; H.C. Deb., col. 980, 800 WA.
43. H.C. Deb., col. 986, 596 WA.
44. H.C. Deb., col. 10, 3-4.
45. H.C. Deb., col. 989, 590-5.
46. See for example the Select Committee on Energy, 1981-82 *The disposal of the British Gas Corporation's interest in the Wytch Farm oil-field*, HC 138.
47. H.C. Deb., col. 8, 554-60; H.C. Deb., col. 10, 21-5.
48. H.C. Deb., col. 971, 891-902.
49. *Guardian*, 28 July 1979.
50. H.C. Deb., col. 983, 606-7 WA.
51. H.C. Deb., col. 24, 15.
52. *Times*, 31 May 1980, 3 June 1980.
53. *Times*, 10 October 1980.
54. H.C. Deb., col. 987, 1446.
55. H.C. Deb., col. 16, 169-252.
56. *Times*, 28 October 1982; *Sunday Times* and *Observer* 30 October 1982; see also *Times* 25 August 1983.
57. 28 October 1982.
58. H.C. Deb., col. 32, 596-601.
59. *Times*, 15 April 1983.
60. H.C. Deb., col. 882, 650; H.C. Deb., col. 969, 1716-1808; H.C. Deb., col. 989, 226-7 WA; H.C. Deb., col. 985, 3; 990, 36 WA; H.C. Deb., col. 26, 600-601.

61. HC 337, 1981-82.
62. H.C. Deb., col. 975, 989-1036.
63. HC 337, 1981-82 and HC 76-ix, 1981-82.
64. H.C. Deb., col. 24, 17-18; see also H.C. Deb., col. 42, 621-2.
65. H.C. Deb., col. 982, 207-10 WA; later H.C. Deb., col. 7, 60-61 WA.
67. *Tidal power from the Severn Estuary*, Energy Paper No 46.
68. H.C. Deb., col. 995, 929-30.
69. HC 401, 1981-82.
70. Select Committee on the European Communities, *The rational use of energy in industry*, HC 83, Session 1982-83.
71. H.C. Deb., col. 25, 6-7 WA.